Schriftenreihe des Forschungsinstituts für Europafragen der Wirtschaftsuniversität Wien

Band 23

Research Institute for European Affairs Publication Series

Volume 23

SpringerWienNewYork

Fritz Breuss, Gerhard Fink and
Stefan Griller (eds.)

Institutional, Legal and Economic Aspects of the EMU

SpringerWienNewYork

Prof. Dr. Fritz Breuss
Prof. Dr. Gerhard Fink
Prof. Dr. Stefan Griller
Research Institute for European Affairs, Wirtschaftsuniversität Wien,
Wien, Austria

Financial support was given by the *Bundesministerium für Bildung, Wissenschaft und Kultur,* Wien

Printed in Austria

Typesetting: Camera ready by editors
Printing: Ferdinand Berger & Söhne Gesellschaft m.b.H., A-3580 Horn
Printed on acid-free and chlorine-free bleached paper
CIP data applied for
SPIN: 10887315

With numerous Figures

ISBN 3-211-83856-2 Springer-Verlag Wien New York

Preface

The Economic and Monetary Union (EMU) of the European Union has been launched quite successfully in 1999. Nevertheless, as an operating economic and political system in practice it is still in its infancy. Only recently, the Euro has been introduced as legal tender, transforming the EMU from a virtual to a real monetary union. The EMU is quite unique in its architecture in many respects. Some of its special institutional, legal and economic aspects are the topics of this book. Of course, it is impossible to analyse the complexity associated with the EMU in all its facets. The asset of this contribution, however, lies in its multi- and interdisciplinary approach. The book consists of four parts.

Part 1 contains three papers which deal with some selective problems in connection with the "institutional and legal set-up of EMU". *Barbara Dutzler* in her contribution on the legal status of the ESCB raises the fundamental question whether the ECB is really already the fourth pillar in the EU. She comes to the conclusion that one cannot support the bold statement, put forward sometimes in the literature that the ECB is a "new Community". *Harald Badinger* and *Barbara Dutzler* analyse the economic and legal possibility how to deal with the undoubtedly existing excess reserves in the Euro system. Economically as well as legally there is no clear answer to this problem. *Stefan Griller* demonstrates in his Austrian case study the problematic practice of "Maastricht conformity" in connection with the EMU excessive government deficit criterion in the case of public undertakings.

Two papers in *part 2* deal with the "fiscal policy framework" and ask for the "room for improvement". *Michael Artis* focuses on the Stability and Growth Pact as a major pillar of the complex co-ordination architecture of fiscal policy in the EMU. The SGP, in his view, is "one of the most remarkable pieces of policy co-ordination in world history". *Andrew Hughes Hallett* and *Nicola Viegi* philosophise in their contribution theoretically on the need for inter-institutional co-ordination in EMU. They do this with a re-evaluation of the theory of optimal currency areas (OCA) and conclude that the choice of the policy regime matters.

Part 3 with three papers covers the monetary policy in the EMU its financial markets and specialities of the payment system. *Fritz Breuss* asks whether ECB's monetary policy is optimal already. He concludes that the ECB's performance was quite remarkable given the external shocks (oil price crises) in the first phase of EMU, but that it could gear its inflation target better to core than headline inflation. *Rudolf Habacht*, *Walter Hoffenberg* and *Aurel Schubert* treat the economic and technical aspects of the specific payment system in the ESCB. They not only look at payments between central banks and money between banks (TARGET) but also on the important cross-border transfers within the euro area. *Gerhard Fenz* analyses the euro as an international currency and possible reasons for its weakness against the US-dollar in the first phase of EMU. As an explanation he puts forward the surge in euro denominated bonds issued by non-EU residents.

Part 4 in two papers is devoted to some aspects of EU enlargement. *Bernhard Mahlberg* and *Ralf Kronberger* examine – under the Optimum Currency Area (OCA) point of view - to what degree which candidate country's business cycle correlates already with those of the EMU. A clear-cut picture does not yet evolve. *Peter R. Haiss* deals in some detail with the financial sector of the candidate countries and finds that the weakness of this sector may well constitute a practical constraint for a full-fledged integration into the EMU.

We want to thank the Austrian Federal Ministry for Education, Science and Culture for their financial assistance granted for the printing of this volume. Last but not least the editors thank *Nurgül Özen* for her patience and professionalism in producing the final text.

Fritz Breuss, Vienna
Gerhard Fink, Vienna
Stefan Griller, Vienna

October 2002

Table of Contents

Part 1:
Institutional and Legal Set-up of EMU

Barbara Dutzler

Institutional Framework of the EMU – Is the ECB a Fourth Pillar?

I. Introduction

The institutional framework of the Economic and Monetary Union (EMU), and the status of the European System of Central Banks (ESCB) has only recently developed into one of the more extensively discussed subjects of European integration.[1] As the

---

[1] *Zilioli/Selmayr* (2000) 591ff, *Torrent* (1999) 1230ff, *Amtenbrink/de Haan* (2002) 69ff, or *Herrmann* (2002) 1ff.

present article argues, this recent attraction is warranted not only because the institutional provisions are finally filled with life and have had to pass the first tests of practicability and viability. It is, moreover, also warranted by the fact that the interactions of the actors are to a large extent the direct result of the structures as introduced by the Treaty of Maastricht. It should not come as a surprise in the "community of law"[2] that *Jellinek's* much-cited concept of the normative power of facts became reality just the other way around, as an example for the "faktische Kraft des Normativen".

Even more significant is the relevance of EMU for the future development of the European Union (EU), in the sense that the structural imbalance between the monetary and economic pillar of EMU and the unique institutional status of the ESCB stimulated debates on the desirability of a political union. This aspect should be borne in mind, when in the following, an analysis of the precise location of the European Central Bank (ECB) and of the doubts on the extent of its integration into the institutional framework of the European Community (EC) as an effect of this very institutional design will be conducted. This analysis is hence an attempt, with a view to the proposals regarding the economic component of EMU (enhanced co-operation, the status of the Eurogroup), to contribute to a well-founded discussion on the parameters of a possible future design of EMU.

II. The Legal status of the ESCB

A.) Preliminary remarks

The task of positioning an independent central bank vis-à-vis the executive, legislative and judiciary is more complicated at an European level due to the the fact that there are no such clearly defined powers as in the classical nation state.[3] The relevance of the degree of separation of the ECB from the EU is said to follow from the different legal consequences of the ECB's position inside the organisational framework and its relationship with the Community institutions and bodies.[4] In this respect, the peculiarity of the institutional provisions of the ESCB, which is not included in the list of Community institutions under Art 7 EC Treaty, gave rise to the rather controversial interpretation of its status as "independent spe-

---

2 "Rechtsgemeinschaft", *Hallstein* (1973) 31ff.

3 *Weinbörner* (1998) 454.

4 *Zilioli/Selmayr* (2000) 592.

cialised organisation of Community law."[5] The ESCB could even be understood as a legal entity similar to the Community itself, hence a *new Community*.[6]

This view is presented with the remark that the *political* concept of the unity of the Union could not be used to undermine the *legal* principle of supranational central bank independence enshrined in Art 108 EC. True, given the intertwining between EMU and the future of European integration,[7] it is far more than a purely legal question, but rather an issue of high political importance.[8] For instance, it is asked, and rightly so, whether the ECB *should* be an independent specialised organisation of Community law.[9] However, the caveat of the use of politically inspired terminology is two-edged, and can be applied to the term *new Community* as well. When it is tried to pin down the hard facts of the legal position of the ECB, regard must be given to both the motivations and the consequences of the views presented hereinafter.

The key issue is whether, with a view to the "fair measure of distance from the Community",[10] Community secondary law is applicable to the same extent to the ECB as to the Community institutions? Is there a substantial and material link between EU/EC and the *affiliated* ECB in a sense that the former is a fully integrated element included and comprised by the latter, or is there only a loose connection, a sort of goal-oriented interlocking (*zielorientierte Verklammerung*)[11] of ultimately disassociated components? These questions require in the first place an overview of the discussion and analysis of the organisational setting of the ECB.

B.) The academic debate

The classification of the ECB and its location in the institutional system of the EC/EU is a difficult issue. At the one end of the spectrum, the ECB is perceived, in spite of its independence guar-

---

5 So *Selmayr* (1999) 170ff; *Zilioli/Selmayr* (2000) 591ff.

6 *Selmayr* (1999) 178, *Zilioli/Selmayr* (2000) 628.

7 See *Snyder* (1994) 99 and (1999) 473.

8 In the sense that "questions of law can never be neatly separated from questions of power and influence", *Schermers/Blokker* (1999) §14.

9 *Amtenbrink/de Haan* (2002) 65ff.

10 *Smits* (1997) 93.

11 See *Pechstein/Koenig* (2000) paras 100-102 on the relationship between EC and EU and the differences between the conceptions of a cloak, roof, and platform construction.

anteed in the Community constitutional charter,[12] as a Community body with a status similar to one of the institutions.[13] Equally, the ECB is also called a *quasi*-organ or institution *sui generis*, and in spite of the deviations from the "classical" organs, its role is compared with the one of the Commission.[14] *Pernice* already qualifies the description of ESCB and ECB as „institutional quintessence of monetary union", integrated as a part of the EC in the EC Treaty, by pointing to their independent charter: The separate embodiment in Art 8 EC and the separate legal personality indicated that the ESCB and the ECB were not institutions of the EC, but autonomous bodies, although similarly fully subject to the Community rule of law.[15]

Slot is already a step further, when stressing that neither the Community rule of law nor the opportunities for judicial control would make the ECB "automatically" part of the institutional framework of the Community. This was due to the power of the ECB under Art 110 EC to make regulations, its independent status by virtue of Art 108 and the exclusion from the enumeration of Community institutions in Art 7 EC.[16]

Selmayr[17] and *Zilioli/Selmayr*,[18] who conceive the ECB as independent international organisation outside the Community, represent the other end of the spectrum.

This last position is certainly the most controversial, and has been rejected for instance by *Hahn/Häde*, who view the ECB as *Gemeinschaftsinstitution mit organähnlicher Stellung*, due to the

---

12 The use of this term goes back to Case 294/83 *Les Verts* [1986] ECR 1339 para 23.

13 "Gemeinschaftseinrichtung mit organähnlicher Stellung", see *Häde* (1999) para 1.

14 *Smulders* (1999) Art 4a para 3, pointing to the responsibility for a Community policy (Arts 105 and 111), independence (Art 108), right of initiative (Art 107 para 5), and custodian of the Treaty (Art 237(d) 2nd sentence). See also *Weinbörner* (1998) 387.

15 So *Pernice* (1997) para 1. This seems to be a modification to the definition in *Pernice* (1993) 1059, which is much closer to the one of *Zilioli/Selmayr* (2000). There, he regarded the ESCB as a quasi autonomous institutional system separate from the EC and its institutions, a "Community within the Community".

16 *Slot* (1994) 232ff. Still, the ESCB was "firmly situated within the Community legal order", ibid 245.

17 *Selmayr* (1998) 138 "selbständige Sonderorganisation", *Selmayr* (1999) 177ff "neue Gemeinschaft".

18 *Zilioli/Selmayr* (2000).

explicit link with the Community as manifested in Art 8 and 105ff EC.[19] *Torrent* raises the objection that the definition of the ECB as a Community of its own would have the result that one could not explain whose central bank the ECB was, a question with only two possible answers: on the one hand, the (manifestly incorrect) opinion that the ECB was the central bank of the participating member states, which would render it an intergovernmental body,[20] or the obvious, that the ECB was the central bank of the European Community.[21] The *unity thesis,* however, provides an additional, third answer, arguing that the ECB has to be considered as the central bank of the European Union: Every attempt to determine the constitutional position of the ECB in respect to the three Communities EC, European Atomic Energy Community (EAEC) and European Community for Steel and Coal (ECSC), would get into serious difficulties as they had ceased to exist and were only areas of activity and competencies of the Union's institutions.[22] The solid constitutional basis provided by the Union's constitutional framework allowed for far reaching organisational and operational autonomy and distinguished the ECB radically from the World Bank with its loose relationship with the UN.[23]

Art 2 EU supports such an interpretation, as the establishment of an economic and monetary union is not an objective in itself, but rather a means to an end,[24] which is the achievement of the Union's objectives as laid down in this very article. Even in a conservative understanding of the Union as just the common roof for the three pillars comprising the European Communities, Common Foreign and Security Policy (CFSP), and Police and Justice Co-operation in Criminal Matters (PJC), it must therefore at least be seen as a for-

---

19 *Hahn/Häde* (2001) 34.

20 Which is implied by the use of the term "unselbständige *zwischenstaatliche* Einrichtung" by *Seidel* (2000) 552.

21 *Torrent* (1999) 1230ff.

22 So *von Bogdandy* (2001) 210.

23 However, *Selmayr* (1999) 177 n. 72 sees an analogy between ESCB and World Bank, which belonged to the UN family but was not obliged to bring its credit policy in line with the resolutions of the GA.

24 *Snyder* (1994) 65. Cf. Art 2 EU: The Union shall set itself the following objectives: to promote economic and social progress [...] through establisment of an economic and monetary union.

mal frame of reference, within which *inter alia* the EC acts in order to realise its objectives.[25]

Insofar as the realisation of the objectives of the Union as regards economic and monetary union by virtue of Arts 2 and 4 EC belong to the Community's field of action, in the organisational structure of which the ECB is embedded, the ECB acts as an independent part of the Community, and not of the Union.[26] It is, however, at the same time exactly because of this "full integration" of the task of establishing an EMU in the Community pillar[27] that the objection that the ESCB and ECB could not be EU institutions as the TEU fails to mention them[28] does not represent an obstacle. Similarly, albeit in the converse sense, the fact that the European Council is only an institution of the EU, but not of the EC, did not prevent its influential role under the multilateral surveillance procedure of Art 99 EC.

Out of these considerations, the point made by *Zilioli/Selmayr* – that classifying the ECB as the central bank of the EU was possible only in the language used by politicians, intended to convey the political message of the unity of the Union's *political* system[29] – is understandable to a certain extent. However, this very argument cannot be applied in order to reject a classification of the ECB as central bank of the *EC*. In contrast, it can be assumed that the insertion of EMU in the first pillar had far-reaching *legal* consequences, and also affects the internal relationship between ECB and Community.

C.) The nature of the link between ECB and Community

During the run-up to EMU, the establishment of a separate economic and monetary pillar juxtaposed to the Treaty on the European Community appeared attractive for a number of reasons: the competencies of the Member States in the field of economic policy, the distrust of the Commission, and the creation of an autonomous monetary authority, the introduction of which in the institutional

---

25 "Formalrechtlicher Strukturrahmen", so *Stadler* (1996) 97. *Weinbörner* (1998) 50 regards EMU as a core element of an "Overall-Union".

26 *Stadler* (1996) 97.

27 *Pipkorn* (1994) 263; *Di Bucci* (1997) 4 (as far as EMU is subject to full juridical control).

28 *Hahn/Häde* (2001) 33. See also Art 5 EUV.

29 *Zilioli/Selmayr* (2000) 600.

scheme appeared problematic.[30] This history explains why also today, the EMU chapter, although inserted in the EC Treaty, appears as a pillar itself.[31]

Nevertheless, as also *Zilioli/Selmayr* stress,[32] the French proposal of a "pilier monétaire" had been rejected by the IGC, as the majority of the Member States opted to make the realisation of EMU a task of the Community.[33] The central argument of the authors is that this location of monetary sovereignty in the first and central pillar, the "heart" of the European Union's temple structure, constituted only a conceptual link, without establishing a deeper organic or even proprietary connection between the EC and the ECB. The ECB was therefore, as shown in the below chart, although within the first pillar and subject to Community law, a "new Community" only *associated* to the Community:[34]

Figure 1: The "new Community" ESCB

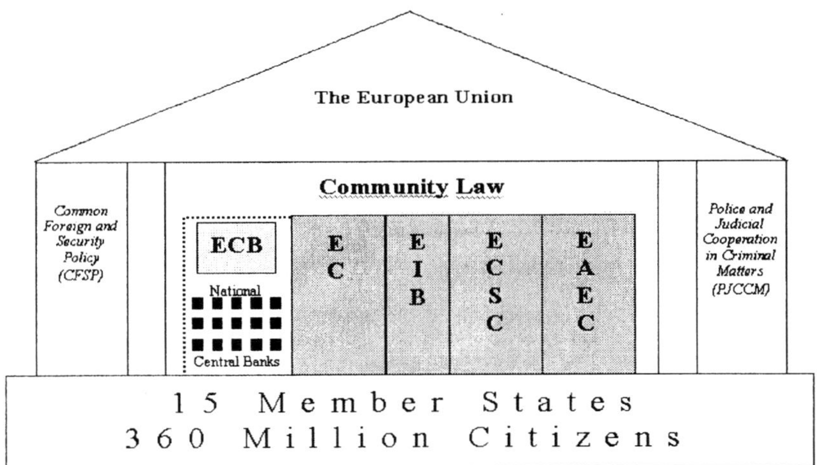

Source: *Zilioli/Selmayr* (2000) 624.

The authors claim that the difference between their view and the European Investment Bank's (EIB) original perception of itself as a

[30] *Louis* (1995) 20.
[31] So the characterisation by *De Witte* (1998) 53.
[32] *Zilioli/Selmayr* (2000) 602.
[33] *Louis* (1997) 591.
[34] *Zilioli/Selmayr* (2000) 621-624.

"third party in relation to the Communities"[35] is the emphasis on the foundation in Community law by which it has been established. The ECB was only subordinated to the European Court of Justice (ECJ) due to its distinct position at the same normative level as and on an equal footing with the Community.[36] Denominating the ECB as a "Community within the Community" would indicate its subordination under the legal person EC viz. the Community institutions, so that only an understanding of the ECB as new Community would meet the requirement of an extensive protection of its independence as envisaged by Art 108 EC.[37] The issue is hence the subordination of the ECB not only to the principles of primary Community law and the jurisdiction of the ECJ, which is accepted, but also to all secondary Community law.

One could, however, argue that the effects of this view are but the same as if the authors had called the ECB a third party to the Community: It can hardly be denied, given the explicit wording of the EC Treaty, that the ECB is bound by the norms of primary Community law which subject it to the ECJ's jurisdiction. Which additonal consequences could have potentially resulted from such an open expression of "secessionist tendencies",[38] in addition to those already claimed by *Zilioli/Selmayr:* the non-applicability of secondary Community law, the assumption of equal rank between ECB and the Community institutions, the claim of *original* in contrast to *derivative* competencies, the denial of non-contractual liability of the Community for the ECB, or the ECB's competence to act as an autonomous actor at the international level within its own field of competence.[39] It is not easy to imagine a more revolutionary thesis of the Community's institutional structure.

III. The arguments in favour and against

A.) Why an analogy with the EIB is appropriate

It might therefore useful to analyse the arguments adduced by *Zilioli/Selmayr* with the hindsight of the dispute on the EIB's legal

---

35 So AG *Mancini's* account in his Opinion on Case 85/86 *Commission v. EIB* [1998] ECR 1281, para 5.

36 *Zilioli/Selmayr* (2000) 624.

37 *Selmayr* (1999) 180.

38 Cf. *Zilioli/Selmayr* (2000) 592 answer to *Torrent's* critique as to the consequencies of their thesis on the institutional unity of the EU.

39 See on this *Zilioli/Selmayr* (1999) 286, 291ff.

status in Case 85/86, where the ECJ was called upon to rule in a case that concerned the flow of income taxes that were withheld from the salaries of the employees of the EIB to the Community budget.[40] There is however the view that due to the close functional and institutional link between the EIB and the EC, as opposed to the functional and institutional separation of the ECB from the policies of the Community, an analogy between EIB and ECB is not appropriate.[41]

It is true that the ECB is different from the EIB in that

- the ECB's independence is not a product of case law, but consecrated in the EC Treaty,
- the EIB shall act *in the interest of the Community* when granting loans and giving guarantees to specific projects,[42] whereas a similar provision for the ECB is missing,
- the composition of the EIB Council by the ministers of the Member States[43] is believed to link it much more to the Community as the organs of the ECB, and
- the Treaty lists the EIB in Part V, Institutions of the Community, whereas it does not mention the ECB there.

In spite of these differences, one cannot *prima facie* exclude the application of the ECJ's jurisprudence on the legal status and non-contractual liability of the EIB. On the contrary, lacking a judgment addressed to the ECB,[44] this caselaw is to be considered with due regard to the institutional differences resulting from the functional differences between a central bank and a bank intended to facilitate the financing of investment programs, as points of reference and benchmarks for an appropriate classification of the ECB. The argument against this analogy, as the decisive paragraphs of the *Commission v. EIB* reveal, seems to be rooted in the content of the judgment:[45]

> It is true that under Article 129 of the Treaty the Bank has legal personality distinct from that of the Community and that it is administered and managed by organs of its own in accordance with its statute. In

40 Case 85/86 *Commission v. EIB* [1988] ECR 1281.

41 So *Selmayr* (1999) 175.

42 Art 267 EC.

43 Art 9.1. EIB-Statute.

44 But see *infra* at 24.

45 Case 85/86 *Commission v. EIB* [1988] ECR 1281 paras 28-30.

> order to perform the tasks assigned to it by Article 130 of the Treaty the Bank must be able to act in complete independence on the financial markets, like any other bank. Indeed, the Bank is not financed out of the budget but from its own resources, which consist in particular of the capital subscribed by the Member States and funds borrowed on the financial markets. Lastly, the Bank draws up annual accounts and a profit and loss account which are audited annually by a committee appointed by the Board of Governors.
>
> Nevertheless, the fact that the Bank has that degree of operational and institutional autonomy does not mean that it is totally separated from the Communities and exempt from every rule of Community law. It is clear in particular from Article 130 of the Treaty that the Bank is intended to contribute towards the attainment of the Community's objectives and thus by virtue of the Treaty forms part of the framework of the Community.
>
> The position of the Bank is therefore ambivalent inasmuch as it is characterised on the one hand by independence in the management of its affairs, in particular in the sphere of financial operations, and on the other by a close link with the Community as regards its objectives. It is entirely compatible with the ambivalent nature of the Bank that the provisions generally applicable to the taxation of staff at the Community level should also apply to the staff of the Bank. This is true in particular of the rule that the tax in question is collected for the benefit of the Communities' budget.

In the next section, the main arguments invoked by the ECB – the independence of instructions, its unclear legal status (no Community institution), its legal personality, and the conduct of monetary policy in its own responsibility, not as a Community agent – will be answered, where appropriate, with the arguments which the ECJ considered as applicable to the EIB.

B.) Art 108 and the degree of independence

As *Amtenbrink/de Haan* note,[46] *Zilioli/Selmayr* seem to regard central bank independence as a sort of legal pre-existing constitutional principle which was implemented in Art 108 EC. In fact, the authors talk of an *effet utile* of Art 108, which would not allow the circumvention through legislative means of the prohibition to give instructions to the ECB,[47] and understand the independence of instruction as laid down in Art 108 EC *only as expression* of the extensively installed autonomy of the ECB.[48] A similar notion seems to be invoked when it is claimed that "in development" (*Ausgestaltung*) of this independence requirement under Art 108 a further intensive co-operation between ECB and the Community institutions in the course of their respective performance of their duties was not permissible.[49]

It is true that the effort of installing an independent European central bank was not confined to introducing the prohibition of instructions into the Treaty. Rather, it was flanked not only by other statutory guarantees of personal, financial, operational and institutional independence,[50] but also left with the task of defining its objective which under Art 105(1) EC is to maintain price stability, and without prejudice to this objective, to support the general economic policies in the Community. Contrary to what is usually assumed,[51] the introduction of these objectives in this order does not *per se* reduce the ECB's degree of political discretion. The EP therefore rightly classifies the ECB as "endowed with operational and goal independence that no other central bank in the world has attained."[52]

---

46 *Amtenbring/de Haan* (2002) 69ff.

47 *Zilioli/Selmayr* (2000) 636.

48 "Ausdruck der umfassend angelegten Autonomie", *Selmayr* (1999) 180, emphasis added.

49 So *Weinbörner* (1998) 456.

50 This is the usual classification, see *Louis* (1999a) 468f; *Smits* (1997) 155ff. For instance, personal independence is guaranteed by Arts 11 and 14.2. ESCB-Statute providing the members of the ESCB decision-making bodies with the necessary security of tenure (term of office, modalities of retirement). Financial independence is ensured by Arts 28, 30 ESCB-Statute so that the ESCB can avail itself autonomously of the appropriate economic means to fulfil its mandate.

51 See for instance *Ver Loren van Themaat* (1996) 14.

52 *European Parliament* (1999) 22.

It seems nonetheless, as if the origin of the problem was a misperception of the degree of independence which has been attributed to the ECB in order to enable it to fulfil its statutory tasks: Although unprecedented and arguably disproportionate, it is not more than the sum of its parts and can be traced back to the fears of inflation due to the establishment of a central bank without reputation in a climate less favourable to stability than in Germany.[53] Other than a fundamental legal doctrine, independence as a legal principle only operates on the basis of the Treaty provisions laying it down and in the framework of other Treaty provisions limiting it.[54] Moreover, central bank independence is a political choice.[55] Even *Selmayr* agrees that the degree of autonomy conferred upon the ECB is not an end in itself, but has merely an auxiliary function to enable the bank to realise the primary objective of price stability.[56] Accordingly, it is out of technical considerations that the ECB was granted independence of instructions, far reaching legislative powers, a budget separate from that of the Community, and similar provisions which all can be amended only under the procedure of Art 48 TEU. There is thus no reason why AG Mancini's conclusion that for the EIB "these arguments have a much lower profile than the Bank thinks and maintains"[57] should not be applicable to the ECB as well.

C.) Attribution of legal personality and exclusion from list of institutions

The ECB is, due to its separate establishment in Art 8 EC, no "institution" of the Community as the five entities mentioned in Art 7 EC.[58] This is, from a systematic point of view, only logical,[59] as institutions usually do not posses legal personality but are integral parts of the EC which as such has legal personality,[60] and in contrast to the ECB in principle act in all areas of activity of the EC.[61]

---

53 So *Majone* (1999) 16; *Louis* (1995) 70.

54 So *Herrmann* (2002) 8.

55 *Amtenbrink/de Haan* (2002) 70.

56 *Selmayr* (1999) 178.

57 Mancini, op. cit *supra* note 35 para 11.

58 *Louis* (1995) 56.

59 *Stadler* (1996) 93ff.

60 *Smulders* (1999) para 3.

61 Both geographically (*Stadler* (1996) 94) as well as regarding comepetencies (*Snyder* (1994) 67).

Out of similar considerations, the Commission had proposed to establish ESCB and ECB in a separate paragraph to Art 7, in order to avoid any confusion between the legal set-up of the institutions and the ESCB with regard to legal personality and the "classical" administrative and financial rules.[62]

On the one hand, this means that the exclusion of ESCB and ECB of Art 7 EC was, far from being a distinct aim at the outset, a result of the independence conferred on it for a "plurality of reasons",[63] and essentially due to the specific feature "legal personality", with which the ECB had been endowed out of similar functional considerations as for the granting of independence.[64] Taking into consideration that central banks must be in the position to act freely in the international financial markets, it is not at all surprising if they enjoy international legal personality.[65] As a part of the legal personality of the Community, the ECB would not have had legal capacity on its own, and not been entitled to acquire or dispose of movable and immovable property or to be a party to legal proceedings, as can be inferred from Art 107 EC and Art 9.1. ESCB-Statute as purpose of this provision.[66] Whereas it is not at all exceptional for the Community to create bodies endowed with legal personality,

---

62 SEC (90) 2500/2, commentary, reprinted in *Krägenau/Wetter* (1993) 194, 204. However, it was the Non-Papers of COREPER, providing rightaway for a whole new Article, which was finally realised. Reprinted in *Krägenau/Wetter* (1993) 218ff.

63 Cf. *Louis* (1999a) 462.

64 See on the legal personality of the EIB AG *Mancini* in Case 85/86 *Commission v. EIB* ECR [1988] 1281, para 11: The justification for the provision in primary legislation that gave the bank legal personality is that once it had been decided to set up the EIB "it was an obvious or even an obligatory step to give it legal personality, if only to enable the new body to operate within the various Member States in the same way as any other credit institution."

65 Cf. *Zilioli/Selmayr* (1999) 277ff: the more independent, the more likely to be awarded with the capacity to act autonomously at the international level.

66 The legal personality that exists is therefore *derivative*, relative and limited, *Herrmann* (2002) 9. That its existence depends on the intention of the drafters – to conduct the tasks conferred upon the ESCB – and on recognition by other subjects of public international law, is also recognised by *Zilioli/Selmayr* (1999) 277.

this never amounted to putting these bodies outside the Community.[67]

As the key issue is the degree of integration of the legal person ECB in the legal person EC, it must be emphasized that the fundamental characteristic of an *organ* (as the Community "institutions" are called in the German version of the Treaty)[68] is that its acts are directly imputable to the organisation of which it forms an integral part.[69] Is the ECB therefore a Community organ, in a technical sense, as was the Court of Auditors prior to being raised to the status of an institution?[70]

In case of the EIB, Advocate General (AG) Mancini rejected its qualification as an organ, as he considered its acts not to be directly imputable to the Community. Nevertheless, he called the connection between the Bank and the Community "functional", similar to the link between public bodies making up the so-called "indirect administration" of the State and the State itself.[71] The ECJ accepted this approach, by referring in its judgment to [now] Art 267 EC, according to which the EIB acts *in the interest of the Community* and thereby "forms part of the framework of the Treaty."[72] For the

---

67 *Torrent* (1999) 1233. Louis talks of a "conception excessive des conséquences de l'attribution de la personalité juridique", *Louis* (1999b) 9 n. 26. *Tizzano* (1998) 403 n. 45 argues that the affirmation of the ECB's legal personality aimed at avoiding dominance by the Community institutions and bodies, in order to enable it to exercise its specific competencies, but it did not aim at the creation of a new subject distinct from the entity in which it was inserted, for which it acted, and without which it would not even be conceivable.

68 See Art 7, Art 10, Art 11, Art 108 EC. It is argued that the term "institutions" does not have a specific content or substance, see *Mancini* op. cit. *supra 35* para 10. There are, however, Treaty provisions directed at Community "institutions" only, as Art 289 or 290 EC. Cf. *Schweitzer* (1999) Art 289 para 9, who deduces from the existence of a special norm for the ECB's seat (Art 37 ESCB-Statute) that it was not an Community institution under Art 7 EC. However, that the decison on the seat of a Community agency is left to the political discretion of the governments of the Member States, and not necessarily determined in the act by which it is established, is not unusual, (recall the discussions on the European Food Agency's seat).

69 *Levi* (1978) 235.

70 So *Amtenbrink* (1999) 166.

71 AG *Mancini, supra 35* para 10.

72 Case 85/86 *supra 40* para 29, emphasis added.

ECB, not only is Art 105 EC devoid of a similar provision. As also Arts 8 and 9 EC on ECB and EIB differ from Art 7 in that they do not contain the requirement to perform the *tasks entrusted to the Community*, the claim that the ECB had an independent and exclusive area of competence acting only exceptionally as a Community agent does not come as a surprise.[73]

D.) Monetary policy as own competence of the ECB

To be concrete, it is argued that monetary sovereignty has never, "not even for a juridical second", been transferred to the legal person EC, but was transferred directly from the Member States to the ECB.[74] Thereby, the ECB would possess originary competencies, not delegated to it by the Community institutions. The "own" objective of maintaining price stability as *lex specialis* to Art 2 EC would exclude the use of the ECB as financial instrument of the Communities.[75]

However, after an examination of Arts 2, 4 and 105 EC this interpretation must be rejected.[76] Under Art 105(1) 3rd sentence, the ESCB is to act in accordance with the principles set out in Art 4 EC. This article refers to the *Member States and the Community*[77] and makes them responsible not only for the introduction of a single currency, but also for the *definition and conduct* of a single monetary policy and exchange rate policy, the primary objective of both of which shall be to maintain price stability and, without prejudice to this objective, to support the general economic policies in the Community.[78] In doing so, Member States and Community are to comply with the guiding principles of stable prices, sound public

---

73 *Selmayr* (1999) 176ff.

74 *Zilioli/Selmayr* (2000) 618. *Pernice* (1995) 1059 seems to express a similar view: "Institutionell wird die WWU zwar in die EG eingebettet, die neuen Kompetenzen werden jedoch nicht – oder nicht nur –, dies erscheint bemerkenswert, auf die EG und ihre Organe übertragen, sondern der Unionsvertrag konstituiert ein von diesen gesondertes, quasi autonomes institutionelles System, das ESZB." However, by pointing to the integration of the System in the EC Treaty, and adding that not the *organs* of the EC, but the ESCB, would be the bearer of monetary sovereignty, there is a remarkable difference. *Ibid*, emphasis added.

75 *Zilioli/Selmayr* (2000) 610ff.

76 For the following cf also *Torrent* (1999) 1231ff, in particular n. 7.

77 "and to nobody else", *Torrent* (1999) 1232.

78 Art 4(2) EC.

finances and monetary conditions, and a sustainable balance of payments.[79]

Thus, how could the *Community* conduct monetary policy if this was the exclusive competence of the "new Community" ECB, unless the term "Community" is read as standing for Community in a broad sense, encompassing all its organs and bodies, even those with a separate legal personality such as the ECB? This reading is supported by the provision of Art 105(2) 1st indent, according to which the ESCB's task is to conduct and implement the monetary policy *of the Community* (and not "of the System"): this task was delegated to the ESCB which has been established for this purpose. Moreover, the ECB not only conducts, by maintaining price stability, a Community objective – see Art 2 EC, which lists sustainable and *non-inflationary* growth as one of the principle aims of the Community[80] – but Art 105(1) EC obliges it also to contribute to the achievement of the objectives of the Community as laid down in Art 2 EC, by supporting the general economic policies in the Community. True, there is a hierarchy between these two goals, as the latter contribution is only without prejudice to the primary objective of price stability, but this does not derogate from the ECB's duty of contributing to the achievement of the objectives laid down in Art 2 EC. Applying without temporal limitation, this permanent obligation establishes a lasting and close link between ECB and Community.

The argument that Arts 2 and 4 EC concerned chiefly the *process* of the establishment of EMU and the introduction of a single currency[81] is no barrier, even though with the application of Art 105 EC "from the beginning of the third stage"'[82] the ESCB is responsible for monetary policy. As has been observed,[83] by virtue of Art 121(3) it is the *Community* to enter the third stage, whereas the

---

[79] Art 4(3) EC.

[80] *Amtenbrink/de Haan* (2002) 68. According to *Stadler* (1996) 95, the ECB is competent to realise this sub-goal (price stability) of the Community.

[81] *Zilioli/Selmayr* (2000) 605 n 65. Note the conceptual similarity with the ECJ's argumentation of the Community's special character in *Costa v. E.N.E.L* (Case 6/64 [1964] ECR 585), in which the ECJ referred to the transfer of powers and limitation of the Member States' sovereign rights by the creation of a body of law.

[82] Art 116(3) 2nd sentence EC.

[83] *Torrent* (1999) 1232.

ECB is not mentioned there. In addition, it would be paradoxical to assume that the ECB conducted a stability-oriented monetary policy just for its own pleasure, and not in the interest and *for* the Community, which established it for this purpose.[84] As a result, the fact that the ECB conducts the tasks conferred upon it independently, without instructions, is irrelevant for the existence of a link, via the objectives, between ECB and Community stronger than a mere "unity of ideals".

Insofar the ECB is a means for the EC to achieve its political aims, and constitutes, as the EIB, "a Community body established by the Treaty."[85] The conduct of the common monetary policy gives the ECB a status similar to an agency.[86] From an institutional point of view, the establishment of an "internal body" (foundation, fund, agency) having a distinct legal personality outside the Community institutional structure laid down in Art 7 EC empowered to autonomously exercise political discretion is only admissible if foreseen in the "constitution" itself.[87] Other than assumed by *Zilioli/Selmayr*,[88] the establishment by primary instead of secondary law is therefore only the appropriate reaction to the limitation posed by "the balance of powers which is characteristic of the institutional structure of the Community."[89] It does not impede the qualification of the ECB as a Community agency. The ECB is hence the bearer of the respective powers,[90] but, as the EP observes, "under the Maastricht Treaty, the policy delegation, target and instrument independence, and powers that the ECB and NCBs have gained are

---

84 Even with due regard to the *sui generis* nature of the Community, one will not be able to reject the "common sense" argument that money is a public good. Even in the third stage of EMU, the *National* Central Banks still form part of the organisational structure of the Member States, on this *Hahn/Häde* (2001) 35; *Häde* (1999) Art 107, § 8 ("Einrichtungen der Mitgliedstaaten") with further references.

85 Case 110/75 *Mills v EIB*, [1976] ECR 955, para 14.

86 *Smulders* (1999) Art 4a para 3 speaks of an "organschaftlicher Status".

87 Examples of such constitutionally created bodies are the EIB and the ECB, so *Lenaerts* (1993) 42, in application of the ECJ's judgment in Case 9/56 *Meroni v. High Authority* [1957-58] ECR 133.

88 *Zilioli/Selmayr* (2000) 608-611.

89 Case 9/56 *Meroni v. High Authority* [1957-58] ECR 133, 152.

90 *Hahn/Häde* (2001) 32.

not their own", but "such powers have been delegated by the political authorities".[91]

E.) Consequences of the institutional particularities

1.) Importance

It may be inferred from above that the view that the institutional location in the organisational structure would not have any impacts on the scope of ECB's discretion[92] must be modified: As a matter of fact, whether the ECB is characterised as "Community institution *sui generis* with own legal personality," as "first fully fledged and independent agency of the Community"[93] or as "specific and autonomous segment of the organisational machinery of the Community"[94] has little practical relevance. Here, the differences are more or less of semantical nature. However, this is different for the more extensively outlined concept of the "independent specialised organisation", which has some remarkable impacts that deserve to be subsequently presented.

2.) Non-contractual liability

In this regard, an important question is the non-contractual liability. To be concrete, under Art 288 para 3 EC, para 2, the non-contractual liability of the Community, applies under the same conditions to damage caused by the ECB in the performance of its duties. In spite of the wording of the Treaty, it is held that, as the ECB was not a "Community agent", Art 108 EC would prohibit that the Community directed the ECB's monetary policy. In the absence of links between the ECB's and the Community's budget, it would be "quite absurd" to hold the Communities liable for damage caused by the ECB.[95] Redress could be sought directly from the ECB, which would have to make good any damage caused by its decision-making bodies in the performance of its duties.[96]

---

91 *European Parliament* (1999) 8; similar *Herrmann* (2002) 8-9.

92 So *Stadler* (1996) 97.

93 "Erste vollentwickelte und unabhängige Behörde der Gemeinschaft", *Smulders* (1999) Art 106 para 28.

94 So *Mancini* for the EIB, *supra* note 35 para 13.

95 *Zilioli/Selmayr* (2000) 638.

96 Cf. *Committee of Central Bank Governors* (1990) 17: "the *ECB* will be liable for the acts and decisions taken by the Council and the Executive Board, and there is thus no legal uncertainty be as to whether the

At this point, reference is made to *SGEEM and Etroy v. EIB,* wherein the ECJ found that although the EIB was neither an institution of the Community nor explicitly mentioned in Art 288 EC,

> "it would be contrary to the intention of the authors of the Treaty if, when it acts through a Community body established by the Treaty and authorized to act *in its name and on its behalf*, the Community could escape the consequences of the provisions of Article 178 and the second paragraph of Article 215 of the Treaty, the intention of which is to reserve for the Court's jurisdiction cases involving the non-contractual liability of the Community as a whole towards third parties."[97]

However, even if it is recalled that the ECB – in contrast to the EIB – is not a financial instrument of the Community, this passage does not serve as a justification to exclude contractual liability of the Community for the ECB: Neither did the ECJ decide on acts, which had not been performed on behalf of the Community, nor did it reveal that it intended to decide thereby, as a question of principle, on the liability for the EIB in general (in contrast, any statement of the law is limited to the case in hand).[98] In addition, the qualification of the EIB by the ECJ, in a prior judgment, as Community body led the AG to the following statement:

> "the Bank's status as an independent legal person *can hardly in itself preclude* an interpretation of the second paragraph of Art 215 [now 288] to the effect that the Bank can render the Community liable, subject, obviously, to the requirement that the actual manifestation of that liability, that is to say, the payment of compensation, must be made out of the

---

Community would have to assume liability for the system." Emphasis added.

97 Case 370/89 *SGEEM and Roland Etroy v. EIB*, [1992] ECR 6211 para 15 (interlocutory judgment), emphasis added.

98 Case 370/89 *SGEEM and Etroy v. EIB* ECR [1993] 2583 para 24: "*in this instance*".

> Bank's own funds and not out of the Community budget."[99]

Furthermore, the AG commented on the fact that only the ECB, but not the EIB, was explicitly mentioned by Art 288 para 3 EC: the ECB, in difference to the EIB, exercised public authority, and this public-law nature of its duties and powers made it necessary not only to include for the Central Bank rules in the Treaty, relating to the jurisdiction of the ECJ, but in addition made it also natural to draw an analogy between the ECB and the Community institutions for the purpose of matters relating to compensation.[100]

As a result for the non-contractual liability of the Community for the ECB's acts, whereas a possible damage would have to be compensated out of the ECB's own funds, the bearer of liability would be the Community.[101] After all, the fact that the ECB by virtue of Art 108 EC conducts the monetary policy of the Community without being subject to instructions, for instance regarding the stance of policy, is a sign of its independence, but does not prevent that the actions of the ECB can ultimately be imputed to the Community.[102] One could compare this approach with the treatment of the acts of the Commission, as Art 108 EC was obviously modelled after the provision of the Commission's independence as laid down in Art 213(2) EC, which however did not put the Commission outside the liability scheme of the Community, not even if it uses its independent right of initiative.[103] This model would, without undermining the operational autonomy or reputation of the ECB, un-

---

[99] AG *Gulmann* in Case 370/89 *SGEEM and Etroy v. EIB* ECR [1992] 6211 para 13, emphasis added.

[100] *Ibid,* para 15.

[101] However, representation before the ECJ usually is taken over by the institution or institutions against which the matter giving rise to liability is alleged, cf. Joined Cases 63 to 69/72 *Hansmoehle v. Council* [1973] ECR 1229, 1247, AG *Lenz* in Case 50/86 *Grands Moulins v Council and Commission* ECR [1987] 4833 para 6ff.

[102] *Hahn/Häde* (2001) 34, but insofar inconsistent with their position at 59, the ECB was liable, as the Community could not be liable for the misconducts of an independent central bank. This view is also presented by *Baur* (2001) 62ff, 66.

[103] This does not limit the existing discretion of the Commission to commence proceedings which excludes the right for individuals to require it to adopt a specific position, cf. Case T-201/96 *Smanor* ECR [1997] II-1081.

derscore the link between the actions of the ECB, as bearer of the Community's monetary policy, and the Community.[104]

3.) The issue of subordination

The second consequence which is assumed to result from the "extensively installed autonomy of the ECB" is the real motivation for denying that the connection between ECB and Community was stronger than a mere "association": the equal footing of the ECB with the three original Communities.[105] This amounts not only to the rejection of sometimes voiced demands for a political mandate,[106] but touches upon the question of subordination under Community secondary law, and sometimes also under the general principles of Community law.[107] As reported by *Louis*, the objective of avoiding that the ECB would be governed by the general rules applicable to the institutions, was in fact the reason that certain Member States refused to include it in the list of institutions under Art 7 EC. These efforts, however, were ineffective, as the ECJ would, irrespective of the qualification as an organ or institution, not hesitate to recur, in case that the applicable legal norms did not foresee a specific arrangement, to the general principles of Community law.[108]

The view that the Treaty did not seek, by not unequivocally putting the ECB on a par with the institutions of the Community, to

---

[104] Cf. Case 85/86 *Commission v. EIB* [1988] ECR 1281, para 30, where the ECJ regarded the general principles of community law applicable on the EIB if they did not undermine the operational autonomy and reputation of the bank as an independent institution on the financial markets, for instance by affecting "the capital or the actual management of the bank".

[105] *Zilioli/Selmayr* (2000) 622.

[106] See *Magnette's* account of the calls made by the EP, *Magnette* (2000) 338.

[107] See *Committee of Central Bank Governors* (1990) 18, invoking arguments to establish the System separately in a new paragraph of Art 7: "In order to avoid any legal uncertainty arising from the possible application to the System of general provisions relating to Community institutions, the Statute contains a special Chapter (VII) which includes the necessary provisions governing the general aspects of the System." Thereby, the application of the general provisions seems to be excluded. *Zilioli/Selmayr* (2000) 623 however underscore the ECB's subjection to the principles of primary Community law.

[108] *Louis* (1995) 56-57.

bind the ECB by the fundamental duty of co-operation of the Community institutions under Art 10 EC, and limited such co-operation to situations expressly laid down by the Treaty,[109] must therefore be rejected: In the light of the legally guaranteed independence of instructions, there cannot be sustainable arguments against a parallel application of general rules, if that should be necessary.

On the contrary, there could be sound reasons to treat the central bank in the same way as the organs of the Community.[110] This consideration seems to guide the approach of positively defining the ESCB as an organ of the Community, which in carrying out the Community's tasks is to co-operate with the institutions and other bodies. This was to happen in accordance with Art 10 EC, which in spite of its wording applied to relations between the ESCB and the institutions and to relations between the ESCB and the Member States.[111] It must be recalled that such a duty to co-operate does not amount to subordination, as the ESCB by virtue of Art 108 EC is protected from being given instructions, also in the form of political medium-term objectives. The room for manoeuvre below this limit, however, is considerable.

4.) Excursus: The OLAF case

Even if *Zilioli/Selmayr* accept the subjection of the ECB under the general principles of Community law, one consequence of their perception of the ECB as being on an equal footing with the Community is that the ECB's subjection under secondary Community law is denied, if they find that secondary law to be inconsistent with

---

[109] So *Weinbörner* (1998) 387ff. Cf also *Pernice* (1999) para 3, pointing to the fact that the political institutions of the Community have, with regard to the ECB, in addition to a complementary law-making capacity only clearly defined rights of participation and information.

[110] Cf. *Slot* (1998) 247, who calls it odd that WTO Agreements concluded under Art 300(7) EC are not binding on the ECB, as this paragraph applies to the "institutions of the Community", whereas agreements concluded in accordance with Art 111(3) EC are binding on the ECB.

[111] *Smits* (1997) 93. Cf. also Case C-65/93 *Parliament v. Council* [1995] ECR I-643 para 23, where the ECJ held that inter-institutional dialogue was "subject to the same *mutual duties of sincere cooperation* as those which govern relations between Member States and the Community institutions." Emphasis added.

the general principles of primary Community law.[112] A concrete case is the Regulation 1073/1999 on the European Anti-Fraud Office (OLAF),[113] or its powers vis-à-vis the ECB, which is a matter *sub judice.*[114] Under the "equal-footing-thesis", the subordination of the ECB under OLAF is regarded as inconsistent with the special status of the ECB in the Community legal order, its functional and institutional independence: Also OLAF, which would as a matter of fact issue instructions in the course of its investigations, was bound by the absolute prohibition of instructions enshrined in primary law.[115]

The second objection against any activity of OLAF on the ECB's premises relates to the fact that fraud prevention under Art 280(1) EC as a shared competence of Community and Member States aims "to protect the financial interests *of the Community*". The Commission considered the protection of the Community's financial interests as provided for in Regulation 1073/1999 to be applicable to the ECB, since it was not restricted to the protection of the Community budget, but had a wider scope and extended to "budgets managed" by the Communities, including also budgets of separate, decentralised Community organisations.[116] Accordingly, the ECB's own budget and financial resources separate from those of the Communities would not preclude the applicability to the ECB of the measures adopted under Art 280(4) EC. However, both the ECB and the EIB refused to submit to the Commission's inves-

---

[112] Cf. *Zilioli/Selmayr* (2002) 631. See also *Schweitzer* (1999) Art 290 para 14 on the ECB's language regime: As Art 290 EC refers to the language regime of the Community *institutions*, the Council's Language Regulation 1/1958 was considered as not applying to the ECB, whereas the ECB's language regime had to be in line with the general principle to treat all Community languages equally. The solution found was that the principles of the regulation apply to the legal acts of the ECB under Art 34 ESCB-Statute, but not to guidelines and instructions, see Art 17.2., 17.6. and 17.8, Rules of Procedure of the ECB, OJL 125 1999, as amended in OJL 314 1999.

[113] Regulation (EC) 1073/1999 of the EP and the Council concerning investigations conducted by the European Anti-Fraud Office (OLAF), OJL 136, 31/05/1999 1-7.

[114] Case C-11/00 *Commission v. ECB*, OJC 122, 29/04/00 8.

[115] *Selmayr* (1999) 171, 180.

[116] So the pleas in law and main arguments of the Commission, published in OJC 122, 29/04/2000, 8. See also Commission Press Release IP/00/22.

tigation agency to carry out investigations on their premises, since OLAF was set up on the basis of the Commission's rules of procedure by virtue of its powers of internal organisation[117] "among its own departments".[118]

With a view to OLAF's extensive powers, its peculiar status as an internal body of the Commission, based on its rules of procedure, poses a problem. By Regulation 1073/1999, the Council formally conferred upon OLAF the powers of investigation which previously had been vested in the Commission under the Regulations 2185/96[119] and 2988/95,[120] comprising both the exercise of the Commission's *external* and *internal* administrative investigation powers. In particular, internally, OLAF may conduct, as long as it complies with the Protocol on Privileges and Immunities, inspections, checks and other measures, which can comprise unannounced and immediate access to the premises of Community bodies and institutions, inspection of the accounts of these institutions and bodies, copy taking and requesting of oral information.[121] The bodies under review are called upon to assist the Office's agents in fulfilling their tasks,[122] and forward to the Office without delay any information relating to illegal activities.[123]

However, according to the ECJ's case law, the purpose of the rules of procedure of a Community institution is to organise the internal functioning of its services in the interests of good administration.[124] Although such measures do not exceed the confines of the power of internal organisation on the ground that they have

---

117 Commission Decision of 28 April 99/352/ EC, ECSC, Euratom, establishing the European Anti-fraud Office (OLAF), OJL 136, 31/05/1999, 20-22, see also Art 218(2) EC: "[t]he Commission shall adopt its Rules of Procedure so as to ensure that both it and its departments operate in accordance with the provisions of the Treaty."

118 So the ECB in recital 7 of ECB/1999/5 (Decision of the ECB on fraud prevention, OJL 291, 12/11/1999).

119 Council Regulation 2185/96 concerning on-the-spot checks and inspections carried out by the Commission, OJL 292, 15/11/1996, 2-5.

120 Council Regulation 2988/95 on the protection of the European Communities' financial interests, OJ L 312, 23/12/1995.

121 Art 4(2) Regulation (EC) 1073/1999.

122 Art 6(6), Reg 1073/1999.

123 Art 7(1), Reg 1073/1999.

124 Case C-69/89 *Nakajima v Council* [1991] ECR I-2069, para 49.

legal effects vis-à-vis third parties,[125] it is clear that the rules governing internal inquiries at other Community institutions and bodies have to respect "the principle of each institution's internal organisational autonomy".[126] Therefore, each institution, body, office or agency was obliged under Art 4(1) of the Regulation 1073/1999 to adopt decisions which should include rules concerning firstly a duty on the part of the staff of the said bodies to co-operate with and supply information to OLAF, and secondly concerning the procedures which OLAF's employees would have to observe when conducting internal investigations, and concerning the guarantees of the rights of persons concerned by such an investigation.[127]

In the following, the EP, the Commission and the Council signed an inter-institutional agreement, according to which they agreed on a standard model which should be entered by all other institutions, and also by the bodies and offices and agencies established by or on the basis of the EC or the Euratom Treaty.[128] The standard model specifies the duty of the institution or body to co-operate with the Office, pass on relevant information and assist the Office's agents by their security office.

All bodies entering the inter-institutional agreement should adopt the model decision without deviating from that model "save where their own *particular requirements* make such deviation a technical necessity."[129] The functional and institutional independence of ECB and EIB was recognised by the Commission as such a particular requirement. It therefore suggested an arrangement similar to the one of the ECJ,[130] which by virtue of an unpublished decision on 26 October 1999 in accordance with Art 4 of Regulation 1073/1999, granted OLAF full access to all documents and information, except for those related to legal proceedings. OLAF's powers were limited only insofar as the registrar of the ECJ serves as the interface between OLAF and ECJ. On the one hand, he is to be informed by ECJ officials and employees, and communicates relevant facts to OLAF, and on the other hand, he

---

125 Case C-58/94 *Netherlands v Council* [1996] ECR-I 2169 para 38.

126 See 4th recital, Reg 1073/1999.

127 Art 4(6) a and b Reg 1073/1999.

128 Inter-institutional agreement of 25 May 1999 between the EP, the Council and the Commission concerning internal investigations by OLAF, OJL 136, 31/05/1999, 15 –19.

129 Inter-institutional agreement paragraph 2, emphasis added.

130 See Commission Press Release, IP/00/22.

has to be informed on any investigations by OLAF at the ECJ's premises. As the duty to co-operate with OLAF is binding on the employees, the ECJ in spite of its *particular requirements* apparently did not see the need to establish an internal audit committee in order to safeguard its independence and specificity.

As a principle, also the ECB is competent to enter into an interinstitutional agreements should its tasks so require.[131] However, not even the invitation of the Cologne European Council to "consider as soon as possible the terms under which the Office may carry out internal investigations and also what form co-operation with the Office might take"[132] could prevent the ECB from issuing a decision on fraud prevention, under which it established the ECB Directorate for Internal Audit and denied OLAF access to its premises.[133] Consequently, the Commission considered the relevant decision not to be compatible with Regulation (EC) 1073/1999 of 25 May 1999 and sued the ECB as well as the EIB.

Without intending to predict the judgment of the ECJ, it should be noted that the Court of First Instance already had to rule on the institutional consequences of OLAF's powers.[134] The Court first shared the concerns of some Members of the EP that the investigations conducted by OLAF could compromise the immunity afforded to the Members of the EP by Art 10 of the Protocol on the Privileges and Immunities, which intended to safeguard their independence in carrying out their duties and to prevent pressure. Consequently, as an interim measure under Art 242 EC, it suspended parts of the EP's Rules of Procedure which had been amended in order to allow for investigations.[135] In particular, the fact that mem-

---

[131] *Smits* (1997) 105.

[132] The European Council "noted with satisfaction" that most of the other bodies, offices and agencies except the ECJ, the Court of Auditors, the ECB and the EIB, had immediately declared their willingness to open their doors where required to an internal investigation by the Anti-Fraud Office, and considered it to be "eminently desirable that all Community bodies should join this interinstitutional initiative," see Conclusions of the Presidency para 35, Press Release No 150/99.

[133] ECB/1999/5, Art 1, 2 and 9.

[134] Case T-17/00 *Rothley and Others v Parliament*, Judgment of 26/02/2002, not yet recorded.

[135] Order of the Court of First Instance of 2. May 2000 in case T-17/00 R, paras 89ff. See for the amended Rules of Procedure of the EP OJL 202, 1999.

bers of OLAF could have access to MEP's offices, in their absence and without their consent, led the Court to conclude that the EP's amended rules of procedure did not contain any specific guarantee with regard to respect for the rights of the MEPs.

However, acting separately under Art 230 para 4 EC for annulment, the Court of First Instance recently dismissed the action as inadmissible, as the MEPs were not individually concerned by the contested measure, which was a "measure of general application" rather than a "decision."[136] In addition, the Court did not find a superior rule of law which could make the action for annulment admissible, as the amended Rules of Procedure let the rules on both independence and immunity of the MEPs unchanged.[137]

As these problems of *locus standi* do not apply to actions brought by the Commission, it will be very interesting whether the ECJ in the pending case on OLAF will have a different stance on the question whether OLAF's investigatory powers infringe a higher rule of law. After all, this is essentially what seems to stand behind the reasoning that a Community secondary law act allowing internal investigations allegedly infringes the higher legal principle of the ECB's independence. However, this is not to say that the ECJ is bound to deliberate on the ECB's institutional status, nor that a rejection of the Commission's application denoted the validity of the positions regarding the ECB as a "new Community". *Au contraire,* OLAF was set up on the basis of Art 218 EC as a body, albeit an independent one,[138] of the Commission, which certainly is a weak legal basis for interfering in the internal administration of other Community bodies which are no Commission "departments". Hence, it is plausible that the ECJ agrees that the "special requirements" of the ECB with regard to the confidentiality of its monetary policy decisions are so demanding that the ECB's refusal to accept

[136] Case T-17/00 para 61.

[137] Case T-17/00 para 73: "the risk cannot a priori be excluded that the Office, in conducting an investigation, might perform an act prejudicial to the immunity enjoyed by every Member of the Parliament. However, if that were to occur, any Member of the Parliament faced with such an act, could, if he considered it damaging to him, avail himself of the judicial protection and the legal remedies provided for by the Treaty."

[138] Whereas the Director is appointed by the Commission, in the exercise of its tasks, OLAF is independent from instructions of the Commission or any government, institution or other body, Art 3 of Dec 99/352.

the jurisdiction of the Commission's agency to carry out investigations on their premises are justifiable.

On the other hand, it should not be forgotten that the ECJ for its own relationship with OLAF did not see the need for the drastic measure of denying access to its premises. More importantly, it cannot accept that the ECB demands for itself the right to establish which Community secondary law is not in line with the general principles of primary Community law and is therefore not binding on it. After all, it is the ECJ which in the interpretation and application of the Treaty ensures that the law is observed.[139] It would therefore add to clarity, if the ECJ used the possibility to rule on the institutional status of the ECB.[140] Given the doubts voiced in the *academia* concerning the ability of the ECJ to provide for a substantial, not only formal or symbolical, link between the ESCB and the Community,[141] it would be an opportunity to show that legal control truly is a counterweight to the ECB's independence.[142] It deserves to be emphasised that the question is not whether the ECB has the right to effectively fight against encroachments into its competencies, but whether this includes the right to reject legislation concerning the inter-institutional relationship outside the field of monetary policy.

IV. Conclusion

It cannot be denied that from a formalistic point of view, a number of Treaty provisions seem to support those calling the ECB a "new Community". For instance, the measure of distance to the Community mechanisms of democratic accountability in the performance of the monetary policy rightly leads to doubts concerning the compatibility of the ECB's autonomy with the democratic prin-

---

139 Art 220 EC.

140 *Torrent* (1999) 1241, calling for a clear-cut decision of the ECJ, "in the interest of knowing [...] to whom the "monetary sovereignty" of the Member States has been surrendered."

141 Inspite of the "unparalleled effort" to bind both monetary policy and its framework, so *Nicolaysen* (1993) 35. See also *Smits* (1997) 502.

142 As submitted by *Louis* (1997) 592. Cf. also *Schmid-Lossberg* (1992) 54, fearing a possible loss of weight of the ECJ, if its control was merely restricted to check whether the Community institutions and bodies acted within their limit of discretion, as this inevitably widened their discretionary margin.

ciple.[143] It must, on the other hand, be doubted that it had been the intention of the drafters of the Treaty to establish a central bank endowed with public tasks which would not be fully integrated in the Community, in the framework of which they had decided to implement EMU.[144]

The legal structures of the Union are very complex, housing a variety of legal persons more reminiscent in structural terms of an old-fashioned "Russian doll" than any architecturally ambitious "temple" or cathedral.[145] This is nevertheless not an argument supporting the separation of the ECB from the EC, but rather contradicting it, as the ECB is just another facet in this variety.[146] Its often-cited "special status" may be comprised as a true child of the political compromises, reflecting the high significance of the process of transferring monetary powers as important sovereign rights to the Community. The asymmetrical structure of EMU has been willingly taken into account,[147] without however neglecting the functional tie between the Community's objectives and the conduct of monetary policy by the ECB as appropriate agent.

Adding a last remark, the efforts to establish the view of a "new Community" ECB and to support the self-image of the ECB as an autonomous entity[148] may be explained by reference to the work of political scientists: There, the notion of a trade-off between the planned (positive) effects of bureaucratic autonomy and its negative

---

143 See *Amtenbrink/de Haan* (2002) 74ff.

144 Cf. *Snyder* (1994) 80: "the accountability of the ECB is due less to the (limited) extent to which it is answerable directly to the Community political institutions or national governments than to the fact that it is locked into a relatively complex institutional structure and set of inter-institutional relations." This "Beziehungsgeflecht" is, however, not of the same quality as the institutional balance at EU level, "where each institution needs to look for the support of others because it is unable to force their hand and make decisions without political consent", *Magnette* (2000) 331. *Au contraire*, it is exactly this what is missing for EMU.

145 *Curtin/Dekker* (1999) 132.

146 See *Tizzano* (1998) 403: "Tali strutturi [...] restano strumenti ed organi di cui il soggetto che le ingloba si avvale, nelle forme di maggiore o minore autonomia volta a volta definite, per la realizzazione die propri obiettivi e deit proprio compiti." Depending on the point of view, this comprising entity was the Community or the Union, ibid n. 45.

147 *Verdun* (1996) 80.

148 Cf. *Selmayr* (1999) 179ff.

side-effects is since the writings of *Max Weber* quite common.[149] Such unintended consequences as unresponsiveness, unaccountability, exploitation of information asymmetries, or even the attempt to maximise autonomy[150] appear thus to be inherent in the institutional set-up within which the ECB is to operate. This is not to say that such consequences are inevitable – at least, it is hoped that they are not, given the practical relevance of the question whether to locate the ECB *within* the EC. It is, however, but in different clothes, the same old story of the appropriate degrees of freedom and tight political constraints, or the search for a balance of powers in a constitutional system.

References

Amtenbrink F. / de Haan J. (2002), The European Central Bank: An Independent Specialised Organization of Community Law – A Comment, CMLRev 39 2002, 65-76.

Baur I. (2001), Die Haftung der Europäischen Zentralbank, Frankfurt 2001.

Bogdandy A. von (2001), Organizational Proliferation and Centralization under the Treaty on European Union, in: *Blokker N. M. /Schermers H. G.* (eds.), Proliferation of International Organizations, Legal Issues, The Hague (et. al) 2001, 177-217.

Christensen J. G. (1999), Bureaucratic Autonomy as a Political Asset, Paper presented at the workshop "Politicians, Bureaucrats, and Institutional Reform", ECPR Uni-Mannheim 26-31 March 1999, http://www.essex.ac.uk/ecpr/jointsessions/Manpapers/w1/Christensen.PDF.

Committee of Central Bank Governors (1990), Draft Statute of the European System of Central Banks and of the European Central Bank, Draft Statute, Introductory Report and Commentary by the Committee of Governors of the Central Banks of the Member States, in: Agence Europe Documents No 1669/1670, 8/12/1990.

---

[149] The crucial aspect being the aspect of how to control political power, see fundamentally *Loewenstein* (1957) 8ff.

[150] See *Christensen* (1999) 7, with further references.

Curtin D. / Dekker I. (1999), The EU as "Layered" International Organization: Institutional Unity in Disguise, in: *Craig P. /de Búrca G.* (eds.), The Evolution of EU Law, Oxford 1999, 83-132.

Di Bucci V. (1997), La Corte di Giustizia, L'Unione Economica e Monetaria ed il Passaggio alla Moneta Unica, 37 *Rivista di diritto europeo* 1997, 3-77.

European Parliament (1999), Report on the constitutional implications of EMU in the context of enlargement, Rapporteur *Barros Moura*, A4-0030/1999 (pdf-Version).

Häde U. (1999), Art 107, in: *Calliess Ch. /Ruffert M.* (eds.), Kommentar zu EU-Vertrag und EG-Vertrag, Neuwied 1999.

Hahn H. J. / Häde U. (2001), Die Zentralbank vor Gericht, ZHR 165, 2001, 30-61.

Hallstein W. (1973), Die Europäische Gemeinschaft, Düsseldorf 1973.

Herrmann C. W. (2002), Monetary Sovereignty over the Euro and External Relations of the Euro Area: Competences, Procedures and Practice, European Foreign Affairs Review 7: 2002, 1–24.

Krägenau H. / Wetter W. (1993), Europäische Wirtschafts- und Währungsunion, Analysen und Dokumente, Baden-Baden 1993.

Lenaerts K. (1993), Regulating the Regulatory Process: „Delegation of Powers" in the European Community, ELR 1993, 23-49.

Levi M. (1978), Sulla Competenza della Corte di Giustizia Comunitaria Nelle Controversie tra la BEI e i Suoi Dipendenti, Rivista di Diritto Europeo, No 2 1978, 229-241.

Loewenstein K. (1957) Verfassungslehre, Heilbronn 1957.

Louis J. V. (1995), L'Union Economique et Monetaire, in: *Louis J. V.* et. al. (ed.), Commentaire Mégret, Le Droit de la CEE, Vol 6, Bruxelles ²1995, 1-165.

Louis J. V. (1997), Union Monétaire et Union Politique. Le Rôle du Juge, in: *Congrés de l'Union des Avocats Européens* at Venice 1996, La Tutela Giurisdizionale dei Diritti nel Sistema Communitario, Bruxelles 1997, 585-596.

Louis J. V. (1999a), Indépendance des Banques Centrales, Séparation des Pouvoirs et Démocratie, in: *Dony M. /Walsche A. de* (eds.), Mélanges en Hommage à Michel Waelbroeck, Bruxelles 1999, 459-481.

Louis J. V. (1999b), Les Relations Internationales de L'Union Economique et Monétaire, EUI Working Paper LAW No 99/10.

Magnette P. (2000), Towards „Accountable Independence“? Parliamentary Controls of the European Central Bank and the Rise of a New Democratic Model, in: ELJ Vol 6 No 4 2000, 326-340.

Nicolaysen G. (1993), Rechtsfragen der Währungsunion: erweiterte Fassung eines Vortrages, gehalten vor der Juristischen Gesellschaft zu Berlin, Berlin 1993.

Pechstein M. / Koenig C. (2000), Die Europäische Union: die Verträge von Maastricht und Amsterdam, Tübingen [3]2000.

Pernice I. (1995), Das Ende der währungspolitischen Souveränität Deutschlands, in: *Due O. /Lutter M. / Schwarze J.* (eds.), FS Everling Bd II, Baden-Baden 1995, 1057-1070.

Pernice I. (1997), Art 4a EGV, in: *Grabitz E. /Hilf M.* (eds.), Recht der Europäischen Union (vormals: Kommentar zur Europäischen Union), EL 10 München 1997.

Pipkorn J. (1994), Legal Arrangements in the Treaty of Maastricht for the Effectiveness of the Economic and Monetary Union, 31 CMLRev 1994, 263-291.

Schermers H. G. / Blokker N. M. (1999), International Institutional Law: Unity within Diversity, The Hague et. al. [3]1999.

Schmid-Lossberg A. (1992), Kontrolldichte im EG-Wirtschaftsrecht, Eine Untersuchung am Beispiel der Rechtsprechung des EuGH zu den Verordungen im Währungsausgleich, Frankfurt am Main 1992.

Schweitzer M. (1999), Art 289, Art 290 EGV, in: *Grabitz E. / Hilf M.* (eds.), Recht der Europäischen Union (vormals: Kommentar zur Europäischen Union), EL 14 München 1999.

Seidel M. (1992), Probleme der Verfassung der Europäischen Gemeinschaft als Wirtschaft- und Währungsunion, in: *Baur J. F. / Müller-Graff P.-Ch. /Zuleeg M.* (eds.), FS Börner, Köln et.al. 1992, 417-430.

Seidel M. (2000), Im Kompetenzkonflikt: Europäisches System der Zentralbanken (ESZB) versus EZB, EuZW Heft 18/2000, 552-554.

Selmayr M. (1999), Die EZB als neue Gemeinschaft – ein Fall für den EuGh?, Europablätter 1999, 170-181.

Slot P. J. (1994), The Institutional Provisions of the EMU, in: *Curtin D.* (ed.), Institutional Dynamics of European Integration, Essays in Honour of Schermers, Dordrecht (u.a.) 1994, 229-249.

Smits R. (1997), The European Central Bank: Institutional Aspects, London 1997.

Smulders B. (1999), Art 4a, Art 106, in: *Von der Groeben H. / Thiesing J. /Ehlermann C.-D.* (eds.), Handbuch des Europäischen Rechts: systematische Sammlung mit Erläuterungen, Baden-Baden ^{5}1999.

Snyder F. (1994), EMU – Metaphor for European Union? Institutions, Rules and Types of Regulation, in: *Dehousse R.* (ed.), Europe after Maastricht An Ever Closer Union?, München 1994, 63-99.

Snyder F. (1999), EMU Revisited: Are We Making a Constitution? What Constitution Are We Making?, in: *Craig P. /de Búrca G.* (eds.), The Evolution of EU Law, Oxford 1999, 417–478.

Stadler R. (1996), Der rechtliche Handlungsspielraum des ESZB, Baden-Baden 1996.

Tizzano A. (1998), La Personalitá Internazionale dell'Unione Europea, in: Diritto dell'Unione Europea 2-3/1998, 377-406.

Torrent R. (1999), To Whom is the European Central Bank the Central Bank of: Reaction to Zilioli and Selmayr, 36 CMLRev 1999, 1229-1241.

Ver Loren Van Themaat P. (1996), Some Propositions on the Legal Aspects of the Planned Economic and Monetary Union in its Political, Economic, and Social Context before and after the Ratification of the Treaty of Maastricht, in: *Snyder F.* (ed.), Constitutional Dimensions of European Economic Integration, The Hague (et.al) 1996, 3-22.

Verdun A. (1996), An "Asymmetrical" Economic and Monetary Union in the EU: Perceptions of Monetary Authorities and Social Partners, Revue d'intégration européenne 1/1996, 59-81.

Weinbörner S. (1998), Die Stellung der Europäischen Zentralbank und der nationalen Zentralbanken nach dem Vertrag von Maastricht, Frankfurt 1998.

De Witte B. (1998), The Pillar Structure and the Nature of the European Union: Greek Temple or French Gothic Cathedral?, in: *Heukels/Blokker/Brus* (eds.), The European Union after Amsterdam, The Hague 1998, 51-68.

Zilioli C. / Selmayr M. (1999), The External Relations of the Euro Area: Legal Aspects, 36 CMLRev 1999, 273-349.

Zilioli C. / Selmayr M. (2000), The European Central Bank: An Independent Specialized Organization of Community Law, 37 CMLRev 2000, 591-644.

Harald Badinger, Barbara Dutzler

Excess reserves in the Eurosystem: an economic and legal analysis[1]

I. Introduction

The introduction of a common European currency and the establishment of an independent European Central Bank (ECB) – two steps of European monetary integration, which had been regarded as "politically very complicated, almost utopian"[2] three decades ago

---

[1] This article partly draws on results from the research project "Excess Reserves in the Eurosystem: An Economic and Legal Analysis of Alternative Uses". Support by the Austrian Science Fund (FWF) – project number P15256 – is gratefully acknowledged.

[2] *Mundell* (1973a) 157.

– became reality on 1 January 1999. Eleven of the 15 Member States of the European Union commenced the Third Stage of Economic and Monetary Union (EMU) and transferred their monetary competence to the European Community. On 1 January 2001, Greece became the twelfth member of the euro area.

This paper addresses the consequences of the euro for the international reserves of the Eurosystem (i.e. the ECB and the national central banks (NCBs) of the countries that have already introduced the euro), both from an economic and a legal point of view. Most previous studies argue that the introduction of the euro generated a considerable amount of excess reserves,[3] although their estimates vary considerably, ranging from one tenth to approximately half of the existing level. Conversely, *Eichengreen* and *Mathieson*[4] even argue that there was a shortage of reserves in the Eurosystem, as a result of the elimination of former reserve assets. Given this broad range of estimates, the first aim of this paper is to systematically re-examine the effects of the euro on international reserves from an ex-post perspective.

Our second objective is to investigate the issue of legal ownership of foreign reserve assets in the euro area and the consequences of this on the ability to dispose of any excess reserves. This reviews the constraints on the independent management of the foreign reserve assets by the NCBs and whether the reserves remaining with the NCBs be used by the individual nations.

Our results show that, accounting for reserve reductions due to the "technical effects" of the Euro, some 40 per cent of the existing reserves can be regarded as excessive. We then consider which organisation, EU member states, the NCBs or the ECB, has authority to manage the official foreign reserves and decide to use them for any other purpose apart from holding and managing them. This paper also discusses the principles to be applied in this case and the question of conformity with the legal norms. In particular, it is the responsibility of the ECB to ensure consistency of foreign reserve management with exchange rate and monetary policy of the ESCB.[5]

---

3 *European Commission* (1990), *Kenen* (1995), *Leahy* (1996), *Breuss* (1997), *Frenkel/Sondergaard* (1999).

4 *Eichengreen/Mathieson* (2000).

5 Art 31.2. Statute of the European System of Central Banks and of the European Central Bank, hereinafter ESCB-Statute.

The rest of the paper is organised as follows. In section two, we describe the implications of the introduction of the euro and estimate the excess reserves generated by monetary unification. In section three we present the legal framework referring to the distribution and use of the ESCB's international reserves and comment on the limits of discretionary use of reserves. In section four, we summarise our results and conclude.

II. The changeover to the Third Stage of EMU and its implications for the Eurosystem's international reserves

The introduction of the euro had a direct and immediate effect on the Eurosystem's international reserves, which is largely a matter of accounting and due to i) the unwinding of official ECU into gold and US-dollar by 1 January 1999[6] and ii) the redefinition of international reserves as of 1 January 1999 as "highly liquid, marketable and creditworthy claims held by the ECB ("pooled reserves") and the participating NCBs ("unpooled reserve assets") on *non-residents* of the euro area and denominated in *foreign currency* (i.e. *in currencies other than the Euro*), plus gold, reserve positions in the Fund and SDR holdings."[7]

The quantitative implications of these technical effects can be seen from Table 1. The unwinding of ECU, which is reflected in the changes from November 1998 to December 1998, led to a considerable increase in gold reserves by approximately 20 per cent in terms of the total (end of) 1998-value and a substantial decrease in foreign exchange reserves by some $37 billion. The exchange of ECU against gold (valued at market prices), however, can only account for $20 billion of this reduction, which indicates that a reduction in reserves took place simultaneously and/or that gold had been exchanged at a higher price. The exchange of ECU against dollar led only to a change in the composition of the foreign exchange reserves and cannot be seen in Table 1.

---

6 The ECU was created by the EMS agreement in 1979 (Article 17) and issued to the central banks of the participating countries through revolving swaps against deposit of 20 per cent of their gold and dollar holdings with the European Monetary Co-operation Fund (later the European Monetary Institute (EMI), and then the ECB). According to Article 23.2 of the EMI Statute and Article 20 of the EMS Agreement the mechanism for the creation of ECUs against gold and US dollars was unwound by the first day of stage three of EMU.

7 *ECB* (2000), emphasis added.

However, the reduction in the level of foreign exchange together with the exchange of ECU into US-dollar, further increased the dominating role of the US-dollar as reserve asset of the European central banks.[8]

---

[8] Although the exact currency composition is kept confidentially by central banks, the dollar share at the beginning of 1999 can be approximated by the following considerations: the US-$ reserves transferred to the European Monetary Institute, which made up some 20 per cent of the EU's total US-$ reserves, amounted to $44,508 million at the end of May 1998 (*ECB Annual Report* (1998) 138); the implied value of the EU's total US-$ reserves made up some 58.3 per cent of the EU's (and as we assume also the Eurosystem's) total foreign exchange reserves. The unwinding of the ECU further increased the dollar share to a level of 66 per cent at the end of 1998. These results are in line with the currency composition of the EU's reserves according to *Masson/Turtelboom* (1997), which is based on aggregate EU-data for 1995, which had been confidentially submitted to the IMF. Further increases in the share of the dollar reserves resulted from the decline in foreign exchange as a result of the redefinition of reserves. Assuming that the dollar reserves were not affected by the redefinition their share was pushed up to a dominating level of 75 per cent at the beginning of 1999.

Table 1: International reserves of the Eurosystem over the period 1998-2001 (million US-$)

	Reserve asset	31.11.1998	31.12.1998	1.1.1999	31.12.1999	31.12.2000	31.12.2001[1)]
(1)	Gold – official price	15450	19702	19958	19348	18219	17682
(2)	market price	94256	115057	116556	116900	109652	111119
(3)	SDRs	5787	6015	6838	4546	4032	4045
(4)	Reserve position	25988	27364	26761	24245	19662	19347
(5)	Foreign Exchange	304015	267237	237548	226250	217792	205323
(6)	Other Reserves	0	0	825	2078	1071	2273
	International reserves						
(7)	incl. gold at official price $\sum(1,3,4,5,6)$	351239	320317	291931	276466	260777	248669
(8)	incl. gold at market price $\sum(2,3,4,5,6)$	430045	415673	388529	374019	352209	342107
(9)	euro claims on non-euro area residents	-	-	10538	4844	3486	5055
(10)	non-euro claims on euro area residents	-	-	8724	14481	14700	21739

Data sources: International Financial Statistics, Euro area statistics (ECB Monthly Bulletin), own calculations. – 1998-values calculated as the sum of the euro area countries. – [1)] 2001-value including Greece. – Official gold price (since July 1974): 35 SDRs/oz. (1oz. = fine troy ounce = 31.10348g).

The effect of the redefinition of reserves is reflected in the changes from December 1998 to January 1999. Former reserve assets, which were denominated in "euro-currencies" (e.g. DM reserves of the *Banque de France*) or held as claims on euro area residents (e.g. a dollar deposit of *De Nederlandsche Bank* with a bank located in Germany) are excluded by the new reserve definition, which led to a decrease in foreign exchange reserves by some $30 billion. This reduction was partly compensated by the two new non-reserve positions "euro claims on non-euro area residents" and "claims in foreign currency on euro area residents", which together made up some $19 billion at the beginning of 1999. One may assume that the remaining gap of $11 billion is accounted for by former reserves, denominated in euro currencies and held as claims on euro area residents (e.g. a DM deposit of the *Banca d'Italia* with a German bank); however, no data on these former reserves is published by the ECB. After the changeover, international reserves amounted to $292 billion, considerably less than $352bn at the end of November 1998. Reserves have since declined to $249 billion at the end of 2001.

Beside these technical effects, the euro had also implications for the "optimal" level of reserves in the euro area. Economic theory suggests that a substantial reduction in international reserves can take place after the formation of a monetary union. The basic arguments can be traced back to the early 70s[9] and are now part of standard textbooks on economic integration:[10] i) After the formation of a monetary union no reserves are needed any more to finance trade between EU countries, which has become "domestic" trade from a monetary perspective. This may be termed the *scale (of foreign trade) effect*. ii) Also, if member states of the currency union are structurally diverse, any balance of payment imbalances may be offsetting, and a pooling of reserves should allow the minimum reserve level to be reduced. This is a classical *portfolio effect*. Further arguments can be made on the elimination of the need to stabilise the exchange rate vis-à-vis the currencies of other members of the currency union, as well as the reduced costs of reserve management after pooling reserves.

---

9 *Mundell* (1973a, 1973b); *Salant* (1973).

10 See for example *Robson* (1993) chapter 9.

In orcer to estimate the likely reserve savings as a result of the euro, we will set up a dynamic panel with fixed-effects for reserve demand of the 12 euro area countries:

$$\ln RES_{i,t} = \alpha_i + \beta_1 \ln IMP_{i,t} + \beta_2 \ln \sigma_{i,t} + \gamma \ln RES_{i,t-1} + u_{i,t} \qquad (1)^{11}$$

where $RES_{i,t}$ = international reserves (incl. gold at the official price) in million US-$, $IMP_{i,t}$ = imports in million US-$, $\sigma_{i,t}$ = standard deviation of the absolute past reserve changes $\Delta RES_{i,T}$ over the last 16 periods (T=t-1, . . . , t-16) in million US-$, $u_{i,t}$ = error term, i = country index (euro area including Greece: 1, . . . , 11; BE and LUX are treated as aggregate for reasons of data availability), t = time index (1, . . . , 17; 1983-1997); the time period includes the last 15 years before the introduction of the euro; the year 1998 is excluded as its data partly reflect the technical effects of the changeover.[12]

Note that both explanatory variables *IMP* and σ are central to the arguments for a reduced reserve demand after the introduction of the euro as outlined above. In our simulation of reserve demand for the Eurosystem we will use the long-run elasticities obtained from the estimation of (1). The effect of the euro will be incorporated through its implications for the explanatory variables, which will be outlined more in detail below.[13]

For dynamic panels, it is well known, that standard panel estimators (as the least square dummy variable estimator (LSDV),

---

11 In the empirical literature on reserve demand, two further variables are usually included in the reserve demand equation: a) the average propensity to import as proxy for openness, or the cost of adjustment to a balance of payments disequilibrium, and b) the opportunity cost of holding reserves. The average propensity to import is omitted here because of its high correlation with the import variable and its theoretical ambiguity. The opportunity costs are also not considered here as – like the majority of previous studies – we could not find a significant measure.

12 Source of the data is International Financial Statistics. Data were downloaded form the databank of the Austrian Institute of Economic Research (WIFO: http://www.wifo.ac.at).

13 This basic modelling strategy draws on *Leahy* (1995). The assumption of parameter stability over the regime shift makes this approach clearly subject to the Lucas-critique. It can be argued that previous empirical work indicates that significant changes in the international monetary system (as the collapse of the Bretton-Woods system) did not fundamentally change the structure of the demand for reserves, see *Frenkel* (1978); *Leahy* (1996).

which uses mean centred variables) yield biased estimates.[14] Of the several dynamic panel estimators suggested, we use the GMM estimator by Arellano and Bond to obtain consistent and efficient estimates of our parameters. Thereby, the fixed effects are eliminated by using first differences; then an instrumental variable estimation of the differenced equation is performed. As instruments for the lagged difference of the endogenous variable all lagged levels of the variable are used, starting with lag two and going back to the beginning of the sample. Consistency of the GMM estimator requires lack of second order serial correlation in the residuals of the differenced specification. The overall validity of instruments can be checked by a Sargan test of over-identifying restrictions.[15] Table 2 summarises the results of our GMM estimation of equation (1).

Table 2: Results of estimation for equation (1) (1983-1997)

dependent variable: $\ln RES_{i,t}$				
	constant	$\ln IMP_{i,t}$	$\ln \sigma_{i,t}$	$\ln RES_{i,t-1}$
Coefficient	-0.015	0.675^{***}	0.343^{***}	0.265^{***}
(t-value)	(-1.32)	(5.07)	(3.60)	(3.01)
long-run coefficient		0.919	0.466	

ρ_1	-4.19^{***}	F-Test	36.77^{***} (5, 159)
ρ_2	-1.46	time period	1983-1997
Sargan (χ^2)	127.39 (39)	no. of obs.	165

***, **, * indicate significance at the 1, 5 and 10 per cent level. – *Arellano/ Bond* (1991) one-step GMM estimates, ρ_1 ... null: no first-order serial correlation, ρ_2 ... null: no second-order serial correlation, Sargan ... null: valid instruments. – Time specific effects: 1987, 1992. – Sample used for estimation includes Greece.

Both the variable *IMP* and σ are highly significant and show the expected sign. The speed of adjustment, implied by the coefficient of the lagged endogenous variable, takes the relatively high value of 74 per cent. The long-run elasticity of reserve demand is 0.92 with respect to trade (*IMP*) and 0.47 with respect to uncertainty (σ).

---

[14] See *Nickel* (1981).

[15] See *Arellano/Bond* (1991).

Tests for serial correlation (ρ_1, ρ_2) and validity of the instruments (Sargan) indicate no missspecification.

The long-run coefficients are now used to simulate the "optimal" reserve demand for the period 1999-2001. In order to set up a long-run reserve demand function for the aggregate Eurosystem, we impose the estimated long-run elasticities and calibrate the intercept to the euro area aggregates of the variables for the end of the estimation period, i.e. 1997. This yields us the following long-run reserve demand equation for the aggregate euro area (*EA*):

$$\ln \hat{RES}_{EA,t} = -5.41 + 0.92 \ln IMP_{EA,t} + 0.47 \ln \sigma_{EA,t} \qquad (2)$$

where $RES_{EA,t} = \sum_i RES_{i,t}$, $IMP_{EA,t} = \sum_i IMP_{i,t}$, and $\sigma_{EA,t} = \sum_i \sigma_{i,t}$, $i = 1, \ldots, 10$. The notation ^ indicates predicted values. Equation (2) is calibrated for the year 1997 (without Greece). The introduction of the euro has yet not been considered in the definitions of the variables for the aggregate Eurosystem as IMP_{EA} and σ_{EA} refer to the hypothetical situation without regime shift.

The *scale (of foreign trade) effect* is incorporated, as after the regime shift, intra-euro area imports cannot be regarded as foreign trade any more. Thus, we can write, with the arrow indicating the changeover

$$IMP_{EA,t} \quad \Rightarrow \quad IMP^{*}_{EA,t} = \sum_i IMP^{EX-EA}_{i,t} \qquad (3)$$

where $IMP^{EX-EA}_{i,t}$ = imports of country *i* from outside the euro area. The * indicates that the definition has been adjusted to account for the regime shift. In 1999, intra-euro area imports accounted for approximately half of the euro area's total imports (see Table 3).

The *portfolio effect* of the monetary union can also be easily incorporated in our simulation using the variable $\sigma_{EA,t}$:[16] After the introduction of the euro, the sum of the individual countries' standard deviations is replaced by the standard deviation of the aggregate reserve changes ($\sigma^{*}_{EA,t}$). As the aggregate change in reserves is given by the sum of the individual countries' reserve changes, the standard deviation of the aggregate can be easily calculated from the individual countries' variances and covariances as follows:

$$\sigma_{EA,t} \quad \Rightarrow \quad \sigma^{*}_{EA,t} = \sqrt{\sum_i \sigma^2_{i,t} + \sum_i \sum_{i \neq j} \sigma_{ij,t}} \qquad (4)$$

where σ_{ij} = covariance between reserve changes of country *i* and country *j*. The effect on reserve demand can be seen by comparing

[16] See *Baker* (1980a, b), *Schiemann* (1986).

the sum $\sigma_{EA,t}$ with $\sigma^{*}_{EA,t}$. Squaring both expressions and simplifying the resulting terms we can deduce that a sufficient condition for a reduction in reserve demand is that $\sum_i \sigma_i \sigma_j > \sum_i \sigma_{ij}$, which can also be written as $\sum_i \sigma_i \sigma_j > \sum_i \rho_{ij} \sigma_i \sigma_j$, where ρ_{ij} is the correlation coefficient between the reserve changes of country *i* and country *j*. As ρ_{ij} can never exceed the value one, reserve demand after formation of a monetary union can at most be equal to the situation before and it will be lower, if at least one country's reserve changes are not perfectly correlated with the other members' reserve changes.[17] In 1999, the value of our uncertainty measure was approximately halved by the portfolio effect of the euro (see Table 3).

The results of our simulation are summarized in Table 3. The upper part of the Table shows the values of our determinants of reserve demand (*IMP*, σ) both for the hypothetical situation without regime shift and for the situation after the introduction of the euro (indicated by the *). Accordingly, two different reserve levels can be simulated. i) Using the values of rows (1) and (3) we can simulate the reserve level that would have materialized, if no regime shift had taken place (6). Alternatively, using the values of (2) and (4) we obtain the "optimal" level after the introduction of the euro (7). The difference between these two levels equals the hypothetical excess reserves, generated by the effect of the euro on reserve demand. Comparison of (6) and (7) shows that the euro has reduced reserve demand by approximately two third (8).

As described at the beginning of this section the euro also led to a considerable decline in reserves by some $50 billion (see Table 1) due to "technical effects". Comparing the simulated "optimal" level (7) with the actual level of reserves (5) yields the actual amount of excess reserves in the Eurosystem. In 2001, excessive reserves made up $86 billion, or 35.4 per cent of the actual level (9). Note, however, that this value has to be regarded as conservative estimate for two reasons. First, in the estimation and simulation, gold is valued at the official price, which clearly understates its actual value. Second, there is also some $22.7 billion of former reserve assets, part of which can also be regarded as excessive assets (see Table 1, positions (9), (10)).

---

17 See *Schiemann* (1986).

Table 3: Simulation of reserve demand with/without regime shift and excess reserves 1999-2001 (million US-\$)

	1999	2000	2001[1)]
(1) $IMP_{EA,t}$	1662953	1752393	1774057
(2) $IMP^{*}_{EA,t}$	842500	917006	937898
(3) $\sigma_{EA,t}$	54791	56312	58939
(4) $\sigma^{*}_{EA,t}$	26573	27447	28135
(5) $RES_{EA,t}$ (actual)	276466	260777	248669
(6) $\hat{RES}_{EA,t}$	376001	399612	412837
(7) $\hat{RES}^{*}_{EA,t}$	143641	157633	162798
(8) *Hypothetical excess reserves* (6)-(7)	232360 (= 61.8 %)	241979 (= 60.6 %)	250039 (= 60.6%)
(9) *actual excess reserves* (5)-(7)	132825 (=48.0%)	103144 (=39.6%)	85871 (=34.5%)

Extra-euro area trade according to the Monthly Bulletin of the ECB; value of imports for 2001 extrapolated. – [1)] including Greece.

In summary, the current level of international reserves in the Eurosystem could be reduced substantially. Approximately one third of the existing reserve level can be regarded as excessive and is on the disposal of the Eurosystem. An obvious question that follows from this result is whether the existing reserve level should in fact be reduced, and, if yes, which would be the best way forward to effect this. It is important to stress that this is not only a question of economic optimality, but also of legal admissibility. Therefore we will go on to investigate the legal framework in the next chapter.

III. The Legal Framework

A. Preliminary remarks

Under Art 105(2) 3rd indent EC Treaty it is the role of the European System of Central Banks (ESCB) to hold and manage the official foreign reserves of the Member States. This is only logical as "with the establishment of the ECB and the adoption of the single currency, it is the euro area as a whole rather than individual participating Member States which need external assets".[18] Despite the seemingly technical rationale of this provision due to its status as accessory right necessary for the implementation of the exchange rate policy of the Community, it nevertheless gives rise to a number of interrelated and complicated questions, which could be categorised as matters relating to horizontal and vertical aspects.

B. The horizontal aspect

1. The structure of the ESCB

The management role of the ESCB with regard to the foreign reserves assets must be reconciled with the fact that the System[19] itself is not a legal person and therefore not entitled to acquire or dispose of movable and immovable property. Legal capacity was given exclusively to the ECB,[20] with the NCBs remaining subject to the relevant provisions in their respective national laws. The result is a two-level system with NCBs and ECB as "integral part" of the ESCB.[21] With the ESCB only providing a roof under which under which the presently 16 different legal personalities co-operate,[22] the relationship between the constituent entities of the System is characterised by subordination of the NCBs under the ECB.[23] When carrying out the tasks of the ESCB, the NCBs, which in this capacity are called "operative arms" of the ECB,[24] are bound by instruc-

---

18 *Central Bank of Ireland* (1999) 32.

19 The term "System" hereinafter stands short for the ESCB, comprising the fifteen NCBs plus the ECB, and is hence not to be mixed up with the term "Eurosystem", which is used by ECB officials to characterise the inner circle of twelve participating NCBs.

20 Art 9.1. ESCB-Statute.

21 See Art 14.3. ESCB-Statute; *Zilioli/Selmayr* (1999) 201ff; *Seidel* (1992) 427 and recently (2000) 552ff argues for a more distinct role of the ESCB.

22 *Stadler* (1996) 88ff; see also *Smits* (1997) 92ff; *Louis* (1995) 56ff; and *Häde* (1999) Art 107, § 2. However, the ESCB is insofar more than only "a term describing the existence of the ECB and the NCBs as integral parts of the System" – so *Committee of Governors of the Central Banks* (1990) 13 – as it is the point of reference for the joint actions of NCBs and ECB in the course of the tasks entrusted to the ESCB under the EC Treaty.

23 *Weinbörner* (1998) 388; see also *Stadler* (1996) 156 ("Befehlsempfänger").

24 *Committee of Governors of the Central Banks* (1990) 14.

tions and guidelines of the ECB,[25] and can be taken before the European Court of Justice (ECJ), if they fail to fulfil an obligation under the Statute.[26]

This does not mean, however, that the NCBs no longer form part of the organisational structure of the Member States.[27] On the contrary, the Treaty speaks of the *National* Central Banks which form the System,[28] even though they can be viewed, in a functional sense, as Community bodies when carrying out ESCB tasks. They are used by the ECB following the logic of the principle of decentralisation in order to ensure that the tasks conferred upon the ESCB under Article 105 (2), (3) and (5) are implemented either by its own activities pursuant to the Statute or through the NCBs pursuant to Articles 12.1. and 14.[29] The residual national character of the NCBs as national bodies is also recognised by Art 14.4 ESCB-Statute, which even explicitly reserves the right for the NCBs to perform, in regard to their own responsibility and liability, functions other than those specified in the Statute. In other words, they may fulfil *public authority functions* in matters relating to money, credit and banking under the respective national laws – for instance, act as an agent of the Member State[30] – as long as these tasks do not interfere with the objectives and tasks of the ESCB.

2. Distribution of reserves between ECB and NCBs

These institutional aspects are not only of abstract theoretical interest, as they help to shed some light on the distribution of competencies regarding the official reserves among the component parts of the System: The transfer of the task to hold and manage the offi-

---

25 Art 14.3. ESCB-Statute.

26 Art 35.6. ESCB-Statute.

27 But so *Seidel* (1992) 425.

28 See also *Hahn/Häde* (2001) 35; *Häde* (1999) Art 107, § 8 ("Einrichtungen der Mitgliedstaaten") with further references. The legal status of the NCBs reflects this: Even if they are not set up as a corporation under public law like the Bundesbank or the Banque de France, but under private law as Aktiengesellschaft (OeNB), as società per azioni (Banca d'Italia), or as public limited company (Banque de Belgique), the State is obliged to hold at least half of the shares (majority).

29 Art 9.2. ESCB-Statute.

30 According to *Issing*, this is one of the four central banking functions, the other three being (i) holding the official currency reserves, (ii) being a bank of the banks, and (iii) emission of notes, see *Issing* (1996) 8-9.

cial currency reserves of the Member States to the *ESCB*, and not to the *ECB*, results in the remaining competencies of the NCBs, as parts of the ESCB, being determined by the *lex specialis* Art 31 ESCB-Statute.[31] The remaining national discretionary power should not be overestimated. The general principle of NCB subordination under the ECB's guidelines and instructions is fleshed out with regard to the reserve management by the NCBs in such a way that except the right of the NCBs to perform transactions in fulfilment of their obligations towards international organisations, all other operations in foreign reserve assets above a certain, unpublished, threshold[32] are subject to the ECB's approval.[33] This is also true for the foreign exchange working balances of the Member States, which they are allowed to continue to manage according to Art 105 Para 3 EC.[34]

The justification for the ECB's exclusive decisional power over the use of reserves is the need to guarantee the effectiveness of the exchange rate and monetary policy of the Community as formulated by the ECB.[35] After all, only a small fraction of the official reserves was transferred to the ECB (50,000 million euro of foreign assets other than Member States' currencies, euro, IMF reserve positions and SDRs,[36] of which 39,566 million, including Greece, were actually transferred),[37] which implies that the danger for the single monetary policy in the Community resulting out of uncoordinated action is considerable, given the sheer size of the official foreign reserves remaining with the NCBs.

---

31 So *Häde* (1999) Art 105 para 32.

32 Only the thresholds for prior notification to the ECB regarding transactions with the foreign exchange working balances of the Member States – 500 million euro – were published in ECB/2001/9, OJL 276 19/10/2001.

33 Art 31.2. ESCB-Statute.

34 See on this *infra C*.

35 See *Weber* (1999) Art 31 para 2.

36 Art 30.1. ESCB-Statute. The key is essentially the same as the key for capital subscription and is based on two objective criteria, GNP and population.

37 A derogation has the effect that the non-participating Member States participate only in the operational costs of the System by an amount of 5% of their capital share respectively, see Art 43.1. ESCB-Statute and Decision ECB/1998/14 and ECB/2000/14. The foreign reserves held by the ECB comprise mainly US-Dollars (30,200 million euro), Gold (5,900 million or 15 %), and Yen, *ECB Annual Report* (1998) 77.

3. The ECB's share

Art 30.1. ESCB-Statute specifies that the *ECB* is "provided by the NCBs with foreign reserve assets", and that it has the "full right to hold and manage" them and to "use them for the purposes set out in the Statute". In the Draft Statute published by the Central Bank Governors, which is very close to the Statute as it stands now, the exact amount to be transferred under this Article was left blank, as a sign for intense discussion going on. The statement in the commentary that, depending on the limit set in Art 30.1., a part of the reserves *might* remain with the NCBs, however, implies that the preference was for a rather high proportion to be transferred, sufficient in any case to ensure the ECB's financial autonomy and credibility.[38]

The rather low fraction which was finally agreed upon can be explained by a fundamental difference between the reserves thus transferred to the ECB (in spite of the resistance of the Bank of England) and the ones remaining with the NCBs. Only the former are subject to full power of disposition by the ECB – although they physically remain at the NCBs, which continue to manage them on behalf of the ECB as its agent[39] – whereas the latter are controlled by the NCBs, subject, however, to approval in case of high value transactions and managed in accordance with the guidelines of the ECB.[40] The need for the ESCB to operate as one system in which all legal persons have the same rights regarding the foreign reserves at their disposal cannot have the effect to give the ECB full rights regarding *all* reserves regardless of whether they were managed by the ECB or the NCBs.[41]

Art 30.1 does not cover this interpretation from both a literal and systematic perspective: The *ECB* is given the full right "to hold and manage the foreign reserve assets *that are transferred to it* and to use *them* for the purposes set out in the Statute." However, the *ECB* does not have the right to hold, manage and use an amount of reserves that goes above the limit specified in the first sentence of Art

---

38 See *Committee of Governors of the Central Banks* (1990) 16, 28.

39 Guideline of the ECB on the management of the foreign reserve assets of the ECB by the NCBs (ECB/2000/1), OJL 207, 17/08/2000, 24. On the compatibility of this decentralised reserves management framework with the Statute see *Louis* (1995) 85.

40 For details see *Levy-Rueff* (2000).

41 But so *Smits* (1999) para 46.

30.1. (EUR 50,000 million). The co-ordination procedure foreseen by Art 31.2. regarding the assets remaining with the NCBs and the exchange rate and monetary policy of the Community clearly foresees limits on the ECB's rights, whereas with full management rights of the ECB over all reserves such an article would not be needed.[42] The same reasoning applies to the possibility of further reserve transfers to the ECB as foreseen by Art 30.4.

A second, related aspect is therefore the precise legal character of the transfer to the ECB, which is an open issue.[43] The Central Bank Governors in the commentary of the Draft Statute first used the term "endowment", but they point to the resistance of the Bank of England which did not see „any necessity to transfer the ownership of the foreign reserves to the ECB" and considered it sufficient that each NCB agreed "to make available a predetermined amount of reserves for the disposal of the ECB."[44] The terms which were agreed upon, "manage and hold", are therefore interpreted as avoiding a sign of a transfer of ownership.[45] Neither Art 30.1 nor 30.3, under which each NCB is credited by the ECB with a claim equivalent to its contribution, are regarded as sufficient in this regard.

It is to be doubted, though, that this fraction of the reserves remains in the ownership of the national entities.[46] *Weber* illustrates these doubts with the hypothetical example of an ECB Governing Council decision in implementation of its competencies under Art 30.3 2nd sentence to determine the denomination and remuneration of such claims. Thereby, the Governing Council could decide that for assets denominated in dollars, the respective claim was to be denominated in dollars, and that the interest rate had to be adjusted to dollar interest rates, or even be paid in dollars. In such a case, the "provision" of the ECB with the foreign reserve assets would not be a transfer of full ownership but could be interpreted as a trust.[47]

---

42 Cf. also the concerns of the *Committee of Governors of the Central Banks* (1990) 17, 28, which originally intended even to make *all* operations with the residual reserve assets, not only those above certain amounts, subject to approval of the ECB.

43 *Weber* (1999) Art 31 para 12.

44 *Committee of the Central Bank Governors* (1990) 27f.

45 *Louis* (1995) 85.

46 But so *Pernice* (1997) para 15.

47 Ibid.

It is not clear whether the fact that the claims of the NCBs are actually denominated in euro and remunerated at the short-term refinancing rates of the System, adjusted to reflect a zero return on the gold component,[48] is sufficient to support the reverse interpretation that it was a transfer of ownership. However, the operation can be understood as a swap transaction under which ownership of different assets is exchanged: foreign reserve assets against corresponding claims in euro. In the absence of any provision under the Statute according to which the NCBs could call these reserves back, the official foreign reserve assets were unconditionally pooled in the ECB's books.

The statistical treatment of the transfer, in line with the European System of Accounts (ESA),[49] supports this interpretation. The concepts and definitions to be used in the statistical information that is reported to the ESCB is described in Annex III of an ECB Guideline,[50] where under the heading "reserve assets" the following sentence can be found: "The pooling of reserve assets will be conducted in the form of outright transfers of ownership," (*Zusammenlegung [...] mittels definitiver Übereignung*, *mise en commun [...] sous forme de transferts complets de propriété*, or *províon [...] mediante transferencias al contado de propriedad*.[51]

Although in the last resort the reserves transferred to the ECB by the NCBs are the *official foreign reserves of the Member States*,[52] the NCBs received a corresponding claim denominated in euro, so that the Member States with the transfer to the ECB effectively lost any rights in this regard.[53] For the reserves remaining with the

---

48 *ECB* (1999) Annual Report 153.

49 Cf. the European system of national and regional accounts in the Community, Council Regulation (EC) No 2223/96 of 25 June 1996, OJ L 310, 30/11/1996, 1 – 469, at 5.25: "The financial assets classified in the category monetary gold and SDRs (AF.1) are the only financial assets for which there are no counterpart liabilities in the system. Therefore, transactions in monetary gold and SDRs (F.1) always involve changes in ownership of financial assets."

50 Guideline of the ECB on the statistical reporting requirements of the ECB in the field of balance of payments and international investment position statistics (ECB/1998/17), OJL 115, 04/05/1999, 47.

51 ECB Guideline (ECB/1998/17), Annex III. 1.7.

52 Art 105(2) 3rd indent and Art 3 ESCB-Statute.

53 This might also explain the reluctance on the part of the Member States to allow a further transfer of official reserves to the ECB above the

NCBs, however, the amount and structure of the reserves actually held and managed is determined nationally. The respective rights of public entities of the Member States and the NCBs, as well as the constraints concerning the management of the reserves posed by the membership in the System, will be discussed in the next chapter.

C. The vertical aspect

1. Ownership by the Member States or the NCBs?

As for the ECB, the words "hold and manage" do not necessarily imply that the NCBs are owners of the *official reserves of the Member States*. The other way round, this provision neither makes the Member States owners of the reserves:[54] This was, and remains, a question of national law. The NCBs' statutes reveals that *all* of them fall short of any provisions that could be interpreted as an intention to transfer not only management rights, but also ownership rights. On the contrary, Art 12.a of the law of the Banco de Portugal, by giving the bank the right to "manage the foreign assets of the country or any other asset *entrusted* to it"[55] may serve as an example for the differentiation between management and ownership. Even if a NCB *owned* the reserves under national law, from an economic perspective, these remain the official foreign reserves of the respective Member State.[56]

Two additional considerations may shed some light on this issue, although from a legal point of view, there is no clear answer possible. First, in the (only speculative) case of a "liquidation" of the central bank, it would be on the state as the main shareholder or owner to decide on the use of the net assets. Second, from a historical perspective, the management of the foreign reserve assets by the

---

limit of EUR 50,000 million, cf. the recent resistance by the EU Council to accept further calls of foreign reserve assets by the ECB as expressed in recital 4 of the Council Regulation (EC) No. 1010/2000 as compared with the ECB Recommendation (ECB/1999/1: reserves do not need to be replenished before further calls, ceiling of 100 billion "appropriate for the time being").

54 So *Smits* (1999) para 39, who also reports attempts during the negotiations to have the wording in a way which would have made the NCBs the owners of the reserves held by them.

55 Banco de Portugal Organic law, approved by law 5/98 of January 31, emphasis added. See also Portuguese version, http://www.bportugal.pt/document/frdocument_p.htm.

56 *Smits* (1999) para 39.

central banks is done in the general interest of the nation, similarly as it is in the general interest of a country to have a currency with which to pay. Formally, the ownership of the reserves therefore lies with the nation as a whole, but is vested in the public authorities (state body or central bank). The objection that the central bank paid for the reserves and accordingly in case of a sale it should be paid an equivalent sum,[57] however, can be rejected: After all, foreign reserves are partly "earned" and partly "borrowed" by the private or public sector[58] and partly consist of retained profits, which ultimately have to be regarded as property of the central bank's stockholders.[59] However, differing between these fractions appears neither feasible nor meaningful, as it does not help to solve the underlying question.

The idealised understanding of ownership may provoke the question whether this concept in the given circumstances is of any practical relevance. The European Monetary Institute (EMI), in its Convergence Report, reminded that those Member States which did not transfer their reserves to their NCBs would not comply with the requirement of the Treaty.[60] Thereby, it reiterated the concerns of the Committee of the Central Bank Governors which saw pressing needs, in order to have all reserves "effectively under the *control* of the ECB", to "bring such assets into the System at the start of Stage Three." The Treaty should therefore stipulate that all foreign reserve assets held by non-central bank entities are to be transferred to the NCBs of the countries concerned.[61]

---

57 So an internal paper of the Bundesbank, cf. *Die Zeit* (2001).

58 I.e. generated by export of goods/services or by capital imports/foreign debts of the government. The OeNB's reserves are from an economic perspective regarded as "borrowed", see *Winckler* (2000) 107.

59 So the Swiss Cantons, Botschaft zur Volksinitiative «Überschüssige Goldreserven in den AHV-Fonds (Goldinitiative), BBl. 2001, 1403, 1412. For the NCBs, on average, 10-20% of the profit generated is attributed to a general reserve fund, 6-10% distributed to shareholders (if any), and the remainder – thus, the lion share – goes to the State.

60 *EMI* (1997) 297f. One example where a NCB was only recently empowered with the management of the official reserves and with the right to transfer parts of these to the ECB is the Banca d'Italia, see Art 7 1 and 2 of the Decreto legislativo 10 marzo 1998, n. 43, Gazzetta Ufficiale n. 61, 14 marzo 1998. The "Ufficio italiano dei cambi" had to be transformed in an instrumental body of the bank, Decreto legislativo 26 agosto 1998, n. 319, Gazzetta Ufficiale n. 206, 04 sett. 1998.

61 *Committee of the Central Bank Governors* (1990) 17.

Control, however, is not the same as ownership, since a precondition for an effective transfer of ownership is the intention to transfer legal property. Nevertheless, control is the focal point, as this is what the task of "holding of the official reserves" implies. There is, for instance, no doubt that the reserves are to be recorded as assets in the central bank's balance sheet, which is for all participating NCBs, in fact, the case. It should be noted that for a central bank to manage the official foreign reserves of a country, it is not explicitly necessary that they are on its balance sheet.[62] The difference between this approach and the transfer of the reserves to the central bank is that once the reserves are shown in an NCB's balance sheet, it has to bear the associated risk.[63]

If profits as well as losses are attributed to the central bank, then consequently, the right of the NCBs to perform "operations in foreign reserve assets"[64] even includes the possibility of a total loss of the foreign currency reserves caused by interventions in the financial markets. Apart from this "involuntary" loss of the reserves, control certainly also includes the right of the NCB to reduce the size or alter the composition of the reserves. With a view to the transfer of sovereign rights in the area of monetary policy to the European level, this constellation – risk attribution at the NCBs and formal ownership of the State – results in the question whether a Member State is free to sell all or part of the reserves. In other words, which rights, if any, emanate from the formal ownership of the State? Does the ultimate ownership of the reserves by the Member States mean that they could compel the central bank to sell an important fraction of them?

2. Limits on ownership rights

The first restriction to the use of reserves by the Member States is usually considered to be the independence of the NCBs, and hence concerns the relationship between NCB and government on the national level. It is therefore useful to pay some attention to the discussion in Switzerland on the competence of the Swiss National Bank (SNB) to transfer 100 million Swiss Francs out of the foreign

62 For instance in Canada, were the Exchange Fund Account holds the foreign reserves, but is managed by the Bank of Canada.

63 The main risks associated with the investment of foreign reserves are exchange rate risk, interest rate risk, credit risk and liquidity risk, for details see *Pankki* (1999) 60.

64 Art 31.2. ESCB-Statute.

reserves to a humanitarian fund (the so-called Holocaustfonds). On the one hand, the SNB's legal experts argued that due to the lack of explicit competencies, due to the amount of money involved – which was too large for a classification as administrative auxiliary work – and due to the foreign policy objectives of such a move, a specific legal basis (Federal resolution) was required to authorise the SNB.[65] The Bundesrat supported this view and submitted an announcement to the Swiss Parliament, in which it proposed such a resolution.[66] The legal Commission of the Nationalrat, however, after a hearing of external legal experts, considered the SNB as solely competent and rejected this move as formalistic and excessive:[67] As Art 2 of the National Bank law vested the SNB with the principal task of pursuing a credit and monetary policy "serving the interests of the country as a whole", the preservation of the dignity of the institution and its reputation was not only in the public interest, but also a condition for the fulfilment of its principal tasks.[68] Otherwise, the purpose and the organisation of the SNB as independent limited company would be contradicted. An authorisation by political forces would negatively prejudge the future political independence of the bank as intended by its statute.[69]

The other side argued that the independence of the SNB was legitimated by its public functions and was defined by law, as it was an independence in the framework of constitutional objectives and legal allocation of duties, and not a quasi unlimited freedom of business practices.[70] To require the SNB to take on further competencies in order to preserve the reputation of the institution would be contrary to the legality principle and the rule of law. A resolution could therefore not have any negative effects on the SNB's independence.[71]

---

65 See *Klauser* (1997).

66 97.051 Botschaft betreffend die Beteiligung der Nationalbank am Fonds zugunsten bedürftiger Opfer von Holocaust/Shoa, 25. Juni 1997, 56 BBl 149. Jahrgang Bd. III, 1361 et seq. (1373).

67 See the discussion as quoted in the Official Bulletin of the Federal Assembly, *Schweizer Ständerat* (1997) 913 et seq.

68 See the argumentation of one of the experts in the NZZ, *Nobel* (1997).

69 *Schweizer Ständerat* (1997) 914.

70 So MP *Rhinow*, *Schweizer Ständerat* (1997) 918.

71 Proponent of these arguments were, however, in the minority, so that it was left to the SNB to "independently" decide to transfer 100 million Swiss francs to the Holocaust-Fund, which it did on 3 November 1997.

This discussion can be transferred with ease to the situation on the European level. With a view to Art 108 EC, whereas it is clear that the Member States no longer have any influence on the management and utilisation of "their" reserves, for instance, by instructing the NCBs how and when the reserves should be used on the foreign exchange markets,[72] the question remains whether the primary law obligation under Art 105(2) 3rd indent EC, vesting the ESCB with the power to hold and manage the official foreign reserves of the Member States, prohibits the Member States from selling a larger fraction of the reserves managed by the NCBs.

The ESCB-Statute contains the principle that to the extent that a sale of reserves has liquidity effects[73] – which is upon the ECB to determine – any reserve transaction has to meet the approval of the ECB.[74] After all,

> "the reason for bringing all foreign reserve assets into the System (i.e. into the NCBs) is to ensure that exchange rate and monetary policy operations are not affected by transactions in official foreign reserve assets undertaken by official bodies outside the System."[75]

Hence, it could be argued that any proposal of utilisation by the Member States concerning operations with foreign reserves above a certain threshold had subject to approval by the ECB, following the procedure under Art 31.2. ESCB-Statute. It can be derived from this article that a prohibition requires a risk assessment of the operation in question and an evaluation whether it poses a damage to the exchange rate and monetary policies of the Community, with the burden of proof resting on the ECB.[76] Given the need for fast decisions concerning the impact of a particular transaction on the monetary

---

72 *Selmayr* (2000) 25.

73 As in case of an outright domestic sale, but not if they are used for foreign debts repayment or "parked" in a fund, see *Burger/Handler* (2001) 420.

74 In a similar way, an excessive sale of gold would probably not be approved, as it could lead to a sharp decline in the gold prices, reducing the value of the ESCB's remaining reserves in monetary gold. As nearly all ESCB members except the Greek and the Danish agreed not to sell more than 2000 tons of gold in the following 5 years (or 400t yearly) each, and only engage in already agreed sales, see *ECB* (1999) Press Release: Joint Statement on Gold, September 1999.

75 So the *Committee of the Governors of the Central Banks* (1990) 20.

76 See *Weber* (1999) Art 31 para 9.

and exchange rate policies, the assessment[77] rests on the Board of Directors as the decision-making body responsible for the current business of the ECB.[78]

However, it may be doubted whether the procedure under Art 31.2., which refers not only to NCB transactions, but also to Member States' transactions with their working balances, is applicable at all. More appropriately, the sale of reserves by an NCB at the wish of a Member State might be regarded as a case not foreseen in the Statute. Not being an issue falling under current business, the decision cannot be left to the Executive Board, but will have to be subject to a Governing Council decision. In any case, though, the decision of the Governing Council is bound to resort to an evaluation of the transaction's compatibility with the ESCB's monetary policy. In other words, a negative decision must be justified by an economic analysis of that transaction's impact.

As a final possible limit on the free use of the reserves by the Member States, Art 101 EC and Regulation (EC) No. 3603/93[79] have to be observed. In particular, central banks must not provide funds to the public sector which result or are likely to result in a debit balance or a claim against that sector, finance its obligations vis-à-vis third parties, or that central banks buy directly debt instruments from the public sector.[80] However, according to Eurostat, under ESA, an "exceptional"[81] transfer of the proceeds of sales of gold or other foreign reserves to governments constitutes a financial

---

77 Cf. the Guideline concerning the Member States working balances, under which the ECB considers the transaction's impact on the liquidity of the euro area banking system. In exceptional circumstances (late notification, adverse market conditions or policy considerations), the ECB may request modification of the timing or manner in which a transaction is to be performed. In "very exceptional" circumstances, the ECB may request the postponement of a transaction, ECB/2001/9 Art 5. This, presumably, does not differ very much for the (unpublished) guideline concerning the NCB's reserve transactions.

78 Art 11.6. ESCB-Statute.

79 Council Regulation (EC) No. 3603/93 of 13 December 1993 specifying definitions for the application of the prohibitions referred to in Articles 104 and 104b (1) of the Treaty.

80 Public sector means Community institutions/bodies, central governments, regional and local public authorities, and other public bodies or undertakings of Member States, Art 3 Regulation 3603/93.

81 I.e., in large size and not related to the exchange rate policy, Eurostat Press Release No 10/97, 3/2/1997.

transaction which has no influence on the measurement of the government deficit as defined for the purpose of the excessive deficit procedure.[82] As the State thereby withdraws equity, a change in the central banks assets only changes the value of the state's shareholding, so that a payment of these proceeds does not fall under the situations described in Art 101 EC.

In order to summarise, whereas national utilisation of reserves and of proceeds out of the sale of reserves is not prohibited under EC law, it is the discretion which the ECB enjoys under Art 31 ESCB-Statute – subject, however, to review by the ECJ concerning legality of acts or failure to act[83] – which is the main limitation to such alternative uses. Reaching an understanding between the NCB and the respective Member State over usefulness and appropriateness of such a move is therefore not only advisable with a view to the credibility of the institutions involved, but also an indispensable requirement for a positive evaluation in the ECB Governing Council.

IV. Conclusions

In this paper we estimated the excess reserves in the Eurosystem and investigated the legal framework for possible reserve reductions. Our estimates suggest that some $86 billion of the reserves actually held by the Eurosystem can be regarded as excessive. These excess reserves, however, are no „free lunch" that could be used arbitrarily. Complex economic feedbacks as well as legal restrictions aggravate the decision, how to transform the exiting reserve overhang into more productive assets. A detailed investigation of the economic consequences of alternative uses is required though beyond the subject of this paper.

As shown in chapter C.2., the economic effects of alternative uses are relevant for an evaluation of their legal admissibility. The lower the impact of such proposals on the liquidity situation in the euro area and on the ESCB's monetary policy, the easier approval without modifications in the timing or manner of the proposal will be gained. It is conditional, of course, on national and international consensus that the proposed use of the assets is more economically efficient and in the public interest than if they remain with the NCBs.

---

[82] Eurostat Press Release No 88/97.

[83] See Art 35.1. ESCB-Statute and Arts 230 and 232 EC.

As concerns a large sale of reserves by an NCB on behalf of a Member State, given that it is the Governing Council to decide on any such request, from a political perspective also the balance of power and alliances in the ECB Governing Council has to be taken into account. It is essential to recall that the Governing Council of the ECB is composed of a majority of national NCB Governors and a minority of supranational members of the Board of Directors. It presumably makes a difference which NCB is concerned and whether it supports the projected sale of reserves. Therefore, pragmatic consensus on national level is likely to produce more effective results than the lengthy, all be it possible, legal dispute settlement procedures applicable in cases of conflicts between the ECB and national governments.

References

Arellano M. / Bond S. (1991), Some Test of Specification for Panel Data: Monte Carlo Evidence and an Application to Employment Equations, in: Review of Economic Studies 58, 1991, pp. 277-292.

Baker S. A. (1980a), European Monetary Union and the Demand for International Reserves: A Note, in: Bulletin of Economic Research 32, 1980, pp. 35-39.

Baker S. A. (1980b), European Monetary Union and the Demand for International Reserves, in: Bulletin of Economic Research 32, 1980, pp. 97-101.

Burger C. / Handler H. (2001), Brauchen wir nationale Zahlungsbilanzen im Euroraum?, in: Wirtschaftspolitische Blätter 4, 2001. 402-422.

Breuss F. (1997), Die gesamtwirtschaftlichen Auswirkungen der WWU in Modellsimulationen, in: *Baumgartner J. / Breuss F. / Kramer H. / Walterskirchen E.* (eds.), Auswirkungen der Wirtschafts- und Währungsunion, Studie des WIFO im Auftrag des Bundesministeriums, Wien 1997, pp. 41-96.

Central Bank of Ireland (1999), Annual Report, http://www.centralbank.ie/publications.asp.

Committee of Governors of the Central Banks (1990), Draft Statute of the European System of Central Banks and of the European Central Bank, Introductory Report and Commentary, in: Agence Europe Documents No. 1669/1670, 8 December 1990.

ECB Annual Report, Several Issues.

ECB Monthly Bulletin, Several Issues.

ECB (2000), Methodological Note: Reserve Assets within the Structure of the Template on International Reserves and Foreign Currency Liquidity, www.ecb.int (statistics /international reserves).

European Commission (1990), One Market, One Money: An Evaluation of the Potential Benefits and Costs of Forming an Economic and Monetary Union, in: European Economy 44, 1990.

EMI (1998), Convergence Report, 1998, http://www.ecb.int.

Eichengreen B. / Mathieson D. J. (2000), The Currency Composition of Foreign Exchange Reserves: Retrospect and Prospect, in: IMF Working Paper No. 131, 2000.

Frenkel J. (1978), International Reserves - Pegged Exchange Rates and Managed Float, Public Policy in Open Economies, a supplementary series to the Journal of Monetary Economics Vol. 9, 1978, pp. 169-195.

Frenkel M. / Sondergaard J. (1999), How Does EMU Affect the Dollar and the Yen as International Reserve and Investment Currencies, in: Research Notes in Economics and Statistics, RN-99-5, Deutsche Bundesbank, 1999.

Gros D. / Schobert F. (1999), Excess Foreign Reserves and Overcapitalisation in the Eurosystem, in: CEPS Working Document No. 128, Center of European Policy Studies, 1999.

Häde U. (1999), Art 105, Art 107, in: *Calliess C. / Ruffert M.* (eds.), Kommentar zu EU-Vertrag und EG-Vertrag, Darmstadt 1999.

Hahn H. J. / Häde U. (2001), Die Zentralbank vor Gericht, ZHR 165, 2001, pp. 30-61.

Issing O. (1996), Einführung in die Geldpolitik, München, [6]1996.

Kenen P. B. (1995), Economic and Monetary Union in Europe: Moving Beyond Maastricht, Cambridge 1995.

Klauser P. (1997), Die Kompetenzen rund um die Nationalbank. Eine Entgegnung an Peter Nobel, Neue Zürcher Zeitung 21. Juni 1997.

Leahy M. P. (1996), The Dollar as an Official Reserve Currency under EMU, in: Open Economies Review 7(4),1996, pp. 371-90.

Levy-Rueff G. (2000), A first assessment of the ECB's management of foreign reserve assets, in: Euro-Ecu 2000, pp. 43-46.

Louis J. V. (1995), L'Union Economique et Monetaire, in: *Louis* et. al. (eds.), Commentaire Mégret, Le Droit de la CEE, Vol 6, Bruxelles [2]1995, pp. 1-165.

Masson P. R. / Turtelboom B. (1997), Characteristics of the Euro, the Demand for Reserves, and Policy Coordination Under EMU, IMF Working Paper No. 58, 1997.

Mundell R. A. (1973a), Uncommon Arguments for Common Currencies, in: *Johnson H. G. / Swoboda A. K.* (eds.), The Economics of Common Currencies, Cambridge 1973, pp. 114-132.

Mundell R. A. (1973b), A Plan for a European Currency, in: *Johnson H. G. / Swoboda A. K.* (eds.) The Economics of Common Currencies, Cambridge 1973, pp. 143-177.

Nickell S. (1981), Biases in Dynamic Models with Fixed Effects, in: Econometrica 49, 1981, pp. 1417–1426.

Nobel P. (1997), Die Kompetenzen rund um die Nationalbank, NZZ 14./15. Juni 1997.

Pernice I. (1997), Art 105 EGV, in: *Grabitz E. /Hilf M.* (eds.), Recht der Europäischen Union (formerly: Kommentar zur Europäischen Union), EL 10 München 1997.

Robson R. (1993), The Economics of International Integration, London [3]1993.

Salant W. S. (1973), Implications for International Reserves, in: *Krause L. B / Salant W. S.* (eds.), European Monetary Unification and its Meaning for the United States, Washington D.C. 1973, pp. 203-236.

Schiemann J. (1986), Der Bedarf an offizieller Währungsreserve als Kriterium für die Bestimmung einer optimalen Währungsunion: Ein theoretischer Ansatz und empirischer Befund für die Länder der Europäischen Gemeinschaft, in: Jahrbücher für Nationalökonomie und Statistik 201(6), pp. 589-604.

Schulze-Steinen M. (1997), Rechtsfragen zur Wirtschaftsunion, Baden-Baden 1997.

Schweizer Ständerat (1997), 97.051 Spezialfonds für Holocaust-Opfer, Herbstsession, Amtliches Bulletin der Bundesversammlung 7. Okt. 1997, 913-922.

Seidel M. (1992), Probleme der Verfassung der Europäischen Gemeinschaft als Wirtschaft- und Währungsunion, in: *Baur J. F. / Müller-Graff P.-C. / Zuleeg M.* (eds.), FS Börner, Köln 1992, pp. 417-430.

Seidel M. (2000), Im Kompetenzkonflikt: Europäisches System der Zentralbanken (ESZB) versus EZB, in: EuZW Heft 18/2000, pp. 552-554.

Selmayr M. (2000), Interventionen zwecks Preisstabilität, in: NZZ 11/10/2000.

Smits R. (1997), The European Central Bank: Institutional Aspects, London 1997.

Smits R. (1999), Art 105, in: *Von der Groeben H. / Thiesing J. / Ehlermann C.-D.* (eds.), Handbuch des Europäischen Rechts: systematische Sammlung mit Erläuterungen, Baden-Baden ^{5}1999.

Stadler R. (1996), Der rechtliche Handlungsspielraum des ESZB, Baden-Baden 1996.

Suomen Pankki (1999), Bank of Finnland Annual Report 1999, http://www.bof.fi/env/ eng/ju/vk99en.pdf.

Weber K. (1999), Art 26-32 Satzung ESZB und EZB (nach Artikel 109m), in: *Von der Groeben H. / Thiesing J. / Ehlermann C.-D.* (eds.), Handbuch des Europäischen Rechts: systematische Sammlung mit Erläuterungen, Baden-Baden ^{5}1999.

Weinbörner S. (1998), Die Stellung der Europäischen Zentralbank und der nationalen Zentralbanken nach dem Vertrag von Maastricht, Frankfurt 1998.

Winckler G. (2000), Optimale Höhe der Reservepositionen der OeNB, in: *Burger Ch. / Handler H.* (eds.), Zahlungsbilanz einst und jetzt, BMWA Wien 2000, pp. 103 – 136.

Die Zeit (2001), Lockruf des Goldes, in: Wirtschaft 41/2001, W. Herz.

Zilioli C. / Selmayr M. (1999), The European Central Bank, its System and its Law, in: Euredia 1999/2 and 3 1999, pp. 187-230 and pp. 307-364.

Stefan Griller

Public Undertakings under the EMU Excessive Government Deficit Criterion*

* I would like to thank *Dr. Barbara Dutzler* for the translation of an earlier German version into English and for valuable comments.

I. Exposition

In recent years, the use of the term "Maastricht conformity" has seen a remarkable rise. In this respect, Austria may serve as an example for most of the EMU Member States. In this country, the term even made its way into the program of the coalition government of the People's Party (ÖVP) and the Freedom Party (FPÖ), which has been holding power since the beginning of 2000.[1] The chapter on budget policy 2000-2003 says that as far as the infrastructure financing companies are concerned, Austrian Railways Infrastructure Financing Comp. (SCHIG) and Motorways Financing Corp. (ASFINAG), the degree of self-financing would be increased considerably. In the subsequent years, the executive boards of both enterprises must propose appropriate measures to the Federal Government in order to "render a contribution to the sustainable relief of the additional strain on the budget." In particular, the executive proposals must include,

> "the reorganisation of the entire railway sector. In the interest of improving competition and to optimise the various business activities, the Austrian Railways' marketing and infrastructural business is to be split. Infrastructural operations are to be joined with those of the Railway Infrastructure Financing Comp. and the Heavy Duty Railways Corp. In the reorganisation process account must be taken of the fact that the conformity with the Maastricht requirements is ensured."[2]

Already on the occasion of the transfer of the Federal stake to the Austrian Motorway and Expressway Company (ÖSAG), and of the Alpine Roads Aktiengesellschaft (ASG) in ASFINAG in 1997,[3]

---

1 To be found at http://www.austria.gv.at/ (visited in May 2002).

2 P 123 of the Coalition Program.

3 The federal law on the transfer of the Federal Government's stake of the Federal road companies in the ASFINAG and the granting of the right of usufruct in favour of this company (ASFINAG-Enabling Act 1997) had been announced as Art I of the Federal law, by which the ASFINAG Act 1982, the BIG Act, the Railways Infrastructure Financing Act, the Federal Road Financing Act 1996, the Federal Ministry Act 1986, the Federal law concerning measures in the range of the Federal road companies, and the Federal Financing Act 1997 were changed (Infrastructure Financing Act 1997, Official Bulletin I 1997/113).

the Government bill clearly emphasised that the aim of the restructuring was to denationalise the debts of ASFINAG, in compliance with the requirements of the convergence criteria.[4]

Also in context of the restructuring of Austria's Property Management Company (BIG), Maastricht conformity was a – quite controversial – issue. Lastly, this topic appeared also in the discussion of the reform of the public housing systems of the Provincial Governments.

Mostly, it is the actual government deficit to which discussions of "Maastricht conformity" refer. However, as far as privatisation decisions are concerned, it plays a comparably minor role.[5] Far more important in this respect is the debt management of the State. Denationalisation decisions often intend, in particular, to shift the debts from the State to a legal entity distinct from the state.[6] This is the focus of this paper.

II. The Debt Criterion in the Framework of Economic and Monetary Union (EMU)

For the decision on the entry in the third stage of EMU, the EC Treaty requires, amongst others, an examination of whether the well-known so-called convergence criteria have been achieved. One of these criteria is the government budgetary position without an excessive deficit. The Treaty, however, is vague in several respects. Contrary to some views, it cannot be upheld that the Member States had to precisely meet the target figures as a precondition for entry. After all, it was only in the case of a decision on entry in the third stage *before* the end of 1996 that the Council would have been required to decide whether "a majority of the Member States fulfil the necessary conditions for the adoption of a single currency", and whether "it is appropriate for the Community to enter the third stage", by taking "due account" to the reports on the matter by the European Monetary Institute (EMI) and by the Commission.[7] This decision, however, was not taken. Instead, and under the procedure of Art 121(4) EC, which was applied at the beginning of May 1998,

---

4 698 Complements to the Stenographic Minutes of the National Council, 20th legislative period.

5 But see on the sale of the Federal real estate to the BIG *infra 92*.

6 On the objectives of privatisation *Hengstschläger* (1995) 166 ff. For examples in addition to those herein dealt with see *Potacs* (1998) para 908 ff, 911 ff.

7 Art 121(3) EC.

the Council had only been required to "confirm which Member States fulfil the necessary conditions for the adoption of a single currency."[8] It was and is hence not convincing to argue that the *necessary* conditions are *only* the convergence criteria in the strict sense, or that *all* those criteria are to be observed *at any rate* and *precisely* by *every* Member State.

This question does not need further attention hereinafter.[9] For our purposes, the essential aspect is the importance of the (negative) criterion of the excessive deficit for the entry into the third stage of EMU, on the one hand, and within the third stage, on the other hand.

As to the first point, taken literally, the Treaty requires "sustainability of the government financial position", apparent from the achievement of a government budgetary position without an excessive deficit. This condition would be fulfilled if, at the time of the examination, the Member State were not the subject of a Council decision that an excessive deficit exists.[10] (Simplifying catchwords: 3% limit for the ratio of the planned or actual government deficit to GDP, 60% for the ratio of government debt to GDP). At the time of examination, eleven EU Member States met this condition ,[11] and therefore entered the third stage of EMU[12] on 1 January 1999. Together with Greece, which followed on later, they introduced the Euro in cash at the beginning of 2002.

As to the second point, namely the importance of sound government finances *within* the third stage, secondary rules have been drawn up in order to ensure proper enforcement of budgetary discipline also after the passage to the third stage of EMU, as a matter of central concern to the EC.[13] If the targets are not met, in the last

---

8 Art 121(4) EC.

9 For details see *Griller* (1997) 223 ff.

10 Art 2 Protocol (No 21) on the convergence criteria.

11 As an example, see 98/309/EC Council Decision of 1 May 1998 abrogating the Decision on the existence of an excessive deficit for Austria, OJL 139, 11/05/1998, 13.

12 98/317/EC Council Decision of 3 May 1998 in accordance with Article 109j(4) of the Treaty, OJL 139, 11/05/1998, 30.

13 Council Regulation (EC) No 1466/97 of 7 July 1997 on the strengthening of the surveillance of budgetary positions and the surveillance and co-ordination of economic policies, OJL 209, 02/08/1997, 1.

resort even fines can be imposed.[14] Of particular importance for our purposes, is that this is not only possible for the *actual government deficit*, but also in case of non-compliance with the *debt ratio* criterion.[15] "'Government deficit (surplus)' means the net borrowing (net lending) (B.9) of the sector of 'general government', …'Government debt' means the total gross debt at nominal value outstanding at the end of the year of the sector of 'general government' (S.13), with the exception of those liabilities the corresponding financial assets of which are held by the sector of 'general government' (S.13)."[16]

In fact, the mentioned Reg. 1467/97 primarily focuses on the actual government deficit, and specifies the exemptions and the calculation of the pecuniary sanctions only for this case. Apart from this, however, according to its wording, the provisions of the Regulation can be applied also if the debt level ratio is exceeded. Even if this interpretation is rejected, in any event, the sanctioning mechanism foreseen in the Treaty itself under Art 104 EC is applicable. Insofar legal certainty is higher (predictability of possible sanctions is better) regarding non-compliance with the actual deficit than with the government debt. The requirement to comply with the reference value applicable in this regard (60%) also in the third stage of EMU is thereby, however, not altered. Hence, the exceeding of the debt ratio criterion by a Member State in the third stage could lead to sanctions by the EC, even if the excess was due not to

---

14 Council Regulation (EC) No 1467/97 of 7 July 1997 on speeding up and clarifying the implementation of the excessive deficit procedure, OJL 209, 02/08/1997, 6.

15 The Treaty terminology is not explicit, but on closer consideration, is hardly doubtful: "Excessive government deficits" under Art 104(1) EC means two things, as can be inferred not only from this provision, but also from Protocol (No 20) on the excessive deficit procedure: the ratio of the actual government deficit to GDP, on the one hand, and the ratio of government debt to GDP on the other hand. The actual government deficit itself is also called "excessive deficit". The term "excessive government deficit" is therefore ambiguous and is used both in a stricter and in a wider sense.

16 Council Regulation (EC) No 3605/93 of 22 November 1993, OJ No L 332, 31/12/1993, 7, as amended by Council Regulation (EC) No 475/2000, OJ No L 58, 3/3/2000, 1.

excessive net borrowing, but to reintegration of denationalised debts before the third stage.[17]

To conclude, the government budgetary position criterion is not only relevant for the entry into the third stage of the EMU, but also for a continuous stability policy of EMU Member States. As a result, the questions, as to which determinants are to be used for its calculation and as to what extent denationalised legal entities are to be considered, are essential for the lawfulness of actions within the third stage.

III. The Classification of Publicly Owned Entities and their Importance on the Calculation of Government Deficit

A. General Remarks

As already sketched out above, the Member States are responsible for "deficits of general government"[18] and have to accept that such deficits, on the one hand, weigh on the qualification for entry in the third stage of the EMU and, on the other hand, may trigger sanctioning measures. According to Art 2 of Protocol (No 20) to the Treaty on the excessive deficit procedure, "government" means general government, that is central government, regional or local government and social security funds, to the exclusion of commercial operations, as defined in the European System of Integrated Economic Accounts (ESA). This definition bears witness to a decision to define the government not on an institutional basis, but "on a functional basis".[19] As the Commission rightly explains,

> "only units of which the principal function is the production of non-market services or the redistribution of resources are included. Accordingly, publicly owned units dealing with commercial operations such as public enterprises are excluded."[20]

From a legal point of view, this situation was created by a Council Regulation on the basis of Art 104(14) EC on the application of the Protocol on the excessive deficit procedure.[21] Thereby, inter

17 However, the reintegration of such debts into government debts will also affect the criterion of new indebtedness under Art 104(2)(a) EC.

18 Art 3 Protocol (No 20).

19 So also the *European Commission* (1998) 145.

20 Ibid.

21 Reg (EC) No 3605/93, as amended by Reg (EC) No 475/2000.

alia, the term "government deficit" is defined according to the ESA in its third edition of 1995 (ESA 95).[22]

"Government" under this approach denotes the – subdivided – sector of general government, "to the exclusion of commercial operations, as defined in ESA 95. The exclusion of commercial operations means that the sector of general government (S.13) comprises only institutional units producing non-market services as their main activity."[23]

The paraphrase provided by the relevant section of ESA is of rather limited assistance, as the general government sector is defined as including all institutional units, which distinct to non-market producers for own final use, were

> "other non-market producers whose output was intended for individual and collective consumption, and mainly financed by compulsory payments made by units belonging to other sectors, and/or all institutional units principally engaged in the redistribution of national income and wealth."[24]

ESA then continues by establishing that in the general government sector, the following institutional entities are to be included:

a) "general government entities (excluding public producers organised as public corporations or, by virtue of special legislation, recognised as independent legal entities, or quasi-corporations, when any of these are classified in the non-financial or financial sectors)...;

---

[22] The third edition is to be applied since 1 September 1999 for the purpose of the Member States' reports to the Commission under the excessive deficit procedure: Art 8 para 2 Council Regulation (EC) No 2223/96 of 25 June 1996 on the European system of national and regional accounts in the Community, OJ No L 310, 30/11/1996, 1. Until that date, the second edition was to be applied; see Art 1 Reg. (EC) 3605/93, in its orginial version.
Meanwhile, ESA 95 was amended by implementing Reg (EC) 1500/2000, OJ No L 172, 12/7/2000, 3, and by Reg (EC) 2516/2000, OJ No L 290, 17/11/2000, 1.

[23] Art 1 para 2 Reg. (EC) 3605/93, as amended. As will be shown, "non-market services" is ambiguous, as it aims at economic capacity as well as at decision-making autonomy of the institution concerned.

[24] 2.68 ESA 95.

b) non-profit institutions recognised as independent legal entities which are other non-market producers and which are controlled and mainly financed by general government;

c) autonomous pension funds..."[25]

At first sight, due to the imprecise phrasing of ESA, in particular concerning sub-para (a) and the undifferentiated exclusion of public producers organised as public corporations or by virtue of special legislation, one could get the impression that such public producers were *never* to be included in the general government sector. This would imply that for such producers, it would be irrelevant whether they mainly produced non-market services or whether they were conducting purely commercial activities. If this was correct, these entities would not even have to be included in the general government sector if they were exclusively engaged in non-market activities.

Opposing such an interpretation is, first, the introductory definition, the intention of which apparently is to include all institutional units in the general government sector that are in a close relationship to the government and engage in non-market services as their main activity. Second, it can be inferred from the so-called sectoral grouping of institutional units in ESA that corporations are only then differentiated from the general government sector if they are market producers.[26]

As a result, public producers are only excluded from the general government sector if their main activity is not the production of non-market services. In simpler terms, under the ESA scheme, the debts of a public producer with legal personality, whose principal activity is the production of non-market services, fall within the general government sector.[27] When a unit performs both non-market and market activities, the classification of the unit inside or outside the general government sector is decided on the basis of the dominant share in its resources between non-market and market sources.[28] Hence, should market elements be predominant, the respective unit will not be included in the general government sector.

A second requirement which must be met in order to avoid a classification inside the general government sector under ESA is the

---

25 2.69 ESA 95.

26 E.g. 2.21 ESA 95.

27 The terminology of ESA deviates from common language, as such a public producer comes under the category of a public corporation.

28 So the *European Commission* (1998) 147.

existence of an "institutional unit". This is "an elementary economic decision-making centre characterised by uniformity of behaviour and decision-making autonomy in the exercise of its principal function."[29] By contrast, entities "which ... have no autonomy of decision in the exercise of their principal function" are to be combined with the units which control them.[30]

The mentioned criteria could therefore – to an extent which will be the subject of the following chapters – lead to the classification of public producers within general government. The legal consequence is the classification of the debts of this unit as government debt.

The two elements, market determination and decision-making autonomy, are to be further specified, as they are essential to the classification of public producers.

B. Market and Non-Market Services

Other non-market producers essentially are institutional units, "whose major part of output is provided free or at not economically significant prices."[31] Decisive for the classification of a unit is the application of the market/non-market rule.

By virtue of ESA 95, production (also of services) is only market production if by looking over a range of years[32] more than 50% of the "production costs" – and not of the current receipts as under ESA 79 – are covered by sales:[33]

> "If less than 50% of the production costs are covered by sales, the institutional unit is another non-market producer... But other non-market Non-Profit Institutions (NPIs) that are controlled and mainly financed by general government are classified to the general government sector."[34]

---

29 2.12. ESA 95. Such a unit either keeps a complete set of accounts, "or it would be possible and meaningful, from both an economic and legal viewpoint, to compile a complete set of accounts if they were required". See also the different definition in the older ESA 78, para 212.

30 2.13. para (c) ESA 95.

31 3.26 ESA 95.

32 3.33 last subparagraph ESA 95.

33 3.32 ESA 95.

34 3.32. para (b) ESA 95. The distinction applied in this paragraph between NPIs and other producers is only relevant for the private sector,

In the text, a further specification of the definition of sales and production costs is given.[35] These provisions, however, do not put into more concrete terms the important question of government payments to the institutional unit. It is only the manual issued by Eurostat[36] which specifies that,

> "payments from general government to public institutional units in respect of actual services provided are to be treated as corresponding to sales in the implementation of the 50% rule when prices are economically significant".[37]

This would apply in two cases: a) when prices paid by the general government to the public producer for actual services are also

---

but irrelevant for classifying public producers, see 3.37 ESA 95 and Table 3.1 ESA 95.

35 3.33 ESA 95. This definition at first sight appears to be redundant, as para(a) (1) seems to request that it is clarified first whether the output is "market", *before* the respective sales can be used for the calculation. Under this condition, the sales cannot clarify the issue of market or non-market. To avoid this result, it may be assumed that the paragraph deals only with the difference between the definition of sales and of output at basic prices, which uses sales only for valuation of market output and costs for non-market output.

36 Eurostat is the "Commission department responsible for carrying out the tasks devolving on the Commission as regards the production of Community statistics" – Art 2 Council Regulation (EC) No 322/97 of 17 February 1997 on Community Statistics, OJ No L 52, 22/02/1997 1. Commission Decision 97/281/EC of 21 April 1997 on the role of Eurostat as regards the production of Community statistics, OJ No L 112, 29/04/1997 56, specified the tasks of Eurostat with respect to the implementation of the Community statistical programme. The provision of the data to be used for the protocol on the excessive deficit procedure can be regarded as one aspect of this task.
On the whole, this situation can be perceived as a delegation to Eurostat of the management and administration of the relevant classification issues of cases under ESA 95 – including decision-making powers; the certainly difficult clarification, even the more concerning statistics, of the mixture of collective responsibility (Art 1 Rules of Procedure of the Commission, OJ No L 308, 08/12/2000 26), empowerment of individual Commissioners with the possibility of subdelegation (Art 13 RoP), and the "delegation" to certain Directors-Generals and Heads of Services (Art 14 RoP) can be omitted here.

37 *ESA Manual* (2002) 15.

charged to similar services (of the same quality) provided by private producers, and b) when, in the absence of private producers in the same kind of activity, the general government pays public units for actual services (rather than through a coverage of costs) in order to have a significant economic influence on the supply and demand.[38] Payments to cover an overall deficit are moreover explicitly excluded by ESA 95.[39]

At this point, it should be mentioned that, as also the Commission notes, the composition of resources (non-market or market) may change over time, so that sectoral reclassifications may be necessary.[40] Should non-market elements prevail in a unit's activity, it may be reclassified from corporate sector back into general government.

C. Decision-Making Autonomy in the Exercise of the Principal Function

Decision-making autonomy in the exercise of the principal function according to ESA 95 means that a "unit must:

a) be entitled to own goods or assets in its own right; it will therefore be able to exchange the ownership of goods or assets in transactions with other institutional units;

b) be able to take economic decisions and engage in economic activities for which it is itself held to be directly responsible and accountable at law;

c) be able to incur liabilities on its own behalf, to take on other obligations or further commitments and to enter into contracts."[41]

As already pointed out above, if there is no such decision-making authority, the entities are "combined with the units which control them",[42] i.e. classified within general government, should it be the controlling subject. Obviously, this provision is of central importance with respect to the evaluation of entities, including those with own legal personality, but which are particularly close to government.[43]

---

38 Ibid.

39 3.33 para (a) ESA 95.

40 *European Commission* (1998) 147.

41 3.12. ESA 95.

42 2.13. para (c) ESA 95 = ESA 79, para 213.

43 At least theoretically, also a government operated entity could be qualified as institutional unit – ESA calls them "quasi-corporations". How-

However, the ambiguity, not to say inconsistency, of ESA, complicates the matter. Whereas the provisions just sketched out above lead to the conclusion that decision-making authority in economic matters is essential for the classification outside general government, other provisions under ESA conflict with this principle. On the one hand, ESA stipulates that entities forming part of a group of units and keeping a complete set of accounts are deemed to be institutional units "even if they have partially surrendered their autonomy of decision to the central body (the holding corporation) responsible for the general direction of the group."[44] On the other hand, within the sector "non-financial corporations", which is distinct from government, there is a sub-sector "*public* non-financial corporations", which is again characterised by the fact that these corporations are "subject to control by government."[45]

The term control is defined by ESA as follows:

> "Control over a corporation is defined as the ability to determine general corporate policy by choosing appropriate directors, if necessary. A single institutional unit ... secures control over a corporation by owning more than half the voting shares or otherwise controlling more than half the shareholders' voting power. In addition, government secures control over a corporation as a result of special legislation decree or regula-

---

ever, the imponderabilities are even larger than presented in the text for corporations. Under 2.13 para (f), ESA defines quasi-corporations as entities which "keep a complete set of accounts and have no independent legal status. However, they have an economic and financial behaviour that is different from that of their owners and similar to that of corporations. Therefore they are deemed to have autonomy of decision and are considered as distinct institutional units." On the other hand, it is said in 2.24 that "the existence of a complete set of accounts, including balance sheets, is not a sufficient condition for market producers to be treated as quasi-corporations. Therefore, partnerships and public producers ... are in general not distinct institutional units because they do not enjoy autonomy of decision, their management being under the control of ... governments which own them." Again, however, "market producers as quasi-corporations" are mentioned as an exception.

44 2.13 para (e) ESA 95.

45 2.28 ESA 95.

> tion which empowers the government to determine corporate policy or to appoint the directors."[46]

Thus, the elimination of decision-making autonomy does not per se preclude the classification of an entity outside general government. As a result, it is not necessarily detrimental to its categorisation within general government if a public undertaking has to observe general guidelines, for instance to allow government to exert a market conform risk control on usual terms, as provided for by the possibilities for intervention under limited liability company law[47] or also by special purpose legislation.[48] The overall idea seems to be that on the whole, there must be economic independence in commercial decisions. After all, the combined effect of the classification criteria used by ESA – the market criterion and the requirement of decision-making autonomy in the principal activity – only allows the conclusion that an institutionalised mechanism of heteronomy, which subjects the decision-making of the public enterprise, always or as a rule, to approval by government, deprives this entity of its decision-making autonomy in the principal activity for the purposes of the ESA system. The result is that its accounts must be included in those of the controlling unit, i.e. general government.

This hardly offers a practical outcome, as it appears to be entirely at the Commission's discretion whether an entity is classified inside or outside general government. In the manual on ESA,[49] the Commission comments on this area of uncertainty. After it describes the principle of decision-making autonomy in the principal activity, it concludes that an institutional unit without decision-making autonomy is to be combined with the unit which controls it. However, then it goes on saying:

---

46 2.26 ESA 95. Also for subsidiaries, this passage specifies what is to be understood under control of voting rights.

47 To take again Austria as an example, this means in particular the powers of the supervisory board concerning the requirement to obtain approval (see § 30j para 5 no. 2 and 5 GmbHG) and those of the General Assembly (§ 35 GmbHG).

48 Many specific pieces of legislation for public enterprises include the right of government to give general instructions on the performance of the legal assignments.

49 This manual was issued in 2002 already in its second edition not least in order to answer the many practical questions on borderline cases.

> "However, a particular case occurs with units which keep a complete set of accounts, have a market activity and whose economic and financial behaviour is similar to that of corporations. These units are deemed to have autonomy of decision and are to be classified, outside the general government sector, in the corporation sector as quasi-corporations."[50]

On the basis of the legal grounds briefly outlined above, there is little certainty of the classification.

D. Financial and non-financial transactions

(1.) To be distinguished from the classification of a legal entity (and its debts) inside or outside the general government sector is the classification of concrete transactions of having or not having impact on government deficit. The issue concerns primarily the current deficit, but has repercussions for the government debt.

A central feature of the calculation of the current deficit is that, contrasting to traditional principles in several countries,[51] so-called *financial transactions* are not taken into account, even if they are undertaken by the state itself. According to ESA, a *financial transaction* is an

> "interaction between institutional units, or between an institutional unit and the rest of the world, by mutual agreement, involving a simultaneous creation or liquidation of a financial asset and the counterpart liability, or a change in ownership of a financial asset, or an assumption of a liability."[52]

Whereas, *non-financial transactions* are:

- *distributive transactions:* transactions by means of which the value generated by production is distributed to labour, capital and government, and transactions involving the redistribution of income and wealth;[53]

---

50 *ESA Manual* (2002) 11. Compare also above in fn 43.

51 For an example, compare again Austria: Regulation of the Federal Ministry of Finance, by which the form and structure of the estimates and settlements of the accounts of Regions and local authorities are determined (Voranschlags- und Rechnungsabschlussverordnung – VRV 1997), Official Bulletin 1996/787.

52 5.02 ESA 95.

53 4.01 ESA 95.

- *transactions in products:* the production of goods and services;[54] and
- *transactions with non-financial non-produced assets:* transactions in particular with land and immaterial assets.[55]

Financial transactions always have counterpart transactions in the system, which may either be other financial transactions or non-financial transactions.[56] The latter, in contrast to financial transactions, enter in the calculation of the net lending/net borrowing B.9. and therefore impact on the deficit. In cases where, however, a transaction and its counterpart are both financial transactions, they change the portfolio of financial assets and liabilities and they may change the totals of both financial assets and liabilities of the institutional units involved or the rest of the world, but they do not change net lending/net borrowing or net worth.[57]

(2.) One consequence is that transactions not only of the general government itself, but also of public producers, i.e. entities which come, irrespective of their eventual legal separation from the state, under the government sector, do not necessarily affect the current government deficit, and consequently also not on government debt. As long as those transactions are *financial* in nature, as for instance the granting of a loan, they have no impact on the government deficit, provided that the counterpart transactions are also of a financial, and not of a distributive, nature.

E. Economic Reality over Legal Form

(1.) Things become more complex by the seemingly increasing trend to "reroute" or "recognise" certain activities following a primarily *economic perspective*, in an effort to lift the "legal veil" and report the "true" economic impact.[58] This may, in some instances, lead to the classification of "non-financial" transactions undertaken by public undertakings as transactions of the government which consequently impact on the net deficit.

On the whole, Eurostat has so far been generous and accepted, for example, the exclusion from general government of cases where the government grants to public enterprises the right to finance,

---

[54] 3.01 ESA 95.

[55] 6.06 ESA 95.

[56] 5.15 ESA 95.

[57] 5.15 ESA 95.

[58] For some critical remarks compare below after fn 91.

construct and exploit public infrastructure.[59] Yearly payments of the State, or even cases in which the infrastructure reverts to general government without further charge at the end of the period of exploitation, do not change this.[60] If however, as can be inferred from a decision on the Italian Railways,[61] the State is obliged by public law to repay the debts of the respective enterprise, the budget of the State specifies each year the amount of repayment, and the debt, issued by the enterprise, is systematically refunded by the State (interest and principal), this debt has to be reclassified in the stock of government debt.[62]

Debts guaranteed in that manner according to Eurostat are hence government debts. This seems to be so regardless of the market or non-market nature of the service in question and the decision-making autonomy of the enterprise in its principal activity. It can be assumed that a state guarantee similar to the one sketched out normally will be associated with some influence of the State and that the market nature will suffer from the elimination of entrepreneurial risk.[63] However, the categorisation of debts guaranteed in this manner as government debts is far from being easily foreseeable – and the press releases in hard cases as a rule lack comprehensible arguments. Taken (theoretically) to the extreme, the debts of a public enterprise, which mainly produces market output and which is autonomous in its decision-making, could nevertheless be classified as general government debts, if there was a particularly far-reaching State guarantee. It is not the concrete decision which is to be criticised, rather the lack of predictability which is problematic.

(2.) Another possible effect of the mentioned *economic perspective* is the reclassification of government transactions with public enterprises.

A recent (Austrian) case concerns the sale of governmental land and buildings to a public enterprise. In this regard, ESA does not

---

59 Compare *ESA Manual* (2002) 182 ff.

60 In particular Eurostat Press Release No 16/97 of 21 February 1997; No 24/97 of 26 March 1997; No 33/97 of 30 April 1997.

61 Eurostat Press Release No 16/97 of 21 February 1997.

62 So also *ESA Manual* (2002) 97 with the explanation that it could be assumed from the outset that this was a liability of the State.

63 This could be considered as a special case of government control, which renders superfluous the detailed examination, whether the unit was still a market producer with decision-making autonomy. Typically, this will not be the case anyhow.

differentiate according to the "character" of an eventual purchaser. It could therefore be assumed that it is not the question *between whom* there is a transaction as long as it is an institutional unit distinct from general government. What should be decisive is the content of the transaction. Thus, financial transactions between the State and separate legal entities in principle do not have an impact on the current deficit, non-financial transactions however do. This is also the general view of the Commission.[64] Accordingly, as a rule, revenues generated from the sale of land and buildings are non-financial transactions and have an impact on the current deficit: Direct sale of a non-financial asset improves the net borrowing/net lending of general government, through a decrease of gross fixed capital formation.[65]

However, in the case of the BIG – which by an Act of parliament was granted the ownership rights of a range of government real estate[66] – the Commission decided differently.[67] It did so irrespective of the fact that it estimated the BIG to be "an institutional unit in its own right", hence not an ancillary unit of general government. The Commission said that although it is 100% government-owned,

> "the degree of control by government over the BIG does not seem to go beyond what is indicated in ESA 95 with respect to institutional units, i.e. fixing the general strategy of the unit without influencing the current management."

The rents earned by the BIG were determined according to market-based valuation methods, so that the BIG therefore was considered a market producer and classified within the "non-financial corporation" sector. Nevertheless, the transfer of property from government to the BIG was to be recorded under "other volume changes in financial assets/changes in classification and structures K10/K12", as it had not been organised as "normal market sale", because of the size of the transaction. In addition, the Austrian State

---

64 *ESA Manual* (2002) 34 ff.

65 See 1.13 para (d) and 6.08 para (a) ESA 95. Compare also *ESA Manual* (2002) 28.

66 See infra note 103.

67 Press Release No 15/2002 – 31. January 2002, Treatment of the transfer of Government real estate to a publicly-owned corporation in Austria.

wanted, according to the Commission, to maintain indirectly the ownership of the transferred property via the State owned company.[68]

The quite staggering result of these short "considerations" is that the BIG on the one hand is seen as sufficiently independent, pursuing activities of a market nature, to be classified as non-financial corporation outside general government, but that its independence at the same time does not suffice to classify the sale of the government real estate other than as a change *within* the capital accounts of the government. The weight of the reference to the "normal market sale" in this context is less than clear. It appears as an unsuitable attempt to negate the transfer of assets by referring to the *content* of the transaction. This cannot be substantiated by pointing to the unusual size of the sale. More promising – under an "economic perspective" – might be the alleged prolongation of the State's right of disposal. However, if the aim is not to "reroute" *every* sale of government assets to public enterprises – which would lack any foundation in ESA 95 – the contention must be that the independence of the BIG in general or in this specific case is not *sufficient*. Still, it is hard to find an explanation which would allow, on the one hand, for a classification of the BIG as a non-financial market corporation, but on the other hand, for the sale to the BIG as a mere rearrangement within the government sector. It is open to speculation to what extent restrictions imposed on the BIG to resale certain of the purchased assets might be of importance. An eventual argument drawing on that point would have to take into account that "indirect ownership" of assets is inevitable with regard to public enterprises, and that a prohibition to sell *certain* of those assets does not necessarily go beyond the fixing of a general strategy. However, it has to be said that no explanation of this kind is offered in the considerations of the Commission. The result is a difference in the required decision-making autonomy with regard to the classification of BIG debts, on the one hand, and the calculation of the current government deficit, on the other hand.The BIG case might be qualified as a borderline case, where it is hard to tell whether the concrete decision is still covered by the impreciseness of ESA, or falls within the Commission's exaggerated approach of "economic reality over legal form". What can be said is that the reasons explicitly provided

68 Ibid.

by the Commission cannot fully justify the result, while eventual additional considerations remain wrapped in mystery.

IV. Aspects of Legal Protection

A. Decision-Making Competencies of the Commission

(1). The provisions of the EC on the avoidance of excessive government deficit are particularly ambivalent concerning the allocation of decision-making powers. On the one hand, it is exclusively the Council, which is competent – on recommendation of the Commission – to decide after an overall consideration "whether an excessive deficit exists."[69] In case of an affirmative decision, the Council can make recommendations, and may, if necessary, "give notice" to a Member State, i.e. set time limits for deficit reduction measures.[70] If the Member State does not observe these recommendations, sanctions, including even fines, may be imposed.[71] On the other hand, the protocol on the excessive deficit procedure sets out that the statistical data "to be used for the application of this Protocol", i.e. for the application of the deficit criterion, "shall be provided by the Commission."[72] Given this legal situation, it is not clear whether the taking of legally binding decisions on the classification of individual transactions and of certain institutional units primarily lies with the Commission, in the course of the production of the statistical data,[73] or with the Council, in the framework of the excessive deficit procedure.

(2.) The Commission, more precisely Eurostat, bases it actions on two Council regulations; one on the application of the Protocol on the excessive deficit procedure,[74] the second on the introduction of ESA 95.[75] The Commission is assisted by two Committees: The

---

69 Art 104 para 6 EC.

70 The right to bring the matter before the ECJ is, however, excluded (Art 104(10) EC). This underscores the highly political character of the whole procedure.

71 Art 104(11) EC.

72 Art 4 Protocol (No 20) on the excessive deficit procedure.

73 *Italianer* (1999) para 103 submitts that the Commission is entitled to change the data supplied by the Member States, in order to guarantee the correct application of the protocol.

74 Reg. (EC) No 3605/93 (see supra note 21).

75 Reg. (EC) 2223/96 (see supra note 22).

Committee on the Statistical Programmes (CSP),[76] and the Committee for Monetary, Financial and Balance of Payments Statistics (CMFB).[77] In EMU matters, the CMFB in practice is more important, as before every controversial decision, its opinion is requested.[78] In practice, the Commission nearly always follows the recommendations of this Committee.

The "decisions" of Eurostat[79] by means of a so-called methodical note are transmitted to the entities and organs concerned, that is, CMFB, Commission, central banks, national statistical offices, but not the Member States as such. The results of CMFB consultation and Eurostat decisions are made public at the same time in the form of press releases.

(3.) It may be doubted whether such a procedure is lawful.[80] For instance, the CSP is not included in the decision-making process, although required by the relevant regulation.[81] This enables the Commission to escape the comitology procedure foreseen therein, whereby in cases of differences of opinion between the CSP and the Commission, the Council is given the possibility to take, within three months, a decision different from the one desired by the

---

76 89/382/EEC, Euratom: Council Decision of 19 June 1989 establishing a Committee on the Statistical Programmes of the European Communities, OJL 181, 28/06/1989 47. The CSP consists of representatives of the statistical institutes of the Member States and is chaired by a representative of the Commission.

77 The Committee had been set up by Council Decision No 91/115/EEC of 25 February 1991 establishing a committee on monetary, financial and balance of payments statistics, OJ No L 59, 06/03/1991 19, amended by Council Decision No 96/174/EC of 26 February 1996. The Committee is composed of one, two or three representatives per Member State, coming from the institutions principally concerned with financial, monetary and balance of payments statistics, up to three representatives of the Commission and up to three representatives of the ESCB. Each Member State, the Commission and the ESCB have one vote each.

78 Art 6 Reg. (EC) 2223/96.

79 See for instance Press Release 15/2002 on the BIG under the heading "New decision of Eurostat on deficit and debt".

80 A good impression of the pragmatic approach applied in this area is given by *van Wijk* (2001).

81 Art 4 Reg. (EC) 2223/96, as amended.

Commission. A similar procedure is missing for the CMFB, whose function is only advisory.[82]

Attempts to read the regulation[83] in the sense that consultation of the CMFB could *replace* consultation of the CSP, are not convincing, in particular not in these cases, where binding decisions of the Commission are at stake. This would assume an intention of the Council to waive its general right to reverse decisions of the Commission in the important field of EMU. Moreover, this would imply that such a fundamental change should be introduced not by amending the relevant authorisation, but merely indirectly by the involvement of a specialised advisory body, the CMFB. Not only is any indication for such an interpretation missing,[84] but it would also be questionable from the perspective of the principle of equality.

The better arguments support the view that the CSP, and hence comitology procedure (in the version of the Management Procedure) is to come into play whenever decisions of the Commission are under discussion.[85] From a systematic point of view, this corre-

---

82 *Van Wijk* (2001) 205 reports that the involvement of the CSP failed due to the opposition of the CMFB, and points to the irregularity that the CMFB is not chaired by a Commission representative, as is the norm with all Committees.

83 Arts 4 and 6 Reg. (EC) 2223/96.

84 Decision 91/115/EEC establishing the CMFB does not clarify the matter, but seems to support the interpretation presented in the text. Art 2 subpara 2 states: "The Committee may be asked to express opinions on the links between monetary, financial and balance of payments statistics on the one hand, and certain other economic statistics on the other, in particular those on which national accounts are based. *The work of this Committee will be coordinated with that of the Statistical Programme Committee*". (emphasis added)

85 Art 4 para 2 and 3 Reg. (EC) 2223/96. The decision-making power goes beyond the points dealt with in Art 2 Abs 2 by reference to "amendments to the ESA 95 methodology which are intended to clarify and improve its content". This seemingly contradictory formulation may be interpreted as authorising the Commission, should there be concrete questions, to restrict the discretion of the Member States regarding the assessment of specific transactions. Insofar, "clarifications of content" are at the same time amendments.

If regarded from the perspective of the separation of power, this comitology procedure can be regarded as an irregularity, insofar as the Council may decide on an isolated case; there are, however, parallels to national mechanisms, according to which usually the Parliaments may

sponds to the principles as laid down in the general Community statistical regime, where the Commission is assisted by the CSP.[86]

(4.) This does not change the responsibility for the production of the data as provided for under the Protocol on the excessive deficit procedure, which, in principle, rests with the Commission.[87] However, this specific task cannot completely reverse the decision-making procedures of the overall scheme of provisions on the drawing up of Community statistics.[88] The Commission is hence responsible for the production of the statistics necessary for the application of the Protocol. To a large extent, it will be able to fulfil this task by processing the data delivered by the Member States. However in cases of conflicts, binding decisions must be made in compliance with the comitology procedure provided for in Reg. 2223/96.

As regards the Council, its primary duty under Art 104 EC (avoidance of excessive deficits) is the evaluation of the statistical data produced beforehand, according to the criteria mentioned in the Treaty. By contrast, the drawing up and eventual decisions on the actual data is the primary duty of the Commission. It does not seem appropriate, however, to deduce from this a strict obligation on the side of the Council to apply the statistics provided by the Commission. At least in cases of grave inconsistencies, it could take issue with the statistical material compiled by the Commission and assess it in a divergent manner.[89] The Commission decisions on statistics, though, cannot be qualified as a provisional measure in-

---

influence the compilation of the settlement of the accounts. Moreover, as just discussed, such a decision usually prejudges decisions on similar matters in all Member States, and insofar is Janus-faced.

86 See Art 19 Reg. (EC) 322/97, see supra note 36.

87 Art 4 Protocol on the excessive deficit procedure.

88 Otherwise, there would be a risk of divergence in the decision-making procedures, on the one hand, regarding the drawing up of the overall EC statistics, and on the other hand, for the purposes of the Protocol.

89 It would otherwise be left to the Commission to determine the Council Decision on the excessive deficit by decisions on the proper accounting method, despite such a far-reaching influence being excluded by Art 104 EC, under which the Commission only has the right to give recommendations.

Most likely it will be very difficult to de facto challenge an accounting decision, which was not contested before, only afterwards at the Council level. In any event, this would result in a divergence between Community statistics and the basis for the Council decision.

tended to pave the way for the final decision, which would be open to review only together with (and if there was) the Council decision.[90] On the contrary, these decisions are far more than a preparatory measure, as they do not only serve as the basis of a possible Council decision. Normally, at the point of the decision on the appropriate accounting treatment, it is neither clear whether such a procedure will be started, nor whether the actual decision will give any rise for such a procedure at all (as the overall development in this context does not matter).

B. Some Remarks on Legal Certainty

As has been demonstrated, the ambiguity and vagueness of the terms of the ESA 95 lead to an exorbitant margin of discretion in regard to both the classification of a certain "unit" and of a certain transaction. Moreover, the combination of the two elements of discretion makes it even more difficult to predict classification decisions.

Ambiguity and vagueness are a general feature of the law and as such inevitable, given that the legislator has to use human language. The crucial question is whether the concrete amount of legal uncertainty in the application of the excessive deficit criterion is resulting from this inevitable effect, or is rather due to insufficient drafting of the rules to be applied. It is submitted that good reasons strike for the latter view. The strained relationship between the contradicting, yet central classification lines for the treatment of public undertakings does not provide for operational solutions from an epistemological point of view. One cause might be that what had originally been set up as a description for good statistics has been transformed into a legally binding instrument which is of crucial importance for the functioning of EMU.

In addition to what has been demonstrated above, a few words shall be added with regard to the *economic perspective* as advocated by the Commission. The Commission refers to a functional approach or to a principle of "reporting economic reality over legal form".[91] The principle is coined in that "it is important sometimes to look through the legal form of an institutional unit or economic flow, and to report the economic reality. This can apply both to the classification of units and to the classification of flows."

---

90 For such a constellation see for instance Case T-64/89, *Automec*, ECR [1990] II-367 para 42.

91 *ESA Manual* (2002) 26.

It has to be acknowleged that the Commission's view can, at least to some extent, be founded in the existing legal framework. 1.38 ESA 95 reads as follows:

> "The system's treatment of most transactions is straightforward; that is, the transactions are recorded in the same way as they appear to the institutional units involved. However, some transactions are rearranged in order to bring out the underlying economic relationships more clearly. Transactions can be rearranged in three ways: rerouting, partitioning and recognising the principal party to a transaction."

Regarding the important aspect of recognising, the "determination" is as follows:

> "When a unit carries out a transaction on behalf of another unit, the transaction is recorded exclusively in the accounts of the principal. As a rule, one should not go beyond this principle ..."[92]

Consequently, the criteria for the classification of units and flows not only are, as demonstrated, ambiguous and vague in itself. Moreover, they are declared relative in their legal significance, and are subject to eventual corrections under the "economic perspective criterion". This criterion is in itself far from providing *additional* elements of clarity, as it aggravates the unclear meaning of the legal text. One might say that as a result the underlying criteria merge and dissolve at the same time. Market criterion, decision-making autonomy, and transaction character thus cannot be scrutinized by applying the ESA text. Rather is the Commission carrying out an evaluation of the underlying "economic reality".

One may therefore contend that Council Reg. 2223/96, a constituent part of which is ESA 95, infringes the principle of the rule of law and the principle of legal certainty, which according to ECJ is one of the fundamental principles of Community law.[93] Judicial review lacks legal significance as long as the standards applied are so ambiguous and vague that most important points are delegated to

---

92 1.41 ESA 95.

93 For instance Joined cases 212 to 217/80, *Salumi*, ECR [1981] 2735 para 10, and in particular Case C-143/93, *Van Es Douane Agenten*, ECR [1996] I-431, in which the ECJ declared a regulation inapplicable. See also Art 6 para 1 EU.

the implementing decision. If the regulation was challenged before the ECJ, it should be declared void in the points addressed, mainly as regards the decision making autonomy criterion and the broad option to "reroute" and "recognise" classifications.[94] As long as those points remain unchanged, and as long as a legal dispute is avoided, the decisions on classification in practice will be the result of a bargaining process, which is worrisome when regarded from the perspective of the rule of law.

C. Possibilities to Challenge Commission Decisions

(1.) As was set out above, decisions of Eurostat in the course of drawing up of Community statistics constitute contestable acts for the purposes of Art 230 EC. Accordingly, they may be challenged by their addressees, in particular by the respective statistical offices. Member States usually do not appear as addressees of such acts. Since they are privileged applicants, they nonetheless may institute proceedings against such decisions. As it cannot be assumed that the Member States are represented by the statistical offices, the two-month period within which proceedings must be instituted only starts from the date on which the act came into their knowledge.

It is, however, not only possible to challenge actual decisions, but also, as indicated above, the remarkably vague Reg. 2223/96, and more precisely, important parts of ESA, which are given binding force by that Regulation. On the occasion of a concrete dispute, a possible violation of the Treaty by this Regulation could be advanced.[95]

(2.) It could be doubted whether accounting decisions do involve binding and hence contestable legal acts of the Commission or Eurostat at all. Alternatively, the production of statistics could be comprised as a mere fact, which serves as the basis for subsequent decisions, for instance under the excessive deficit procedure.[96]

That the production of Community statistics has a significance of its own,[97] and requires legal decisions in controversial cases, however, points to the opposite. This cannot only be inferred from the decision-making practice of Eurostat, but also from Reg. 2223/96, which qualifies clarifications of the content as binding

---

94 Art 230 and Art 241 EC.

95 Art 241 EC.

96 Though, contractual liability in accordance with Art 288 EC would be possible.

97 Art 285 EC, introduced by the Treaty of Amsterdam.

acts. This could impinge on the interests of the Member States in many ways, particularly if the principles of "impartiality, reliability, objectivity [or] scientific independence"[98] are not observed. Thereby, a wrong picture of the overall situation could be created, which distorts the factual situation and harms the Member State – for instance by reducing its credit worthiness. The reference to decisions on statistics in the course of the selection procedure for the third stage of EMU is thus only a supplementing, but not the decisive, argument in favour of the qualification of such finding as legal acts.

It is established case law that it is not the nature or form, but the content of the measure that opens it for judicial review.[99] Accordingly, against all acts or decisions an action for annulment may be brought under Art 230 EC, which bring about a distinct change in the legal position of the applicant.[100] There is no doubt that, in particular, controversial Eurostat decisions fulfil this requirement. There, the reports by the Member States or their statistical offices may even be changed,[101] which affects the interest in a correct presentation of the Community statistics. The dubious form of these decisions is consequently irrelevant.

V. The Example of the Austrian Bundes-Immobiliengesellschaft (BIG)

A. Outline of the Legal Status

The Bundes-Immobiliengesellschaft (BIG) was set up by a special law in 1992 (BIG-Act)[102] and is 100% government owned. This has not been changed by the Federal Real Estate Act enacted at the

---

98 Art 285 para 2 EC. See also Art 10 Reg. (EC) No. 322/97.

99 E.g. Case C-57/95, *France/Commission*, ECR [1997] I-1627, para 7.

100 E.g. Case 22/70, *AETR*, ECR [1971] 263 para 38/42, Case C-303/90, *Code of Conduct*, ECR [1991] I-5315, Guiding Principles 1, or also T-64/89, *Automec*, ECR [1990] II-367 para 42.

101 For instance in the decision on the BIG, Eurostat news release No 15/2002: "... The transfer has therefore no impact on the general government deficit... This has the effect that the debt of the BIG is not to be included in the debt of the general government sector."

102 Federal law on the establishment of a Property Management Company with limited liability and the disposition over government real estate including buildings with flats, Official Bulletin 1992/419 as amended by 1997/113.

end of 2000.[103] An important change brought about by the new law is, however, that the BIG gains the ownership in the largest part of the real estate, of which it previously had the right of usufruct.[104] For this acquisition of property, which takes place in several tranches, the BIG has to pay the Federal government a fee amounting to EUR 2.398 million.[105] The second important change, which will not be discussed in detail, is the spin-off of the management of the Federal government property by setting up a 100% subsidiary of the BIG, the Immobilienmanagementgesellschaft (IMB).[106] Already by the Infrastructure Financing Act 1997, the range of the properties managed by the BIG was substantially increased. At the same time, the BIG was required by law to assume a series of liabilities of the Autobahnen- und Schnellstraßen-Finanzierungs-Aktiengesellschaft (ASFINAG) from credit operations in order to finance building constructions of the Federal government, which led to a considerable stock of debts for the BIG.[107]

The primary subject of BIG's business activity is the provision of real estate for Federal government, in accordance with its requirements, such as: the acquisition, the use, the management, the renting-out and the sale of real estate and buildings, the construction and maintenance of the latter as well as key services in the running of a building.[108] These tasks are to be carried out by the BIG's own staff or by staff of its subsidiaries, i.e. mainly those of

---

[103] Federal law, by which the building and real estate management of Federal government is reorganised and Federal property is disposed of (Federal Real Estate Act, BundesimmobilienG) and by which the Federal Ministry Act 1986 as well as the ASFINAG-enabling Act 1997 is changed, Official Bulletin I 2000/141.

[104] § 13 BundesimmobilienG.
Already earlier, the BIG had been entitled to make a tender to Federal government for real estate for which it had the right of usufruct, regarding ownership, construction rights or other rights. The compensation offered was to be determined by an expert opinion of the Ministry of Finance. The Finance Minister was also legally enabled to accept such offers (§ 3 para 2 BIG-Act).

[105] § 14 BundesimmobilienG.

[106] § 6 BundesimmobilienG.

[107] § 3 para 1 and § 3a BIG-G as amended by BGBl 1997/113. The State guarantees by virtue of § 36 para 3 of the new BundesimmobilienG remain in force.

[108] § 2 BundesimmobilienG.

IMB.[109] On "market conditions", and if justifiable from an economic perspective, the BIG may satisfy the demand for space of the Federal government by renting back the objects listed in an annex to the law, adapt them if necessary, and acquire new premises in case of building projects of Federal government.[110] A further task is also the sale at "at least reasonable prices".[111] The overall objective, as can be inferred from the law, is to reorganise the real property assets and demands of the Federal government according to economic and market-oriented principles.[112]

The Federal government concludes individual lease contracts with the BIG for the transferred objects, whereas lease contracts, which had been concluded under the prior usufruct agreements remain in force.[113] Without further need of approval, the BIG enters into the existing agreements between the Federal government and third parties. This is the same for rights and duties under building projects, which are already started or are in the way of planning, but which have not yet been finished.[114] Also administrative, but seperate units (legal persons different from the Federal government) were enabled to conclude "market" lease contracts with the BIG, if they had used transferred property without a specific contract. Otherwise, they had to vacate these properties by 31 August 2001 at the latest.[115]

In BIG's articles of association, a supervisory board with at most four representatives of capital, elected by the General Assembly, is to be foreseen. The articles of association may make certain legal transactions subject to approval by the supervisory board. Approval is, in any case, foreseen for sales of real estate, which due to the value of the property in case or for cultural or security reasons is to be regarded as significant.[116]

---

109 § 4 para 1 BundesimmobilienG.

110 § 4 para 1 BundesimmobilienG.

111 § 4 para 4 BundesimmobilienG. See also § 2 para 1 BIG-Act.

112 § 1 para 1 BundesimmobilienG. Other objectives mentioned there include the tightening of deep-rooted historical structures, the promotion of cost awareness of the users, in order to make sure that there is a rational use of the resources, and instruments of synergetic assessment of demand.

113 § 19 BundesimmobilienG.

114 § 17 BundesimmobilienG.

115 § 20 BundesimmobilienG.

116 § 3 BundesimmobilienG.

De facto, the activities of the BIG based on these provisions include:

- management and maintenance of transferred properties based on market estimates.
- running of assets in order to improve the structure of earnings (renting to third parties).
- preparation and settlement of a sale or any other utilisation of Federal government-owned buildings – but only in a very limited number of cases.
- construction of buildings and refurbishments. Quite often, in such cases, there are already project agreements of the Austrian Republic, into which the BIG then enters. Subsequently, on the one hand the planning is continued, and on the other hand, a lease contract with a government unit is concluded. Only afterwards, the construction work is conducted.

B. Legal Evaluation

Based on this legal situation, most notably because of the repeated requirement of market-conformity of the BIG activities, it seems appropriate to classify it under the non-financial corporation sector for the purpose of ESA, irrespective of its close relationship to the Federal government. Its principal activities are not non-market services, but on the contrary, the BIG orients its business activities by the realities of the property market. In particular, rents, as well as decisions on the optimum management and utilisation, including the construction of buildings and refurbishment, have to comply with market principles. As a matter of fact, the so-called 50% criterion is easily met by the BIG.[117]

Certainly, the far-reaching control of the Federal government over both the General Assembly (due to limited company-law) and the supervisory board (by virtue of § 3 BIG-Act) cannot be denied. Thus, the economic independence of the BIG could be doubted due to the fact that renting contracts nearly exclusively were concluded with the State,[118] which therefore has a quasi-monopoly as a buyer.

---

[117] So also Eurostat, see supra at page 80.

[118] See BIG (2000) 6. The revenues flowing from the contracts concluded with the State are even large enough to completely cover the construction activities of the BIG, which were financed by loans taken up on the capital markets, see 9. This closeness to the State and its State-related functions were the reasons for Moody's to assign the BIG an

However, with a view to the discussed impreciseness of ESA, this is in itself no reason to negate the so-called Maastricht-conformity of the BIG design. It can also be added that market-conformist behaviour of the BIG to an increasing extent is induced by the pressure from administrative units trying to minimize their expenses for the rental of offices. As a result, the debts of the BIG are not to be included in the debt of the general government sector.

As discussed and citizised above,[119] this did not hinder the Commission to "reclassify" the mentioned sale of governmental real estate to the BIG as a pure rearrangement of the capital accounts of general government.

VI. Final Remarks

The elimination of governmental control over public undertakings is no condition for the "Maastricht conformity" of the construction, i.e. for the elimination of the entities' debts from general government debts. The establishment of a separate legal entity is sufficient to achieve this task. However, this is only true as long as the conduct of the undertaking is based on "market" criteria and takes place "autonomously". Theoretically, these conditions could even be met by a government operated entity. With a view to the ambiguity of the appraisal criteria, though, this approach cannot be recommended. Moreover, it should also be borne in mind that the Commission feels authorized, under an economic perspective, to "reroute" or "recognise" transactions performed by public undertakings, which can cause effects on the actual government deficit.

On the whole, the ambiguity and vagueness of the applied criteria appear highly problematic from the perspective of the rule of law, which is a general principle of EU law. The predictability of classification decisions by the Member States, and also the Commission is not guaranteed. For almost every legal entity operating under governmental influence objections against the exclusion from governmental debts and from the actual deficit – to be raised by the Commission – are arguable. For this reason, there seems to be urgent need of amending and clarifying the ESA.

AAA-issuer rating, see http://edi1.ediorg.at/redak/upload/-799965/Rating_(Moody%27s).pdf (accessed in May 2002).

119 See above after fn 67.

References

BIG (2000), Bericht über das Geschäftsjahr 2000, Bundesimmobiliengesellschaft, http://edi1.ediorg.at/redak/upload/-799965/BIG GB2000.pdf.

European Commission (1998), Euro 1999, 25 March 1998, Report on progress towards convergence and its recommendation with a view to the transition to the third stage of Economic and Monetary Union (COM(98)), 1999.

ESA 95, European System of Accounts ESA 1995, Eurostat, Publication Office Luxembourg 1996.

ESA Manual (2002), ESA95 manual on government deficit and debt, Statistical Office of the European Communities, Luxembourg 2002.

Griller St. (1997), Blockademöglichkeiten gegen die Einführung des Euro? in: Journal für Rechtspolitik 1997, 221ff.

Hengstschläger J. (1995), Privatisierung von Verwaltungsaufgaben, in: VVDStRL 54 1995, 165ff.

Italianer A. (1999), Kommentar zu Art 104c EGV, in: *von der Groeben H. / Thiesing J. / Ehlermann C.-D.* (eds.), Kommentar zum EU-/EG-Vertrag Baden-Baden III[5] 1999.

Potacs M. (1998), Öffentliche Unternehmen, in: *Raschauer B.* (ed.), Grundriss des österreichischen Wirtschaftsrechts 1998, Rz 901ff.

Van Wijk H. (2001), Bridging the Fault Lines. The Early Years of the Committee on Monetary, Financial and Balance of Payments Statistics, 2001 (not obtainable in book trade).

Part 2:
Fiscal Policy Framework - Room for Improvement?

Michael J. Artis

The Stability and Growth Pact: Fiscal Policy in the EMU

I. Introduction

The Stability and Growth Pact must rank as one of the most remarkable pieces of policy coordination in world history. Its construction makes it in some respects comparable to the founding of the Bretton Woods system. The theory of policy coordination teaches that when policy actions carry significant externalities, there is a general case for coordination to obtain better outcomes. But there is a forbidding cost to continuous real-time coordination. It may be preferable to expend a one-time investment cost in setting up a system, following rule-bound co-ordination thereafter with a minimum of costly interventions subsequently. The Bretton Woods analogy is quite interesting. Nations agreed at Bretton Woods to abide by a system of fixed exchange rates with escape clauses allowing for exchange rate revaluation or devaluation in defined cases. In running the set-up it proved useful to arrange for systematic monitoring and surveillance (through OECD's Working Party 3). The discipline of the fixed rate system was seen in later expositions of the theory of coordination as a device which could bring the participants closer to the cooperative solution. The temptation to renege was kept within bounds by the dominance of the hegemonic power, the United States.

Something like this can be seen to apply to the Stability and Growth Pact. This also enforces a rule-bound co-ordination, with an accompanying surveillance procedure, which has the capacity to bring the system closer to the cooperative solution. But there is no hegemon to enforce continued adherence to the system; instead, the SGP itself embodies a formal punishment mechanism and enlists the power of the markets in its aid. In the end, of course, the Bretton Woods system succumbed to tensions that could not be resolved; and it collapsed. It is possible to see some tensions building in the SGP now; and some adaptations will be needed at some time in the future.

This paper aims to uncover some of these tensions though it is not its objective to predict an imminent collapse. The following sections are devoted, first, to explaining the institutional and the "theory" background to the SGP and its provisions and, second, to a brief evaluation of its achievements. After that we endeavour to set out what appear to be the principal tensions.

II. Background to the Stability and Growth Pact

In the formal institutional sense the background to the SGP is provided by the fiscal criteria in the Treaty on European Union, more commonly known as the Maastricht Treaty. Those criteria provided reference values of 3% and 60% respectively, for the budget deficit and government debt ratio, the first (but not the second) of which were carried over directly into the provisions of the Stability and Growth Pact. The Maastricht Treaty offered these reference values as targets to be achieved, for they were accompanied by "escape clauses", allowing a country still to participate in the Monetary Union even in the event that its budget deficit and debt ratios were above the reference values. For the budget deficit ratio the escape clause would "forgive" an excess over the reference value if "either the ratio has declined substantially and continuously and has reached a level that comes close to the reference value or, alternatively, the excess over the reference value is only exceptional and temporary and the deficit remains close to the reference value". For the debt ratio "forgiveness" would require that "the ratio is sufficiently diminishing and approaching the reference value at a satisfactory pace". Then, "if a Member State does not fulfil the requirements under one or both of these criteria, the Commission shall prepare a report. The report shall also take into account whether the government deficit exceeds government investment expenditure and take into account all other relevant factors, including the medium term and budgetary position of the Member State." Much of this wording was to reappear in the Stability and Growth Pact.

The important point about the Maastricht criteria was that they were clearly aimed at bringing into line those States whose fiscal history gave rise to concerns about solvency and they did so in a context in which a strong incentive was offered for the States in question (most notably, Italy) to take corrective action. It has been remarked, from this point of view, that had the Treaty not existed, it would have had to have been invented. In this context the invective reserved for the criteria by economists with other goals in view was perhaps misplaced. As we shall argue below, the Maastricht fiscal criteria (even though more honoured in the breach than in full compliance) were hugely successful.

The institutional precedent afforded by the Maastricht criteria offers a clue also to the purpose of the Stability and Growth Pact. Because observance of the Maastricht criteria could rely on the incentive afforded by successful participation in the Monetary Union, the question naturally arose as to what mechanism could be used to sustain compliance with the essentials of the criteria after the Union had been formed.

This accounts for why the Stability and Growth Pact incorporated its own punishment mechanism. But the Stability and Growth pact, being intended to apply to the fiscal policies of the countries after the Union had been formed, necessarily has some other goals to meet beyond that of securing the solvency of the member governments. These other goals must include, above all, some reference to the regulation of the relationship between monetary and fiscal policy. To appreciate the range of issues that this involves, it is essential to consult the economics literature in the area.

III. The interaction between fiscal and monetary policy in a monetary union

The European Monetary Union possesses an unusual constitution in that it offers 12 independent sovereign national governments, 12 fiscal authorities and a single independent Central Bank. Other monetary unions typically have a single central government, a single fiscal authority and a Central Bank. Nowadays it is common to find that that Central Bank has a degree of independence ("instrument independence"), from the government and in many cases there is some kind of federal fiscal structure, where lower tiers of government enjoy some tax-raising and expenditure rights, usually accompanied by a restriction on borrowing rights, a degree of formal redistribution via the federal budget and – as an accidental output - a built-in inter-regional stabilization function. The EMU set-up is some way away from this; but the SGP represents a formal system of regulation that takes the EMU set-up in the direction of the "representative" monetary union as we have described it.

Economic analysis stresses the following features of the interaction between fiscal and monetary policy in a monetary union. First, there is the issue of externalities, or spill-over effects. The fact that the monetary union coincides with a Single Market arrangement should mean that fiscal expansion in one country will have important spill-over effects on other countries, through the integration of the goods market. Actually, empirical analysis suggests that this effect is weaker than might be supposed, which in turn implies that the domestic employment-creating effects of expansionary fiscal policy are still of considerable concern to the relevant fiscal authority (which in turn suggests that expansionary fiscal policy remains attractive).[1] At the same time the normal brakes on expansionary fiscal policy at home seem to be weakened in the monetary union context. For any individual country the normal accompanying features of expansionary fiscal policy (at least when monetary policy is unchanged) are to be found in rising interest rates and a rising exchange rate; in the monetary union context these effects will appear at the level of the Union as a whole. At first sight, at any rate, these arguments suggest a tendency towards over-expansionary fiscal policy. Another externality arises from the (presumed) effect of capital market integration, as a result of which Union-wide financial institutions will progressively increase their presence, holding the debt of various Union governments in their portfolios and thus exposing all other countries to a solvency risk arising in any one of them. Moreover, there may be a greater risk of a solvency crisis arising not only because fiscal expansion may appear more attrac-

---

1 Actually, the most recent work using VAR techniques of analysis *Perotti* (2002), seems to come up with very small estimates of fiscal policy effects. If these are confirmed in further estimates it could change the seriousness with which fiscal-monetary policy interaction is viewed.

tive, but also because the implicit guarantee of debt redemption that applies when the country concerned is outside the union (that the Central Bank in the last resort will lend the domestic currency in whatever quantity is required) is no longer present (see *Mackinnon* (1994)) for an original exposition of this point).

All these arguments, and one other, suggest that a framework involving fiscal restraint is going to be needed. This additional argument arises from the need that may be perceived to shield the Central Bank's independence from a determined bid by governments to "call the shots" in the making of macroeconomic policy.

It might be argued that the statutory independence of the European Central Bank – which is greater than that of any other Central Bank in the world on all the normal scoring systems – is sufficient to banish this threat. But it has been well emphasised (e.g., by *Lohmann* (1996)) that the ECB's statutory independence is in the first instance "paper" independence. The European Central Bank lacks a history and a constituency of support to which it can appeal in struggles against the (after all, democratically elected) governments of the day. This might be argued to reinforce the case for a restrictive fiscal policy framework.

Naturally there are also some strong arguments in the contrary direction. One is simply a contingent argument. It happens that when the EMU began it did so against the background of some justified concern for the solvency of some governments – but once this is rectified, it should be "business as usual". Another points to the increasing integration of goods markets to suggest that the attractions, domestically, of expansionary fiscal policy may be waning in the longer run. The local government of the City of Manchester, for example, does not see strong employment reasons for an expansionary fiscal policy. Local fiscal expansion will simply spill-over in too large a measure. Most important of all, though, is the fact that the ability for national governments to follow a discretionary fiscal policy (not necessarily an expansionary one) attracts a premium in circumstances when they no longer can use monetary policy and where the country might suffer from an asymmetric shock, or where the European Central Bank might be construed (correctly or not) as taking insufficient action.

A. Provisions of the Pact

How do the provisions of the Pact stack up against the considerations rehearsed above? A useful summary of the provisions, preserving the language of the original texts, can be found in *Artis/Winkler* (1998), but here we may note the main features as follows. First, the countries agree to aim at a medium term fiscal position of balance or small surplus in their budget deficit ratios. Second, they aim to avoid positions in which the current deficit ratio exceeds 3%. Third, when such "excessive deficits" are realized, the Pact foresees a formal punishment mechanism coming into action in the event of persistent flouting of the Council's recommendations for correction of the deficit. (A position of excessive deficit may not be declared in certain cases even when the current deficit exceeds 3%, generally in conditions in which a severe recession can be recognized). Finally, the signatories to the Pact undertake to submit their fiscal projections on a regular basis to a surveillance procedure, in which the Commission has the duty to advise the Council on how well the projections meet the criteria. The 3% reference value of the Maastricht Treaty for the budget deficit ratio appears in the Pact as a maximum not to be exceeded, whilst the Treaty's debt ratio criterion is not repeated in the Pact. Most of the Pact's provisions can be described as adding detail to the excessive deficit procedure introduced in the Treaty, bringing in sanctions and clarifying the circumstances in which those sanctions might be waived or applied. The inclusion of a medium term target of balance or small surplus in the budget deficit ratio is new in the Pact and can be argued to constitute a firm declaration that debt ratios will be brought under control. In fact, as the deficit in question is measured inclusive of interest payments achievement of the goal implies, over the long term, zero or even negative debt positions.

Early interpretations of the Pact found its rationale to lie mainly in the strengthening it provided of the independence of the European Central Bank. *Artis/Winkler* (1998) used the phrase "negative co-ordination" to indicate that the Pact embodies policy co-ordination in the rule-bound sense, where the objective of restraint seems to be the key. Then the danger which some commentators perceived (e.g., *Allsopp/Vines* (1996); *Eichengreen* (1997)) was that the Pact could prove *too* restrictive, in circumstances where many countries were already close to the 3% limit, and would rob countries of a necessary degree of flexibility to respond to recessionary conditions. Whilst the worst result anticipated in this criticism failed to materialize, the critical line of argument provoked a constructive response. That response consisted in interpreting the "medium term" balance target as a target for the "cyclically adjusted" balance and then in arguing that the "built-in stabilizers" could be relied upon to allow countries to avoid breaching the 3% limit. Estimates of the built-in stabilizer effect are produced by each of the major international economic policy-advisory institutions – the IMF, OECD and the EC – and differ little between themselves. The methodology pre-specifies unemployment compensation expenditures as the only cyclically-varying spending item and then additionally computes the sensitivity of the various tax revenues to variations in the output gap, on the basis of the existing tax schedules. In total, this allows an estimation of the sensitivity of the budget ratio to cyclical changes in the output gap on the maintained assumption that neither tax nor spending schedules, as such, display cyclical sensitivity.[2] By designating a "worst outcome" output gap, it is possible then to compute a fiscal programme which is guaranteed to avoid infringing the 3% limit on the current deficit even in bad states of the world (see *Artis/Buti* (2000)). The hope is that the slope of the schedule, given by the built-in stabilizer estimate, then allows for an adequate amount of fiscal buffering to occur. Figure 1 illustrates the argument.

2 *Melitz* (2000) has shown that this assumption is factually incorrect; governments show evidence of responding to the inflow of tax revenues during cyclical expansions by spending more.

Figure 1: The 3% limit, the medium term aim and the built-in stabilizers

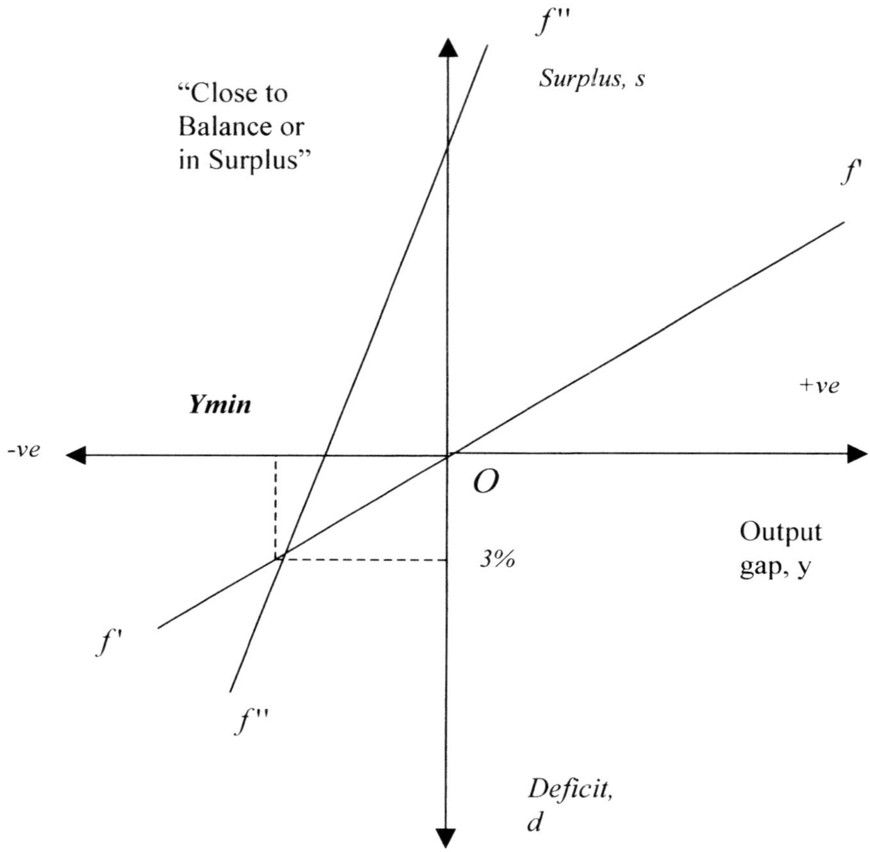

The Figure shows how the fiscal programme of a country (denoted by the *ff* schedules) should be chosen so as to secure a current deficit in "the worst case" (*Y min*) that does not exceed the 3% limit. The slope of the fiscal programme is given by the built-in stabilizer estimate (*ds/dy)* where s is the budget surplus ratio and y is the deviation of output from trend (the output gap). The value of the cyclically adjusted surplus can be read from the point on the *ff* schedules corresponding to a zero output gap. Countries with high built-in stabilizers need to aim for bigger surpluses than those with a low degree of built-in stabilization.

A stylized view has emerged then that, at least to a first approximation, the combination of the SGP and the independent Central Bank provide an ideal allocation of responsibilities. The ECB will take care of common shocks, whilst asymmetric shocks are buffered by the built-in stabilizers in the fiscal systems of the countries concerned. This is the picture conveyed, for example, by *Alesina et al* (2001) in their review of the macroeconomic framework of the EMU. The qualification above "to a first approximation" is well-placed however. For the framework to produce the best results, the ECB must provide an acceptable (and accurate) appreciation of the conjunctural position of the Eurozone economy and its prospects, the national governments need to change their cyclical behaviour in favour of the "artificially" constructed model provided by the built-in stabilizers whilst the stabilizers need to be shown to be capable of dealing with a variety of shocks more or less successfully;[3] finally, the output gap must be the most significant determinant of inflation.

B. Achievements of the Pact

What has the Pact achieved? The following is a tentative list of achievements of the Pact.

First and most important, the Pact has achieved some credibility. The public surveillance procedures have acquainted markets with what is going on, and added transparency in a hitherto obscure area. The credibility of the procedures means that a "rogue" country has to take into account the possibility of painful market sanctions on aberrant behaviour (likely more credible than the formal sanctions embodied in the Pact). Perhaps the first test of the credibility of the formal procedures was arrived at when the Commission asked the Council of Ministers in 2002 for permission to send an "early warning" to Portugal and Germany; whilst this permission was withheld, the intervention secured a renewed promise from the countries concerned that they would adhere to the parameters of the Pact. It was generally agreed that the credibility of the Pact was preserved.

---

3 *Brunila et al* (2002) have examined the potential performance of the built-in stabilizers, concluding that they are best addressed to temporary demand shocks (which is as it should be), and are quite significant in quantitative terms.

Second, the course of fiscal policy has consolidated the achievements of the Maastricht Treaty in securing solvency. The decline in the ratio of debt to GDP at the level of the Eurozone as a whole has been gradual, but steady, from a peak in 1997: in 1980 the ratio of gross debt to GDP for the Euro Area members stood at 35.1%, by 1985 it had risen to 53.8% and by 1997 it stood at 75.3%. Then it fell to 72.6% in 1999, and to 70.2 and 69.1 in the subsequent two years and is forecast to fall further to 68.6 and then 67.2 % in 2002 and 2003.[4]

Third, the conversion of the "medium term" into "cyclically neutral" and the apparent agreement on cyclical adjustment procedures implicit in discussions of the outcome of the Seville Council meeting (June 2002) and explicitly mentioned in the EC's Public Finance Report 2002 mark an advance in economics-friendly presentation of the issues.

Fourth, there has been no obvious conflict between fiscal policy and the European Central Bank. The latter institution has been allowed the freedom to establish its credentials and the meaning of its independence without having to battle with the governments.

The above looks like – and surely is - a significant list of achievements. Some observers would argue that the list is marred by evidence of "fiscal reform fatigue", and it is true that there has been some backsliding on the promises made for fiscal positions by 2004, whilst two countries – Germany and Portugal - are even close to the 3% limit on the 2002 estimates. Two observations are in order here: first, it is true that some countries have used the initially good growth experience in the early years of EMU to reduce taxes rather than to pay down their debt or trim the budget as a whole, perhaps illustrating that the SGP is in the words of *Charlie Bean* (see *Bean* (1998)) "all sticks and no carrots"; second, the selection of the particular year 2004 as the "medium term" perhaps should not be taken too seriously – 2004 may well not be a year of zero output gap. The targets should have been set – and perhaps in future will be - for cyclically adjusted quantities, not the current deficit. One reaction to these backslidings has been to call for a tightening of the SGP's procedures (as in *Feldman* (2002)), or for the introduction of spending rules and perhaps a debt target. The latter

---

4 The figures and the forecasts are drawn from the EC's Spring 2002 forecasts; see *European Economy* (no 2/2002).

would repair what seemed at the time of the construction of the Pact a notable omission, in light of the Maastricht treaty debt criterion – but at that time the medium term target of balance or slight surplus was not yet taken as seriously as it has been since. Even so, the authors of one careful empirical exercise (*Fatas/Mihov* (2002b)) have not detected evidence of fiscal reform fatigue and the threatened infringements are not (yet, at least) general.

Despite the positive achievements listed above there are signs of growing tensions that suggest the need for some adaptation of the SGP.

IV. Tensions in the SGP

The most obvious tension arises simply from the fact that the key figure in the SGP, the 3% budget deficit limit, has no intrinsic, analytically defensible, rationale. *Bini-Smaghi et al.* (1994) have given a "fly-on-the-wall" account of its origins. The main point about the choice of this figure is that it set a tough, but achievable, target which was adequate to stem the threat of insolvency. The figure is also one for a current, interest-inclusive, definition of the deficit. The argument for preferring such a definition is generally that methods of cyclical adjustment are not agreed and could open the door to manipulation. Set against the fact that this definition allows heterogeneous items of revenue (from income taxes to the proceeds of privatization) to be lumped together, the objection does not seem a powerful one.

But again, where the need for a reduction in government debt is of paramount importance, it can be argued that the heterogeneity of revenues does not matter, and that cyclical adjustment is irrelevant. From any other point of view, though, the definition of the deficit and the choice of reference value appear arbitrary beyond belief: this point was made in many of the early discussions of the Maastricht criteria (see, for example, *Buiter/Corsetti* (1993)). The most analytically defensible framework for deficit target setting is provided by the so-called "Golden Rule", under which investment expenditures, which provide a future stream of returns, can reasonably be financed by bond issue, whilst current expenditures should be matched by tax revenues, on a cyclically adjusted basis. Such a framework is currently in use in the United Kingdom, as well as – in different forms - in some other countries of the EU. A particular reason for taking it seriously is represented by the imminent enlargement of the EU. Economic theory suggests that in the early stage of development public sector infrastructure investment may have a key role to play in the growth process. The accession countries should not be prevented from exercising their judgement in this matter by the presence of arbitrary numbers in the SGP. A standard reason quoted for not proceeding in the manner suggested has been the argument that what constitutes an investment expenditure is, at the margin, a debatable matter, and that this could open the door to undesirable creative accounting. Yet, this would seem an area where international co-ordination on standards could be most profitable.

A second source of tension arises from the perception that reliance on the built-in stabilizers alone may not be sufficient in conditions in which a country may be hit by an asymmetric shock (or, where the response of the ECB to a common shock may be perceived to be inadequate). Ceding monetary sovereignty may be argued to raise, not reduce, the premium on cyclically-oriented fiscal policy. In Finland and in Sweden some interest has been shown in developing the use of the variable payroll tax as an instrument for dealing with asymmetric shock: the payroll tax can be argued to be the fiscal instrument most capable of replicating the effects of an exchange rate change. More generally, the dividing line between formal built-in stabilizers and cyclically-oriented fiscal discretion[5] can be argued to be somewhat fuzzy, at least if the latter is bounded in some formal manner so that persistence is contained; the timing of the response of the fiscal intervention is also important. In current suggestions, the institutional vehicle proposed is designed to mimic the speed of reaction of a Central Bank, with tax intervention power being assigned on a limited basis to a "fiscal bureau", charged with a clear stabilization objective. The need for a lengthy process of prior parliamentary approval must be avoided in these proposals. *Simon Wren-Lewis* (2002) provides a well-argued case for this type of fiscal intervention facility.

A third source of tension is present in the demand for "co-ordination" between the fiscal authorities and the European Central Bank. Such a demand has been latent in the formation of the "Euro-

---

[5] Sometimes "discretion" is identified with fiscal policy action which has no counter-cyclical aim (e.g., *Fatas/Mihov* (2002a)), which is obviously not what is at issue here.

Group" of finance ministers of the Eurozone countries and will receive a significant formal, constitutional boost so soon as the Nice Treaty is adopted (or the relevant parts of that Treaty become somehow incorporated in the practices of the EU). Whilst it has been emphasized here that the SGP *is* coordination, and of a highly significant type, what proponents have in mind is an extension in which regular meetings would be held with the European Central Bank, and fiscal and monetary policy intervention might as a result be co-ordinated in some "real-time" sense. Analysts have viewed this with some apprehension (in particular see *Alesina et al* (2001)), as it might prefigure a loss of independence for the ECB, but there is both substantial political power and some economic sense behind the demand. The political power derives from the simple fact that to a politician adhering to the rules of the SGP must seem like the task of a subordinate actor, whilst the challenge of curbing the independence of the ECB, perhaps in the name of democracy, looks an interesting one. Economic analysis could suggest some benefits in a dialogue between the fiscal and monetary authorities, if only in the direction of an exchange of information. Avoiding the positive mistakes of faulty diagnosis of the economic conjuncture, for example, could pay handsome dividends. Some have argued that the lack of a visible "fiscal authority" for Europe has damaged the Euro on foreign exchange markets, and although this is hard to believe, the fact that the Eurozone lacks the normal accoutrements of a sovereign nation in this respect may contribute to a lack of understanding.

The tensions highlighted here are clearly of quite different kinds. Their resolution at the moment is actually blocked by the credibility achieved for the current set-up. There is a fear that even by discussing these issues openly that credibility will be lost; this encourages the short term resolution of problems arising by "make-do" compromises. This will do for a while and it would, indeed, be foolish to compromise the credibility of the SGP and its achievements. But sooner or later, the tensions highlighted here will need to be addressed and resolved.

References

Alesina A. / Blanchard O. / Gali J. / Giavazzi F. / Uhlig H. (2001), Defining a Macroeconomic Framework for the Euro Area, Monitoring the European Central Bank, No 3, CEPR, London 2001.

Allsopp C. / Vines D. (1996), Fiscal Policy and EMU, in: National Institute Economic Review, No 158, 1996, pp. 91 –107.

Artis M.J. / Buti M. (2000), Close to Balance or in Surplus – a Policy-Maker's Guide to the Implementation of the Growth and Stability Pact, in: Journal of Common Market Studies, No 38, pp. 563-91.

Artis M.J. / Winkler B. (1998), The Stability Pact: Safeguarding the Credibility of the European Central Bank, National Institute Economic Review, No 163, pp. 87-98 .

Bean C. (1998), Discussion, in: Economic Policy, No 26, 1998, pp. 104-107.

Bini-Smaghi L. / Padoa-Schioppa T. / Papadia F. (1994), The Transition to EMU in the Maastricht Treaty, Princeton Essays in International Finance, No 194, 1994.

Brunila A. / Buti M. / in't Veld J. (2002), Cyclical Stabilization under the Stability and Growth Pact: How effective are the automatic stabilizers?, Bank of Finland Discussion papers, 6.2002.

Brunila A. (2002), Fiscal policy: Coordination, discipline and stabilization, Bank of Finland Discussion papers, 7.2002.

Buiter W. / Corsetti G. / Roubini N. (1993), Excessive Deficits: Sense and Nonsense in the Treaty of Maastricht, Economic Policy, No 16, 1993, pp. 58-100.

Buti M. / Giudice G. (2002), Maastricht's Fiscal Rules at Ten, in: Journal of Common Market Studies, forthcoming.

Eichengreen B. (1997), Saving Europe's Automatic Stabilisers, in: National Institute Economic Review, No 159, 1997, pp. 92-98.

Fatás A. / Mihov I. (2002a), The Case for Restricting Fiscal Policy Discretion , CEPR Discussion papers, No. 3277, 2002.

Fatás A. / Mihov I. (2002b), Fiscal Policy and EMU, *mimeo*.

Feldmann H. (2002), The Stability and Growth Pact Justification, Implementation, Reform Proposals, in: (eds.) *Caesar R. / Scharrer H-E.*, European Economic and Monetary Union: An Initial Assessment, Nomos Verlagsgesellschaft, 2002 Baden- Baden.

Lohmann S. (1996), Quis custodiet ipsos custodes? Necessary Conditions for Price Stability in Europe, in: *Siebert H.* (ed.) Monetary Policy in an Integrated World Economy, 1996, pp. 139-60.

McKinnon R.I. (1994), A Common Monetary Standard or a Common Currency for Europe? Fiscal Lessons from the United States, Scottish Journal of Political Economy, No 41/4, 1994, pp. 337-357.

Melitz J. (2000), Some cross-country evidence about Debt, Deficits and the Behaviour of Monetary and Fiscal Authorities, European Economy, Reports and Studies, No 2, 2000, pp. 3-21.

Perotti R. (2002), Estimating the Effects of Fiscal Policy in OECD Countries, *mimeo*, European University Institute.

Wren-Lewis S. (2002), Fiscal Policy, Inflation and Stabilization in EMU, paper for workshop on the interactions between fiscal and monetary policies in EMU, March 2002.

Andrew Hughes Hallett, Nicola Viegi

On the Need for Inter-institutional Coordination in EMU: a re-evaluation of the theory of optimal currency areas

I. Introduction

By now there is a significant literature on economic coordination between countries, and some of it is devoted to the particular issues of coordination between the European economies as they enter their new regime of monetary union.[1]

However, just as the policy framework and development of the European economy changes because it becomes more closed with the single currency, and because its policy options become restricted through a single monetary policy, so the need for intercountry coordination reduces with a single currency.[2] To an important extent, that is now built in as part of the EMU policy regime. But, by the same token, the room for policy manoeuvre will also have become restricted compared to what we have been used to, and that will tend to produce less stable outcomes for those who suffer different shocks or have structures different from the European average.

To prevent that becoming a problem, and to restore economic performance to a level at which countries can profit from the advantages of full monetary integration, we will need to create closer coordination between the institutions of the monetary union instead.[3] In this paper we examine how that might happen, and the importance of making it happen when there is not sufficient inter-institution coordination. To do that we use a simple two country model of monetary union. There are therefore three sets of institutions involved: a single Central Bank, two national governments, and two national wage bargaining organisations. They select monetary, fiscal and wage setting policies respectively. They are independent institutions; but they may take more or less coordinated approaches to national economic performance by altering the way in which they select their policies and the degree to which they allow conflicts to appear between them.

Asymmetries between countries or institutional objectives are then introduced by the possibility of asymmetric shocks or divergent preferences over a common set of objectives. Our results then show very clearly the need for inter-institutional coordination, and how it may be achieved. Moreover, we are able to represent all our

---

1 See *Mooslechner/Schürz* (2001) for a recent survey.

2 *Italianer* (2001).

3 *Demertzis et al* (1999b).

results in terms that are now familiar from the theory of optimal currency areas.

II. The Model

A. Monetary Policy

The objective of the paper is to analyse how different asymmetries affect the design and conduct of economic policy in EMU. The model therefore must have a single monetary policy, which is set to fix the level of prices for the union as a whole. That policy will be derived by minimising a generic quadratic objective function of the form:

$$\min_{\pi} L = \frac{1}{2}\left[(\pi)^2 + \gamma(y_a - k)^2\right] \tag{1}$$

where $\gamma \geq 0$ is the relative importance, in the Central Bank's view, of stabilising output levels across the union as a whole. So a conservative Central Bank is one with a small value of $\gamma \to 0$, and a more liberal one will have a larger value of γ. But in all cases that follow, the Central Bank will be independent of other policy makers.

Next, y_a is the average level of output in the union, with target value $k \geq 0$.[4] Aggregate supply in the two countries constrains the average level of output that can be achieved in the union:

$$y_a = \frac{1}{2}(y_1 + y_2) = \pi - \frac{1}{2}(w_1 + w_2) - \frac{1}{2}(t_1 + t_2) + \frac{1}{2}(e_1 + e_2) \tag{2}$$

This relationship therefore constrains the minimisation of (1). We assume that the ECB's monetary policy controls inflation directly, and that wages (w_1, w_2) are set nationally on the basis of the domestic labour market institutions. Finally the fiscal policy variables, (t_1, t_2) are defined as net tax revenues in countries 1 and 2 respectively. So $t_j < 0$ means a fiscal deficit in country j. Likewise (e_1, e_2) represents the supply shocks to those two countries.

---

4 For an extensive justification of the presence of $k > 0$, see *Persson/Tabellini* (1990) or *Blinder* (2000). That assumption is usually employed to correct for tax distortions, or any other market rigidities which would make labour markets clear at below their full employment level. But note that $k = 0$ is allowed here too. So the possibility that k may be positive is not crucial to the results which follow.

Those shocks will have the usual properties of zero mean and constant variance.

This aggregate supply function is just a multicountry version of the supply function popularised in this literature by *Barro / Gordon* (1983), or *Alesina / Gatti* (1995). Since wages will be set as a function of expected inflation – the function itself depending on the labour market institutions at hand – equation (2) is simply a union-wide supply function, extended to include fiscal policy in the manner of *Debelle / Fischer* (1994). Hence $1/2(w_1 + w_2)$ transmits the effects of expected inflation π^e. But, because of the timing issue described below, wages will actually be set ahead of the determination of y_a. That means π^e will be the inflation rate which the wage setters and private sector expect, at the beginning of the period, to hold at the end of that period and the start of the next. Thus $\pi_t^e = E(\pi_{t+1} | I_t)$ where I_t is the information set available at the start of period *t*. That means our supply function is, in fact, a simple variant of the New-Keynesian Philips curve - which emphasises forward looking behaviour in wage and price setting[5] in a way which is well suited to modelling the European economy.[6] As such, it incorporates the micro-foundations of monopolistic competition between firms, the staggered wage-price setting of Calvo contracts, and quadratic adjustment costs. Optimal wage contracts would then produce a relationship[7] like (2).[8]

B. Wage Bargains and Fiscal Policy

Wage changes in this model represent the expected changes in production costs. We assume that wage bargainers determine their own desired level of wage inflation in each of the labour market regimes studied below; and that they do so on the basis of what they expect to be the outcomes (in terms of inflation and employment) of whatever monetary and fiscal policies the Central Bank and fiscal

---

5 *Roberts* (1995).

6 *Gali et al* (2001).

7 The output variables y_a, and y_1 and y_2 in what follows, will be measured as deviations from their natural rates - hence the signs in (2). And the fiscal variables can be converted, at some complication to the algebra, to deviations from their expected values if fiscal policy is expected to have only temporary effects, see *Demertzis et al* (1999a).

8 *Rotemberg/Woodford* (1998).

authorities can be expected to choose in their own interest. This means we have a *hierarchical game* in which independent monetary and fiscal authorities play a Nash game among themselves, while playing a Stackelberg game with respect to the wage setters. This step is necessary to ensure that the Central Bank is fully independent in setting its policy (instrument independence). Target independence is also implied since the Bank sets its own target values, including the relative priority parameter γ.

However the two governments, and by extension their electorates, are likely to be interested in their own (domestic) output levels, and the differences between them:[9]

$$y_d = \frac{1}{2}(y_1 - y_2) = -\frac{1}{2}(w_1 - w_2) - \frac{1}{2}(t_1 - t_2) + \frac{1}{2}(e_1 - e_2) \tag{3}$$

This expression for the difference in income levels makes clear what has always been argued by the optimal currency area (OCA) literature for a long time. If the shocks are asymmetric, asymmetries in labour market or in the use of fiscal policy, could be used to reduce the differences between countries.

C. The Timing of Decisions

The moves of our game are as follows: first unions, or individuals, set wages; then shocks occur; and finally monetary and fiscal authorities set their instruments in a non cooperative manner. Consequently, the ECB maximises (1) subject to (2), while the two fiscal authorities maximise their own national objective functions using their fiscal instruments:[10]

$$\min_{t_j} L_j = \frac{1}{2}\left[(\pi)^2 + (t_j)^2 + \beta(y_j - k)^2\right] \tag{4}$$

for $j = 1, 2$, subject to the same *national* supply functions that underlie (3). The parameter $\beta > 0$ determines the importance, as the governments see it, of output stabilisation relative to inflation

---

9 This technique of dividing the analysis up between the sums and the differences of national outputs is due to *Aoki* (1976). In our context it has the advantage of distinguishing clearly the policy domains of the different actors (the ECB targets the European averages, while national governments and national unions target the national levels). This technique therefore has the advantage that it allows us to isolate the asymmetric effects of different policies.

10 See *Svensson* (1997).

control or deficit control. If following *Rogoff* (1985), we wish to examine the world of conservative Central Bankers, we must set $\gamma < \beta$. Then minimising (1) and (4) for $j = 1, 2$ *conditional* on the wages set according to whichever labour market regime is in place, yields a sequence of three optimal reaction functions - one for each player:

$$\pi = \frac{\gamma}{1+\gamma}\left[\frac{1}{2}(w_1 + w_2) - \frac{1}{2}(t_1 + t_2) + k - \frac{1}{2}(e_1 + e_2)\right] \quad (5)$$

and $$t_j = \frac{\beta}{1+\beta}\left[\pi - w_j - k - e_j\right] \qquad \text{for } j = 1,2. \quad (6)$$

Solving this system of three equations in three unknowns, we have:

$$\pi = \frac{\gamma}{1+\gamma+\beta}\left[\frac{1}{2}(w_1 + w_2) + k - \frac{1}{2}(e_1 + e_2)\right] \quad (7)$$

$$t_1 = -\frac{\beta}{1+\beta+\gamma}\left[w_1 + k - e_1\right] + \frac{\beta}{1+\beta+\gamma}\left[\gamma\frac{(w_1 - w_2)}{2} + \gamma\frac{(e_1 - e_2)}{2}\right] \quad (8)$$

$$t_2 = \frac{\beta}{1+\beta+\gamma}\left[w_2 + k - e_2\right] - \frac{\beta}{1+\beta+\gamma}\left[\gamma\frac{(w_1 - w_2)}{2} + \gamma\frac{(e_1 - e_2)}{2}\right] \quad (9)$$

Equations (8) - (9) show the pressure which is put on fiscal policy by the presence of asymmetric shocks or asymmetries in the labour market. Because the monetary policy operates on the European averages only, fiscal policy (or the level of wages as a proxy for relative production costs) will have to intervene to make up and stabilise any differences in income levels.

The equilibrium which emerges from equations (7) - (9) is therefore conditioned on the wage formation process present in each country. We analyse two possible regimes. Both are symmetric; one with full centralisation of wage bargaining, and one with complete decentralisation in the labour market. But like other authors in this area, we do not include an explicit budget constraint in our model. Instead we constrain fiscal policy by placing *explicit* penalties on the use of fiscal policy by the fiscal authorities: see (4). Standard theory would then produce a feedback rule, in the context of the sequential decision making of our model, which satisfies the sufficient conditions required for long term solvency and the "cash in advance" constraint.[11] That, in effect, endogenises expenditures and their financing costs. Consequently, we do not need to report the components of the budget constraint or debt in what follows: each t_j is simply the net revenue stream, which is required to guarantee solvency *and* the cash in advance constraint.

III. Regime 1: Non Cooperation with decentralised labour markets

A. The Optimal Policies

In our model workers move first, setting a one period wage contract before any shocks appear and before fiscal and monetary policies are set. However, in this regime, the labour markets are identical in the two countries and atomistic. Therefore increases in nominal wages will be set such that they will equal the inflation rate expected at the beginning of each period,[12] i.e.

$$w_j = \pi^e \tag{10}$$

Assuming rational expectations, substituting equations (7) - (9) in (10), and solving out the resulting system of equations, we obtain the expected rates of wage and price inflation:

$$w_j = \pi^e = \frac{\gamma}{1+\beta}k \tag{11}$$

Substituting this equilibrium value into the reaction functions of the policy authorities, we obtain the actual levels of inflation and taxation for the two countries, respectively:

$$\pi = \frac{\gamma}{1+\beta}k - \frac{\gamma}{1+\beta+\gamma}\frac{(e_1+e_2)}{2} \tag{12}$$

$$t_j = -\frac{\beta}{1+\beta}k + \frac{\beta}{1+\beta+\gamma}e_j + \frac{\beta}{1+\beta+\gamma}\left[\gamma\frac{e_j-e_i}{2}\right] \tag{13}$$

This will give an average European income equal to:

$$y_a = \frac{\beta}{1+\beta}k + \frac{1}{1+\beta+\gamma}\left[\frac{(e_1+e_2)}{2}\right] \tag{14}$$

---

11 See *Canzoneri et al* (2000).

12 w_j is measured here as a deviation from an exogenous trend in productivity growth.

This is the output level targeted by the Central Bank, and is a function of the average supply shocks. The difference in output levels, however, is driven by the differences between those shocks:

$$y_d = \frac{1+\gamma(1-\beta)}{1+\beta+\gamma}\left(\frac{e_1-e_2}{2}\right) \tag{15}$$

B. Asymmetric shocks: absolute vs. relative stabilisation

Equation (15) shows the importance of the OCA literature quite clearly. The more similar the shocks, the smaller the differences in regional income levels, and the smaller the need for regional stabilisation.

But it does not follow that the tax reactions are also smaller or less reactive. They may be, but that requires the domestic shock (i.e. e_j in (13)) to be small, as well as the differences between those shocks $\left(e_j - e_i\right)$ to be small. Those two terms define the absolute and the relative stabilisation problems respectively. Thus fiscal policy has to deal with both absolute and relative stabilisation problems, whereas monetary policy only has to deal with absolute stabilisation. Hence monetary policy needs to be directed at the stabilisation of the aggregate cycle (Keynesian style), while fiscal policy does all the regional stabilisation work: see (14) and (15) respectively. But if the single monetary policy cannot deal with the former (absolute stabilisation) problem very satisfactorily, then fiscal policy will have to become more active and deal with both problems at once. And, to prevent instrument overload, policy makers will naturally look elsewhere for an additional instrument. Interventions in the labour market are then the obvious candidate.

C. Output Stability, Policy Volatility, and the Theory of Optimal Currency Areas

An analysis of expected values and variances of the five main policy variables $\left(\pi, t_1, t_2, y_a, y_d\right)$ allows us to say something about the interrelation between the shocks and the various target variables; and also to show how the economy's stability is affected by the policy preferences of the Central Bank and the governments. We have, for example

$$E(\pi)=\frac{\gamma}{1+\beta}k \quad ; \quad E(t_j)=-\frac{\beta}{1+\beta}k \quad ; \quad E(y_a)=\frac{\beta}{1+\beta}k \quad ; \quad \text{and} \quad E(y_d)=0.$$

Hence the expected and average outcomes are not different from the single economy case. But the variability of these outcomes is strongly affected by the nature of the shocks, and by their similarity across countries when monetary policy is set centrally. For example:

$$V(\pi)=\frac{1}{4}\left(\frac{\gamma}{1+\beta+\gamma}\right)^2\left(\sigma_1^2+\sigma_2^2+2\rho\sigma_1\sigma_2\right) \tag{16}$$

$$V(t_1)\frac{1}{4}\left(\frac{\beta}{1+\beta+\gamma}\right)^2\left((\gamma+2)^2\sigma_1^2+\gamma^2\sigma_2^2-2\gamma(\gamma+2)\rho\sigma_1\sigma_2\right) \tag{17}$$

$$V(t_2)=\frac{1}{4}\left(\frac{\beta}{1+\beta+\gamma}\right)^2\left((\gamma+2)^2\sigma_2^2+\gamma^2\sigma_1^2-2\gamma(\gamma+2)\rho\sigma_1\sigma_2\right) \tag{18}$$

$$V(y_a)=\left(\frac{1}{1+\beta+\gamma}\right)^2\left(\sigma_1^2+\sigma_2^2+2\rho\sigma_1\sigma_2\right) \tag{19}$$

$$V(y_d)=\left(\frac{1+\gamma(1-\beta)}{1+\beta+\gamma}\right)^2\left(\sigma_1^2+\sigma_2^2+2\rho\sigma_1\sigma_2\right) \tag{20}$$

From relations (16) - (20) we can see the importance of the degree of correlation between the shocks, ρ, in the determination of the behaviour of the policy instruments and target variables. In fact these results reaffirm the conclusions of the Optimal Currency Area literature. The main point is that inflation, and hence the application of monetary policy, will be more variable than in the closed economy or single country case. This is because the shocks of a second country have to be taken into account. Hence the higher the degree of integration between the regional shocks, and the more suitable are the countries for forming a monetary union, the more of each shock will be transmitted from one member economy to another.

Fiscal policy, likewise, has to be more active because it too has to deal with the additional sources of volatility caused by foreign shocks. But, unlike monetary policy, it will be *less active* the closer is the integration between those shocks, since regional (i.e. relative) stabilisation will then be less important. As a result, aggregate output will be *more volatile* than in the single economy case; and more so the stronger are the reinforcing effects of similar shocks hitting the two member economies. That follows from the behaviour of the common monetary policy. But the differences in income levels will show less variation if those shocks are more integrated, *especially* if fiscal policy becomes more active (i.e. as β rises).

D. Overall Performance: the political consequences

The characteristics described above are also reflected in the expected loss function (welfare indicator) of each country and for the Central Bank. Considering first the Central Bank, its expected loss function is:

$$\min_{\pi} L = \frac{1}{2}\left[(\pi)^2 + \gamma(y_a - k)^2\right]$$

$$E(L) = \frac{\gamma(1+\gamma)}{2}\left[\frac{1}{(1+\beta)^2}k^2 + \frac{1}{4(1+\beta+\gamma)^2}\left(\sigma_1^2 + \sigma_2^2 + 2\rho\sigma_1\sigma_2\right)\right] \tag{21}$$

But at the national level, considering that

$$y_1 = y_a + y_d$$

$$y_2 = y_a - y_d$$

we have:

$$y_1 = \frac{\beta}{1+\beta}k + \frac{1}{(1+\beta+\gamma)}e_1 + \frac{\gamma(1-\beta)}{(1+\beta+\gamma)}\left(\frac{e_1 - e_2}{2}\right) \tag{22}$$

$$y_2 = \frac{\beta}{1+\beta}k + \frac{1}{(1+\beta+\gamma)}e_2 + \frac{\gamma(1-\beta)}{(1+\beta+\gamma)}\left(\frac{e_2 - e_1}{2}\right) \tag{23}$$

Evaluation with a generic loss function of like:[13]

$$LP_j = \frac{1}{2}\left[(\pi)^2 + (t_j)^2 + \lambda(y_j - k)^2\right] \tag{24}$$

implies that the loss functions faced by the voters in each economy are:

$$E(LP_j) = \frac{1}{2}\left[\frac{y^2 + \beta^2 + \lambda}{(1+\beta)^2}k^2 + A\sigma_j^2 + B\sigma_i^2 + 2C\rho\sigma_j\sigma_i\right] \tag{25}$$

where

$$A = \left(\frac{1}{1+\beta+\gamma}\right)^2\left[\frac{y^2}{4} + \frac{\beta^2(2+\gamma)^2}{4} + \frac{\lambda(2+\gamma+\gamma\beta)^2}{4}\right]$$

---

[13] In this general formulation λ may be equal to β, the governments' relative priority. Or it may be equal the relative priority of the electorate's median voter λ. See *Demertzis et al* (1999a) for the importance of this distinction. Thus LP_j is either the government's or the electorate's social welfare function.

$$B = \left(\frac{1}{1+\beta+\gamma}\right)^2 \left[\frac{\gamma^2}{4} + \frac{\beta^2\gamma^2}{4} - \frac{\lambda\gamma^2(1-\beta)^2}{4}\right], \text{ and}$$

$$C = \left(\frac{1}{1+\beta+\gamma}\right)^2 \left[\frac{\gamma^2}{4} + \frac{\beta^2\gamma(\gamma+2)}{4} + \lambda\frac{\gamma(1-\beta)(2+\gamma(1-\beta))}{4}\right]$$

Inspection of equation (25) shows that being in a monetary union has worsened the overall performance of each individual economy to the extent that each has to absorb the disturbance caused by the transmission of foreign shocks (σ_i^2 in (25)) as well as the disturbances caused by their own shocks (σ_j^2 in (25)).[14] Most of the cost is from domestic shocks since A > B in all cases. That is also a standard result from optimal currency area literature: one has to share in the macroeconomic pain (of adjustment) if one wants to share in the microeconomic gains of integration. But the extent to which one has to share in that macroeconomic pain depends critically on the correlation between shocks (ρ), on the monetary policy responses to correlated shocks (γ), and on the degree of fiscal activism (λ, β). However the foreign shocks, and the degree of their integration with domestic shocks, only play a role when monetary policy is actively stabilising (i.e. only when $\gamma \neq 0$).

To those observations, we can add that the voters' preferences will only substantively affect the systematic part of the problem and the own shocks part (since the λ term offsets the other terms in B,

---

14 The first term in (25), representing the systematic part of the problem, is identical to the single economy case, *Demertzis et al* (1999a). Therefore there is no change in the nonstochastic part of the problem due to monetary union. It is the stochastic part, or the extra volatility which we have to contend with, which has changed with the formation of the currency union. This must necessarily change the design of economic policy, and alter the value of having a conservative Central Banker in particular. Moreover since the changes are all in the stochastic terms, and not in the deterministic elements, monetary union may also have the effect of changing the trade off between lower inflation and output stabilisation - possibly removing the "lower inflation at no cost" result of *Alesina / Gatti* (1995). Thus equation (25) is the crucial result. It shows that the choice of policy regime (e.g. conservative or not) and the impact of the optimal currency area conditions are not generally independent.

and B and C are positive but decreasing in moderate to large values of λ and β respectively). Hence the voters attention is likely to remain fixed on domestic economic outcomes; not on foreign problems or even the Europe-wide level of performance.

Secondly, the fact that domestic performance has been worsened by entry into the currency union, compared remaining insulated and outside, we have a simple demonstration of *Agell's* (1999) hypothesis that greater integration naturally leads to more rigid labour markets in an attempt to provide insurance (if not protection) against the fact that the domestic economy is now subject to a range of shocks over which the domestic policy instruments can no longer exercise any effective degree of control.

E. Political Dependence: Sensitivity to Variations in the Priorities

We can now study the impact of *asymmetries in preferences*. To do that we compute the sensitivity of our results to changes in the policy makers' preferences as measured by their relative priorities for output stabilisation. This is simply an exercise to see how the policies and the stability of a monetary union might vary as new policy makers or new governments come into office.

In practice we would probably be most interested in what happens if more liberal (less inflation adverse) governments appear; or if more conservative (more inflation adverse) Central Bank policies were introduced. We can evaluate those possibilities by signing the corresponding partial derivatives with respect to β and γ. The results are collected together in Table 1. The first panel shows the effect on the aggregate (Europe wide) variables, where E denotes an expected value and V its variance. The second panel shows the effect on national output levels and on the differences between them.

Table 1: The Sensitivity of the Outcomes to Variations in Policy Priorities (The Impacts of an Increase in β or γ).

	β	γ		β	γ
$E\pi^*$	-	+	Ey_d	0	0
$V\pi^*$	-	+	Vy_d	-	-
Et_j	-	0	Ey_1	+	0
Vt_j	-	?	Vy_1	-	-
Ey_a	+	0	Ey_2	+	0
Vy_a	-	-	Vy_2	-	-

Note: the term $\partial Vt_j / \partial\gamma$ can be signed only in special cases; for example where $0 \geq \rho$ and $\beta \geq 1$ when it is positive. In other cases, the sign is ambiguous or could be opposite for the two countries.

From Table 1 we get some insight into why different sets of policymakers might wish to adopt different policy preferences over the same set of policy targets. We can see that more liberal governments (higher values of β) will reduce both average inflation and its variability; and also increase aggregate output while reducing its fluctuations. The explanation for this apparent paradox is that inflation would then become lower on average. This is because, as governments use fiscal policy more vigorously to stabilise output, not only does the Central Bank have to react by tightening monetary policy to recover the balance between inflation losses and output stabilisation that it prefers. It has to do more than that because, with the Central Bank's anticipated reaction to a rise in β, the private sector will reduce their inflationary expectations - which causes output to rise again. So the Central Bank has to overreact.[15] That is to say, a liberal government can always get what it wants with respect to output, while also getting better inflation results, by pushing the Central Bank into overreacting with its monetary policy. That is a „lower inflation at no cost" result. But that arises be-

---

[15] *Demertzis et al* (1999a) show that this happens because the Central Bank has to have a steeper optimal reaction function in order to overcome the variations in inflation expectations, as well as inflation itself, given the fiscal responses. This has the consequence that the two policy instruments have to become strategic substitutes.

cause the governments coordinate to get it, not because the Central Bank is conservative.

Conversely, and more in line with conventional wisdom, a more conservative Central Bank (a lower value of γ) will reduce average inflation and its variance, simply because it will use this instrument less vigorously to achieve the output objective. Output variance will therefore rise, as *Rogoff* (1985) argues.

Differences with the standard single economy results emerge in the second part of the Table. Varying priorities do not affect the differences in income levels; but more liberal governments will reduce the likely variations in those differences, while a more conservative Central Bank will extend the range of those differences. Similarly liberal governments will increase the expected output levels in both countries while reducing their variability. But a more conservative Central Bank will produce no improvements on average, while making national incomes more volatile. That may make a conservative Central Bank unpopular, especially where its legitimacy remains an issue.

This last, rather unhelpful result shows that the benefits of a conservative Central Bank are not without cost in a world with fiscal policies.

F. Asymmetric Shocks under Different Political Regimes:

Finally, the expressions for y_1 and y_2 in (22) and (23) show that an increase in β would decrease the impact of an asymmetric shock on national incomes, and hence on any differences between them. This means more liberal governments would indeed undertake more regional stabilisation. This remark refers to the impact of a country specific shock of given size on the domestic economy ($e_1 - e_2$ for y_1, and $e_2 - e_1$ for y_2).

On the other hand, a more conservative Central Bank (a smaller value of γ) would cause a given level of asymmetric shocks to have a larger impact on national incomes (if $\beta \geq 1$) and on the differences between them – whatever fiscal policies may try to do in mitigation. That's a new result. It says that a more conservative Central Bank will exaggerate the impact of asymmetries in a monetary union if national governments are rather liberal, but it will help contain them if the governments are conservative too.

IV. Regime 2: Non Cooperation with two centralised unions

We now switch to our second regime. Monetary union is still in place, but we now assume that both countries have a single centralised union - and that national wages will be set according to the objectives of those unions. This is again a symmetric regime: both countries have the same wage bargaining arrangement in which a single union set wages according to the conditions in their own labour market.

A. Optimal Policies and Output Volatility

Because the hierarchical structure of the game has not changed, the Central Bank and governments have the same reaction functions as before:

$$\pi = \frac{\gamma}{1+\gamma+\beta}\left[\frac{1}{2}(w_1+w_2)+k-\frac{1}{2}(e_1+e_2)\right] \tag{26}$$

$$t_j = -\frac{\beta}{1+\beta+\gamma}\left[w_j+k-e_j\right]+\frac{\beta}{1+\beta+\gamma}\left[\frac{\gamma}{2}(e_j-e_i)\right] \tag{27}$$

However, each union still determines the wage rate at the beginning of each period. And each union aims for the full employment and also a certain level of real wage, as exemplified in the following objective function:[16]

$$\min_{w_j} L_{uj} = \frac{1}{2}E\left[(w_j-\pi)^2+\delta(y_j-k)^2\right] \tag{28}$$

The first term represents the Union's desire to preserve the real wages of its members (measured as a deviation from some exogenous productivity trend). The second shows the unions desire to stabilise output, and hence the employment of its members. That is, if δ increases, unions care more about employment. But if it falls, they care more about the real wage level of their members. Employment objectives like these translate into output stabilisation in our framework.[17] So this regime is the first in which wages (or

---

[16] See *Holden* (2000) or *Danthine/Hunt* (1994) for this specification.

[17] We do not consider the alternative formulation in which real wages are used as a supplementary form of monetary policy. This would involve giving the unions an explicit inflation objective; or giving them an explicit opportunity and framework within which they can coordinate with the Central Bank. That is a scenario for a subsequent paper. For

production costs, or interventions in the labour market) could become an additional policy instrument. Inserting the supply function equations, and solving for the expected values of taxes and inflation, we have the following reaction functions for the unions

$$w_j = \pi^e - \frac{\delta}{1+\delta}\left(t_j + k\right) \tag{29}$$

where $\delta = 0$ implies the decentralised bargaining regime as a special case.[18] Next, substituting the three reaction functions (26) - (27) into (29) we obtain the equilibrium wage as:

$$w_j = -\frac{\delta(1+\gamma)+\gamma(1+\delta)}{1+\delta+\beta}(k) \tag{30}$$

That gives the following equilibrium levels of inflation and taxation (putting (30) back into (26) and (27)):

$$\pi^* = \frac{\gamma}{1+\gamma+\beta}\left[\left(1-\frac{\delta(1+\gamma)+\gamma(1+\delta)}{1+\delta+\beta}\right)k - \frac{1}{2}(e_1+e_2)\right] \tag{31}$$

---

now, we continue with the hierarchical form of our game, with a particular form of objective function for the unions. That makes the wages a supplement to fiscal policy and raises the possibility of greater coordination between the unions and their respective governments.

18 This reaction function could be misleading, because it implies that a centralised union would always fix real wages below the level of a fragmented labour market. This is true only if we restrict the parameter δ to be greater than 0. If we allow $\delta < 0$, we can consider the case in which the unions try to achieve an increase in real wage, i.e. has a target nominal wage different from the expected inflation. Although not strictly correct (it violates the second order conditions for a minimum for the Trade Unions), this simplification does not change the basic implication of our results: that monetary union increases the power associated with a monopolistic union. However, how far this monopoly power would be used is an open question. Varying δ allows us to consider both the case where the unions try to increase the real wage extracted for the members, and the case where they try to stabilise employment at home at expense of employment abroad. That allows us to classify the cases where the unions, or the labour market policies more generally, act in their own private or national interests as $\delta \le 0$; and the cases where they act more in the social interest as $\delta > 0$.

$$t_j^* = \frac{\beta}{1+\beta+\gamma}\left[\left(1-\frac{\delta(1+\gamma)+\gamma(1+\delta)}{1+\delta+\beta}\right)k-e_j\right]+\frac{\beta}{1+\beta+\gamma}\left[\frac{\gamma}{2}(e_j-e_i)\right] \quad (32)$$

From these expressions it is clear that the labour market characteristics do not affect the way in which policies react to shocks. This is because wages are set before any shock occurs. Wages, therefore, represent a structural characteristic of the economy and can be used to influence economic policy only in so far as economic policy seeks to reach structural objectives (in this case represented by the parameter k).

As a result of all this, the variances of the policies will be the same as in regime 1. And the impact of asymmetric shocks will also be the same. Similarly the same variance and covariance elements of the objective function values in (21) and (25) apply. Consequently, in this regime too, monetary union leads to more variable output and inflation levels. But the systematic part of the policy outcomes does change. If $\delta > 0$, which means the Trade Unions care about output stabilisation, it is easy to check that this regime will lead to lower inflation rates and smaller fiscal deficits on average.[19] This is because, with an extra instrument coming into play, output can be stabilised with the available domestic policies.

That means the Central Bank is free to devote more resources to inflation control, and the fiscal authorities more effort to deficit stabilisation. In other words, labour market interventions can be used to substitute for other policy instruments.

On the output side, there is again no systematic differences in national incomes. But substituting for w_j, t_j and π from (30), (31) and (32) in (2), we can write:

$$y_a = [\Omega(1-\Phi)+\Phi]k \quad (33)$$

where

$$\Omega = \frac{\beta+\gamma}{1+\gamma+\beta}, \Phi = \frac{\delta(1+\gamma)+\gamma(1+\delta)}{1+\delta+\beta}$$

This allows us to deduce that aggregate income may be larger or smaller than with decentralised bargaining, depending on the parameter values. For example, if γ is small and β fairly large ($\beta > 0.62$), then y_a will fall on average. That is the case of a con-

---

[19] Compare (31) with (12); (29) with (13); (30) with (11). These results hold for all parameter values.

servative Central Bank but liberal governments. Conversely, if β and γ are both small (both the policy authorities are conservative), then y_a will rise on average. Finally if δ is large enough,[20] meaning that the unions are strongly committed to the stabilisation of their own economies; rather than to the preservation of real wages across the union, then y_a will again fall.

B. Institutional Conflicts Change the Value of Having a Conservative Central Banker

We can compute the sensitivity of these average outcomes to variations in β, γ and δ. The results are collected together in Table 2 below.

Table 2: The Sensitivity of the Outcomes to Changing Priorities in Regime 2 (Institutional Conflicts)

	β	γ	δ
$E\pi^*$	$+^b$	$-^a$	$-$
Et_j	$+/-^c$	$+$	$+$
Ey_a	$-^a$	$-$	$+$
Ey_i	$-$	$-$	$+$
Ew_j	$+$	$-$	$-$

Notes

a = positive if $\gamma < (1+\beta)\left(\sqrt{\dfrac{2+2\delta}{1+2\delta}}-1\right) < (1+\beta)/\sqrt{1+2\delta}$;

i.e. where β is large and γ is small (or δ small).

b = negative if (but not only if) $\delta \le \gamma$.

c = positive if $\gamma \ge (1+\beta)/(1+2\delta)$.

From Table 2 we can see that liberal governments will generate higher wages. But a more conservative Central Bank, or more self-interested Trade Unions, will also produce higher wages on average.

---

20 In fact if $\delta > \gamma(2\beta^2-\gamma-2)/[1+2\gamma(1-\gamma-2\beta(\gamma+\beta)-\beta(1+\beta+2\gamma))]$ on the plausible assumption that the denominator of this expression is positive.

That is perhaps as expected, since a more conservative Central Bank will trigger larger wage claims as a reaction to the anticipated loss in output and output stability - this is the converse of the over-reaction hypothesis discussed below Table 1. And greater self-interest among union members will produce the same result. Conversely, a more liberal Central Bank and more public spirited Trade Unions will generate lower wage rises, on the Scandinavian model of the 1980s perhaps, because their more "socially responsible" approach would trigger fewer adverse reactions elsewhere in the economy. Institutional coordination, in the form of centralised bargaining and shared objectives (if not outright cooperation), can therefore be very valuable in this scenario.

C. Is it possible to get "Lower Inflation at No Cost"?

What do these results imply for inflation performance? Evidently a more conservative Central Bank would actually have the effect of increasing inflation on average, unless it is already rather conservative (i.e. $\gamma \leq (1+\beta)/\sqrt{1+2\delta}$), or unless the unions are sufficiently self-interested $\left(\delta \leq \frac{1}{2}\left[(1+\beta)^2/\gamma^2 - 1\right]\right)$ – a sufficient condition – or the governments themselves are rather liberal $\left(\beta \geq \gamma\sqrt{1+2\delta} - 1\right)$. It may be that these inequalities will be satisfied in practice (it appears likely if γ starts off fairly small), but it is by no means guaranteed. So it appears that *Rogoff's* conservative Central Banker result could be relatively easily overturned once fiscal policy by fairly conservative governments or wage bargaining by socially minded trade unions are allowed. In fact it may only survive in a world of rather liberal governments, and where the Central Bank is already very conservative.

That result then produces a potential trade off between output levels and inflation, driven by the differing priorities over monetary, fiscal and wages policies. Evidently increasingly liberal governments (γ and δ fixed) will succeed in reducing $E(y_a)$ if the Central Bank is also liberal; or if β is currently small, or δ large and γ large. But they will also produce higher inflation at the same time – at least if δ is sufficiently lager than γ, which seems likely in a conservative setting. Nevertheless increasing fiscal conservatism does not start to produce the more favourable "lower inflation at no cost" result since a sufficient for a fall in β to lower average inflation rates is $\delta > \gamma$ by a sufficient margin; but a necessary condition for a fall in β not to reduce average incomes is is $\gamma \geq (1+\beta)/\sqrt{1+2\delta}$, or $1+2\delta \geq (1+\beta)^2/\gamma^2$. These two conditions are likely to conflict if γ starts off relatively small, or if δ is rather small. Similarly, the lower inflation at no cost result associated with a conservative Central Bank never holds in the presence of an active fiscal policy since $\partial E(y_a)/\partial\gamma > 0$ eliminates the „at no cost“ part. Indeed a conservative Central Bank will only secure lower inflation rates in this framework if γ is already small: $\gamma < (1+\beta)/\sqrt{1+2\delta}$.

D. The Social Contract as a Policy Regime

The results above, especially the last one, suggest that there can be advantages in a social compact, Scandinavian style, once in a monetary union with economies with different shocks and institutions with different priorities. Of course, with an independent Central Bank, such a compact may only be concluded with (and between) governments. But fiscal policy lends itself naturally to such a set up. It is easy to see that $\partial E(t_j)/\partial\delta > 0$ for all values of the other parameters. That means a wages policy can always be substituted for fiscal policy (and vice versa), although not always with the same level of efficiency. That gives us the basis for arguing that fiscally constrained governments will find an incentive to intervene in their labour markets, or to create an institutional structure in which the wage bargainers do that for them, when it comes to employment and output stabilisation policies.

Consequently European governments may well find themselves moving towards a social contract framework in EMU: that is to a system of more centralised wage bargaining and less market flexibility than before, rather than the other way round. However, it is important to note that the use of wages policies does not necessarily guarantee greater fiscal discipline. More liberal governments would increase the average fiscal deficit, i.e. make $E(t_j)$ more negative, if the Central Bank is very conservative and the trade unions rather self-interested. That happens if $\gamma \leq (1+\beta)/(1+2\delta)$ or if $\delta < (1+\beta-\gamma)/2\gamma$ respectively, ine-qualities that are not difficult to satisfy when γ or δ are not large. Thus fiscal deficits will appear when there is a conservative Central Bank and the unions won't help with preserving employment, so that fiscal policy has to bear the brunt of output stabilisation. But they are less likely to appear if the Bank is more liberal, or the wage bargainers more public spirited. These results hold for any type of government.

E. Overall Performance Under This Regime

The objective function values are too complicated to analyse directly in this case. But we can evaluate them numerically. The welfare of the median voter can be obtained by substituting the three equilibrium expressions (30) - (32) into the loss function LP_j. This will therefore become a function only of the parameters of the model

$$LP_j = LP_j(\lambda, \beta, \gamma, \delta, k)$$

Numerical simulations then allow us to visualize how different parameter values affect the welfare of a representative individual, in comparison to the case of perfect decentralization analysed before. Again we can abstract from the effects of shocks because, as noted above, the stochastic elements and shock variances are the same in both regimes.

Figure 1: The Welfare Effect of Having Centralised Trade Unions

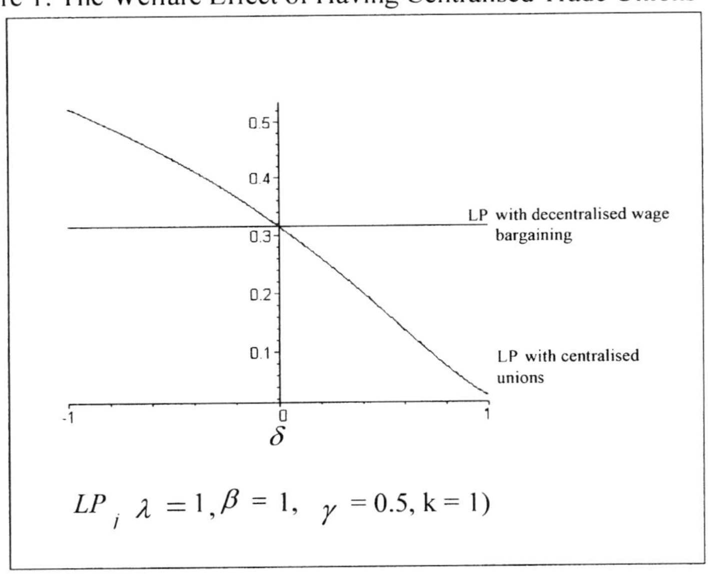

The typical outcome of that comparison, as wage bargaining behaviour varies from the self-interested to the most socially beneficial, is given in the figure above.

It is clear from this that centralisation produces a benefit, from the welfare point of view, only if wage bargaining can be used to achieve aggregate output objectives $(\delta > 0)$. Otherwise, as conjectured by *Calmfors / Driffill* (1988), its power will conflict with the objectives of the economic policy maker, making everybody worse off. This is our $\delta \leq 0$ case, where unions are concerned only to raise real wages.

V. Conclusions

We have used a small but standard theoretical model to formalise and restate one aspect of the theory of optimal currency areas; namely the consequences for a currency union, whether euroisation in Europe or a unilateral one as in the case of dollarisation in Latin America, of asymmetries in shocks, in institutional structures or in preferences. Although our model has been extended to include fiscal policy and different degrees of wage flexibility, we get a concise restatement of all the usual results with respect to asymmetries. And we get some new results:

- The choice of policy regime matters. That is to say the degree of conservatism in monetary policies, the labour market institutions adopted, and the "social contract" made with the unions or fiscal policy makers are crucially important. The incidence of the optimal currency area conditions, and hence the success of a certain union or the suitability of a certain country as a member, will vary systematically with those choices. That is why we say inter-institutional coordination is crucial.
- OCA theory is therefore not independent of the type of policy regime chosen to go with it. One simple illustration is that asymmetries in shocks appear to interact with asymmetries in preferences, to make the impact of both together larger than the sum of either alone. For example a conservative Central Bank exaggerates the impact of any asymmetric shocks on the individual economies.
- The symmetry of shocks may be a necessary condition for a successful union, but it is not sufficient. If the shocks are too large, the reduced set of instruments available may not be able to cope with the results. To prevent policy overload, policy makers are then likely to look for additional instruments at the national level - and a social compact with the unions, in order to regulate the labour markets, is an obvious candidate.
- With decentralised labour markets, a currency union will increase the volatility of output and inflation - the more so, the clo-

ser integrated are the shocks. However the degree of integration appears to have more effect on the distribution of the benefits, and it only matters if monetary policy is active in helping to stabilise output.

- In the same regime, more liberal governments will help reduce the variations in income differentials, while a conservative Central Bank increases the range of such differences. Similarly the variability of the underlying output levels is reduced by liberal governments, but increased by a conservative Central Bank. Consequently, both in levels and in differences, the *Alesina / Gatti* result of "lower inflation at no cost" fails in a conservative monetary union with restricted fiscal policies.
- Introducing centralised wage bargaining shows that labour market policies can be used to substitute for (but not supplant) fiscal policies. However socially minded wage bargainers can undermine and overturn the advantages of having a conservative Central Banker; that is, national output levels may fall and inflation rise if governments are conservative and trade unions public spirited. Hence *Rogoff's* famous result does not survive in a monetary union with fiscal policy unless the governments are liberal and trade unions are self-interested. This appears to be the result of a divergence between private and social welfare.

References

Agell J. (1999), On the Benefits from Rigid Labour Markets, Norms, Market Failures and Social Insurance, in: Economic Journal Vol. 109/1999, pp. 143-164.

Alesina A. / Gatti R. (1995), Independent Central Banks: Low Inflation at No Cost, in: American Economic Review 85(2)/ 1995, pp. 196-200.

Aoki M. (1976), Optimal Control and Systems Theory in Dynamic Economic Analysis, Amsterdam 1976.

Barro R. / Gordon D. (1983), A Positive Theory of Monetary Policy in a Natural Rate Model, in: Journal of Political Economy 91/1983, pp. 589-610.

Blinder A. (2000), Central Bank Credibility: Why do we care? How do we build it?, in: American Economic Review 90/2000, pp. 1421-31.

Calmfors L. / Driffill J. (1988), Bargaining Structure, Corporatism, and Macroeconomic Performance, in: Economic Policy No: 6/1988, pp. 14-61.

Canzoneri M. / Cumby R. / Diba B. (2000), Is the Price Level Determined by the Needs of Fiscal Solvency?, in: American Economic Review 2000 (forthcoming).

Danthine J. / Hunt J. (1994), Wage Bargaining Structure, Employment and Economic Integration, in: Economic Journal Vol. 104/1994, pp. 528-42.

Debelle G. / Fischer S. (1994), How Independent Should the Central Bank Be?, in: *Fuhrer J.* (ed), Goals, Guidelines and Constraints Facing Monetary Policy Makers, Federal Reserve Bank, Boston 1994, MA.

Demertzis M. / Hughes Hallett A. / Viegi N. (1999a), An Independent Central Bank faced with Elected Governments, CEPR Discussion Paper Series No: 2219, Centre for Economic Policy Research, London 1999.

Demertzis M. / Hughes Hallett A. / Viegi N. (1999b), Can the ECB be Truely Independent? Should it Be?, in: Empirica Vol. 26/1999, pp. 217-40.

Gali J. / Gertler M. / Lopez-Salido J. (2001), European Inflation Dynamics, in: European Economic Review 45, Vol. 7/2001, pp. 1237-70.

Holden S. (2000), Monetary Regimes and the Coordination of Wage Setting, Department of Economics, University of Oslo, Norway (mimeo).

Italianer A. (2001), The Euro and Internal Economic Policy Coordination, in: *Hughes Hallett A. / Mooslechner P. / Schürz M.* (eds), Challenges for Economic Policy Coordination within European Monetary Union, Kluwer, Boston and Dordrecht 2001.

Mooslechner P. / Schürz M. (2001), International Macroeconomic Policy Coordination: Any Lessons for EMU?, in: *Hughes Hallett A. / Mooslechner P. / Schürz M.* (eds), op. cit.

Persson T. / Tabellini G. (1990), Macroeconomic Policy, Credibility and Politics, Harwood Academic Publishers, Amsterdam 1990.

Roberts J. M. (1995), New Keynesian Economics and the Phillips Curve, in: Journal of Money Credit and Banking Vol. 27, No: 4/1995, pp. 975-84.

Rogoff K. (1985), The Optimal Degree of Commitment to an Intermediate Monetary Target, in: Quarterly Journal of Economics Vol. 99/1985, pp. 1169-1189.

Rotemberg J. / Woodford M. (1998), An Optimisation Based Econometric Framework for the Evaluation of Monetary Policy, NBER Technical Paper No: 233, NBER, Cambridge 1998, MA.

Part 3:
Monetary Policy, Financial Markets and Payment Systems

Fritz Breuss

Is ECB's monetary policy optimal already?

I. Introduction

Given the external conditions the Economic and Monetary Union (EMU) of the European Union (EU) has been quite a success so far. When the EMU started its third stage with 11 out of 15 EU member states in January 1999, the European and US business cycle were still on an upswing. GDP growth was satisfactory, inflation was low, even some kind of convergence of the European business cycle was visible. However, the high value of the Euro at the start was not sustainable, its exchange rate against major currencies depreciated continuously. Then, in 2000, oil prices increased sharply, fuelled inflation in the industrial world and initiated a faltering of the cycle in the second half of that year, starting in the USA and followed by Europe. In 2001 (Greece became the 12th member of Euroland), the decline continued, accelerated by the terrorist attacks on the World Trade Center on September 11, 2001. On the eve of the change-over from a "virtual" Euroland to a real one (the Euro became legal tender as of January 2002), the world economic situation is characterized by a unique constellation: the triad (USA, EU and Japan) are in recession simultaneously. The recession hitting the euro area can be seen largely as a symmetric shock experienced by all Member States.[1] However, whereas the USA and Japan are counteracting with an active fiscal policy, the EU and Euroland in particular are standing aside. Fiscal policy, still decentralized and in the responsibility of the EU member states has to fulfill – in a complicated co-ordination process - the targets of the Stability and Growth Pact (SGP), which should result in a balanced budget over the cycle. Monetary policy, conducted centrally by the European Central Bank (ECB) reacted by reducing interest rates, but more backward than forward looking and – compared to US's Fed - partly too late. So, Europe can only hope that the upswing in the USA will spill over and induce an export-led growth.

The major argument which is put forward in this paper is that the ECB's reaction to the first external shock, the oil price surge in 2000 and 2001, was quite satisfactory but not optimal.[2] The second

---

1 For this interpretation, see *Begg/Canova/De Grauwe/Fatás/Lane* (2002) p. 12.

2 In our analysis, optimality is not understood as the theoretical outcome of an optimization process (for an integrated approach of such con-

chapter – after a short description of the economic policy framework in EMU - discusses the two pillar strategy of the ECB and its performance so far. It questions whether really two pillars are necessary and estimates a specific Taylor rule to understand the interest-rate setting of the ECB. The implications of the oil price shock are the topic of the third chapter. It is demonstrated that this temporary supply shock led to an asymmetric impact on Euroland's Member States and hence increased inflation and output dispersion. In the fourth chapter the economic outcome of an alternative monetary policy reaction to this shock is analyzed. It turns out that the overall economic performance could have been improved when targeting not headline but core inflation. Conclusions are drawn in section five.

II. ECB's Two Pillar Strategy in Action

A. The asymmetric economic policy framework in EMU

The introduction of the euro and the conduct of the single monetary policy by the independent European Central Bank (ECB) have fundamentally changed the framework within which the European Community and its Member States conduct their economic policies.[3] Building on the existing framework of the Single Market, the specific design of Economic and Monetary Union (EMU), as laid down by the Maastricht Treaty (now in the version of the Nice Treaty), transfers the competence for monetary and exchange rate policies to the Community level (see the EC Treaty chapter entitled "Monetary policy" – Title VII, Chapter 2), while leaving the responsibilities for fiscal policies (see the EC Treaty chapter entitled "Economic Policy" - Title VII, Chapter 1), labor market and employment policies (see the EC Treaty chapter entitled "Employment" – Title VIII) and for many microeconomic and structural policies in the hands of the national or subnational authorities. In contrast to the USA with its coherent centralized economic and monetary policy framework (although the US states have some autonomy) in EMU we are confronted with a complex system of multi-level economic governance – characterized by the interplay

---

cepts, see e.g. *Clarida/Jordi/Mark* (2001) but the empirical demonstration via model simulations that an alternative monetary policy would have led to a better overall economic outcome in the Euro area.

3 *Eijffinger/de Haan* (2000) and *Issing et al.* (2001) describe ECB's policies in detail.

of central monetary policy-making and decentralized economic (mainly fiscal) policy-making. This asymmetry may be either considered as a "design flaw"[4] or as a strength for the EU.[5]

Due to this asymmetric design, the EC Treaty foresees a structured interaction among policy-makers, ranging from more or less constraining forms of policy co-ordination (e.g. via the Stability and Growth Pact - SGP)[6] to a free play of competing policy designs. As EU Member States regard their economic policies as a "matter of common concern" (EC Treaty, Article 99(1)), they shall co-ordinate them. Economic policy-co-ordination (postulated in EC Treaty, Article 4 and Article 99) is necessary to avoid potential negative spillovers across countries and across policies.[7] It is executed in a complicated multilevel process.[8] In order to give coherence to the overall economic policy framework, the EC Treaty establishes the annual Broad Economic Policy Guidelines (BEPG; see EC Treaty, Article 99(2)) as the principal and overarching policy instrument for the co-ordination of economic policies at Community level. These guidelines, which – with due respect for the independent and statutory mandate of the ECB – do not apply to monetary policy, render

---

4 See *Breuss* (2000b) p. 275.

5 See *ECB* (2001b) p. 54.

6 *Canzoneri/Cumby/Diba* (2001) within a new "fiscal" theory of price determination approach, come to the conclusion that a common currency area is not viable if fiscal policy in two or more of the EMU members is Non-Ricardian. They find that constraints written into the SGP are sufficient for a Ricardian regime. In a Ricardian regime, fiscal policy has discipline in the sense that current and/or future primary surpluses are actively adjusted to satisfy the government's public sector's present value budget constraint (PVBC) for any real value of current government liabilities. In this regime, monetary policy provides the nominal anchor, and the price level is determined in a conventional manner. Non-Ricardian regimes, by contrast, lack fiscal discipline. For a thorough analysis of the SGP, see *Brunila/Buti/Franco* (2001). Although it would make more intellectual sense to apply deficit ceilings to the cyclically-adjusted budget instead of the SGP target of a balanced total budget, the calculation of potential output is controversial. Therefore *Begg/Canova/De Grauwe/Fatás/Lane* (2002) p. 13, suggest "to delegate to an independent body the production of estimates of trends in potential output in Member States".

7 See *ECB* (2001b) pp. 55-56.

8 See *ECB* (2001b) p. 65; (2000b) 285 ff.

operational the fundamental principles of close co-ordination. BEPG is the pivot of the more specialized co-ordination and consultation process of multilateral surveillance (for fiscal policy – via the SGP with stability and convergence programs on the budgetary stances (debt/deficit data); employment policy – via the "Luxembourg Process" with employment guidelines and National Action Plans; micro/structural policies – via the "Cardiff Process" with multilateral review of economic reforms; macroeconomic dialogue among social partners, governments, ECB, Commission – via the "Cologne Process"; "open method of co-ordination" – via the "Lisbon Process" providing a more coherent setting of targets and periodic monitoring and evaluation of the results) and gives the principal policy messages. The role of monetary policy in the overall economic policy framework is unique. Although the single monetary policy represents a fundamental pillar of the system of economic governance in the euro area and the ECB is part of the overall economic policy framework there is no overall co-ordination of economic and monetary policy in EMU. There is only a structured exchange of information and views with other policy-makers (e.g. in the major co-ordination body, the Economic and Financial Committee ; see EC Treaty, Article 114(2)). However, the contacts between the independent ECB and the finance ministry are to be understood only as a non-binding open policy dialogue and should be "... in no way misunderstood as an ex ante co-ordination of monetary and fiscal policy stances. In the same vein, the regular and structured dialogue between the ECB and national governments clearly excludes any ex ante policy co-ordination or joint agreements aimed at achieving a predetermined policy-mix."[9] This attitude of only an informal policy dialogue may of course lead to non-optimal outcomes with respect to an overall[10] (monetary and fiscal policy) co-ordination.[11] In contrast to the US system, the EMU is

---

9 *ECB* (2001b) p. 64.

10 See *Breuss/Weber* (2001).

11 *Beetsma/Debrun/Klaassen* (2001) investigate the circumstances under which co-ordination may be desirable. It turns out that co-ordination is beneficial when the correlation of the shocks hitting the various economies is low. Generally, the scope for fiscal co-ordination is larger under asymmetric shocks, because the ECB remains passive as average inflation in the union is unaffected.

missing an arrangement of fiscal federalism.[12] Even more, the individual responsibility of the Member States in the field of budgetary policy is explicitly underscored by the EC Treaty's "no bail-out" clause (Article 103), which stipulates that neither the Community nor any Member State shall be liable for the commitments of another Member State.

B. Two or only one pillar in ECB's monetary policy strategy?

In October and December 1998 the Governing Council of the ECB announced the main elements of its stability-oriented monetary policy strategy to the public. The strategy guides the single monetary policy of the Eurosystem, i.e. the ECB and the national central banks (NCBs) of the Member States which adopted the euro. The stability-oriented strategy of the Eurosystem consists of three main elements: a quantitative definition of the Eurosystems's primary objective, namely price stability (EC Treaty, Article 105(1)), and the "two pillars" of the strategy used to achieve this objective. These pillars are represented by giving money a prominent role (pillar one), as signaled by the announcement of a quantitative reference value for the growth rate of a broad monetary aggregate (M3), and by a broadly based assessment of the outlook for price developments (pillar two) and risks to price stability in the euro area as a whole .[13]

In contrast to the Fed, the Governing Council of the ECB has adopted a concrete definition for price stability: "price stability shall be defined as a year-on-year increase in the Harmonized Index of Consumer Prices (HICP) for the euro area[14] of below 2%".[15]

---

12 Whether fiscal federalism is something one should worry about in EMU is an open question. For a discussion of the different arguments, see *Breuss* (2000a).

13 See *ECB* (1999a).

14 *De Grauwe/Piskorsi* (2001) investigate whether it makes a difference as far as the effectiveness of alternative loss functions of the ECB is concerned whether its policy is based on the union-wide aggregates (as is done in practice) or on the national data (on output, inflation and interest rates) of the member states. The main conclusion is that the monetary policy strategy of the ECB based on the union-wide aggregates may be a reasonable proxy of the optimal policy rule based on the national data of the member states.

15 *Benigno* (2001) investigates the optimal monetary policy in a currency area within the framework of a two-region, general equilibrium model

Price stability according to his definition "is to be maintained over the medium term".[16] However, the ECB did not exactly define the length of the "medium term". Setting a fixed target has the advantage of credibility, the disadvantage is the loss of flexibility. A medium-term orientation of monetary policy ensures genuine and meaningful accountability. It implies the need for monetary policy to have a forward-looking, medium-term orientation. It also acknowledges the existence of short-term volatility in prices, resulting from non-monetary shocks to the price level.[17] Nevertheless, as will be seen, in practice these sound arguments are mere wishful thinking. If the primary objective is satisfied, the ECB shall support the general economic policies of the EU, laid down in Article 2 of the EC Treaty (" ... to promote a harmonious, balanced and sustainable development of economic activities, a high level of employment and of social protection, equality between men and women, sustainable and non-inflationary growth, a high degree of competitiveness and convergence of economic performance, a high level of protection and improvement of the quality of environment, the raising of the standard of living and quality of life, and economic and social cohesion and solidarity among Member States"). Thus the Treaty gives the ECB a "double mandate".[18]

---

with monopolistic competition and price stickiness. His framework delivers a simple welfare criterion based on the utility of the consumers that has the usual trade-off between stabilizing inflation and output. Only if the two regions share the same degree of nominal rigidity, the optimal outcome is obtained by targeting a weighted average of the regional inflation rates. These weights coincide with the economic size of the regions (which is done when calculating the actual HICP inflation for the euro area). If the degrees of rigidity are different, the optimal plan implies a higher degree of inertia in the inflation rate. But an inflation targeting policy, in which higher weight is given to the inflation in the region with higher degrees of nominal rigidity, is nearly optimal. Highest wage rigidity can be found in Spain, Belgium-Luxembourg, Finland, Ireland and Germany. The highest wage flexibility was measured in France, Italy and Austria; see *Benigno* (2001) p. 52.

16 See *ECB* (1999a) p. 46.

17 E.g. the result of indirect tax changes or variations in international commodity – in particular oil – prices; see *ECB* (1999a) p. 47.

18 See also *Begg/Canova/De Grauwe/Fatás/Lane* (2002) p. 11.

Table 1: Macro-economic performance of EU Member States (averages 1999-2001)

	Euro area ins and outs	GDP, real annual %-change	HICP[1)] inflation annual %-change	Unem-ploy-ment rate (in %)	General governm. budget balance (in % of GDP)	Gross public debt (in % of GDP)	Current account (in % of GDP)
Belgium	*B	2.77	2.07	7.57	-0.17	110.97	4.80
Denmark	DK	2.20	2.37	4.83	2.60	47.10	2.50
Germany	*D	1.83	1.70	8.10	-0.97	60.53	-0.63
Greece	*EL	3.93	2.87	11.10	-0.97	101.90	-4.00
Spain	*E	3.63	3.13	14.33	-0.43	60.70	-2.93
France	*F	2.67	1.40	9.80	-1.50	57.73	1.80
Ireland	*IRL	9.60	3.93	4.53	3.07	40.73	-0.57
Italy	*I	2.10	2.33	10.43	-1.10	110.93	0.43
Luxembourg	*L	6.40	2.47	2.33	4.73	5.53	20.03
Netherlands	*NL	2.90	3.17	2.90	1.30	57.00	4.97
Austria	*A	2.30	1.63	3.83	-1.17	63.37	-2.83
Portugal	*P	2.83	3.10	4.13	-1.87	53.90	-9.20
Finland	*FIN	3.40	2.33	9.73	4.53	44.67	6.80
Sweden	S	3.17	1.53	6.10	3.23	57.90	3.57
United Kingdom	UK	2.43	1.12	5.57	2.23	42.60	-2.00
EU-15	EU	2.53	2.10	8.33	-0.03	64.80	0.00
Euro area	*EUR	2.57	2.10	9.03	-0.70	70.57	0.23

[1)] HICP = Harmonized Index of Consumer Prices.

Source: Autumn 2001 Forecasts for 2001-2003, European Economy, Supplement A, No. 10/11 – October/November, Brussels, 2001.

As one sees from table 1, the inflation rate objective in the first years of EMU was nearly fulfilled in the euro area as a whole with a HICP inflation rate of 2.1% on average 1999-2001. However, the dispersion over the Euroland member states was considerable, ranging from 1.4% in France to 3.9% in Ireland. Since the early nineties one sees a strong convergence of inflation rates starting with a standard deviation value for EUR-12 (euro area with 12 member states) of over 5 in 1990 to below one in 2001. The expectation of a "zero dispersion" for the EU as a consequence of the "law of one price" due to the impact of the Single Market (more competition on an integrated market) and additionally because of the Single Currency in the EMU is an illusion.[19] But also the other macro variables – be it GDP growth (varying from 1.8% in Germany to 9.6% in Ireland with an EUR-12 average of 2.6% over the period 1999-2001) or unemployment (varying from 2.3% in Luxembourg to 14.3% in Spain with an EUR-12 average of 9% between 1999-2001) – still exhibit considerable differences in Euroland. Besides the progress made in bringing down inflation, due to the pressure of the SGP the fiscal position of the member states of Euroland improved considerably. However, whereas some countries have already reached surpluses in their budget balances (e.g. Luxembourg and Finland with +4 ½% of GDP, Ireland with +3% - all countries with higher than average GDP growth in the last years), some countries still have a – albeit minor – deficit position (e.g. France, Germany, Italy with around –1% of GDP). Similarly, the debt to GDP ratios are still above 100% of GDP in Belgium, Greece and Italy, whereas all the other Euroland member states are already below or close to the Maastricht reference value of 60% of GDP (see table 1).

An important factor behind the increase in inflation in 2000 and 2001 has been import price development, in particular oil price and exchange rate movements. The euro depreciated against the US-Dollar continuously after the start of EMU in 1999, resulting in a decline of around 25% (see figure 1). Whether the dispersion of inflation within the euro area is only due to diverging business cycles or whether the higher inflation is an equilibrium phenomenon due to the working of the Balassa-Samuelson effect is undecided.[20]

---

[19] The European Commission *EU* (2001c) demonstrated why the "law of one price" (an integrated market with no transport costs product prices expressed in the same currency should not geographically differ) in the EU fails and is also an elusive goal when taking the US economy as a benchmark. There are many factors behind the large and persistent price dispersion in the EU: the Balassa/Samuelson effect; growing importance of services; price-setting behavior for branded goods depending on local preferences. In 1998, price dispersion was higher in the EU (15%) than in the USA (12%). However, EU price dispersion declined – due to the Single Market – during the 1990s.

[20] Whereas *Alesina/Blanchard/Gali/Giavazzi/Uhlig* (2001) pp. 16-18, dismiss the Balassa/Samuelson effect (relative price increase of fast-growing (catching-up) countries – more precisely as a consequence of

Additionally, the oil price shock certainly has hit the Member States of Euroland asymmetrically, as will be demonstrated in chapter 3 when investigating the economic impact of the first external shock. The world oil price which is still denominated in US-Dollars increased from 11 $/barrel in the first quarter of 1999 to a peak of 30.3 $/barrel in the third quarter of 2000. The terrorist attack on the World Trade Center on September 11, 2001 only very temporarily accelerated the oil price rise and prices plummeted afterwards in view of a drastic demand shortage because of the recessions in the USA and in Europe. In figure 2 the actual development of the world oil price since 1996 is contrasted with a "smoothing" of the price development since 1999. This implies an oil price increase over this period of around 30%. As a consequence, energy prices contributed somewhat more than half of the 2.1% rise in overall HICP inflation in the euro area in 1999-2001.[21] Although there are many concepts to calculate "core" inflation (see ECB, 2001a for an overview),[22] the most prominent and widely used method is that which extract the most volatile components of overall ("headline") HICP inflation. Excluding unprocessed food and energy, the so defined "core" HICP inflation[23] was below the ECB target of 2% (see figure 3) and around one percentage point lower than "headline" HICP in-

---

faster growing productivity in the tradable sector compared to the non-tradable sector of an economy) as quantitatively relevant for the inflation dispersion in Euroland; *Reutter/Sinn* (2000) find that as a result of the Balassa/Samuelson effect relative prices change rapidly between and within the euro countries. They derive a minimum inflation rate for Euroland (compatible with the requirement that no country face a deflation) of 0.94% for EUR-11 and of 1.13% for an enlarged Euroland (EUR-21). Within EUR-11 the minimum inflation varies between 0% in Germany and 2.7% in Finland and 2.4% in Ireland, 1.5% in Spain and Italy, 1.4% in the Netherlands, Austria and France, 0.8% in Belgium and Portugal; *Reutter/Sinn* (2000) p. 13.

21 See *ECB*, Monthly Bulletin (June 2001) p. 37; see also *EU* (2001a) p. 45.

22 *Cristadoro/Forni/Reichlin/Veronese* (2001) propose an index of core inflation for the euro area that exploits information from a large panel of time series (400) on disaggregated prices, industrial production, labor market indicators, and financial and monetary variables. The indicator serves as a reliable forecaster of the euro area HICP at one and two years horizon.

23 See *ECB*, Monthly Bulletin (June 2001) p. 37.

flation.[24] Such or similar reflections are undertaken by the ECB in its context of the "second pillar" of monetary strategy via a broadly based assessment of the outlook for price developments. As will be argued in this paper, the concentration on "core" instead of "headline" HICP inflation would have optimized monetary policy and resulted in a better overall economic outcome in the EU – at least in the period 2000-2001.

Figure 1: Euro exchange rates
(national currencies per Euro; 1999M01 = 100)

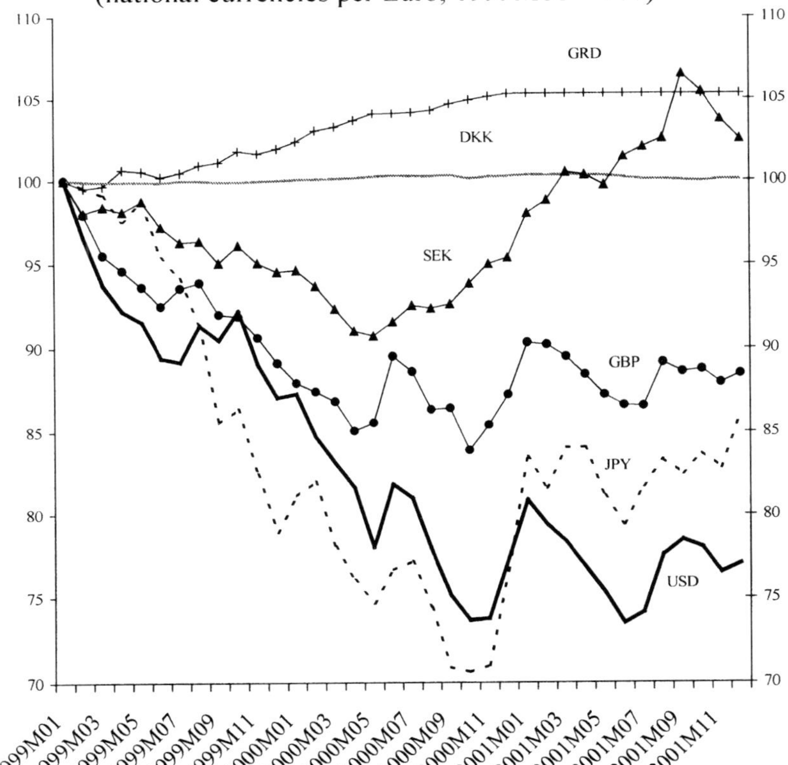

Source: European Central Bank (ECB), 1999-2001.

[24] See *ECB* (2001a) p. 58.

Figure 2: World oil price (Brent crude spot; USD/barrel)

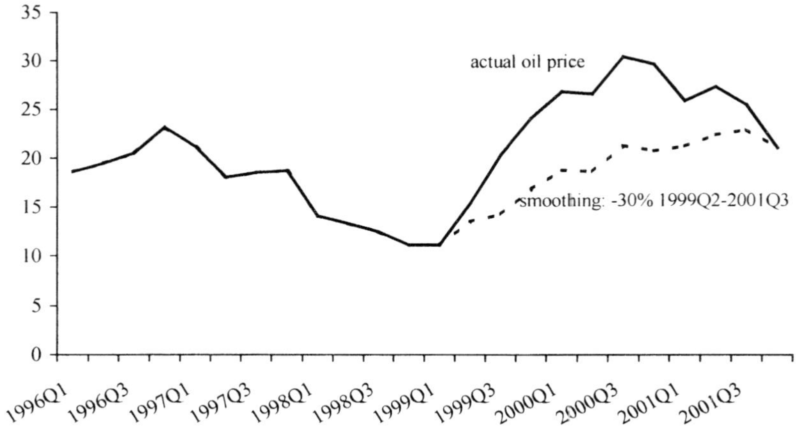

Source: Oxford Economic Forecasting world model.

Figure 3: HICP inflation rates in the euro area– headline and core (in %)

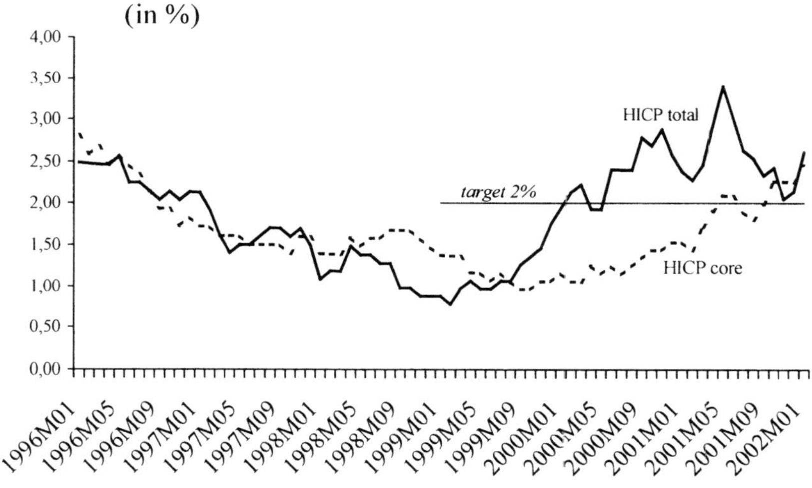

Source: OECD, Main Economic Indicators (several issues)
HICP = Harmonized Index of Consumer Prices ("headline" = total index)
HICP "core" = HICP total excluding energy, food, tobacco, alcohol.

Before analyzing the concrete monetary policy reaction of the ECB to the first external shock (the sharp oil price increase), the importance of the "first pillar" of monetary strategy, the prominent role for money, defined as the annual growth rate of the broad monetary aggregate (M3) is looked at. On December 1, 1998 the Governing Council of the ECB has chosen to announce a reference value for the aggregate M3, defined in an encompassing manner to include not only currency in circulation and the conventional deposit components of broad money, but also both the shares/units of money market funds (MMFs) and debt securities issued by monetary financial institutions.[25] The announced reference value was derived from the quantity theory of money, based on the following medium-term assumptions:[26] Mv = PQ. P is the inflation rate (HICP), defined as below 2%; Q is the trend of real GDP growth in the range of 2-2.5% per annum; v is the velocity of circulation of M3 which, in the medium term, appears to be declining by 0.5-1% each year. Taking into consideration that the actual trend decline in velocity is likely to lie below the stated values, this results in an annual growth of M (M3) of 4.5% per annum, the reference value set by the Governing Council for M3. A look at figure 4 indicates that since the start of EMU the actual growth has deviated from the simple self-declared reference value most of the time. M3 growth exhibited a continuous decline since the mid-eighties,[27] from annual rates of over 10% to 7% in the early nineties and declining to 5% at the eve of the third phase of EMU starting in 1999. When, however, the reference value for M3 is missed so often, one may ask whether one should not give up this "first pillar" anyway. Some, like *Svensson*[28] mean that "the first pillar is actually a brick". In its third report "Monitoring the European Central Bank" *Alesina et al*[29] are somewhat more mild in evaluating the M3 pillar. First, they remark that it may be somewhat absurd to talk about monetary policy without talking about money. However, in its mission, to maintain price stability in the medium term, the growth rate of M3 can only be a servant in this quest and not a target in itself. Whether it is a useful servant,[30] has to be evaluated. However, they conclude by stating, that "to demonstrate the overriding importance of price stability, it

---

25 MFIs: see *ECB* (1999b) p. 35.

26 See *ECB* (1999a) pp. 48-49.

27 See *ECB* (1999b) p. 37.

28 See *Svensson* (2000) p. 97.

29 See *Alesina/Blanchard/Gali/Giavazzi/Uhlig* (2001) pp. 47-48.

30 Given that the longer-term trends in the growth of money stock M3 are only very loosely correlated with the annual rate of consumer price inflation; see *ECB* (1999b) p. 39.

would be useful to move the growth rate of M3 to the side".[31] In its fourth report "Monitoring the European Central Bank" *Begg et al*[32] call it already the "poison pillar". In spite of two adjustments in the M3 series (removal of non-resident holdings of money market fund shares/units and of short-term debt instruments in May 2001 and October 2001 respectively)[33] the monetary pillar is for many reasons of no use at all. On the one hand, it is no good guide for signaling inflation[34], on the other hand money demand is highly volatile. This is the principal reason that most central banks discarded monetary targeting long ago. Lastly, the monetary pillar detracts from the ECB's successes and hence could erode credibility.[35]

For a while, the ECB treated the exchange rate with benign neglect. It has argued, correctly, that its task is to maintain price stability in the euro area, not to target a particular exchange rate. But in September 2000, a joint intervention by the ECB and the Federal Reserve to shore up the weak euro – mainly because the coincidence of boosting oil prices and devaluation of the euro could endanger the main objective of price stability in the euro area - was publicly discussed and then implemented for the first time. The effect was only fleeting: after a short blip, the euro depreciated even further. The decline of the euro stopped only with news that the economy in the United States has started to slow down. A striking example was the very short-lived blip after September 11, 2001. Should the ECB be concerned about exchange rate fluctuations? *Alesina et al*[36] answer with a qualified no. No, because official interventions are small in comparison to the amounts traded daily on the foreign exchange rate markets. No, unless the ECB's intervention signals a shift in policy and such a signal is enough to change market beliefs. And the EC Treaty lays down that any exchange

---

31 See *Alesina/Blanchard/Gali/Giavazzi/Uhlig* (2001) p. 48.

32 See *Begg/Canova/De Grauwe/Fatás/Lane* (2002) pp. 18-21.

33 See *ECB*, Monthly Bulletin (November 2001) p. 10.

34 *Begg/Canova/De Grauwe/Fatás/Lane* (2002) p. 21, demonstrate that across 100 countries the long-run relation between money growth and inflation (1970-99) is very strong. However, the cross-section of the countries over the same period with low inflation countries – like the present Euroland countries - (inflation rates below 5%) the relation is only very weak.

35 See *Begg/Canova/De Grauwe/Fatás/Lane* (2002) p. 18.

36 See *Alesina/Blanchard/Gali/Giavazzi/Uhlig* (2001) p. 40.

rate policy should be consistent with the primary objective of the ECB's monetary policy, which is to maintain price stability. Article 111 of the EC Treaty foresees a close interaction between the EU Council and the ECB with regard to the exchange rate policy.[37]

Figure 4: Growth of money M3 in the euro area (EUR-12) (annual growth in %, seasonally adjusted)

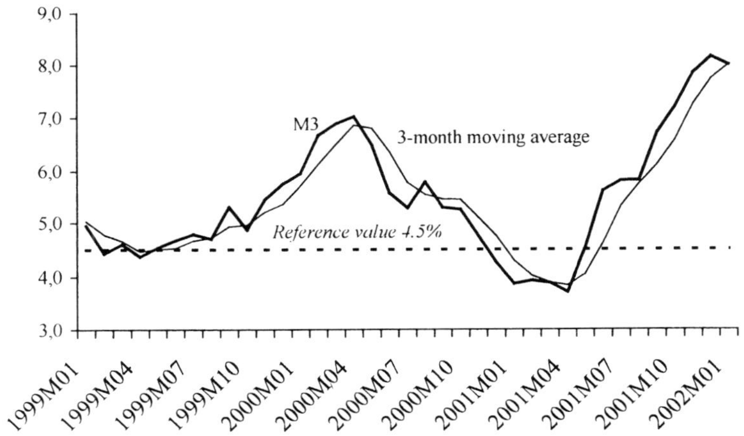

Source: OECD, Main Economic Indicators (several issues).

C. How does the ECB set interest rates?

The Governing Council of the ECB sets three kinds of interest rates: a) those for main refinancing operations, b) those for marginal lending facility (over-night money) and c) those for deposit facility. The main instrument in the following analysis is the interest rate for main refinancing operations (MFO). In figure 5 a comparison of the development of ECB's MFO with the main instrument of US's Board of Governors of the Federal Reserve System (in the following shortened "Fed"), the Federal Funds rate is made.

---

37 E.g. to conclude formal agreements on an exchange rate system for the euro in relation to non-Community currencies or to formulate general orientations for exchange rate policy; see also *ECB* (2001b) pp. 57-58.

Figure 5: Interest rates in the euro area and in the USA

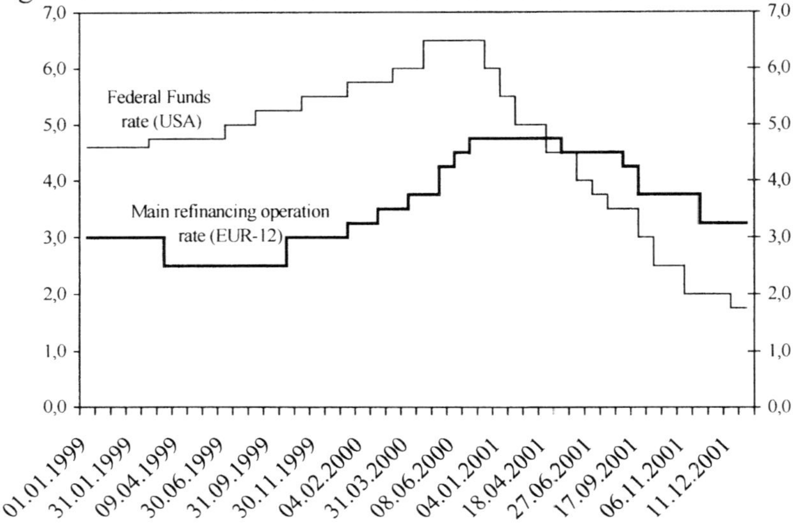

Sources: ECB and USA Federal Reserve Board.

The ECB started with an interest rate for MFO of 3% and made the first interest rate cut in April 1999 to 2.5%. In November 1999 it raised the rate again to 3% and thereafter several times up to the peak of 4.75% in October 2000. After staying on this level for seven months, in May 2001 the ECB began to cut the rates consecutively down to 3.25% which has been maintained since November 2001. The Federal Funds rate already stood higher at the beginning of 1999 (at 4.6%) and was increased progressively to a peak of 6.5% in May 2000. After staying at this level for four months from January 2001, the Fed cut the rates in several steps to 1.75% in December 2001, the lowest level since the Second World War.[38] Shortly after the terrorist attacks on the World Trade Center,

[38] *Begg/Canova/De Grauwe/Fatás/Lane* (2002) p. 45, deal with the popular allegation that the ECB cut interest rates both too little and too late when the recession became obvious in 2001. They conclude in favor of the ECB, however, that the faster reductions in interest rates in the USA in 2001 than in Europe reflected a more rapid deterioration in economic conditions (sharper drop in GDP growth) rather than any systematic difference in how the ECB and the Fed respond to new information. Therefore they find that the 2001 cuts in ECB interest rates were "business as usual".

on September 17, 2001, in a co-ordinated action the Fed and the ECB cut their interest rates by ½ percentage point. Additionally, in a transatlantic financial close co-ordination the ECB and the US Federal Reserve agreed upon on a swap arrangement on September 12, 2001 in order to facilitate the functioning of financial markets and provide liquidity in US dollars. The ECB was eligible to draw up to USD 50 billion on a swap line that expired on October 13, 2001. In exchange, the Fed of New York would receive euro deposits of an equivalent amount at the ECB.[39] All in all the September 11, 2001 increased uncertainty for policy making in addition to the general phenomenon of rising uncertainty near turning points in the business cycle.[40]

As a first observation, figure 5 gives the impression that – given the different inflation and growth performance of both regions - the ECB is following the Fed in setting their interest rate with a time lag – although the periodicity of the lag seems not to be fixed. In effect, a test for the period since January 1999 shows that the Federal Funds rate Granger-causes ECB's interest rate for MFO with a lag of four months. Looking only on the 3-months interest rates one finds that US's interest rates Granger-cause Euroland's interest rates with a lag of three months. It is therefore not implausible to consider Fed's interest rate policy in the reaction function of the ECB.

---

[39] *ECB* Monthly Bulletin (November 2001) p.17, for the detailed report on the utilization of the swap line. This example of an internationally coordinated monetary policy is a rare example where it makes sense. According to *Issing* (2001) such responses should only occur under extreme circumstances. *Begg/Canova/De Grauwe/Fatás/Lane* (2002) pp. 26-30, in a survey of policy co-ordination in the new open economy macroeconomics literature conclude, that there is no simple answer as to the benefits of policy co-ordination. E.g., increased financial integration may reduce the gains from policy co-ordination. Also the sources of co-ordination gains differ across model specifications. And, a commitment by central banks to rules-based monetary strategies can do much to improve performance relative to a discretionary regime, with the marginal gain to implementing a coordinated approach correspondingly smaller.

[40] For a discussion of theoretical and practical arguments of interest rate decisions in an uncertain environment, see *Begg/Canova/De Grauwe/Fatás/Lane* (2002) pp. 31-46.

Taylor's (1993, 2001) original feedback policy rule described monetary policy under Greenspan:[41]

(1) $$i_t = \bar{r} + \pi_t + \gamma_1(\pi_t - \pi^T) + \gamma_2(y_t - y^*)$$

where i_t is Fed's nominal interest rate in quarter t; $\bar{r}$ is the steady-state equilibrium value of the short-term real interest rate (the "natural rate"); π_t is the actual inflation rate in quarter t; π^T is the inflation target; y_t is actual output in quarter t; y^* is potential output; γ_1, γ_2 are coefficients, determining the degree of the interest rate reaction of the Fed to deviations of inflation and output from its targets. Taylor did not estimate this equation, but calibrated it. He suggested the same weights for both coefficients $(\gamma_1 = \gamma_2 = 0.5)$. He also assumed that the "natural" interest rate and the inflation rate target were both equal to 2 $(\bar{r} = \pi^T = 2)$.

As the ECB has as its primary objective maintaining price stability, the same weights for inflation and output targeting are obviously not adequate for Euroland. *Alesina et al*[42] experimented with several variations of Taylor's rule. Simply calibrating the Taylor rule would have called for a tighter policy than that actually pursued by the ECB. Similarly, a simplified Taylor rule, called π-rule, because only inflation targeting (the first term of equation (1)) is considered, would also have led to a tighter monetary policy stance – at least after the rate cut in April 1999. The continuing substantial inflation differentials within the euro area could cause conflict, if the National Central Bank (NCB) governors simply exclusively pursued their national interests and pushed for interest rate decisions that are consistent with inflation in their home country, rather than in the euro area as a whole. *Alesina et al* clearly rule out that hypothesis by calculating the hypothetical interest rates for all member states of Euroland implied by their simple π-rule. The interest rate set by the ECB at the beginning of EMU falls right in the middle of the distribution of the hypothetical national interest. Over time, however, the aggregates of hypothetical national interest rates lay above the actual ECB interest rate, with Ireland accounting for the largest deviation, followed by the Netherlands – in line with the inflation performance since 1999. The assumption of nationalist

41 See also *Schuberth* (2000) p. 24.

42 See *Alesina/Blanchard/Gali/Giavazzi/Uhlig* (2001) 27 ff.

voting would have introduced a contractionary bias in the ECB policy, which was not the case. Furthermore, the ECB appears to have pursued an interest rate policy that has been more attuned to inflation developments in three countries (France, Germany, and Austria), than to those in the euro area as a whole.[43] Finally, *Alesina et al*[44] try an ad hoc "hybrid rule", whereby the ECB responds quite aggressively (with a coefficient as high as 2) to both core inflation and the inflation forecasts (both expressed in terms of deviations from target, and receiving equal weights; assuming a steady-state real rate of 2.5%). This rule appears to track the actual pattern of interest rates in EMU much better. It takes into consideration the transitory price increase due to the oil price development and also implies a forward-looking behavior by the ECB. In 2001, however, the "hybrid rule" deviated systematically from ECB target.[45] Therefore *Begg et al*[46] try a "new rule" which weights core HICP and GDP growth with coefficients of 2.0 and 0.8 respectively, assuming that the long-run real rate is 2.0%, the core inflation target is 2.0% and target output growth is 1.2%. This "new rule" appears to do a much better job then the "hybrid rule" at least in 2001.

In the following the Taylor rule for ECB's behavior since 1999 is not calibrated but econometrically estimated. The time of experience may be too short, to derive already sound conclusions on ECB's policy making. The ECB is of course still in stage of experiencing. Future analyses may therefore come to different conclusions than those presented here for the first three years of EMU. Two kinds of reaction functions are offered. The first is a dynamic form of the traditional Taylor rule as defined in equation (1) but with a dynamic specification, taking into account the lagged dependent interest rate variable[47]:

(2) $$i_t^{ECB} = \alpha + \gamma_1\left(\pi_t - \pi^T\right) + \gamma_2\left(y_t - y^*\right) + \rho i_{t-1}^{ECB}.$$

---

43 See *Alesina/Blanchard/Gali/Giavazzi/Uhlig* (2001) pp. 30-31.

44 See *Alesina/Blanchard/Gali/Giavazzi/Uhlig* (2001) p. 34.

45 See *Begg/Canova/De Grauwe/Fatás/Lane* (2002) p. 44.

46 See *Begg/Canova/De Grauwe/Fatás/Lane* (2002) p. 44.

47 *Goodhart* (1999) successfully estimated Taylor Rules with lagged interest rates for the Bank of England (1992-1998). A significant coefficient on lagged interest rates (as in our estimates in table 2) – in particular in times of high uncertainty as in 2001 - indicates a cost of adjusting interest rates. When shocks occur, the short-run response of interest rates is less than the long-run response.

We use the GMM estimation procedure yielding (asymptotically) correct standard errors with instruments – primarily the lagged values of inflation and output gap (see table 2 for details). In this equation – which will be called the "baseline reaction function" – we define the constant term $\alpha = \bar{r} + \pi_t$ and introduce the lagged dependent variable. i_t^{ECB} is the monthly interest rate of the ECB for main refinancing operations (MFO). π_t is the monthly rate of HICP inflation. π^T is set at 2%, the official inflation rate target of the ECB. y_t is the monthly index of industrial production seasonally adjusted. y^* is the Hodrick/Prescott trend of y_t. The first cut of interest rates by the ECB in April 1999 by 500 basis points is not easily explained economically. It might have been rather a politically motivated decision following the demands by the former German minister of finance with some time lag. Therefore we introduce a dummy variable to catch that decision. Several attempts to estimate the parameters for the inflation gap in a forward looking approach as *Clarida/Gali/Gertler* (1998) did for the G3 (Germany, Japan, and the US) and the E3 (UK, France, and Italy) for the period 1979-1993 by substituting the inflation gap by an expression like $\gamma_1(E[\pi_{t+n}/\Omega_t] - \pi^T)$ were not successful.[48] n would be the horizon of the inflation forecast that is considered by the ECB. *Clarida et al*[49] used one year, so that with monthly data, $n = 12$. This procedure would be too short for the first phase of EMU. E is the expectation operator and Ω_t is the information available to the ECB at the time it sets interest rates.

The estimated constant (long-run value 4.02) of equation (2) represents the steady-state value of the real short-term interest rate plus the inflation rate $(\bar{r} + \pi_t)$. The long-run coefficients (see table 2) reflect the main preferences of the ECB pretty well: price stability is given much more weight (0.80) than deviations from potential output (0.25).

An alternative estimation of the Taylor rule explaining the interest rate setting of the ECB – here preferred – additionally introduces as explaining variable the lagged Federal Funds rate.

(3) $$i_t^{ECB} = \alpha + \gamma_1\left(\pi_t - \pi^T\right) + \gamma_2\left(y_t - y^*\right) + \gamma_3 i_{t-4}^{Fed} + \rho i_{t-1}^{ECB}.$$

48 See also *Clarida* (2001).

49 *Clarida/Gali/Gertler* (1998) p. 1042.

The specification and instrumentation are equivalent to that in equation (2). Based on the Granger causality tests we introduce the Federal Funds rate with a lag of four months.[50] This reaction function – we call it "alternative reaction function" - fits better the actual interest rate development in EMU (see table 2 for the estimated coefficients). Again the long-run coefficients indicate the preference pattern of the ECB (more weight to inflation targeting than to output targeting). But now the ECB seems to follow the policy steps by the Fed. Such a behavior of young institutions like the ECB is plausible because it has to be cautious in building up credibility and competence.

A comparison of the "baseline" with the "alternative" reaction function (see figure 6) shows that the "alternative" Taylor rule better explains the turning point of ECB's interest rate policy in Spring 2001 than the "baseline" Taylor rule. The latter would have exhibited a kind of "overshooting" whereas the former explains quite well the actual development of the MFO.

---

[50] In this context one could consider the interaction of the ECB and the Fed as a two-country monetary policy game where the reaction functions of both countries (central banks) depend on each other's reaction; see *McKibbin/Sachs* (1991) p. 160. In a symmetric case (when both, the USA and Euroland are assumed to be of equal size) a cooperative policy stance would lead to a better overall outcome than a noncooperative (Nash-Cournot) policy stance: output would be higher, interest rates would be lower. In a noncooperative equilibrium, each country perceives that it can be made marginally better off by appreciating its currency and exporting inflation to the foreign country. Because both countries pursue this strategy in the symmetric case, the exchange rate does not change, but policies are overcontractionary. Considering the estimated adjusted Taylor reaction function of equation (3) and assuming that the Fed sets interest rates according to the original Taylor rule without taking the ECB action into account, one could rather think of a monetary policy game à la Stackelberg rather than of a Nash-Cournot game, seeing the Fed as the leader and the ECB the follower in monetary policy actions.

Table 2: ECB reaction functions (Taylor rules)

Dependent variable: i_t^{ECB}	α	γ_1	γ_2	γ_3	ρ	Dummy variable 4M1999	R^2-adj DW
Headline inflation:							
Baseline:	0.86	0.17	0.05	-	0.79	-0.43	0.956
Eq.(2)	*(10.72)*	*(3.99)*	*(8.20)*		*(35.67)*	*(3.56)*	2.11
Long-run coefficients	4.02	0.80	0.25	-	-	-	
With Fed FR:	0.34	0.12	0.04	0.16	0.69	-0.53	0.963
Eq. (3)	*(3.39)*	*(3.88)*	*(3.51)*	*(8.01)*	*(38.90)*	*(4.70)*	2.28
Long-run coefficients	1.08	0.39	0.12	0.50	-	-	
Core inflation:							
Baseline:	0.17	0.05	0.02	-	0.96	-0.50	0.941
Eq. (2')	*(1.24)*	*(1.25)*	*(1.56)*		*(32.57)*	*(10.35)*	1.77
Long-run coefficients	4.75	1.39	0.56	-	-	-	
With Fed FR:	0.43	0.65	0.08	0.27	0.59	-0.44	0.945
Eq. (3')	*(1.63)*	*(6.26)*	*(3.77)*	*(9.13)*	*(10.46)*	*(3.63)*	1.50
Long-run coefficients	1.06	1.60	0.20	0.67	-	-	

Estimation method: GMM – Generalized Method of Moments. The dependent variable is ECB's interest rate for main refinancing operations (MFO); Fed FR is the US federal funds rate. t-values are in parenthesis below the estimated coefficients. Monthly data; the sample is 1999:01 – 2001:12. The instruments are: $p_{t-1},.....,p_{t-4}$, $wp_{t-1},.....,wp_{t-1}$, $y_{t-1},.....,y_{t-4}$, $b_{t-1},.....,b_{t-3}$, where p is the inflation gap as the deviation of actual inflation rate from target for the HICP (headline in Eq. (2) and (3)) and for core inflation in Eq. (2') and Eq. (3')), wp is the annual inflation rate of world commodity prices in USD (HWWA index), y is the output gap measured as the deviation of actual from trend (HP method) and b is business tendency survey for manufacturing in Euroland (OECD data).

The major argument put forward here is that the ECB could have contributed to a better overall economic outcome in the last two years if it – instead of sticking to the total (headline) inflation rate, measured by the HICP – would have reacted to the "core" inflation rate in Euroland. First we will demonstrate that the Taylor rule based on the core inflation rate would have resulted in a one percentage point lower interest rate level. Second we simulate the macroeconomic effects of such a less restrictive monetary policy in chapter 4.

If one re-estimates the Taylor rules of equations (2) and (3) by substituting the "core" HICP inflation rate for π_t , one gets the following results (see table 2). The same estimation method (GMM with the same instrument structure – but now with lagged core inflation rates) and the same specification is applied and the equations with core inflation are called (2') and (3') respectively. The estimated parameters for equation (3') – the "alternative Taylor rule approach" - considering the Fed FR gives a better overall result. However using Fed's FR indicates the strong dependency from the US policy making (long-run coefficient 0.67). The correct way to estimate the potential interest rate when targeting (autonomously) the inflation rate gap is the "baseline Taylor rule approach" of equation (2'). The results show that the estimated coefficients for the inflation and the output gap are of low statistical significance. Estimating the interest rate path with the parameters of equation (3') show a much lower interest rate level for MFO (see figure 6). On average, the ECB's interest rate would have been lower by around one percentage point from the second quarter 2000 to the third quarter 2001.[51] At the end, however, the Taylor rule with core inflation would have resulted in a somewhat higher interest rate level as the actual ones.

---

[51] For a similar evaluation with a Taylor rule, taking "core inflation" as the relevant inflation rate for the normative rule, see the European Commission, *EU* (2001a) pp. 56-57, although the Taylor rule used there is not made explicit.

Figure 6: ECB interest rate policy and Taylor rules
(ECB interest rate for MFO)

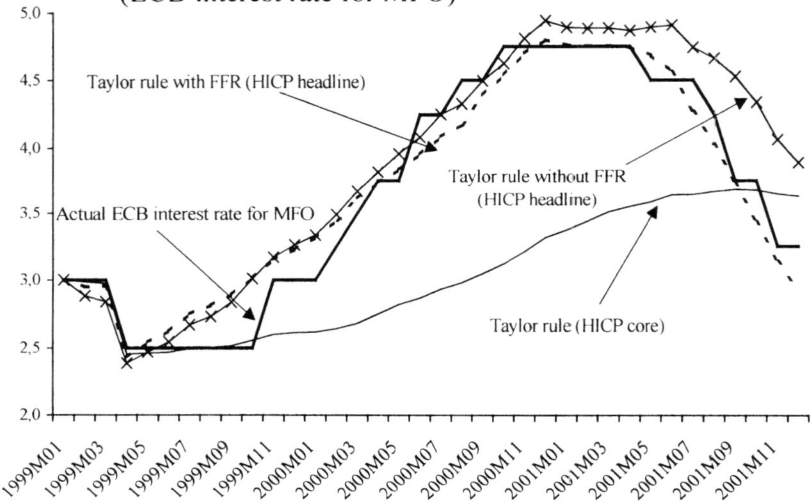

Source: Own calculations based on data from the ECB.

III. The economic impact of the first external shock in EMU

World oil prices started to increase when EMU started into its third stage in the first quarter 1999 at a level of 11.1 US-dollar per barrel (Brent crude spot oil). The oil price peaked in the third quarter 2000 at a level of 30.3 $/barrel. Since then it has declined gradually, exhibiting a very short-lived jump after September 11, 2001 and declined afterwards when the economic outcome in the industrial world became more and more gloomy. As a consequence of the conflict of Israel with the Palestinians in Spring 2002 the oil price started to climb again. As was demonstrated already (see figure 3) the oil price hike since 1999 together with the depreciation of the euro translated into an additional increase of headline HICP inflation in the euro area since mid-1999 of around one half of a percentage point and during 2000, until autumn 2001 of more than one percentage point.

With the oil price hike of 1999-2001 – a classical temporary supply shock - Euroland experienced the first baptism of fire. What was the macroeconomic outcome inside Euroland and outside of it? In order to estimate this one has to make an assumption as to a "normal" development of oil prices in this period. We assume a smoothing path between the second quarter of 1999 up to the third quarter of 2001. The effect of the oil price increase from this "normal" path of 12% in 1999Q2, 30% from 1999Q3 to 2000Q4, 18% from 2001Q1 to 2001Q2 and 10% in 2001Q3 was simulated (see figure 3).

Box 1: NiGEM – A world macro model

The simulations were carried out by the NiGEM world macro model of the National Institute of Economic and Social Research.[52] The model consists of the standard demand- and supply-side specifications with spill-overs via foreign trade. The model covers – among all industrial and many developing countries - all EU countries (except Luxembourg). So, one can differentiate between the 11 euro area countries and the three pre-ins (Denmark, Sweden and the United Kingdom). The simulations were done here with the rational forward-looking option for long rates, wages, exchange rates, equity prices and inflation. When the exchange rate is forward-looking its current value is determined by the current interest rate differential and on temporaneous expectations of the exchange rate next period. As policy options the European aggregation is chosen, that means European exchange rates for the Euroland members are fixed against each other and movements of interest rates are the same for the Euroland countries. Interest rates and exchange rates are then determined according to "European targeting", where monetary policy is determined by Euroland economic conditions (an alternative would be "German targeting" – a reminder of the EMS system). This option proxies EMU where the ECB decides monetary policy but allocates weights to economic conditions in all the countries included in the Euroland aggregation. There are several interest rate options: a) Nominal GDP and inflation targeting; this proxies best the "two pillar" strategy of the ECB and is used in the following simulations; b) Inflation targeting only looks at deviations from inflation target; c) Taylor rule.[53]

Given the chosen assumptions of the oil price hike of around 30% in the period 1999 to 2001 the model simulations executed with the NiGEM world macro model (for a model description, see

[52] NIESR, London; see *Barrell/Dury/Holland* (2001).

[53] Source: http://www.niesr.ac.uk/models/nigem/nigem.htm

box) resulted in the following macroeconomic impact for the Euro area as a whole (see figure 7).[54]

Real GDP in Euroland decreased by 0.4 percentage points until the end of 2001 and leveled off thereafter. HICP inflation increased by 0.8 percentage points. The oil price shock also contributed to a depreciation of the euro against the USD by 0.3%. The Euro area's current account deteriorated by 0.8 percentage points of GDP due to the negative terms-of trade effects of the shock. Also the budget policy was negatively affected by around 0.4% of GDP. Short-term interest rates, the unemployment rate and the debt to GDP ratio increased. Overall, the oil price shock hit the economy of Euroland adversely.[55]

---

[54] *Hunt/Isard/Laxton* (2002) simulate the macroeconomic effect of hypothetical 50 per cent oil price shock over the period 2000-2010 with IMF' MULTIMOD. They distinguish between a temporary (50 per cent oil price increase in the first year), a persistent shock (first two years) and a permanent shock over the whole period. Instead of Taylor rules, they use monetary policy reaction functions with forward-looking inflation-forecast-based (IFB) rules. Additionally, they study the effects/costs of the optimal reaction of monetary policy to oil price increases by considering the difficult pass-through of oil prices into core and headline inflation. The pass-through of oil prices into core inflation depends heavily on the kind of shocks (temporary versus permanent). A Delayed monetary policy reactions – because of the uncertainties about the effects of oil-price increases on core inflation - might affect the process of inflation expectations. The assumed forward-looking monetary policy reaction function of MULTIMOD implies that adjustments to changes in the output gap and the inflation forecasts occur with no delay. Delaying the policy reaction – that is, holding the short-term nominal interest rate constant and allowing inflation expectations to rise – has expansionary effects on GDP in the short run but leads to a much sharper interest-rate response by the third year, with subsequent contractionary effects on GDP.

[55] In its standard shock analysis with the INTERLINK model the OECD (see *Dalsgaard/André/Richardson* (2001)) finds that a 50% oil price increase (corresponding to a $12 ½ rise if the oil price is $25 per barrel) results in a decline of real GDP in the euro area of 0.4% in the first and 0.2% in the second year after the shock. Inflation goes up by 0.6% in the first and 0.2% in the second year. Similar, but somewhat lower effects are found for the USA and for Japan. In a comparable exercise the European Commission *EU* (2001a) p. 28, simulating a $12 increase in oil prices with their QUEST world macro model, real GDP in the

The aggregate impact of the first external shock to Euroland is one aspect, but the oil price shock affected differently real GDP of the Member States of the euro area (see figure A1) and those of the pre-ins area of the EU (see figure A2).

In the euro area (see figure A1) the biggest negative GDP impact is found four Ireland, Spain and Austria (all exhibiting a decline of GDP of 0.8 percentage points until the end of 2001), followed by France and Italy (-0.6 percentage points). Portugal, Finland, Belgium, the Netherlands and Germany were hit the least by the shock (between –0.1 and –0.2 percentage points). Nevertheless, the oil price shock increased the dispersion of the Euroland business cycle or stopped its convergence (see table 1). The pre-ins (see figure A2) - at least those countries – which more or less appreciated their currencies against the euro (the United Kingdom and Sweden) could isolate their economies from the negative impact of the oil price shock. The others, which either fixed their exchange rate to the euro (like Denmark) or participated in the ERM-II (like Greece in 1999 and 2000, before entering EMU in 2001) exhibited a negative output effect of the oil price shock (Greece, however, improved after the short-term negative impact).

---

euro area would decrease by 0.2 in the first year, by 0.4 in the second year and by 0.2 percentage points in the third year after the shock; inflation would increase by 0.7 in the first, by 0.4 in the second and by 0.2 percentage points in the third year.

Figure 7: Euro area: Macro-economic effects of a world oil price shock (30% increase 1999Q2-2001Q3)

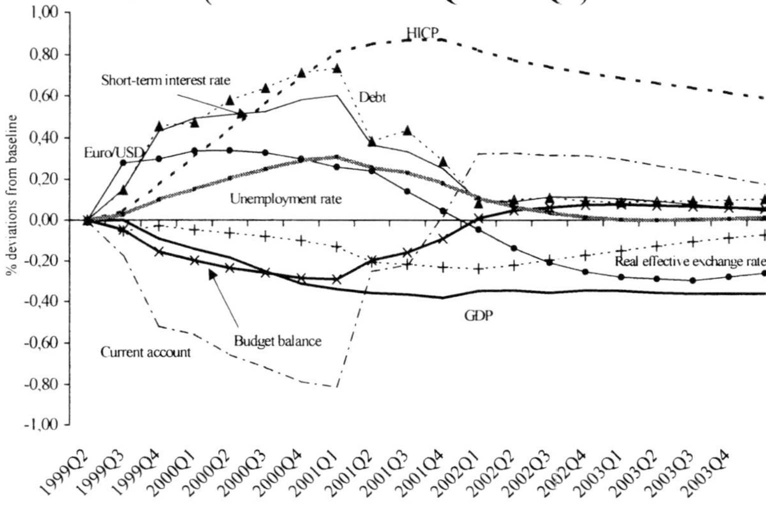

Source: Own calculations with the NiGEM world macro model.

Similarly to the output impact, the oil price shock increased dispersion of the inflation performance in Euroland. With the exception of Ireland, it worked against the dispersion which one would have expected from the Balassa/Samelson effect. This external shock brought the amazing divergence process of price inflation in Euroland to a stop in 2000. The oil price shock increased HICP inflation rates by 1.8% in Ireland, by over 1% in France and Italy and below 1% in the other euro area countries. The lowest inflation effect was felt in Portugal and Spain (below the average Euroland effect; see figure A3). Out of the pre-ins countries (see figure A4), Denmark (+1.2 percentage points) exhibited an inflation shock above Euroland average, the United Kingdom inflation increase of 0.8 percentage points coincided with Euroland average, those of Sweden and Greece was below average, although Greece's inflation performance deteriorated after fixing its exchange rate when entering the EMU in 2001.

IV. A better outcome by an alternative monetary policy reaction?

What are the conclusions after the first external shock to Euroland for monetary policy? First, one could be satisfied with the actual policy reaction by the ECB. Second – and this position is preferred here – one could look for ways to optimize monetary policy. In order to mitigate the oil price shock, monetary policy could have reacted not only to total ("headline") HICP inflation but to "core" inflation. This would also be consistent with the second pillar of the "two pillar" strategy, namely a broad analysis of all price developments. By sticking only to headline inflation – because its rate already overshot the self-declared target of 2% (see figure 3) – monetary policy was too tight during the past two years. As the 2000/01 oil price shock was a classical temporary supply shock, also theory would have suggested for targeting core inflation.[56]

How should the monetary policy stance be evaluated? In practice this is often done by many NCBs (for an overview of the different approaches and problems associated, see *Gerlach/Smets* (2000)) as well as by private banks with the so-called Monetary Conditions Index (MCI). The MCI combines the transmission of two channels of monetary policy: the interest rate and the exchange rate channel. The MCI represents the relative size of the interest rate and exchange rate impacts in a country on either output (real GDP) and inflation. A ratio of X to 1 implies that a change in the exchange rate by X percent has the equivalent impact to a 100 basis point change in the interest rate. Thus the larger the ratio the weaker is the relative impact of the exchange rate. Generally, large and relatively closed economies such as the USA or Japan are thought to have ratios of around 10 to 1 and very open (small) economies around 2 or 3 to 1.[57] The MCI is defined as

---

56 See *Begg/Canova/De Grauwe/Fatás/Lane* (2002) p. 17. According to them a permanent supply shock (e.g. a rise in oil price) shifts the short-run supply curve to the left and reduces full-capacity (potential) output. As output exceeds its new long-run level, inflation increases. The correct response is to increase interest rates in order to reduce aggregate demand. In case of a temporary supply shock (as the 2000/01 oil price shock), however, full-capacity output remains unaffected. The shift of the short-run supply curve brings output below capacity and hence is no risk for inflation. The correct response of the central bank is not to react. Such a policy rule can be implemented by formulating the targeting strategy in terms of "core inflation", which ignores the effects of temporary supply shocks on inflation.

57 See *Mayes/Virén* (2000) p. 201.

(4) $$MCI_t = \sum_s w_s \left(P_{st} - P_{s0}\right),$$

where the P_s are variables related to monetary policy actions $(1,....,s)$ A_j (j indicating the actions available: interest rates in levels, exchange rates in log form) thought to affect demand (real GDP, Y) or inflation (π). Thus there will be relationships of the form

(5) $$Y = f(P_{1,...,s}, X), \qquad \text{or}$$
$$\pi = g\left(P_{1,...,s}, X\right),$$

X representing all the other variables in the model that also have an impact on demand (real GDP, or inflation). The weights w_s will be computed from the partial derivatives of the appropriate elements in f (or g) including due allowance for the dynamic structure. An MCI is thus conditional on a particular model of the economy. Normally, MCIs are computed on the basis of the effects on real GDP.

Mayes/Virén (2000) suggest that the MCI for the euro area will be only 3.5 (compared to 10 for the USA and 6.0 used by the European Commission in its Autumn 2001 Forecast; see *EU* (2001b) p. 6). My calculations with the NiGEM world macro model confirm the value derived by *Mayes/Virén* (2000) of around 3.0. The European Commission in its Autumn 2001 forecasts for 2001 to 2003[58] evaluates the monetary conditions for the euro area. By combining real interest rates (approximated by the difference between the 3-month rate and core inflation) and real exchange rates (based on unit labor costs in manufacturing), the Commission derives the monetary conditions index (MCI) as a synthetic measure of the change in monetary conditions vis-à-vis a reference period. The loosening in monetary conditions in the euro area since January 1999 were mainly due to the real depreciation of the euro, which only slightly reverted in the first three quarters of 2001. In contrast, since mid-1999 real interest rates increased and only since the end of 2000 have they decreased. At the end of 2001 the real interest rates have returned to their starting level due to gradually increasing core inflation, and the recent cuts in policy rates. As a result mone-

---

[58] See *EU* (2001b) p. 6.

tary conditions remain – according to the European Commission - conductive to growth.

The gradual increase of the MCI, indicating a continuous loosening of ECB's monetary policy stance since 1999, does not preclude that it could not have been improved by a more adequate policy reaction after the oil price shock. The ECB – although it can (and did) intervene in foreign exchange markets – use only one "instrument" for monetary policy, namely the ability to exert substantial control over short-term interest rates. The ECB therefore cannot exert any lasting control over the mix of monetary conditions between interest rates and the exchange rate. As the European Commission confirms, the easing of monetary conditions, measured by the MCI came from the euro depreciation.[59]

What would have been the macroeconomic outcome of a monetary policy of the ECB, oriented to the core inflation? Instead of raising interest rates a decrease – as derived in subchapter C - would have been adequate. In order to simulate the effects of a looser monetary policy the impact of a one percentage point cut in the short-term interest rate of the euro area in the period 2000Q2 to 2001Q3 is simulated with the NiGEM world macro-model.

---

59 My simulations of a sustained 10% depreciation of the Euro vis à vis the US-Dollar with the NiGEM world macro model indicate the following result: real GDP increased by 1% in the first, by 1.2% in the second, by 1% in the third and by 0.9% in the fourth year. Inflation increased by 0.4% in the first, by 1.1% in the second, by 1.9% in the third and by 2.5% in the fourth year. Behind the sustained 10% depreciation of the euro the real effective exchange rate of the euro depreciates by 4.2% in the first, by 3% in the second, by 2.1% in the third and by 1.3% in the fourth year.

Figure 8: Euro area: Macro-economic effects of an interest rate cut (1% decrease of short-term interest rates in the euro area 2000Q2-2001Q3)

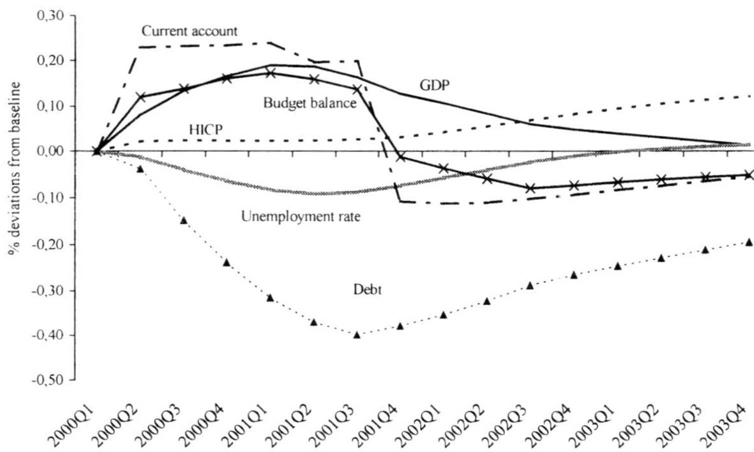

Source: Own calculations with the NiGEM world macro model.

In the euro area as a whole a looser monetary policy (a 1% cut of short-term interest rates over seven quarters) would have resulted in a slight increase of real GDP (+0.2 percentage points),[60] a decline in the unemployment rate (of around 0.1 percentage points) and the debt to GDP ratio (by 0.4% of GDP), an improvement in the current

60 *Dalsgaard/André/Richardson* (2001) find with the OECD INTERLINK model that a sustained drop in short term and long term interest rates of 1 percentage point with fixed exchange rates leads to an increase in real GDP in the euro area of 0.4 percentage points in the first year and increasing to 0.6 percentage points in the second year and staying at that level thereafter. The transmission effects of interest rate cuts on the real economy and the price system, simulated with the NiGEM model are the higher, the longer lasting such cuts are. This is due to the forward-looking behavior of agents assumed in the model. If, e.g. the short term interest rates are cut not only over one year, but sustained over a period of seven years, real GDP increases by 0.8% in the first, by 1.3% in the second, by 1.4% in the third and by 1.3% in the fourth year. HICP inflation increases by 0.2% in the first, by 0.4% in the second, by 0.7% in the third and by 1.2% in the fourth year. By contrast *Mihov* (2000) p. 383, finds output responses to a 1% interest rate cut over the same period of only half of that size with a simple VAR model.

account (by 0.2% of GDP) and in the fiscal balance (below 0.2% of GDP) and interestingly without much increase of inflation – below 0.1 percentage points till 2002 and thereafter up to 0.1 percentage points compared to base line (see figure 8). The interest rate cut of one percentage point would have led to an immediate depreciation of the euro against the dollar by the same amount leading to a real effective depreciation of the euro of 0.7%, but declining shortly thereafter. The peak of the transmission of the expansionary monetary policy to the real economy (GDP) is reached after 5 quarters, those of inflation peaks after 16 quarters after starting with the monetary shock. This is in line with other simulations of the transmission of monetary policy in the literature (see e.g. *Mihov* (2001) with a VAR model approach).[61]

Again the interesting aspect of this exercise is the different impact in the Euroland member states. As the economies of Euroland are far from being equal and fully synchronized as far as the business cycle of real GDP is concerned (see table 1), the transmission of monetary policy to output (and other macro variables) must be different. As figure A5 shows, a more expansionary monetary policy over the last two years would have resulted in higher GDP stimulation in Germany and Austria than in Portugal or Belgium. The real GDP effects spreads from ¼ percentage points to only 0.1 percentage points. Additionally, the speed of adjustment differs between the Euroland Member States. Although the overall impact of a one percentage point increase of short-term interest rates is

[61] For an overview of the main determinants of the transmission of monetary policy to output and the different transmission channels (interest rates, exchange rates, credit and bank lending, balance-sheet), see EU (2001a) p. 58. The numerous attempts to estimate the extent of possible asymmetries in output and price responses to the single monetary policy across Euroland countries (via empirical macroeconomic models) have not provided a consistent and robust picture of cross-country differences in monetary transmission and they are affected by methodological problems (Lucas problem). This state of affairs has revamped interest in microeconomic studies comparing economic and financial structures across countries, as they are ultimately responsible for any differences in the way monetary impulses are transmitted throughout the economy; see *EU* (2001a) pp. 57-59; *Clements/Kontolemis/Levy* (2001) and *Suardi* (2001); *Angeloni/ Kashyap/Mojon/Terlizzese* (2001) for an overview of the present status of research for Euroland.

very modest, it nevertheless would have resulted in a mitigation of the downturn of the business cycle in the euro area. However, the experiment also indicates that each monetary shock leads to a general disturbance of the process of the synchronization of the European business cycle,[62] often claimed as being necessary to fulfill the OCA (optimum currency area) criteria.[63]

In the pre-ins area of the EU, only the United Kingdom exhibited slight negative spill-overs from the interest rate cut in Euroland, a result consistent with the classical two-country Mundell-Fleming model with flexible exchange rates. The other pre-ins (Denmark, Greece and Sweden) hat effects comparable with those of Euroland average (see figure A6).

The inflation effects of the temporary interest rate cut are generally very modest. Only Ireland (see figure A7) stands out at the beginning. But even in the medium run the inflation increasing

---

62 Many attempts to find a "common European business cycle" have failed so far; see a recent exercise by *Breitung/Candelon* (2001). Accordingly, the common cycle hypothesis is clearly rejected for U.K. (industrial production) data whereas some weak evidence for a joint cyclical pattern is found for France, the Netherlands, Austria and Germany. *Artis/Zhang* (1999) show that the business cycle affiliation of the Exchange Rate Mechanism (ERM) member countries has shifted from the United States to Germany since the formation of the ERM. In the same period, however, the United Kingdom's business cycle affiliation did not change. In contrast, *Inklaar/de Haan* (2001) in an empirical study covering the years 1960-1997 find no relationship between exchange rate stability (e.g. EMS period) and business cycle synchronization.

63 *Mihov* (2001) p. 385, demonstrated that neither a complete symmetric transmission mechanism of monetary policy nor a complete synchronization of the business cycle is a necessary condition for the functioning of a currency union. The diversity across five EMU countries he analyzed is not uniformly larger than across US regions. In fact, the USA is more diverse than the five EMU countries. May be that not ex ante OCA criteria (the intensity of trade with other members; the correlation of domestic business cycles with other members) have to be fulfilled when entering a monetary union, but that it is enough to fulfill them ex post. *Frankel/Rose* (1998) favor this position. As international trade patterns and international business cycle correlations are endogenous, they conclude that countries with closer trade links trend to have more tightly correlated business cycles. Hence, they derive the "endogeneity of the OCA criteria".

effect is not higher than 0.15 percentage points. The dispersion of the inflation effects is weaker than those of real output effects. With the exception of the United Kingdom (where it is slightly negative) the inflation effects are similar in the pre-ins countries (see figure A8).

V. Conclusions

Overall, the ECB managed monetary policy quite satisfactorily in the first phase of EMU. However, one may ask whether monetary policy really was optimal. The estimated Taylor reaction function indicates that monetary policy was rather backward than forward-looking. On the one hand it reacted with a lag to the actions of US's Fed. On the other hand it was overly cautious as it was targeting total HICP inflation. In this paper it is argued and also demonstrated with model simulations that a monetary policy that targets inflation measured by total HICP was not optimal given the fact that Euroland was confronted with the first external (oil price) shock. The oil price shock led to an increase in headline inflation of over one percentage point in 2000/2001. By setting interest rates according to the underlying or "core" inflation the monetary policy stance could have been looser without risking additional inflation. The latter is demonstrated in simulation experiments with a world macro model. For the future the ECB could – without giving up the "two pillar" strategy – orient its policy reaction more to "core" than to total inflation. Of course one could argue that it is difficult to orient monetary policy forward-looking as most of the price forecasts – in particular those for commodity prices (and therefore also those for crude oil) – are chronically false. In fact, the OECD as well as the European Commission in their 1999 December forecasts underestimated the oil price development for the year 2000 by 25% to 30% and those for the year 2001 by around 10%. In 2000, they gradually adjusted their forecast to the correct values!

References

Alesina A. / Blanchard O. / Gali J. / Giavazzi F. / Uhlig H. (2001), Defining a Macroeconomic Framework for the Euro Area: Monitoring the European Central Bank 3 (MECB3), Center for Economic Policy Research (CEPR), London, 2001.

Angeloni I. / Kashyap A. / Mojon B. / Terlizzese D. (2001), Monetary Transmission in the Euro Area: Where Do We Stand?, Paper prepared for the conference: "Monetary Policy Transmission in the Euro Area", European Central Bank, pp. 18-19, December 2001.

Artis M. J. / Zhang W. (1999), "Further Evidence on the International Business Cycle and the ERM: Is There a European Business Cycle?", in: Oxford Economic Papers, Vol. 51, No. 1, January 1999, pp. 120-132.

Barrell R. / Dury K. / Holland D. (2001), Macro-Models and the Medium Term. The NIESR experience with NiGEM, National Institute of Economic and Social Research, London (unpublished paper), June 2001.

Begg D. / Canova F. / De Grauwe P. / Fatás A. / Lane P.R. (2002), Surviving the Slowdown: Monitoring the European Central Bank 4 (MECB4), Center for Economic Policy Research (CEPR), London, 2002.

Beetsma R. / Debrun X. / Klaassen F. (2001), Is Fiscal Policy Coordination in EMU Desirable?, in: CEPR Discussion Paper Series, No. 3035, London, October 2001.

Benigno P. (2001), Optimal Monetary Policy in a Currency Area, in: CEPR Discussion Paper Series, No. 2755, London, April 2001.

Breitung J. / Candelon B. (2001), "Is There a Common European Business Cycle? New Insights from a Frequency Domain Analysis", Deutsches Institut für Wirtschaftsforschung (DIW), in: Vierteljahreshefte zur Wirtschaftsforschung ("Business Cycle Research in the European Economic and Monetary Union"), Heft 3/70, 2001, pp. 331-338.

Breuss F. (2000a), "Flexibility, fiscal policy and stability and growth pact", in: *Fourth ECSA-World Conference* – The European Union and the EURO: economic, institutional and international aspects, European Commission, Luxembourg 2000, pp. 98-126.

Breuss F. (2000b), "Die Wirtschafts- und Währungsunion und ihre Folgen", in: *Breuss F. / Fink G. / Griller St.* (eds.), Vom Schuman-Plan zum Vertrag von Amsterdam: Entstehung und Zukunft der EU, Springer-Verlag, Wien/New York, 2000, pp. 273-309.

Breuss F. / Weber A. (2001), "Economic Policy Coordination in the EMU: Implications for the Stability and Growth Pact", in: *Hughes-Hallet A. / Mooslechner P. / Martin Sch.* (eds.), Challenges for Economic Policy Coordination within European Monetary Union, Kluwer Academic Publishers, Boston/Dordrecht/London, 2001, pp. 143-167.

Brunila A. / Buti M. / Franco D. (eds.) (2001), The Stability and Growth Pact. The architecture of fiscal policy in EMU, Palgrave, Basingstoke, 2001.

Canzoneri Matthew B. / Cumby Robert E. / Diba Behzad T. (2001), "Fiscal discipline and exchange rate systems", in: The Economic Journal, Vol. 111, No. 474, October 2001, pp. 667-690.

Clarida R. (2001), "The Empirics of Monetary Policy Rules in Open Economies", in: International Journal of Finance and Economics 6(4), October 2001, pp. 315-323.

Clarida R. / Gali J. / Gertler M. (1998), "Monetary policy rules in practice. Some international evidence", in: European Economic Review Vol. 42, No. 6, June 1998, pp. 1033-1067.

Clarida R. / Gali J. / Gertler M. (2001), "Optimal Monetary Policy in Open versus Closed Economies: An Integrated Approach", in: The American Economic Review 91(2), May 2001, pp. 248-252.

Clements Benedict J. / Kontolemis Zenon G. / Levy J. (2001), Monetary Policy Under EMU: Differences in the Transmission Mechanism?", in: IMF Working Paper No. 102, Washington 2001.

Cristadoro R. / Forni M. / Reichlin L. / Veronese G. (2001), A Core Inflation Index for the Euro Area", in: CEPR Discussion Paper Series, No. 3097, London, December 2001.

Dalsgaard Th. / André Ch. / Richardson P. (2001), Standard Shocks in the OECD INTERLINK Model, in: OECD Economics Department Working Paper No. 306, September 6, 2001.

De Grauwe P. / Piskorski T. (2001), Union-Wide Aggregates versus National Data Based Monetary Policies: Does it Matter for the Eurosystem?, in: CEPR Discussion Paper Series No. 3036, London, November 2001.

Goodhart C. (1999), "Central Banks and Uncertainty", Bank of England Quarterly Bulletin, February 1999.

ECB (1999a), "The stability-oriented monetary policy strategy of the Eurosystem", in: ECB Monthly Bulletin, January 1999, pp. 39-50.

ECB (1999b), "Eura area monetary aggregates and their role in the Eurosystem's monetary policy strategy", in: ECB Monthly Bulletin, February 1999, pp. 29-46.

ECB (2001a), "Measures of underlying inflation in the euro area", in: ECB Monthly Bulletin, July 2001, pp. 49-59.

ECB (2001b), "The economic policy framework in EMU", in: ECB Monthly Bulletin, November 2001, pp. 51-65. *Eijffinger Sylvester C.W. / de Haan J.* (2001), European monetary and fiscal policy, Oxford University Press, Oxford 2001.

EU (2001a), The EU Economy 2001 Review, in: European Economy No. 73, Brussels 2001.

EU (2001b), Autumn 2001 Forecasts for 2001-2003, European Economy, Supplement A, in: Economic Trends No. 10/11 – October/November, Brussels 2001.

EU (2001c), Price levels and price dispersion in the EU, European Economy, Supplement A, in: Economic Trends No. 7 – July, Brussels 2001.

Frankel J. /Andrew Rose K. (1998), "The Endogeneity of the Optimum Currency Area Criteria", in: The Economic Journal Vol. 108, No. 449, July 1998, pp. 1009-1025.

Gerlach St. / Smets F. (2000), "MCI's and Monetary Policy", in: European Economic Review Vol. 44, No. 9, October 2000, pp. 1677-1700.

Hunt B. / Isard P. / Douglas L. (2002), "The Macroeconomic Effects of Higher Oil Prices", in: National Institute Economic Review No. 179, NIESR, London, January 2002/1, pp. 87-103.

Inklaar R. / de Haan J. (2001), "Is there really a European business cylce? A comment", in: Oxford Economic Papers 53, pp. 215-220.

Issing O. (2001), "The Challenge for Monetary Policy: a European Perspective", www.ecb.int visited April 2002 (key speeches).

Issing O. / Gaspar V. / Angeloni I. / Tristani O. (2001), Monetary policy in the Euro area: strategy and decision-making at the European Central Bank, Cambridge University Press, Cambridge, 2001.

Mayes D. / Virén M. (2000), "The exchange rate and monetary conditions in the Euro Area", in: Weltwirtschaftliches Archiv/ Review of World Economics, Heft 2, Band 136, June 2000, pp. 199-231.

McKibbin Warwick J. / Sachs J. D. (1991), Global Linkages: Macroeconomic Interdependence and Cooperation in the World Economy, The Brookings Institution, Washington, D.C., 1991.

Mihov I. (2001), "Monetary policy implementation and transmission in the European Monetary Union", in: Economic Policy No. 33, October 2001, pp. 369-406.

Reutter M. / Sinn H.-W. (2000), The Minimum Inflation Rate for Euroland, in: CESifo Working Paper Series No. 377, Munich, December 2000.

Schuberth H. (2000), Monetary Policy Rules in Europe: Which Rule for the Eurosystem?, Dissertation at the Vienna University of Economics and Business Administration, April 2000, 24 ff.

Suardi M. (2001), "EMU and asymmetries in the monetary policy transmission", EC DG ECFIN, in: Economic Papers No. 157, Brussels, July 2001.

Svensson Lars E.O. (2000), "The First Year of the Eurosystem: Inflation Targeting or Not?", in: American Economic Review 90(2), 2000, pp. 95-99.

Taylor John B. (1993), "Discretion versus Policy Rules in Practice", in: Carnegie-Rochester Conference Series on Public Policy, 1993 (39), pp. 195-214.

Taylor John B. (2001), The Role of the Exchange Rate in Monetary Policy Rules, draft, Stanford University, 2001.

Appendix:

Figure A1: Euro area: GDP effects of a world oil price shock (30% increase 1999Q2-2001Q3)

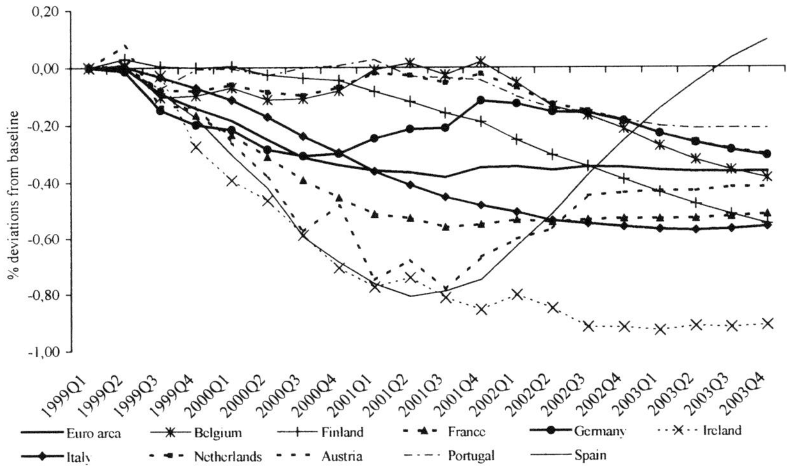

Source: Own calculations with the NiGEM world macro model.

Figure A2: Pre-ins area: GDP effects of a world oil price shock (30% increase 1999Q2-2001Q3)

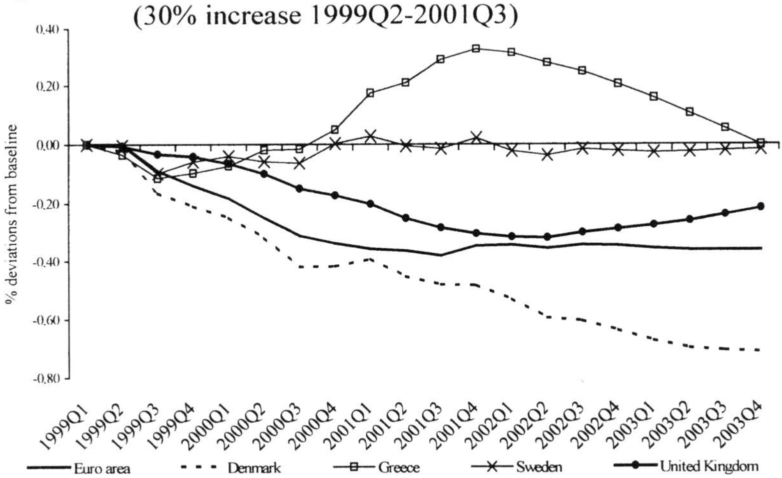

Source: Own calculations with the NiGEM world macro model.

Figure A3: Euro area: HICP inflation effects of a world oil price-shock (30% increase 1999Q2-2001Q3)

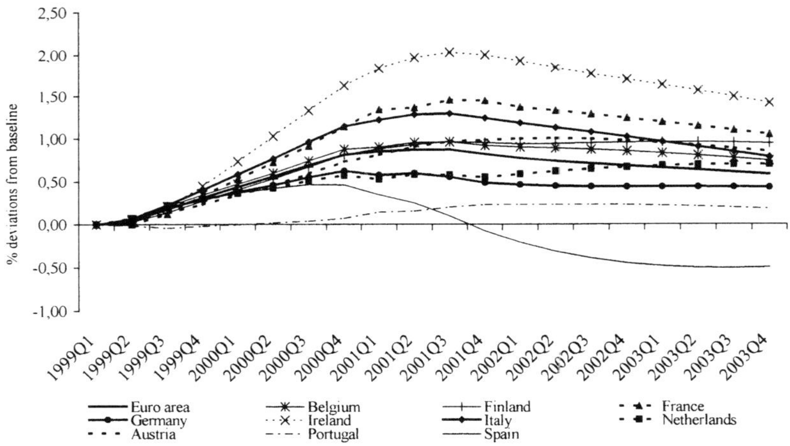

Source: Own calculations with the NiGEM world macro model.

Figure A4: Pre-ins area: HICP inflation effects of a world oil price shock (30% increase 1999Q2-2001Q3)

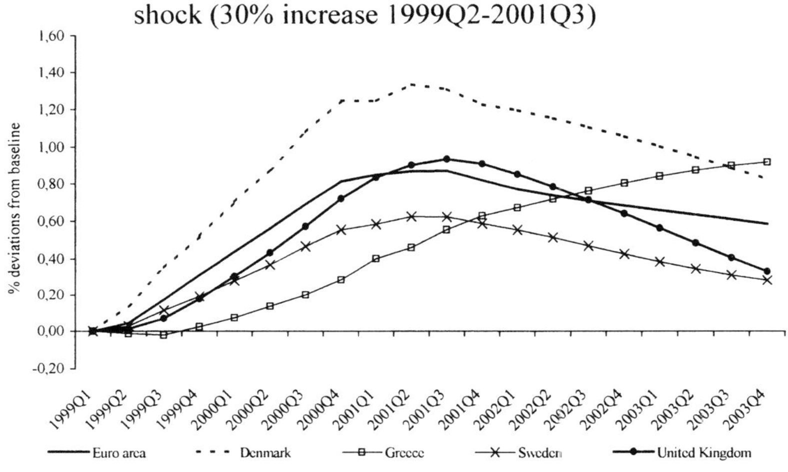

Source: Own calculations with the NiGEM world macro model.

Figure A5: Euro area: GDP effects of an interest rate cut (1% decrease of short-term interest rates in the euro area 2000Q2-2001Q3)

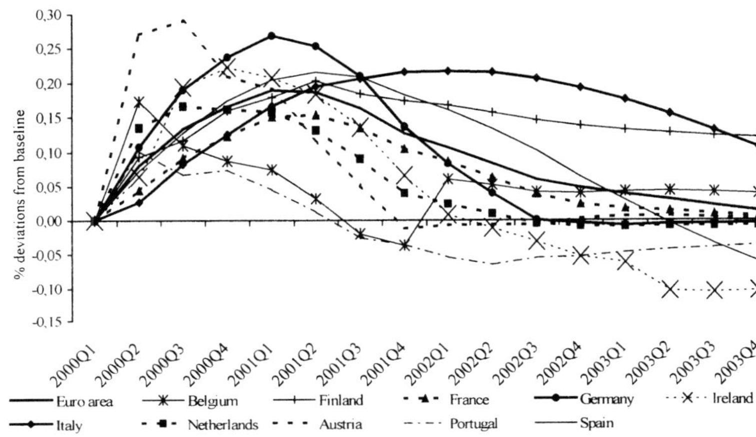

Source: Own calculations with the NiGEM world macro model.

Figure A6: Pre-ins area: GDP effects of an interest rate cut (1% decrease of short-term interest rates in the euro area 2000Q2-2001Q3)

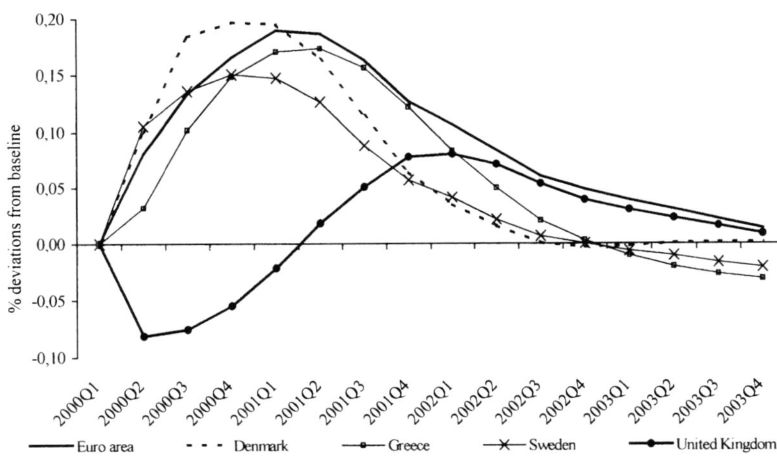

Source: Own calculations with the NiGEM world macro model.

Figure A7: Euro area: HICP inflation effects of an interest rate cut (1% decrease of short-term interest rates in the euro area 2000Q2-2001Q3)

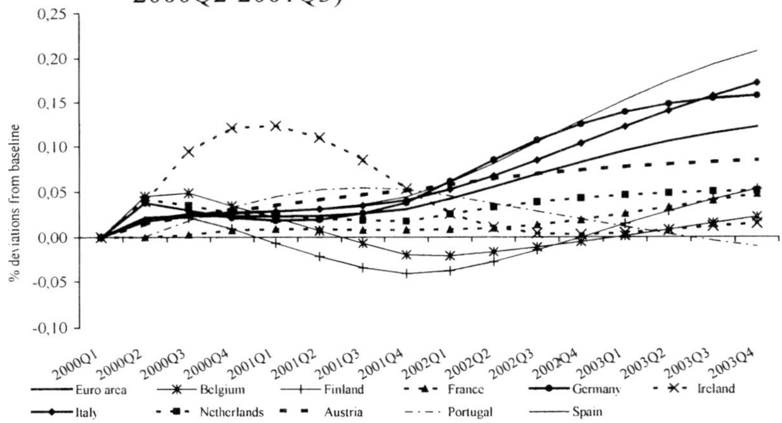

Source: Own calculations with the NiGEM world macro model.

Figure A8: Pre-ins area: HICP inflation effects of an interest rate cut (1% decrease of short-term interest rates in the euro area 2000Q2-2001Q3)

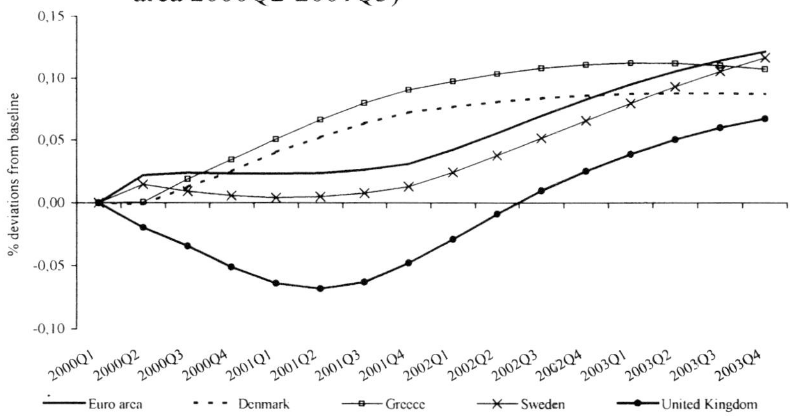

Source: Own calculations with the NiGEM world macro model.

Rudolf Habacht/ Walter Hoffenberg/ Aurel Schubert

EMU and Issues in European Payment Systems

I. Introduction

Efficient and secure payment systems in the euro area are crucial elements of the Single Market and of Economic and Monetary Union. Payment systems are of special concern for central banks, both from a monetary stability as well as from a financial stability perspective. A malfunctioning of the payment infrastructure could affect i) the stability of financial institutions or markets, ii) the confidence of the users in payment instruments, and in general, the confidence of the public in the currency, and iii) the implementation of monetary policy. Therefore, central banks always have been involved in payments systems, both in retail (at least with respect to currency) as well as wholesale systems. With the establishment of Economic and Monetary Union in Europe the issue of efficient and reliable payment systems has gained in importance.

The topic of payments systems can be approached from an operational or from a supervisory point of view. In this article we will try to deal with both aspects.

On an operational level one has to distinguish between retail payments systems and wholesale or large-value systems. Retail systems are of special interest from a Single Market as well as from a consumer protection perspective, while large-value systems have special relevance for monetary policy implementation and financial stability aspects.

Therefore, the EU Treaty and the Statute of the European System of Central Banks (ESCB) and the European Central Bank (ECB) recognise the promotion of the smooth functioning of payment and settlement systems as one of the basic tasks of the Eurosystem.[1] Consequently, this article also focuses on the Eurosystems´ oversight perspective and policy stance and illustrates their implementation at national level with the example of Austria.

As a third perspective, this article also touches briefly on the role of payments information for collecting statistics on cross-border flows for the compilation of balance-of-payments statistics.

II. The institutional framework in Europe

A. The Central Banks - The ESCB

Defining the role of the European System of Central Banks (ESCB) the Maastricht Treaty states in the Article 105 (2), that one of

> *"..the basic tasks to be carried out through the ESCB shall be to promote the smooth operation of payment systems".*

The Statute of the European System of Central Banks and of the European Central Bank, which as an annexed Protocol is an integral part of the Treaty, explicitly grants regulatory powers to the ECB and allows for the operational involvement of the ESCB in payment systems by stating in Article 22, that

> *"..the ECB and national central banks may provide facilities, and the ECB may make regulations, to ensure efficient and sound clearing and payment systems within the Community and with other countries."*

This applies to both retail and large-value payment systems.[2]

B. EU Council and the EU Parliament

The EU Council and the EU Parliament have – based on the assignment of powers by the Treaty - adopted several legal acts relevant for the field of payment systems:

1. Directive 97/5/EC on cross-border credit transfers

The objective of the "Directive 97/5/EC of the European Parliament and of the Council of 27 January 1997 on cross-border credit transfers" is to make credit transfers within the Single Market in euro rapid, reliable and inexpensive. Especially the phenomenon of

---

[1] The term "Eurosystem" refers to the ECB and the national central banks of the - at present - twelve countries participating in the third stage of European monetary union.

[2] See *ECB* (2001a), p. 52.

"double charging", i.e. the charging of both the sender and the receiver of a transfer, even in cases where the sender had committed to paying all charges, should be prohibited. The Directive applies to cross border credit transfers up to a value of € 50.000 ordered by individuals as well as enterprises and executed by (credit) institutions. This means the Directive is primarily targeted at retail payment transactions. This Directive states that:

- The institution has to provide comprehensive information on conditions (costs, execution time) for cross border credit transfers prior to the payment order. This information should be available to the customer in writing, where appropriate by electronic means, and in readily comprehensible form.
- A cross border transfer should be credited to the beneficiary's account within five banking business days following the date of acceptance of the transfer by the institution.
- Unless otherwise stipulated, the "OUR" clause applies to the charging of fees for the payment order. This means, any intermediary or receiving bank should not charge any additional fees, in particular not to the beneficiary.
- In the case of non-execution of a credit transfer, the accepting institution should – without prejudice to any other claim which may be made - re-credit the amount of the ordered transfer, up to € 12.500, to the originator within 14 banking business days after the day of the originator's request.

2. The Settlement Finality Directive

The „Directive 98/26/EC of 19 May 1998 on settlement finality in payment and securities settlement systems" applies to i) systems (i.e., a formal arrangement between at least three participants), ii) participants of those systems, iii) collateral security provided in connection with the participation in a system or operations of the central banks in their functions as a central bank.

The principal objectives of this Directive are:

- to eliminate the main legal risks to which payment and securities settlement systems are exposed,
- to ensure that the smooth functioning of a system cannot be compromised by the application of a foreign insolvency law,
- to enhance the legal certainty of collateral.

The main provisions of the Directive are:

- the moment of opening of insolvency proceedings shall be the moment when the relevant judicial or administrative authority handed down its decision,
- transfer orders and netting shall be legally enforceable and, even in the event of insolvency proceedings against a participant, shall be binding on third parties, provided that transfer orders were entered into a system before the moment of opening of such insolvency proceedings,
- a transfer order may not be revoked by a participant in a system, or a third party, from the moment defined in the rules of the system;
- Member states shall specify the systems which are included in the scope of this Directive and shall notify them to the Commission.

3. Regulation (EC) No 2560/2001 on cross-border payments in euro

The "Regulation (EC) No 2560/2001 of the European Parliament and of the Council of 19 December 2001 on cross-border payments in euro" aims to ensure that charges for cross border payments in euro are the same as those for (domestic) payments in euro within a Member State. Its intention is to contribute to the creation of a "single payment area" as a complement to the single currency area of the euro and the internal market. For many years already the Commission and the Parliament had criticised the high charges for small value cross-border payments. Various studies had shown that in 2001 the average price of a cross-border transfer of € 100 in the Union had been € 24.[3] Also, the use of Automated Teller Machines (ATMs) in another country of the Union than the home country continued to be more expensive, even when the same currency - euro - is being withdrawn. At the same time, the alignment of charges for cross-border payments with those for payments at national level should not lead to a higher level of charges for payments at national level.

This Regulation does not apply to cross border payments made between institutions for their own account.

---

[3] Study on the Verification of a Common and Coherent Application of Directive 97/5/EC on Cross-Border Credit Transfers in the 15 Member States - Transfer Exercise, Report for the Commission of the European Communities (DG MARKET), Retail Banking Research, London, 17 September 2001.

The main provisions of the Regulation are:[4]

- With effect from 1 July 2002, charges levied by an institution with respect to cross border electronic payment transactions in euro up to € 12.500 shall be the same as the charges levied by the same institution in respect of corresponding payments in euro transacted within the Member State in which the establishment of that institution executing the cross border electronic payment transaction is located.
- With effect from 1 July 2003, charges levied by an institution in respect of cross border credit transfers in euro up to € 12.500 shall be the same as the charges levied by the same institution in respect of corresponding payments in euro transacted within the Member State in which the establishment of that institution executing the cross border electronic payment transaction is located.
- With effect from 1 January 2006 the amount € 12.500 shall be raised to € 50.000.

"Cross border credit transfers" are defined as "transactions carried out on the initiative of an originator via an institution or its branch in one Member State, with a view to making an amount of money available to a beneficiary at an institution or its branch in another Member State; the originator and the beneficiary may be one and the same person."

"Cross border electronic payments" are defined as i) cross border transfers of funds effected by means of an electronic payment instrument, other than ordered and executed by institutions, where "electronic payment instrument" itself is defined as a remote access payment instrument and electronic money instrument that enables its holder to effect one or more electronic payment transactions, and ii) cross border cash withdrawals by means of electronic payment instrument and the loading (and unloading) of an electronic money instrument at cash dispensing machines and automated teller machines at the premises of the issuer or at an institution under contract to accept the payment instrument.

- An institution shall make available to its customers in a readily comprehensible form, in writing, including, where appropriate, in accordance with national rules, by electronic means, prior information on the charges levied for cross-border payments and for

[4] The statistical aspects of this Directive are being discussed in the last part of this paper.

payments effected within the Member State in which the establishment is located.

4. The E-Money Directive

The "Directive 2000/46/EC of the European Parliament and of the Council of 18 September 2000 on the taking up, pursuit of and prudential supervision of the business of electronic money institutions" is introducing a minimum set of harmonised prudential rules for electronic money issuance.

The Directive defines "electronic money" as a monetary value i) stored on an electronic device, ii) issued on receipt of funds of an amount not less in value than the monetary value issued, iii) accepted as means of payment by undertakings other than the issuer.

Regarding the redeemability it states, that a bearer of electronic money may, during the period of validity, ask the issuer to redeem it at par value in coins and notes or by a transfer to an account free of charges other than those strictly necessary to carry out the operation. A minimum threshold for redemption may not exceed € 10.

Electronic Money Institutes (as defined in the Directive 2000/12/EC of 20 March 2000 relating to the taking up and pursuit of the business of credit institutions) shall have an initial capital not less than € 1 million, and they shall have at all times own funds which are equal to or above 2% of the higher of the current amount or the six months' target total amount of the institution's financial liabilities related to the outstanding electronic money.

5. Recommendation on Electronic payment instruments

The "Commission Recommendation of 30 July 1997 concerning transactions by electronic payment instruments and in particular the relationship between issuer and holder (97/489/EC)", applies to i) transfers of funds, other than those ordered and executed by financial institutions, effected by means of an electronic payment instrument, ii) cash withdrawals by means of an electronic payment instrument and the loading (and unloading) of an electronic money instrument, at devices such as cash dispensing machines and automated teller machines and at the premises of the issuer or an institution who is under contract to accept the payment instrument.

The Recommendation describes aims in the field of:

- Minimum information contained in the terms and conditions governing the issuing and use of an electronic payment instrument,
- Information subsequent to a transaction,

- Obligations of the holder,
- Liabilities of the holder,
- Obligations of the issuer,
- Liabilities of the issuer,
- Notification of loss or theft,
- Settlement of disputes.

C. Banking federations and associations

Most of the banks in the EU are organised into national federations and organisations. These national organisations and federations are organised on the European level in the European Banking Federation, the European Association of Co-operative Banks, and the European Savings Banks Group. These European Credit Sector Associations (ECSAs) play an important role in negotiating with the third parties (e.g. Commission, ECB) on behalf of their members.

III. Central bank systems

A. Real-time gross settlement systems

The central banks have clear policy interests in the smooth functioning of both payment systems and, more generally, of the financial system as a whole. They therefore developed in the beginning of the 90s concepts to improve efficiency and stability in payment systems.

Along these lines, a report entitled "Minimum Common Features for Domestic Payment Systems"[5] was published in November 1993. The report established ten principles covering the areas that required specification in terms of minimum common features: access conditions, risk management policies, legal issues (including the need for a legal basis for central bank oversight), standards and infrastructures, pricing policies and business hours. One of the main risk reduction policies was that an RTGS system should be set up in each EU country for the relevant national currency, into which as many large-value payments as possible should be channelled. Such systems should settle across accounts at the central bank and have

---

5 Report to the Committee of Governors of the Central Banks of the Member States of the European Economic Community on "Minimum Common Features for Domestic Payment Systems" prepared by the Working Group on EC Payment Systems, November 1993.

sound legal, technical and prudential features, which are compatible across EC member states.

This constituted the promotion of RTGS processing within the EU and also formed the basis for linking national RTGS systems in order to have a cross-border RTGS system ready by the start of EMU. This resulted in the Trans-European Automated Real-time Gross settlement Express Transfer (TARGET) system that successfully started its operations on 4 January 1999.

At the same time, from a monetary policy perspective a single monetary policy - especially for a large area like the euroarea - requires an efficient large-value payment system. Only if central bank money can move within seconds from one corner of the monetary area to any other is a single monetary policy with a single overnight interest rate possible. Funds have to move from financial markets with excess liquidity to areas with need for more liquidity within moments.

The basic features of a real time gross settlement system are:

- The payment transactions are processed gross, e.g. one by one without any calculation of net balances.
- The settlement takes place real time, e.g. when the RTGS-system receives a payment order, it processes it immediately (if there is coverage on the account to be debited),
- once the payment is settled, it is irrevocable.

The aim of RTGS-systems is to exclude systemic risks from the payment mechanism. In (non-RTGS) clearing systems payments in the first step are processed on a net basis, bilateral or multilateral balances are calculated, but the settlement takes place in the second step some time later, usually at the end of the day. A liquidity problem or even an insolvency of one participant is only obvious at the time of settlement. If such a participant fails to fulfil his liabilities vis à vis other participants, those other participants might get into troubles fulfilling their own liabilities due to the missing incoming funds. The resulting wave of problems is known as the "Domino Effect" and could affect the whole system.

In RTGS-systems no bilateral clearing balances and therefore no unexpected failures of participants can occur. Consequently the central banks want systemically relevant payments (i.e. high value payments which could cause problems as described above) to be processed via their RTGS-Systems.

Figure 1: RTGS-Systems

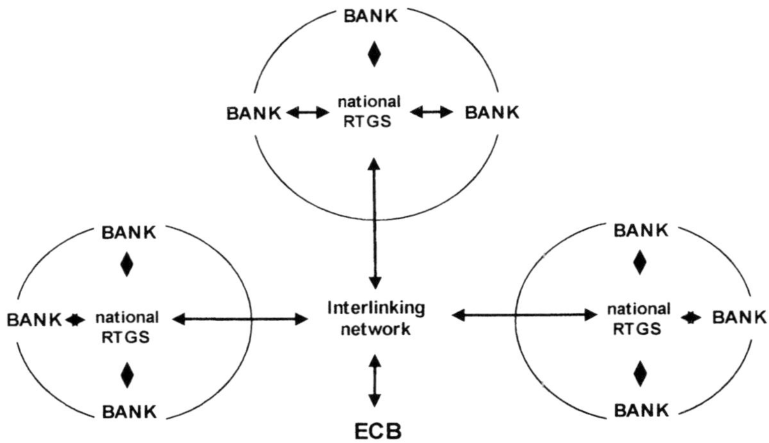

Source: OeNB

B. TARGET

The decision to construct a Trans European Interbank Express System (TARGET) consisting of 15 national RTGS-Systems and the ECB payment mechanism (EPM) was taken by the Council of the European Monetary Institute (EMI) in March 1995. These systems were developed in the years 1995 to 1998. At the beginning of 1999, for the start of the European Monetary Union all 16 components were interconnected forming the TARGET-system.

TARGET was developed to meet three main objectives:

- To provide a safe and reliable mechanism for the settlement of cross border payments on an RTGS-basis,
- to increase the efficiency of intra-EU cross border payments,
- to serve the needs of the monetary policy of the Eurosystem (i.e. the ECB plus the national central banks of the countries which form the Euro area).

The rules governing TARGET can be found in the "Guideline of the European Central Bank of 26 April 2000 on a trans-european automated real-time gross settlement express transfer system (TARGET)." This guideline contains rules for the access criteria, the pricing, the time and days of operation, the payment rules, intraday credit provisions, and the reimbursement scheme.

As participants are admitted:

- Supervised credit institutions as defined in the first indent of Article I of the First Banking Coordination Directive (now incorporated in the Directive 2000/12/EC), which are established in the European Economic Area (EEA),
- Treasury departments of central or regional governments of Member states active in the money markets,
- Public sector bodies of Member states authorised to hold accounts for customers,
- Investment firms established in the EEA which are authorised and supervised by a recognised competent authority, and
- Organisations providing clearing or settlement services subject to oversight by a competent authority.

Today TARGET is one of the largest payment systems in the world:

- About 5000 participants, e.g. almost all EU credit institutions have access using a highly efficient service for time-critical and/or high-value payments,
- The total number of payments processed in TARGET per day on average is 211.274 (2001),
- The average value of a cross border interbank payment is about € 10,8 million (2000),
- The average value of a cross border customer payment amounts to about € 1,1 million (2000).

IV. Private cross border payment systems

A. EBA EURO 1/ STEP1/ STEP2

1. EURO1

EURO 1 is a multilateral large-value EU-wide payment system for euro credit transfers. It processes credit transfers only. The system is governed by the Euro Banking Association (EBA), which is a co-operative undertaking covering EU-based commercial banks and EU branches of non-EU banks.

Clearing banks from all the EU Member States and five non-EU countries (Australia, Japan, Norway, Switzerland, and the U.S.) are participating in the system.

EURO1 operates under the “Single Obligation Structure (SOS)”, a legal structure where participants agree to enter a contractual agreement that on each settlement day, at any given time, each participant will have only one single payment obligation or claim with respect to the community of other participants as joint debitors/creditors. This single obligation or claim is calculated continuously until the end of the day, when the settlement takes place in central bank money at the ECB.

This settlement process starts after cut off time (presently 4 p.m.) with the clearing banks in a debit position paying their single obligation via TARGET into the EBA settlement account at the ECB. After all amounts due have been received, the ECB pays under instruction of EBA the claims to the clearing banks in a credit position via TARGET again.

2. STEP1

STEP1 is a short term solution for cross border retail payments within a pan-European payment system. The processing of payments takes place in STEP1, the resulting settlement in EURO1. It has been available since 20 November 2000.[6]

The service was developed to rapidly enable banks to comply better with the EU-legislation concerning the reduction of charges within the European Union by offering an advanced technical solution simplifying the operations and so lowering the costs for participating banks.

To achieve this the following objectives should be met: i) shorten the payment execution time, ii) foster the use of industry standards to enhance straight-through processing in the banks, and iii) develop European business practices in relation to cross-border retail payments.

3. STEP2

STEP2 is a project aiming at establishing a pan-European automated clearing house processing mass payments in the sense of inter-bank settlement of commercial and retail payments. Operations should start end of 2002. Participation in STEP2 will be restricted to banks established in the EU and will be possible either as settling members or as non settling members (user members and third party members).

The payment orders planned for processing in STEP2 are i) commercial transfers in euro, ii) non-time critical, iii) formatted according to agreed technical standards.

---

6 The Eurosystem explicitly welcomed the STEP 1 initiative as having the potential to improve cross-border retail payments services; *ECB* (2001a), p. 55.

The initial service offered, the first release, will be for processing credit transfers through the system with direct debit processing being offered in a second release.

STEP2 generates for each bilateral payment obligation a settlement payment message for processing in EURO1. Bilateral payment obligations between Settling Participants are settled automatically via EURO1 funds transfers. Bilateral payment obligations between Non-Settling Participants are settled within given limits through EURO1 banks appointed as STEP2 Settlement Banks by each Non-Settling Participant.

B. Eurogiro

Eurogiro is a co-operation of more than 30 postal and giro organisations in the EU, the United States, Japan and since January 2002 also China. It is an electronic payment system created in 1989 for business and private customers processing cross border credit transfers and cash-on-delivery orders.

The system works the way that the participants act as correspondents for each other, e.g. payments are executed through reciprocal accounts which the correspondents hold for each other. Defined standards regarding formats and time scales are mandatory for each member. Payments are settled on a gross basis once a day bilaterally by the members concerned. Execution time is usually for credit transfers three business days and for cash payment orders five business days.

C. S-Interpay

S-Interpay was established in 1994 as a co-operation of the German savings banks and their central institutions, the Landesbanken/Girozentralen. The system provides cross border payment services available to all members of the European Savings Banks Group and, in principle, also to other commercial banks.

In general, one bank per country acts as central correspondent for that country. This correspondent collects all cross border payment orders transferring them to the central participant in the foreign country, where these payments are channelled into the relevant local system. The exchange of payments between correspondents takes place on the basis of file transfers. Cover payments are made via TARGET or EURO1.

D. TIPANET

Transferts Interbancaires de Paiement Automatisés (TIPANET) is a network of co-operative banks from eight countries in Europe and Canada. It is a cross border bulk payments system, processing credit transfers, direct debits and cheques. The maximum amount of a transaction that can be transferred corresponds to the balance-of-payments reporting threshold in the receiving country. Execution time for cross border payments is usually two days.

Similar to other systems, in TIPANET a local correspondent collects all payments, converting them into the internal format and sending them to the foreign correspondent in the form of payment batches. The settlement takes place via the reciprocal accounts which the correspondents hold for each other.

E. Correspondent Banking

The traditional correspondent banking is strongly affected by the concentration process triggered by European Monetary Union. The different payments system initiatives and structural consolidations in the financial sector lead to a substantial decrease in the number and importance of bilateral correspondent banking relationships.

V. Payment Systems Oversight in the Eurosystem

The Treaty and the Statute of the European System of Central Banks (ESCB) and the European Central Bank (ECB) recognise the promotion of the smooth functioning of payment and settlement systems as one of the basic tasks of the Eurosystem. In general terms, oversight establishes the regulatory framework according to which payment systems should be designed, operated and governed and ensures that the framework is implemented. Payment systems oversight is aimed at a given system rather than at individual participants. The objectives of oversight are to protect the financial system from systemic risks and to foster the efficiency and soundness of payment systems and payment instruments.

A. The evolutionary path

The process was mainly initiated by G10 central banks with the adoption of the Lamfalussy report in 1990.[7] This report underlined the risks which net settlement systems could trigger for financial stability and set out six minimum standards multilateral netting systems should comply with. The six Lamfalussy Standards called for a worldwide substantial redesign of the main features of any large-value net settlement system. The report also set out five principles for co-operative oversight of cross-border and multi-currency

[7] *BIS* (1990).

netting and settlement schemes. The intention of these principles was to provide a mechanism for mutual assistance among central banks in carrying out their individual duties according to their shared objectives of promoting the safety and efficiency of interbank payment and settlement arrangements. Moreover, the principles provide a framework for the allocation of responsibilities between central banks and the relevant supervisory authorities. They may be considered as the launch of the modern concept of oversight.

EU central banks' awareness towards risk and efficiency in payment systems was accelerated in the context of the realisation of the Single Market and the preparations for EMU. With the Second Banking Co-ordination Directive[8] banks acquired more flexibility as regards how they could organise cross-border activity and participate in payment systems located in other EU countries. In order for EU banks to operate outside their country of incorporation with competitive equality, it was necessary that they would be allowed access to this country's payment system on an equal footing with national institutions. EU central banks co-operated closely to ensure that differences between national payment systems did not create risks for the integrity and stability of national and cross-border payment systems. They also wished to ensure that these differences would not distort competitive conditions or create opportunities for regulatory arbitrage. The overall aim was to cater for a level playing field.

Along these lines, the above mentioned report "Minimum Common Features for Domestic Payment Systems"[9] was published in November 1993 with its recommended risk reduction policy of setting up RTGS systems in each EU country. This resulted - as

---

8 Second Council Directive 89/646/EEC of 15 December 1989 on the coordination of laws, regulations and administrative provisions relating to the taking up and pursuit of the business of credit institutions (amending Directive 77/780/EEC); now superseded by Directive 2000/12/EC of the European Parliament and of the Council of 20 March 2000 relating to the taking up and pursuit of the business of credit institutions, as amended by Directive 2000/28/EC of the European Parliament and of the Council of 18 September 2000.

9 Report to the Committee of Governors of the Central Banks of the Member States of the European Economic Community on "Minimum Common Features for Domestic Payment Systems" prepared by the Working Group on EC Payment Systems, November 1993.

mentioned above - in the Trans-European Automated Real-time Gross settlement Express Transfer (TARGET) system of the ESCB.

With a view to the introduction of the euro in 1999, all large-value payment systems operating in the EU were assessed against the Lamfalussy standards in 1998, and were found compliant.

The bases for the Eurosystem's oversight policy in the area of electronic money are the 1994 "Report to the EMI Council on Pre-paid Cards" and the 1998 "Report on electronic money". The latter report sets out seven minimum requirements for the issuance of electronic money: Issuers of e-money must be subject to prudential supervision. E-money schemes must be legally solid and transparent. They must fulfil an adequate technical security. Protection against criminal abuse must be taken into account. E-money schemes must provide monetary statistics to central banks. Issuers have to be legally obliged to redeem e-money against central bank money at par and central banks must have the possibility to impose reserve requirements on the issuers of electronic money.

Finally, in January 2001, the G10 Governors endorsed the report entitled "Core Principles for Systemically Important Payment Systems".[10] This report extends the Lamfalussy standards to apply more broadly to systemically important payment systems of all types, not only to systems that involve multilateral netting. It complements the Lamfalussy standards with four new principles. In addition, it explains the key role of central banks and sets out their responsibilities in applying the Core Principles, i.e. assessing existing payment systems against the Core Principles and initiating or promoting action to ensure that they are implemented. It also re-emphasises that the central bank, in promoting payment system safety and efficiency through the Core Principles, should cooperate with other central banks and with any other relevant domestic and/or foreign authority. The Core Principles report is included in the set of minimum standards the Eurosystem uses for its common oversight policy on payment systems.[11]

---

[10] *BIS* (2001).

[11] The International Monetary Fund and the World Bank have also adopted these standards for their consultations under the Financial Sector Assessment Programme (FSAP).

B. The legal and institutional framework

Article 105 (2) and (4) of the Treaty establishing the European Union (the Treaty)[12] as well as Articles 3[13] and 22[14] of the Statute of the European System of Central Banks and of the European Central Bank (the Statute) provide the legal basis for the oversight activities of the Eurosystem. Over the past few years, specific provisions related to oversight have also amended the statutes of several national central banks (NCBs; e.g. Austria, Belgium, Spain, Greece, France, Ireland and Italy).

On the basis of the Statute the Governing Council of the European Central Bank is the decision-making body responsible for the performance of the tasks of the Eurosystem in the field of oversight of payment systems.

Whenever the functioning of payment systems affects: i) the implementation of monetary policy, ii) systemic stability, iii) establishment of a level playing field between market participants, iv) cross-border payments within the Eurosystem and with other countries, the Governing Council of the ECB formulates the common oversight policy stance by determining the objectives and setting the standards with which payment systems have to comply.

In areas not specifically covered by the common oversight policy, policies defined at the NCB level apply within the framework of the objectives and core principles defined at the Eurosystem level.

The enforcement of the common oversight policy stance is ensured by the NCBs in relation to payment systems legally incorporated in their jurisdiction (e.g. national retail payment systems). Systems without a clear national base are overseen by the central bank of the country where the system is legally incorporated unless the Governing Council of the ECB decides otherwise.

The common oversight policy stance can be ensured by ECB legal acts in accordance with Article 22 of the Statute of the ESCB or

---

12 "The basic tasks to be carried out through the ESCB shall be [...] to promote the smooth operation of payment systems."

13 "In accordance with Article 105(2) of this Treaty, the basic tasks to be carried out through the ESCB shall be: [...] to promote the smooth operation of payment systems."

14 "The ECB and national central banks may provide facilities, and the ECB may make regulations, to ensure efficient and sound clearing and payment systems within the Community and with other countries."

by informal tools (e.g. moral suasion).[15] An appropriate co-ordination and reporting framework ensures consistency in the implementation of oversight policies.

As far as national payment systems are concerned, the respective national central bank is responsible for an ongoing monitoring of new developments that may have an influence on the safety and efficiency of the system. It includes the assessment of the possibly changing nature and scale of financial risks as well as the monitoring of other activities (e.g. the consolidation process). National payment systems with foreign participation require a close co-operation and co-ordination with the ECB and other national central banks involved. They contribute to ensuring a common understanding, harmonised approaches and a level playing field for market participants.

In considering the importance of close institutional co-operation the ECB and the NCBs of the Eurosystem, in their capacity as overseers of payment systems, and the EU banking supervisory authorities agreed on a "Memorandum of Understanding" (MoU). The MoU is a non-legally binding arrangement which has been in place since April 2001. Taking into account both the new institutional environment created by the establishment of the Eurosystem and the Eurosystem's oversight framework, its focus is on an exchange of information in relation to large-value interbank funds transfer systems, in order to ensure the soundness and stability of such systems and of their participants (credit institutions and investment firms). In the future the Memorandum may also serve as a starting-point for organising co-operation on retail payment systems, including e-money schemes.

In short, payment systems oversight has become a core function, payment systems oversight has become an integral part of the Eurosystems′ widen responsibility for monetary and financial stability, both for the ECB and the NCBs. By identifying potential risks posed by the design and operation of payment systems and, where necessary, by taking corrective action central banks will clearly contribute to the sound and smooth evolution of the European payment schemes.

The next part of this article concisely illustrates how this payment system oversight function is going to be performed in Austria,

---

15 So far the Eurosystem practice has shown a clear preference for the latter.

where for this purpose a new legal and organizational framework has been given to the Oesterreichische Nationalbank (OeNB) as from April 2002.

C. Payment Systems Oversight in Austria

1. Legal Basis and Scope of Application

The OeNB performs payment systems oversight on the basis of Article 44a Nationalbank Act.[16] In addition to providing the mandate to inspect the payment systems systemic stability, Article 44a among others specifies disclosure obligations as well as the OeNB's possibility to issue regulations or carry out inspections. Moreover, it specifies a strict organisational separation of responsibilities to prevent a conflict of interest within the OeNB. On principle, all payment systems which fall under Article 44 para. 4 are subject to payment systems oversight.[17]

2. Oversight Principles and Methods

Within the Eurosystems framework, the OeNB specifies and publishes minimum criteria on systemic stability for all types of payment systems.[18] These spell out the principles on systemic stability of payment systems, on which the disclosure of qualitative information and inspection are based. The catalogue covers three main areas:

- *Legal risks*

  Every payment system should have a clearly defined legal basis, of which participants[19] should be informed. The terms and conditions of the system should cover all rights and obligations of using the payment system and should be legally enforceable with respect to all participants.

- *Financial risks*

  All participants should have a clear understanding of the credit and liquidity risks arising from the operation of or participation in the system. Proof shall be furnished that participants and private

---

16 See Finanzmarktaufsichtsgesetz (Financial Market Supervision Act), Federal Law Gazette I no. 97/2001, Amendment of the Nationalbank Act 1984.

17 This definition includes Securities Settlement Systems and Securities Trading Systems.

18 This public documentation is in line with the *IMF* (2000).

19 Operators, commercial participants and private users of the payment system.

users are informed about any financial risks. Operators should ensure that all participants are capable of taking on and managing specified financial risks. The terms and conditions of the payment system should provide for well-defined responsibilities for all participants to hedge and contain financial risk. Payment systems should provide prompt final settlement, at minimum at the end of the day of value. The assets used for settlement should preferably be a claim on the OeNB. Where other assets are used, the operator shall ensure that they carry little or no credit or liquidity risk.

- *Organizational and technical risks*

In order to guarantee confidentiality and the integrity of the payments handled by the system, the operator shall make use of state-of-the-art IT security. The system should ensure a high degree of security and operational reliability. Apart from the necessary IT security measures, appropriate organizational and personnel measures should be taken. Above all, suitable contingency arrangements for timely completion of daily settlement in the event of failure and disruptions should be made and well documented. The system should provide for transparent and effective governance and control.

The application of these principles to the various categories of payment systems operating in Austria is specified in specifically tailored modules.

Payment system operators have to demonstrate compliance with the criteria by submitting appropriate documentation. Appropriate documentation consists above all in documents specifying the legal standards on which the operation of the system is based and their enforceability with respect to all participants, the terms and conditions of the payment system and other legal documents. Technical security and reliability are to be evidenced by the submission of a comprehensive description (system policy) of the basic structure of the system, the environment in which it is used, its security and internal system control and of opinions of certified auditing agencies confirming the asserted fulfillment of security requirements.[20]

In addition, in the near future the OeNB will use a reporting system for payment system statistics to judge the systemic relevance of payment systems. Those payment system statistics are

---

[20] The OeNB will have the right to use the services of external experts and national or international auditing agencies.

intended to provide reliable data about the number and value of transactions processed by payment systems at quarterly intervals.

VI. Payments systems and balance of payments statistics

A reason that has been frequently cited by banks to justify their high fees for cross-border retail credit transfers is the obligation to report such transfers for balance-of-payments (b.o.p.) statistics.[21] Especially, since in some countries a manual handling is still necessary for this reporting. However, as the ECB had concluded in 2001, the major causes for the inefficiencies - leading to high costs and long execution times - in the cross-border payments were the internal organisation of banks and the communication interface with the customer. Non-standardised customer interfaces and a low degree of automation in banks' internal systems[22] explained a large part of the costs.[23]

What is the link between cross-border transfers and the balance of payments?

Balances of payments measure the economic links between a country and the rest of the world. They are important indicators for monetary policy as they show capital inflows as well as outflows from a monetary area. Therefore, the ESCB needs to compile comprehensive and reliable monthly, quarterly and annual balance of payments statistics.[24] But these statistics are also important to answer questions linked to international trade and trade policy like those concerning the competitiveness of an economic area. From a monetary policy perspective with the creation of the common currency the focus has shifted from the *national* level to the *euro area* level. The euro area balance of payments is an important element within the two pillars of the Eurosystem's monetary policy strategy. However, *national* balances of payments remain important indicators for structural economic analyses, as well as indispensable for

---

21 See *ECB* (2001a), p. 56.

22 See *ECB* (2001a), p. 53. In addition, the euro area country that does not rely on a bank settlement based balance-of-payments collection system, Ireland, showed the second highest average cost for cross-border retail credit transfers in the euro area (after Portugal).

23 *Hans van der Velde*, President of Visa EU is quoted to have said, "Banks charge horrendous amounts to send money to other countries - they just have absolutely arcane systems across borders" (*Financial Times*, 18 March 2002).

24 See *ECB* (2000).

computing the "rest of the world accounts" of the national accounts. National accounts such as GDP are needed as a reference value in the Stability and Growth Pact or as GNP for fourth-resource purposes.

In order to be able to compile reliable balances-of-payments and to supply the ECB with the required statistical information traditionally most countries have relied on banks reporting cross-border financial transfers (bank settlements) - not only their own ones but also on behalf of their customers.

Now the Regulation (EC) No 2560/2001 on cross-border payments in euro states that:

Member States shall remove with effect from 1 July 2002 at the latest any national reporting obligations for cross-border payments up to € 12.500 for balance-of-payments statistics.[25] With effect from 1 January 2006, it is planned (subject to a review by mid-2004) that the threshold will be increased up to € 50,000.

With this, most of the retail transfers will no longer be reported by the banks to the balance-of-payments compilers. Therefore, in order to avoid an unacceptable loss in data quality and to continue to compile reliable balance-of-payment information the respective national compilers have to develop alternative sources of information, replacing (fully or partly) the banks settlement based compilation systems. Several NCBs have already started to develop new systems based primarily on direct reporting as well as surveys. In case of direct reporting the (mainly large) companies that perform cross-border business, e.g. in services or financial transactions, have to report those directly to the balance-of-payments compilers. In case of surveys the compilers regularly survey a representative sample of businesses or individuals about their cross-border activities and then estimate on this basis the overall amount of transactions. Commercial banks will only have to report their own cross-border business.

This major change in compilation systems requires time and good preparation. It will lead to a shifting of burden from commercial banks to enterprises (and individuals) as well as the balance-of-payments compilers. Fortunately, after intensive lobbying by the

---

25 The Committee on Monetary, Financial and Balance of Payments Statistics (CMFB) had already agreed in June 2000 on a common exemption threshold of € 12,500 from January 2002 for those Member Countries making use of settlement-based reporting by banks on behalf of their customers.

European statisticians with the aid of the European Central Bank[26] it was possible to get the text of the Regulation amended from the initially set - premature deadlines - to 1 January 2006, a more realistic date. After all, the ECB together with the European Commission are the prime users of - high quality - European balance-of-payments information. They need accurate balance-of-payments data for decision making, both in the area of monetary policy as well as for international negotiations in the field of foreign trade in goods and services.

VII. Conclusions

With 1 January 2002 the Single Currency became (physical) reality for about 305 million citizens of the euro area. This transformed the euro area into a domestic payment area for cash payments in euro. However, the Single Currency is not yet accompanied by a Single Payment Area, at least as far as retail payments are concerned.

For payments in central bank money between banks, a uniform payment area has largely been achieved through TARGET, already in 1999, although the price for cross-border transfers (within the euro area) is (still) considerably higher than for domestic transfers. As regards cross-border retail payments in commercial bank money, until mid 2001 the banking sector had not given sufficient attention to this important aspect of the changeover to the euro,[27] despite more than ten years of pressure from the European Commission and the European Parliament. It was then - mainly on the basis of new initiatives of the Commission and the Parliament - that serious progress has started to be made. However, it will take a few more years until a Single European Payments Area will complement the Single Currency.[28] This will then finally create a truly "domestic" payment area for the euro and thus crown Economic and Monetary Union.

---

[26] See *ECB* (2001b).

[27] *ECB* (2001a), p. 54.

[28] In the beginning of April 2002 , the Féderation Bancaire de l'Union Euroéenne (FBE) together with some other European associations of the banking sector announced their intention to create a Single Payments Area by 2010 (*Neue Zürcher Zeitung*, 3 April 2002).

References

Bank for International Settlements (1990), Report of the Committee on Interbank Netting Schemes of the Central Banks of the Group of Ten Countries, Basle 1990.

Bank for International Settlements (2001), Report of the Committee on Payment and Settlement Systems on "Core Principles for Systemically Important Payment Systems", Basle 2001.

European Central Bank (2000), Guideline of the European Central Bank of 11 May 2000 on the statistical reporting requirements of the European Central Bank in the field of balance-of-payments statistics, the international reserves template and international investment position statistics, ECB, 2000/4.

European Central Bank (2001a), Towards a uniform service level for retail payments in the euro area, Monthly Bulletin, February 2001, pp. 51-58.

European Central Bank (2001b), Opinion of the European Central Bank of 26 October 2001 at the request of the Council of the European Union on a proposal of the European Parliament and of the Council on cross-border payments in euro, CON, 2001/34.

International Monetary Fund (2000), IMF Code of Good Practices on Transparency in Monetary and Financial Policies, 2000.

Gerhard Fenz*

The euro as an international currency and its depreciation against the US-dollar

I. Introduction

The euro established itself immediately as the second most important international currency ahead of the Japanese yen but still well behind the US dollar. In many aspects the euro mainly inherited the role of Deutsche mark played before the start of EMU stage three. This holds particularly for its use as a vehicle currency on foreign exchange markets and its use by monetary authorities as an anchor, intervention and reserve currency. A notable exception is the success of the euro on international debt securities markets. Right from its introduction in 1999 on the euro captured a market share similar to that of the US dollar. It is generally agreed that the success of an international currency depends primarily on its importance on international financial markets as financing and investment currency. Other functions especially those in the public sector tend to follow developments in the private sector. Thus the prospects of the euro to play an even more important role as an international currency in the future seems to be excellent.

* I wish to thank *Fritz Breuss* and *Gerhard Fink* for helpful comments and discussion. All remaining errors are mine.

II. Functions of international currencies

The functions a national currency fulfils at the international level are similar to the functions of money within a country: It can serve as a medium of exchange, as a unit of account and as a store of value (see Table 1). In addition *Krugman/Obstfeld* (1993) distinguish between functions in the private and public sector. With respect to international transactions of the private sector an international currency is used to solve the "double coincidence of wants" problem at the level of currency exchange by serving as a vehicle through which currency exchange is made indirectly at lower costs. If a currency is used for denomination purposes in international trade it serves as an international unit of account. The international store of value function in the private sector is associated with international financing and investment decisions.

Table 1: Functions of international currencies

Functions	Private sector	Public sector
Medium of exchange	Vehicle currency	Intervention currency
Unit of account	Denomination	Currency peg
Store of value	Portfolio allocation	Reserve currency

Source: *Krugman/Obstfeld* (1993); *Hartmann* (1998).

In the public sector currencies used by monetary authorities for interventions on foreign exchange markets fulfill the function as a medium of exchange. Closely linked to this decision is the store of value function determining the currencies suitable as international reserve. Finally, the international role as a unit of account is associated with currency pegs.

Decision by private market participants concerning the denomination of international financial assets and the invoicing of international trade are decisive for the strategy of central banks' exchange rate policies. Monetary authorities tend to follow developments in the private sector. Close financial and international trade links constitute the driving force behind the choice of a currency as an anchor and its use as a reserve and intervention currency.

III. The role of the euro as an international vehicle currency

Consider a simple three country model where each country has its own currency: country *A* has currency *a*, country *B* currency *b* and country *C* currency *c*. The demand for and the supply of currencies reflect the desires of agents to make payments to the other countries. Assume that these structures of payments are given[1] and that all payments are expressed in units of one currency so that they can be directly compared. Figure 1 gives an example for a structure of payments:

Fig.1 Structure of payments

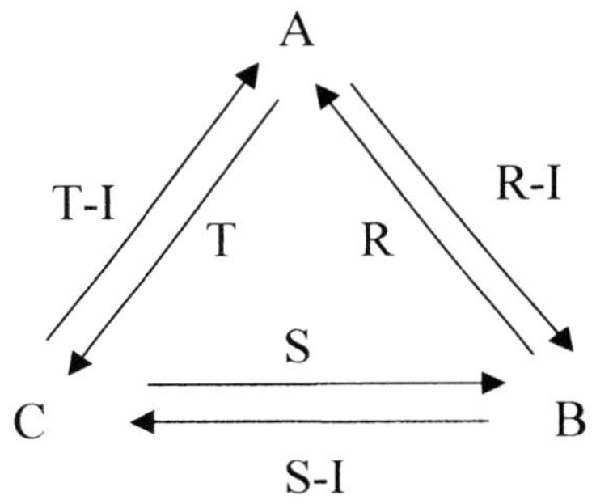

Country *A* wants to make payments worth *R-I* to country *B*, country *B* wants to make payments worth *R* to country *A* ... . Thus, for example, country *A* runs a surplus of *I* on the market *A/B*. Assuming that all countries must have a balanced current account implies that county *A* runs a deficit of *I* and country *B* runs a surplus of *I* with country *C*. Thus the imbalances on all three markets are equal which is of course only a special feature of a three country model.

Given the structure of payments the next step is to look at the actual transactions on the currency markets - the structure of exchange. The currency markets will clear if the demand for each currency by foreign agents equals the supply from domestic agents, who want to make payments in foreign currency. In the absence of transaction costs this structure is not determined. But even without transaction costs it is not possible to carry out exchanges only through direct exchange. Since foreign exchange markets would not clear in this case some of the exchange must take place indirectly via a third currency. *Krugman* (1980) shows that the introduction of transaction costs reduces the possible exchange patterns to six structures of exchange, two for each currency serving as the vehicle

---

1 Assuming that the structure of payments is given turns out to be identical to ignoring feedback's from the structure of exchange, the actual currency flows, on the structure of payments.

currency. In figures 2 and 3 the two equilibria with currency *a* being the vehicle currency are shown:

Fig. 2 partial indirect exchange

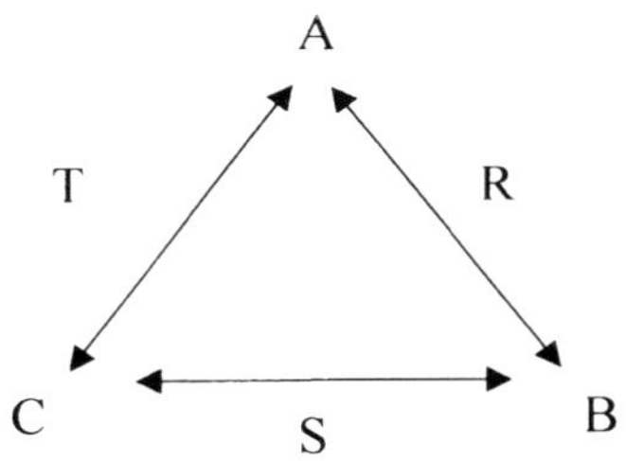

Fig. 3 total indirect exchange

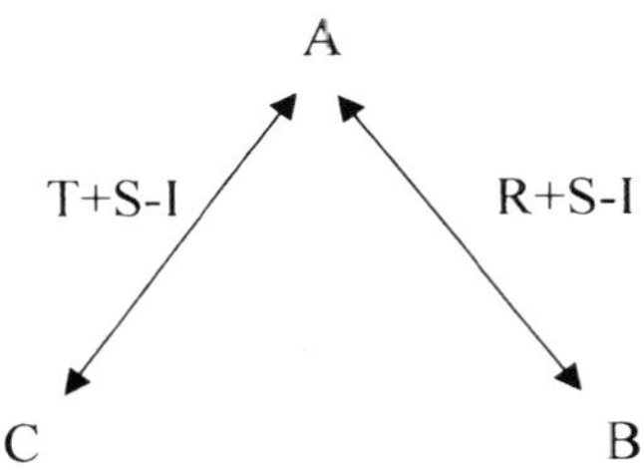

Let T_{ab}, T_{ac} and T_{bc} denote the unit transaction costs on the three bilateral foreign exchange markets. Currency *a* will be the vehicle currency if $T_{ab}<T_{bc}$ and $T_{ac}<T_{bc}$ holds. If the indirect exchange on the currency market *b/c* is more expensive than the direct exchange ($T_{ab} + T_{ac} > T_{bc}$) the equilibrium exchange structure will be one like in figure 2 which in the following is called partial indirect exchange. If indirect exchange is less expensive ($T_{ab} + T_{ac} < T_{bc}$) the equilibrium structure will be as in figure 3 called total indirect exchange. In the case of partial indirect exchange only the minimum necessary amount, the amount of imbalance *I*, is exchanged indirectly, while in the case of total indirect exchange the currency market *b/c* disappears and any exchange between country *B* and *C* is done via the vehicle currency *a*. If indirect exchange through currency *a* is cheaper than indirect exchange through currency *b* or *c*, currency *a* will play a limited role as an international medium of exchange even if direct exchange is less costly than indirect exchange. Some indirect exchange is needed if the structure of payments is not balanced otherwise the currency markets do not clear. The costs of this indirect exchange are minimized if the structure of exchange fulfils the above inequalities.

The example of a three country model shows that it depends crucially on transaction costs on foreign exchange markets which currencies will be used as vehicle currencies. Transaction costs on the other hand are determined by the volatility of exchange rates and by trading volumes since foreign exchange markets are characterized by thick market externalities.

The Bank for International Settlements published in March 2002 the latest Triennial Central Bank Survey on Foreign Exchange and

Derivative Market Activity (*BIS* (2002)) based on data for April 2001. The overall results show a remarkable trend reversal on foreign exchange markets. Contrary to previous periods global foreign exchange market turnover declined markedly between 1998 and 2001 from 1490 to 1200 billion USD. The decline was especially pronounced on spot markets with trading volumes more than 30% lower than in 1998. Volumes on swap markets declined by 10% while forwards experienced a slight increase. This confirms the trend of increasing market shares of derivative products in foreign exchange markets.

Table 2: Global foreign exchange market turnover:
Daily averages in April, Bill. USD

	1989	1992	1995	1998	2001
Spot transactions	317	394	494	568	387
Outright forward	27	58	97	128	131
Foreign exchange swaps	190	324	546	734	656
Estimated gaps	56	44	53	60	26
Total traditional turnover	590	820	1190	1490	1200
Turnover at April 2001 exchange rates	570	750	990	1400	1200

Source: *BIS* (2002), p. 4.

According to the BIS several factors explain this downward trend. The emergence of electronic brooking was the main technical innovation in spot markets. It reduced the need of direct trading among foreign exchange dealers. Also the ongoing process of consolidation and concentration in the banking sector as a whole contributes to declining trading volumes. Additionally the trend of concentration and internationalization in the corporate sector implies a centralization of corporate treasury and an increase in exposure netting. Finally, the introduction of the euro eliminated intra-euro foreign exchange transactions which accounted for about 10% of total turnover. As a consequence the share of the euro in global foreign exchange turnover declined sharply to 38% in 2001 compared to the aggregate level of its predecessor currencies of 53% in 1998. But it is higher than the share of the Deutsche mark was in 1998 (30%) and the euro established by far as the second most important currency. In contrast the market shares of all other important international currencies increased slightly indicating that shifts in market shares are solely caused by the elimination of trading between the euro's legacy currencies.

Table 3: Currency shares of global foreign exchange turnover

	1989	1992	1995	1998	2001
US dollar	90 %	82 %	83 %	87 %	90 %
Euro[2]	33 %	55 %	60 %	53 %	38 %
Deutsche mark	27 %	40 %	36 %	30 %	
Japanese yen	27 %	23 %	24 %	20 %	23%
Pound sterling	15 %	14 %	9 %	11 %	13 %

Source: *BIS* (2002), p. 7.

According to foreign exchange turnover the role of the euro as a vehicle currency is still very much limited to the exchange with the US dollar on the one hand and to a regional level on the other hand. Trading between the US dollar and the euro accounted for 30% of global turnover, 6 percentage points less than for the euro's legacy currencies in 1998. Nevertheless it is the deepest currency market well ahead of the dollar/yen market (20%). The limitation to a regional level is well illustrated by the foreign exchange turnover in selected countries between the respective local currency on one side and the US dollar or the euro on the other side. Even in Western European countries the dominance of the US dollar is still unrivalled. The share of the euro ranges from just 1% in the United Kingdom to 21% in Sweden. Surprisingly even in Denmark the only country joining the new exchange rate mechanism (ERM II) at the moment the share of the euro does not exceed 18%. The euro is only well established as a vehicle currency in several accession countries. In Hungary (68%) and in Slovenia (55%) the euro managed to rank first and also in the Czech Republic (40%) the share is remarkably high whereas it plays only a minor role in Poland (5%). In Russia the euro captured less than 1% market shares. The relevance of the euro in other regions is small.

2 Previous to 1999: Aggregate EMS currencies turnover.

Table 4: Foreign exchange turnover in selected countries in April 2001, Local currency against:

	Total in Bill USD	USD in %	EUR in %
Denmark	7.819	76	18 %
Norway	8.210	86	11 %
Sweden	14.063	56	21 %
Switzerland	24.215	77	18 %
United Kingdom	122.852	83	1 %
Czech Republic	1.522	57	40 %
Hungary	188	28	68 %
Poland	5.507	80	5 %
Slovakia	390	76	23 %
Slovenia	91	10	55 %
Russia	4.158	98	1 %
Turkey	285	89	11 %
Australia	26.839	96	1 %
Canada	25.675	88	1 %
Japan	109.708	93	6 %
New Zealand	2.794	90	2 %
Singapore	11.600	98	1 %

Source: *BIS* (2002), Statistical Annex, Table E.7.

Transaction costs can be measured directly by bid-ask spreads on spot markets. The data displayed in Tables 5 to 7 refer to average daily spreads as published by Bloomberg. They have to be interpreted with some caution as quoted spreads do not necessarily coincide with actual spreads in the interbank market which can be considerably lower. Still it is believed that they reflect cost developments in the foreign exchange market rather well on average. The most striking fact is the remarkable increase in spreads – as measured by the mean (see table 5) - for the by far deepest market the US dollar / euro currency pair. Compared to the US dollar / euro market in 1999 and the US dollar / Deutsche mark market in 1998 spreads of the US dollar / euro currency pair soared up by 3 basispoints until 2001. Less surprising is the increase in spreads on the euro / yen market which is in line with the marked decrease in trading volumes compared with Deutsche mark / yen volumes before the start of the EMU stage three in 1999.[3] In sharp contrast

[3] See *ECB* (2001) p. 14.

spreads on other currency markets with either the US dollar or the euro on one side remained rather stable since the introduction of the euro.

Table 5: Spreads in basispoints: Mean value

	1995[1]	1996	1997	1998	1999	2000	2001	2002[2]
DEM/EUR-USD	7,35	4,89	3,54	4,20	4,18	5,20	7,55	6,15
GBP-USD	3,52	4,57	4,42	5,44	4,50	5,40	5,11	4,77
GBP-DEM/EUR	11,40	9,35	4,51	5,09	6,35	5,53	5,45	6,15
JPY-USD	6,98	5,79	4,77	5,74	6,02	5,56	5,92	4,03
JPY-DEM/ EUR			9,28	9,66	5,54	9,27	12,40	11,22
AUD-USD	7,70	6,86	6,93	10,61	8,63	9,08	9,45	9,95
AUD-DEM/ EUR		13,68	8,72	11,37	16,31	15,87	17,18	16,64

1) Dec. 11, 1995 – Dec. 31, 1995. 2) Jan. 2, 2002 – Feb. 8, 2002.
Source: Bloomberg, own calculations.

However, higher US dollar / euro spreads can not be explained by a decline of liquidity. They are rather a result of the surge in volatility in this specific foreign exchange market and thus most probably a temporary phenomenon. Rising uncertainty with regard to the exchange rate between the dollar and the euro in the course of the economic slowdown in 2001 may be one of the driving forces. Median spreads as displayed in table 6 are less influenced by outliners thereby reflecting market assessments more accurate than average values. Large upward deviations of mean from median values are also indicating periods of higher volatility and uncertainty. Clearly average US dollar / euro spreads have been higher than their median levels. This pattern is also confirmed by the implied volatility of the dollar / euro exchange rate measured by the conditional standard deviation of an GARCH(1) process as shown in figure 4.

Table 6: Spreads in basispoints: Median

	1995[1]	1996	1997	1998	1999	2000	2001	2002[2]
DEM/EUR-USD	6,95	4,51	2,91	3,29	4,67	5,07	5,90	5,65
GBP-USD	3,24	4,49	3,71	4,90	3,18	6,23	6,73	5,55
GBP-DEM/EUR	10,36	8,04	5,24	5,08	6,57	6,06	6,19	6,15
JPY-USD	4,90	4,71	4,20	4,30	4,23	4,59	6,53	3,78
JPY-DEM/EUR			9,41	9,47	5,56	9,07	11,03	10,16
AUD-USD	6,75	6,34	6,60	8,06	7,75	8,55	9,68	9,67
AUD-DEM/EUR		12,19	7,74	9,50	16,29	15,86	17,25	17,07

1) Dec. 11, 1995 – Dec. 31, 1995. 2) Jan. 2, 2002 – Feb. 8, 2002.
Source: Bloomberg, own calculations.

Table 7: Spreads in basispoints: Differences between mean value and median

	1995[1]	1996	1997	1998	1999	2000	2001	2002[2]
DEM/EUR-USD	0,40	0,38	0,63	0,91	-0,49	0,13	1,65	0,50
GBP-USD	0,28	0,08	0,71	0,54	1,32	-0,83	-1,62	-0,78
GBP-DEM/EUR	1,04	1,30	-0,72	0,01	-0,22	-0,53	-0,74	0,00
JPY-USD	2,08	1,08	0,57	1,44	1,79	0,97	-0,62	0,25
JPY-DEM/EUR			-0,13	0,19	-0,02	0,20	1,38	1,05
AUD-USD	0,95	0,53	0,33	2,55	0,88	0,53	-0,24	0,28
AUD-DEM/EUR		1,49	0,98	1,87	0,02	0,01	-0,07	-0,44

1) Dec. 11, 1995 – Dec. 31, 1995. 2) Jan. 2, 2002 – Feb. 8, 2002.
Source: Bloomberg, own calculations.

Figure 4: Volatility of dollar / euro exchange rate

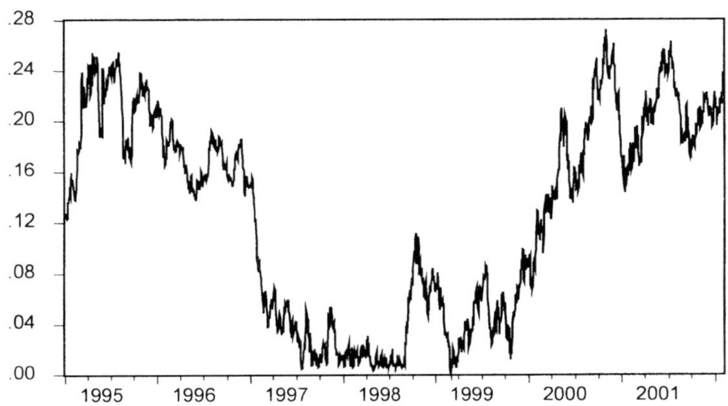

Source: Bloomberg, own calculations.

IV. The role of the euro as an anchor currency

According to statistics on official exchange rate policies the weight of the euro as an anchor currency is still strongly determined by its legacy currencies, especially the French franc and the Deutsche mark. According to *IMF* (2001) and *ECB* (2001) figures, 56 countries officially align their exchange rate at least partially with the euro (see table 8). This set of countries includes those with very close links to the euro like the currency board in Bulgaria as well as those with loose ones like the currency peg to special drawing rights in Saudi Arabia.

Especially countries with strong economic linkages use the euro as a currency anchor. This holds in particular for Eastern European accession countries and countries in the CAF franc zone. Outside these two regions the euro is only used as one of several currencies in a basket. The role of the euro as a currency anchor in Asia seems to be very limited. Moreover the aggregate GDP of the 56 countries together amounts only to 4% of world GDP.

Table 8: Exchange rate regimes using the euro

EXCHANGE RATE REGIME	NUMBER OF COUNTRIES	COUNTRIES
No separate legal tender (entitled to use the euro as official currency)	5	Mayotte, Monaco, Saint-Pierre-et-Miquelon, San Marino, Vatican City
Euroisation	3	Andorra, Kosovo, Montenegro
Currency board	4	Bosnia-Herzegovina, Bulgaria, Estonia, Lithuania
Currency peg to euro	18	Cyprus, Denmark, Cape Verde, Comoros CFA franc zone: Benin, Burkina Faso, Cameroon, Central African Republic, Chad, Congo, Côte d'Ivoire, Rep. of Equatorial Guinea, Gabon, Guinea-Bissau, Mali, Niger, Senegal, Togo,
Currency peg to SDR	8	Latvia, Bahrain, Jordan, Libyan Arab Jamahiriya, Myanmar, Qatar, Saudi Arabia, United Arab Emirates
Currency peg to a basket including the euro	8	Iceland, Kuwait, Malta, Bangladesh, Morocco, Seychelles, Vanuatu, Botswana
Crawling peg / band	3	Hungary, Israel, Tunisia
Managed floating with respect to the euro / basket including euro	7	Burundi, Croatia, Czech Republic, FYR Macedonia, Poland, Slovak Republic, Slovenia

Source: *ECB* (2001), p. 42.

The choice of official exchange rate regimes is also closely linked to the use of a currency as foreign exchange reserve asset. According to the *IMF* (2001) the introduction of the euro led to an arithmetic decline in the euro's share in international reserves. From January 1, 1999 on previous holdings by euro area members of other euro area members legacy currencies do no longer count as official reserve assets. This caused a decline of the euro share in world foreign exchange reserves to 12,7% at the end of 2000 compared to a combined share of euro legacy currencies of 14,8% at the end of 1998. Similar to the Deutsche mark before 1999 the euro is the second most important reserve currency ahead of the Japanese yen with 5,3% but well behind the US dollar with 68,2%. The role of the euro as an reserve currency is more important in developing countries (14,6%) than in industrial countries (10,2%).

Official exchange rate regimes do not necessarily tell much about actual exchange rate policies. Better insights of exchange rate policies can be gained by analyzing actual exchange rate movements. If movements of the exchange rate between a certain currency (X) and the US dollar (USD) can be mainly explained by movements of the exchange rate between the US dollar and the euro (EUR), this would indicate that the euro is used as an anchor currency. This sensitivity can be calculated by regressing changes in the exchange rate with respect to the dollar ($\Delta(E_{X,USD})$) on a constant (α) and on changes of the exchange rate between the euro and the US dollar ($\Delta(E_{EUR,USD})$) as shown in the following equation:[4]

$$\Delta(E_{X,USD}) = \alpha + \beta\Delta(E_{EUR,USD})$$

A high coefficient of determination indicates that the actual exchange rate policy follows the euro while in case of a low coefficient the US dollar is the attractor. Figure 5 shows the results for two different time periods, 1995 to 1998 and 1999 to February 2002, in order to track changes over time. Exchange rates of countries above the 45 degree line tended to move closer with the euro in the period 1999-2002 than in the period 1995-1999 while countries below the line moved closer with the dollar.

---

4 See *Galati/Tsatsaronis* (2001).

Figure 5: Exchange rate sensitivities with respect to the euro and the US dollar

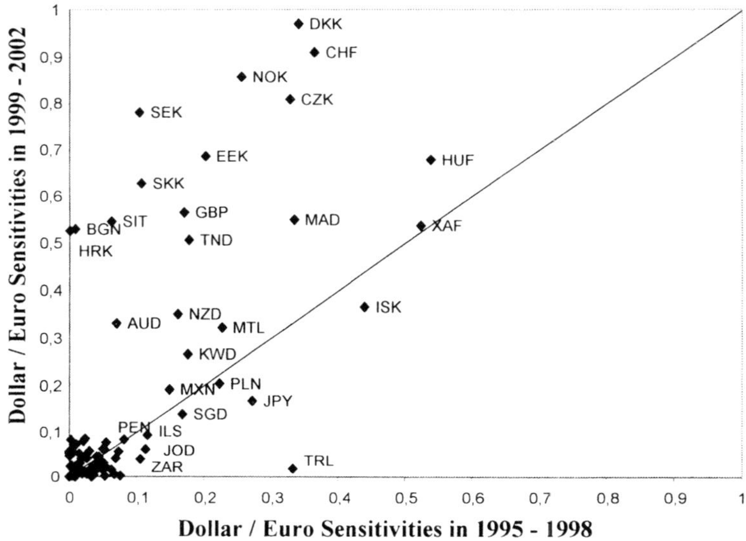

AUD: Australia, BGN: Bulgaria, CHF: Swiss, CZK: Czech, DKK: Denmark, EEK: Estonia, GPB: Great Britain, HRK: Croatia, HUF: Hungary, ILS: Israel, ISK: Island, JOD: Jordanian, JPY: Japan, KWD: Kuwait, MAD: Morocco, MTL: Malta, MXN: Mexico, NOK: Norway, NZD: New Zeeland, PEN: Peru, PLN: Poland, SEK: Sweden, SIT: Slovenia, SKK: Slovakia, SGD: Singapore, TND: Tunisia, TRL: Turkey, XAF: Central African Republic , ZAR: South Africa.

Source: Bloomberg, own calculations.

The currencies of the Western European countries Denmark, Switzerland, Norway, Sweden and to a lesser extent the United Kingdom closely track the euro. With the notable exception of Denmark none of these countries' currencies is officially pegged to the euro. The second region closely connected to the Euroarea encompasses the accession countries to the European Union. Both groups of countries intensified their currency links to the euro in recent years. Unexpectedly the sensitivity of the Australian and the New Zeeland dollar increased over time. But this is in line with the reported improvement in liquidity on these bilateral foreign exchange markets.[5]

Overall actual exchange rate movements clearly show the still rising importance of the euro as a anchor currency. Nevertheless the

[5] See *ECB* (2001).

role of the euro is still limited to regions with close historical and/or economic links and is not of a global character as it is the case for the US dollar.

V. The role of the euro as an international financing and investment currency

In judging the success of the euro as an international financing currency we have to look at international debt securities markets. Before starting with a detailed analysis it is necessary to define which security market segments are covered by the term "international debt securities". We use data from the BIS international securities statistics and follow their definition. The BIS provides data for domestic and international debt securities which are further disaggregated along the categories bonds and notes and money market instruments:

Table 9: The BIS definition of debt securities markets

	Issues by Residents	Issues by Non-Residents
In Domestic Currency	A	B
In Foreign Currency	C	D

A = Domestic bonds; B = Traditional foreign bonds; C + D = Euro-Bonds; B + D = External or cross-border bonds; B + C + D = International Bonds.
Source: *BIS* (1995).

The BIS definition of international debt securities include Euro-Bonds and Euro-notes (D + C) and traditional foreign bonds (B) plus the corresponding segments of money market instruments. Thus, only issues by residents in their domestic currency (A) are excluded.[6] The BIS provides data for outstanding amounts in current dollar terms and for announced and net issues in dollar terms of the date of announcement. Announced new issues are a good indicator of current judgements by market participants, net issues give the actual amount of new external financing volume and outstanding amounts measure the importance of debt securities during the recent past. A disaggregation by the currency of issue is available representing the most important statistical source for our analysis. Thus, for example, new net issues of euro denominated international debt securities cover all euro denominated issues except those by residents of the euro area (A). Additionally available are data for outstanding amounts, net issues and announced issues by national-

6 Due to the lack of data international notes cover only the segments C and D, i.e. Euro-Notes.

ity of issuer. International debt securities by US-nationality issuer cover for example: issues by US borrowers on the US market in foreign currencies (C); issues of US borrowers on a foreign market in the currency of that market (B, an euro issue in Frankfurt for example); and issues by US borrowers on a foreign market not in the currency of that market (D, a Japanese yen or US dollar issue in Frankfurt for example). Unfortunately these data are not further disaggregated by currencies. But, assuming that segment B is an important component, an increase of US-nationality issues would indicate additional US external financing activity in foreign currencies, most probably either in yen or in euro. A simultaneous increase in euro denominated international issues and in US-nationality issues therefore indicates increased financing activities of US borrowers on euro denominated international securities markets.

The introduction of the euro could well turn out to be a watershed concerning the structure of international bonds, notes and money market instruments markets. The euro did successfully challenge the leading role of the US-$ as an international financing currency on international debt securities markets.

Our analysis is based on quarterly data from the Bank of International Settlements starting in the fourth quarter of 1993 until the fourth quarter of 2001 measured in current dollar terms. During the whole period outstanding amounts of international debt securities denominated in US-dollar exceeded amounts in euro - since 1995 US dollar bonds increased their lead. With the introduction of the euro in 1999 *announced issues* in euro, the best indicator of judgements by market participants, increased dramatically. In all quarters in the period 1999 to 2001 announced issues in euro were higher than in any other quarter during the analyzed time period. Annual increases in the years 1999 to 2001 amounted to 107%, 105% and 158% with respect to the year 1998.[7] The gap to issues denominated in US dollars narrowed markedly despite the fact that activities on dollar markets were high as well and the euro depreciated by 25% against the dollar within three years.

This pattern is also confirmed by *net issues* in euro and US dollar. Table 10 reproduces the figures for net issues of total interna-

---

7 Percentage increases would be even larger if an arithmetic correction for cross border issuance within the Euroarea before the introduction of the euro would be taken into account. See *Detken/Hartmann* (2000).

tional debt securities by currency while table 11 and 12 disaggregate along the sub-categories bonds and notes and money market instruments. Again in each quarter the activity of euro denominated issues is higher than before the start of EMU stage three. In several quarters actual amounts raised on international euro denominated markets surpassed US dollar issues (1999 Q4, 2001 Q1 and 2001 Q4, see table 10). Net issues in euro denominated debt securities in 1999 yet were slightly higher than US dollar issues. After a back-slide in 2000 euro issuance activity recovered again in 2001. The euro and the US dollar market shares seem now to have stabilized at similar size.

Table 10: Int. Debt Securities (Bonds, Notes and Money Market Instruments): Net Issues by Currency, Bill. USD

	1Q 98	**2Q 98**	**3Q 98**	**4Q 98**	**1Q 99**	**2Q 99**	**3Q 99**	**4Q99**
USD	120,3	146,5	83,6	60,0	148,9	163,2	144,8	73,7
EUR	61,5	73,7	58,4	29,2	132,1	155,4	141,0	116,9
Total	197,9	233,1	151,6	93,8	316,9	366,5	331,7	226,3
	1Q 00	**2Q 00**	**3Q 00**	**4Q 00**	**1Q 01**	**2Q 01**	**3Q 01**	**4Q01**
USD	131,8	143,0	152,6	154,1	158,5	158,9	110,0	122,9
EUR	123,7	109,2	102,0	108,4	163,7	135,2	76,6	143,7
Total	297,5	315,9	317,2	312,8	328,4	295,4	177,1	270,1
	1998	**%**	**1999**	**%**	**2000**	**%**	**2001**	**%**
USD	410,4	61%	530,6	43%	581,5	47%	550,3	51%
EUR	222,8	33%	545,4	44%	443,3	36%	519,2	48%
Total	676,4	100%	1241,4	100%	1243,4	100%	1071,0	100%

Source: *BIS* (1999-2002).

This development can be mainly ascribed to the sub-category of international bonds and notes. The US dollar share dropped from 62% in 1998 to 48% in 2001 while the euro share increased from 33% to 44% (see table 11). Shifts in market shares are even more dramatic in the smaller sub-category of international money market instruments (see table 12). But since these markets are much more volatile they are not an appropriate indicator of long run developments.

Table 11: Int. Bonds and Notes: Net Issues by Currency, Bill. USD

	1Q 98	2Q 98	3Q 98	4Q 98	1Q 99	2Q 99	3Q 99	4Q99
USD	113,9	141,7	78,1	65,3	141,1	167,2	142,0	75,3
EUR	62,4	74,3	54,8	23,1	113,5	153,2	130,6	111,9
Total	188,6	232,9	133,3	91,5	268,7	353,3	292,8	191,1
	1Q 00	**2Q 00**	**3Q 00**	**4Q 00**	**1Q 01**	**2Q 01**	**3Q 01**	**4Q01**
USD	136,2	137,0	141,8	139,4	157,6	161,1	118,8	120,1
EUR	121,9	104,0	96,5	103,1	150,1	135,8	80,2	136,8
Total	276,9	273,3	274,9	266,2	326,2	321,6	222,7	279,9
	1998	**%**	**1999**	**%**	**2000**	**%**	**2001**	**%**
USD	399,0	62%	525,6	48%	554,4	51%	557,6	48%
EUR	214,6	33%	509,2	46%	425,5	39%	502,9	44%
Total	646,3	100%	1105,9	100%	1091,3	100%	1150,4	100%

Source: *BIS* (1999-2002).

Table 12: Int. Money Market Instruments: Net Issues by Currency, Bill. USD

	1Q 98	2Q 98	3Q 98	4Q 98	1Q 99	2Q 99	3Q 99	4Q99
USD	6,4	4,8	5,5	-5,3	7,8	-4,0	2,8	-1,6
EUR	-0,9	-0,6	3,6	6,1	18,6	2,2	10,4	5,0
Total	9,3	0,2	18,3	2,3	48,2	13,2	38,9	35,2
	1Q 00	**2Q 00**	**3Q 00**	**4Q 00**	**1Q 01**	**2Q 01**	**3Q 01**	**4Q01**
USD	-4,4	6,0	10,8	14,7	0,9	-2,2	-8,8	2,8
EUR	1,8	5,2	5,5	5,3	13,6	-0,6	-3,6	6,9
Total	20,6	42,6	42,3	46,6	2,2	-26,2	-45,6	-9,8
	1998	**%**	**1999**	**%**	**2000**	**%**	**2001**	**%**
USD	11,4	38%	5,0	4%	27,1	18%	-7,3	9%
EUR	8,2	27%	36,2	27%	17,8	12%	16,3	-21%
Total	30,1	100%	135,5	100%	152,1	100%	-79,4	100%

Source: *BIS* (1999-2002).

The surge in issues on international debt security markets was due to higher activity of both US and euro area borrowers (see table 13–15). According to figures by *nationality of issuer* both increased their financing activity right after the start of EMU stage three. US borrowers increased their issues of international debt securities by 67% from 287,1 Bill US-$ in 1998 to 480,4 in 1999 and remained at about that level in the next two years (see table 13). Issuance by euro area borrowers on the other hand surged up by 150% from 208,5 Bill US-$ in 1998 to 519,8 in 1999 and further to 559,4 in 2000 before declining to 429,0 in 2001. In absolute terms the increase of issues by euro are borrowers was larger in the sub-category bonds and notes (see table 14) while it was more pronounced in relative terms in money market instruments (see table 15).

Table 13: Int. Debt Securities (Bonds, Notes and Money Market Instruments): Net Issues by Nationality of Issuer, Bill. USD

	1Q 98	2Q 98	3Q 98	4Q 98	1Q 99	2Q 99	3Q 99	4Q99
USA	60,5	100,3	67,9	58,4	127,8	140,1	129,0	83,5
Euroarea	75,1	61,5	48,8	23,1	125,1	148,9	134,6	111,2
Total	197,9	233,1	151,6	93,8	316,9	366,5	331,7	226,3
	1Q 00	**2Q 00**	**3Q 00**	**4Q 00**	**1Q 01**	**2Q 01**	**3Q 01**	**4Q01**
USA	92,3	108,0	141,1	125,8	153,2	121,1	94,8	114,4
Euroarea	136,2	147,8	136,5	138,9	147,1	100,7	65,9	115,3
Total	297,5	315,9	317,2	312,8	328,4	295,4	177,1	270,1
	1998	**%**	**1999**	**%**	**2000**	**%**	**2001**	**%**
USA	287,1	42%	480,4	39%	467,2	38%	483,5	45%
Euroarea	208,5	31%	519,8	42%	559,4	45%	429,0	40%
Total	676,4	100%	1241,4	100%	1243,4	100%	1071,0	100%

Source: *BIS* (1999-2002).

Table 14: Int. Bonds and Notes: Net Issues by Nationality of Issuer, Bill. USD

	1Q 98	2Q 98	3Q 98	4Q 98	1Q 99	2Q 99	3Q 99	4Q99
USA	61,1	97,7	62,3	55,9	114,8	131,9	129,7	77,7
Euroarea	68,9	67,1	43,3	17,7	97,0	143,6	108,6	80,2
Total	188,6	232,9	133,3	91,5	268,7	353,3	292,8	191,1
	1Q 00	**2Q 00**	**3Q 00**	**4Q 00**	**1Q 01**	**2Q 01**	**3Q 01**	**4Q01**
USA	93,9	112,1	122,0	117,9	149,8	126,8	108,5	123,4
Euroarea	122	107,0	123,4	115,0	140,0	115,4	77,1	117,0
Total	276,9	273,3	274,9	266,2	326,2	321,6	222,7	279,9
	1998	**%**	**1999**	**%**	**2000**	**%**	**2001**	**%**
USA	277,0	43%	454,1	41%	445,9	41%	508,5	44%
Euroarea	197,0	30%	429,4	39%	467,4	43%	449,5	39%
Total	646,3	100%	1105,9	100%	1091,3	100%	1150,4	100%

Source: *BIS* (1999-2002).

Table 15: Int. Money Market Instruments: Net Issues by Nationality of Issuer, Bill. USD

	1Q 98	2Q 98	3Q 98	4Q 98	1Q 99	2Q 99	3Q 99	4Q99
USA	-0,6	2,6	5,6	2,5	13,0	8,2	-0,7	5,8
Euroarea	6,2	-5,6	5,5	5,4	28,1	5,3	26,0	31,0
Total	9,3	0,2	18,3	2,3	48,2	13,2	38,9	35,2
	1Q 00	**2Q 00**	**3Q 00**	**4Q 00**	**1Q 01**	**2Q 01**	**3Q 01**	**4Q01**
USA	-1,6	-4,1	19,1	7,9	3,4	-5,7	-13,7	-9,0
Euroarea	14,2	40,8	13,1	23,9	7,1	-14,7	-11,2	-1,7
Total	20,6	42,6	42,3	46,6	2,2	-26,2	-45,6	-9,8
	1998	**%**	**1999**	**%**	**2000**	**%**	**2001**	**%**
USA	10,1	34%	26,3	19%	21,3	14%	-25,0	31%
Euroarea	11,5	38%	90,4	67%	92,0	60%	-20,5	26%
Total	30,1	100%	135,5	100%	152,1	100%	-79,4	100%

Source: BIS (1999-2002).

Several reasons were discussed as potential explanations of the successful start of the euro on international debt security markets as an international financing currency:

1. In the wake of the Asian and Russian Crisis a flight to quality emerged boosting demand for bonds supplied by issuers from well rated countries like the USA and the EU. Issues of emerging countries have been very low in 1999.

2. The general trend to disintermediation can explain the increased volume of total international debt securities. The fact that disintermediation in Europe is far less advanced than in the USA could be - in the wake of a catching up process – a potential source of additional activity on European capital markets. As a matter of fact the European corporate bond sector witnessed increased issues of debt securities and most of these offers were placed on international markets: Net issues of international debt securities by euro area-nationality corporates were more than four times higher in 2001 than in 1998: They increased from 21,5 Bill US dollar to 87,7. US corporates on the other hand issued international debt securities worth 23,5 Bill. US dollar in 1998 and 72,5 in 2001. Also international issues by European financial institutions experienced significant growth from 171,7 Bill US dollar in 1998 to 451,4 in 1999 before dropping to 325,0 in 2001. The rise by US financials was less spectacular from 178,4 Bill US dollar in 1998 to 194,3 Bill US dollar in 2001. In contrast US government and state agencies increased their international issues markedly from in 85 Bill. US dol-

lar 1998 to in 216,9 in 2001 while euro area government borrowers issues remained rather constant with 15,4 Bill. US dollar in 1998 and 16,7 in 2001. Thus European corporate and financial borrowers and US corporate and public borrowers made intensive use of international capital markets to meet their financial needs.

3. Recent years were a period of huge and spectacular mergers in Europe. The external capital needs to finance these deals were partly met on international euro denominated debt securities markets.

4. Low interest rates in Europe made it very attractive for international borrowers to raise financial capital in euros. Especially until early 2001 interest rates in the USA were higher motivating US borrowers to become active on euro denominated markets.

5. Finally and most important, the introduction of the euro created an international financial market which because of its size, liquidity and depth is an interesting alternative to the dominating US market. Sinking transaction costs and considerations about risk diversification boosted the demand for and supply of international bonds. Since the development was not a continuos process but characterized by a sudden jump in the volume of euro denominated international bonds, notes and money market instruments already in the first quarter of 1999, neither cyclical economic factors nor exchange rate movements serve as possible explanations. The liquidity and market depth of the new and large currency area together with the favorable interest rate structure for borrowers, led to a marked increase in financing activity right after the introduction of the euro.

We showed that the euro immediately established itself as an international financing currency. In net issues of international debt securities the euro reached a market share of 48% only slightly lower than the US dollar with 51%. US borrowers seeking favorable financing conditions in Europe seem to have strongly stimulated this development. As reported by the European Commission[8] US borrowers issued international bonds denominated in euro worth 37,1 Bill. euro in 1999, 56,9 Bill. euro in 2000 and 71,4 Bill. euro in 2001. In 2001 US borrowers accounted for almost 15% of

---

[8] Figures by the European Commission published in "Monthly Note on the Euro-Denominated Bond Markets", are not directly comparable with BIS data since only issues of an amount of 50 Mill. Euro or more and of a maturity of one year and more are included.

all international euro denominated issues. But who bought these papers? Did international demand for euro denominated papers develop as quickly as supply? Only if this is the case the euro would also have established as a successful international investment currency. Unfortunately available data concerning the investment side are very limited. According to *Detken/Hartmann* (2000) and *ECB* (2001) the role of the euro as an international investment currency could not keep pace with its successful emergence as an international financing currency. Their arguments are based on the lower growth of international bank assets compared to international debt securities and on survey data among global fund managers indicating that the introduction of the euro did not lead to any dramatic change in portfolio allocation decisions of fund managers. Although the data are weak and have to be interpreted with caution we may draw the conclusion that the huge increase in euro denominated international debt securities was mainly absorbed by investors from the euro area.

The implications of the successful emergence of the euro as an international financing currency on the US dollar / euro exchange rate are the topic of the next section.

VI. The depreciation of the euro as the result of its success?

Long-run parity conditions like relative purchasing power (PPP) theory and the international Fischer effect (IFE) would have suggested the dollar to depreciate against the euro since its introduction in 1999. Inflation rates and interest rates were on average higher in the USA than in the euro area. Also many market participants and exchange rate analysts were puzzled by the decline of the euro by more than 24% until the end of 2001, especially as US saving rates were historically low and current account deficits high.

The gap between the euro as a success story as international financing currency and its more modest role as a currency for international investment may help to solve the puzzle. As pointed out before low interest rates in Europe compared to US levels and the creation of a new, liquid and deep international financial market by the introduction of the euro motivated international borrowers especially from the US to become active on international euro denominated markets. Most of the additional supply of euro denominated securities was absorbed by European investors. The consequence of this financing strategy, not anticipated by market participants, was – ceteris paribus - a depreciation of the euro versus the dollar. First, a good deal of the euro denominated financial capital raised by US borrowers was converted into US dollars on foreign exchange markets thereby directly affecting the exchange rate. Second, the relative increase in the supply of euro denominated assets led - according to the short run portfolio model as shown below – to a depreciation of the euro in order to guarantee market clearing on international debt securities markets.

Contrary to the monetary approach the portfolio asset model regards home-currency securities as imperfect substitutes for foreign-currency securities. Risk aversion of portfolio holders may motivate this pattern. Thus, uncovered interest rate parity does not prevail. As usual we assume a home asset preference. Differentials between home and foreign interest rates reflect mainly exchange rate risks.[9]

In traditional approaches to the portfolio model the outstanding amount of home-currency securities either reflected cumulated government or cumulated current account deficits. In a world with integrated international financial markets this strict currency distinction is no longer valid. Especially large multinational enterprises can issue securities denominated in any international currency.

For our purpose it is convenient to view financing decisions and thereby the supply of home- and foreign-currency securities as exogenous and concentrate on the endogenous variables exchange rate and interest rate. They adjust to changes in the exogenous stock variables to clear markets. In figure 6[10] we present a graphical analysis of the portfolio asset model for the case of a relative increase in the supply of euro denominated debt securities. This shifts the equilibrium condition for domestic bonds, the BB schedule, to BB′ and the equilibrium conditions for foreign bonds, the FF schedule, to FF'. The equilibrium condition on the money market (MM) is not affected. The increase in the *relative* supply of home-currency securities (i.e. the relative increase in euro denominated vs. dollar denominated international debt securities) is the exogenous shock we wish to analyze.

---

9 As in many empirical studies differences due to credit risk differentials between securities issued by foreign and home borrowers are ignored.

10 Graphically the effects are only shown for the euro area. The effects for the USA are a mirror image.

Figure 6: Effects in the short run portfolio model

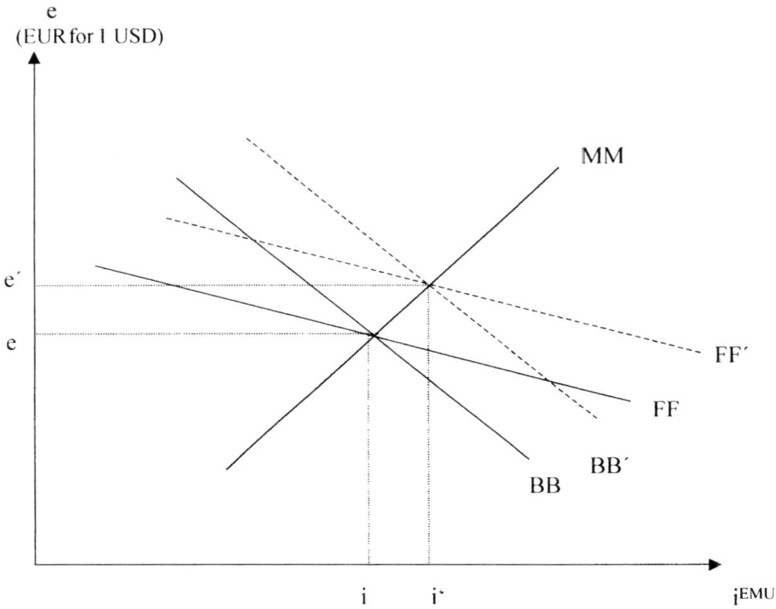

As shown this leads undoubtedly to a depreciation of the euro against the US dollar. A devaluation of the home currency increases wealth (see equation 4) and thereby the demand for home-currency securities (see equation 1). But the depreciation also increases the value of foreign bonds. Assuming preferences for a balanced portfolio concerning the value of stocks of foreign and domestic securities held by investors, the increased value of foreign bonds decreases demand for them. Thus we reach a new equilibrium with a depreciation of the home currency (euro) from *e* to *e'*. The effect on euro area interest rates is positive in our graphical example, the size of the increase depends on wealth and interest rate elasticities of the demand functions for money, euro currency bonds, and US currency bonds.

Home country (euro area) Foreign country (USA)

(1) $B = b(\overset{+}{r}, \overset{-}{r^* + E(\dot{e})}, \overset{+}{W})$ $\quad B^* = b^*(\overset{+}{r - E(\dot{e})}, \overset{-}{r^*}, \overset{+}{eW^*})$

(2) $F = f(\overset{-}{r}, \overset{+}{r^* + E(\dot{e})}, \overset{+}{W})$ $\quad F^* = f^*(\overset{-}{r - E(\dot{e})}, \overset{+}{r^*}, \overset{+}{eW^*})$

(3) $M = m(\overset{-}{r}, \overset{+}{W})$ $\quad M^* = m^*(\overset{-}{r^*}, \overset{+}{eW^*})$

$$(4) \quad W = B + eF + M \qquad eW^* = B^* + eF^* + eM^*$$

$$(5) \quad B = B + B^* \qquad F = F + F^*$$

$\bar{B}$ and $\bar{F}$ denote the stocks of home- and foreign-currency bonds, b (b^*), f (f^*), m (m^*) denote home (foreign) demand for home-currency bonds, foreign currency bonds and money. $E(e)$ and e indicate the expected exchange rate and the exchange rate, r and r* the home and foreign interest rates, W and W^* home and foreign wealth.

Effects of the composition of wealth on the foreign exchange rate are a crucial feature of the portfolio asset model. Similar to the effects of a sterilized intervention by monetary authorities a shift in the composition of wealth in the euro area from dollar to euro denominated bonds induces a depreciation of the euro[11] (see *Branson/Henderson* (1998); *Breuss* (1998); *Isard* (1995) for a detailed analytical treatment). Thus the model correctly predicts a depreciation of the euro. Since the real side of the economy is not modeled important factors determining exchange rates as for example inflation, current accounts and output growth are not considered. Thus implications by this model are only valid in the short run.

Within the short run portfolio asset model also a temporary phenomenon associated with the euro cash changeover can be dealt with which also affects the exchange value of the euro. During the first half of the nineties an increasing amount of Deutsche marks and to a lesser extent also of Austrian shillings and Finish marks circulated in Eastern Europe and in Turkey as people in those countries had little confidence in the stability of their own currencies. Due to uncertainties concerning the unwinding of the cash changeover part of these stocks were converted to other stable or to home currencies in the years before 2002. *Sinn/Westermann* (2001) show that in the case of the Deutsche mark this behaviour goes hand in hand with the strong fall in the share of the Deutsche mark in Euro-12 currency in circulation. This drop is reinforced by the conversion of black money held outside Germany. Both factors caused an increase in the supply of Deutsche mark in Germany which obviously was absorbed by the Bundesbank to prevent interest rates from falling. As a side effect the interventions by the Bun-

[11] In this very simple version of the portfolio asset model the production side is not modeled. Therefore output and price changes are not analyzed.

desbank neutralized any direct effect on the exchange rate. But the open market operations increased the stock of German treasury bills in the private sector thereby increasing the supply of bonds denominated in Deutsche mark / euro. As shown above in the framework of the portfolio asset model such shifts in the stock of assets cause an depreciation of the Deutsche mark / euro.

VII. Conclusions from a historical perspective

Britain was the largest trading nation until the end of the 19th century and the British pound was uncontested in its use for indirect currency exchange, as denomination currency for international debt securities and as unit of account in terms of which commodity prices were set. Even until the first world war when the USA have already emerged as the worlds leading economic nation the British pound kept its dominating role in international goods and financial markets. Between the two world wars the position of the Sterling as the only major international currency started to weaken but it was not before the end of the second world war that this decline accelerated sharply. Thus, the British pound dominated international goods and financial markets much longer than the economic power of the UK would have suggested reflecting huge inertia and hysteresis effects in the use of international currencies.[12] In the second half of the 20th century only the US dollar was omnipresent. The international role of other currencies like the Deutsche mark and the Japanese yen was limited to a more regional level. Even major regime shifts like the break down of the Bretton Woods system did not jeopardize the position of the US dollar as the economic and political strength of the USA was unrivaled worldwide.

Due to economies of scale in the use of international currencies history matters and existing structures in international goods and financial markets tend to persist for a long time. Only major shocks like the rise of the USA to the leading global economic nation (and the synchronous fall of the UK) at the beginning of last century can give rise to a new market structure. The introduction of the euro certainly constitutes a major shock to international markets and may well lead to a shift to a new equilibrium.

Against this historical evidence the emergence of the euro as an international currency in its first three years must be assessed as promising. Although persistency characterized many aspects of

---

[12] See *Rey* (1997).

international currency markets since the introduction of the euro in 1999 some remarkable changes can be observed as well.

As an international financing currency the euro had a brilliant start. Announced issues of international euro denominated debt securities - a good indicator of judgements by market participants - increased dramatically in 1999. Market shares rose abruptly by 11 percentage points to 32% compared to the previous year. A similar upsurge took place in the net issuance of euro denominated international debt securities. The share of net issues denominated in US-dollar dropped from 61% in 1998 to 43% in 1999 while the euro share increased from 33% to 44%. After a small backslide to 36% in 2000 net issues of euro denominated international debt securities recovered to 48% in 2001 just falling short of the US dollar market share by 3 percentage points. Since this development was not a continuous process but characterized by a sudden jump in the volume of euro denominated debt securities already in the first quarter of 1999, neither cyclical economic factors nor exchange rate movements serve as possible explanations. The creation of a new deep and broad market and favorable financing conditions in Europe made it very attractive for international borrowers to raise financial capital in euro. According to the short run portfolio model these shifts in the supply of euro and US dollar denominated international debt securities may well have triggered the depreciation of the euro against the US dollar. Additionally temporary effects caused by the return flow of money holdings of euro legacy currencies (mainly Deutsche mark) from Eastern Europe and Turkey to the euro area in the course of the cash changeover help to explain the puzzle of the euro depreciation.[13]

On international foreign exchange markets and in its use as an anchor and reserve currency the euro inherited mainly the role the Deutsche mark played before. Thus it established immediately as the second most widely used international currency in these aspects. The percentage share of the euro of average daily turnover on global foreign exchange markets in April 2001 reached 38% compared to 30% of the Deutsche mark in 1998. But it is well below the aggregate level of its predecessor currencies mainly because of the elimination of intra-euro trading volumes. Transaction costs - measured by spreads on foreign exchange markets - increased in recent past. This seems to be a consequence of rising trading costs

[13] See *Sinn/Westermann* (2001).

following a consolidation process in the banking industry. As an anchor currency the role of the euro is mainly limited to two regions: Europe and former French colonies in Africa.

The further development of the euro as an international currency will be decided on international financial markets. If its success as an international financing currency will be prolonged its relevance with respect to other roles an international currency fulfills will increase. The vision of a bipolar world currency system in which the US dollar and the euro are equally important seems no longer unrealistic. But historical evidence concerning inertia and hysteresis effects suggest that this can be a long process. In the near future the US dollar will remain the unrivaled number one as an international currency. An important political task in order to support the further success of the euro as an international currency remains the elimination of existing obstructions to a really united European financial market.

References

Branson H. W. / Henderson W. D. (1990), Specification and Influence of Asset Markets, in: *Jones W. R. / Kenen B. P.* (eds.), Handbook of International Economics, Vol.2, North-Holland/ Amsterdam, 1990, pp. 750-805.

BIS (1995), The BIS Statistics on International Banking and Financial Market Activity, Basel, August 1995.

BIS (1999-2002), Quarterly Review: International Banking and Financial Market Developments, several issues, Basel, 1999-2002.

BIS (2002), Triennial Central Bank Survey on Foreign Exchange and Derivative Market Activity in 2001, Basel, 2002.

Breuss F. (1998), Außenwirtschaft Band II, Monetärer Teil - Schwerpunkt Wirtschafts- und Währungsunion, Springer-Verlag, Wien-New York, 1998.

Detken C. / Hartmann Ph. (2000), The Euro and International Capital Markets, in: CEPR Discussion Paper No. 2461, May 2000.

Dominguez K. / Frankel J. (1990), Does Foreign Exchange Intervention Matter? Disentangling the Portfolio and Expectations

Effects for the Mark, in: NBER Working Paper No. 3299, March 1990.

ECB (2000), Annual Report, Frankfurt, 2000.

ECB (1999-2000), Monthly Bulletin, several issues, Frankfurt, 1999/2000.

European Commission (1999-2001), Monthly Note on the Euro-Denominated Bond Markets, several issues, 1999/2000/2001.

European Commission, "Quarterly Note on the Euro-Denominated Bond Markets", several issues, http://europa.eu.int/comm/economy_finance/publications/bond_markets (March 2002).

Galati G. / Tsatsaronis K. (2001), The impact of the euro on Europe's financial markets, in: BIS Working Paper No.100, Basel, July 2001.

Hartmann Ph. (1998), Currency Competition and Foreign Exchange Markets, Cambridge, 1998.

IMF (2001), Annual Report of the Executive Board for the Financial Year Ended April 30, 2001, Washington D.C., http://www.imf.org/external/pubs/ft/ar/2001/eng/index.htm, September 2001.

Isard P. (1995), Exchange rate Economics, Cambridge, 1995.

Krugman P. / Obstfeld M. (1993), International Economics, Theory and Policy, 3rd edition, Chicago, 1993.

Krugman P. (1980), Vehicle Currencies and the International Structure of exchange, in: Journal of Money, Credit, and Banking, vol. 1, no. 3, August 1980, pp.513-26.

Merill Lynch (2000), Size and Structure of the World Bond Market: 2000, April 2000.

Obstfeld M. / Rogoff K. (1996), Foundations of International Macroeconomics, Massachusetts Institute of Technology, 1996.

Rey H. (1997), International Trade and Currency Exchange, in: Discussion Paper No.322, Centre for Economic Performance, London, February 1997.

Sinn W.-H. / Westermann F. (2001), Why has the euro been falling?, in: CESifo WP No. 493, May 2001.

Part 4:
Enlargement and EMU

Bernhard Mahlberg, Ralf Kronberger

Eastern Enlargement of the European Monetary Union: An Optimal Currency Area theory view

I. Introduction

On January 1st 1999, eleven member states of the European Union commenced stage three of European Monetary Union (EMU), fixed the exchange rates of their national currencies and introduced the Euro as their single currency. Two years later, on January 1st 2001, Greece became the twelfth member of EMU. On January 1st 2002, the national central banks together with the European Central Bank (ECB) began circulation of Euro notes and coins and started to withdraw national currencies. This was finished by the end of the February 2002 and since March 1st 2002, the Euro has been the only legal means of payment for almost 320 million people in the twelve EMU countries.

In 1989, the Communist regimes collapsed throughout the region of Central and Eastern Europe. Besides the subsequent establishment of democracies in these societies, the Central and Eastern European countries (CEEC) started to transform their economies from planned to market systems. In addition, they have oriented their interests towards the European Union (EU). Since 1994, ten CEEC have applied for EU membership and, from 1998 the European Commission has been negotiating with the first group of five countries (the "Luxembourg Group"). At the Helsinki Council meeting in December 1999, the EU decided to start negotiations with the rest of the CEEC (the "Helsinki Group"). Last June in Gothenburg, the European Council set itself the goal of completing the negotiations with some of the candidate countries by the end of 2002. First accessions should start at the beginning of 2004. Part of the accession process is the ratification of the Treaty of Maastricht[1] and accordingly, the member states are obliged to participate in the European Monetary Union if they fulfill all criteria.[2] This is also valid for the CEEC. Consequently, the question of EMU preparedness in the CEEC is becoming more and more important.

The Maastricht criteria are not identical to the Optimal Currency Area criteria as derived from economic literature. This branch of literature dates from 1961 when Mundell introduced in his seminal paper the theory of Optimum Currency Area (OCA). An OCA is characterized by a group of countries for which forgoing the exchange rate mechanism, as an instrument of correcting asymmetric shocks, is compensated by other economic policy instruments. In this paper, we address the issue whether the CEEC are a part of a European OCA or not. One of the OCA criteria is the similarity of business cycles among the countries participating in a currency union. The business cycles of the CEEC, as measured by the development of the Gross Domestic Product (GDP) and the Industrial Production (IP) index, are analysed and compared with the cycles of EU member states.

---

[1] In this analysis candidate countries Cyprus and Malta are not dealt with.

[2] The United Kingdom and Denmark are exempt due to an opt-out clause. Sweden is not a member, as it did not participate in the European Monetary System.

II. Accession Criteria for EU and EMU membership

In 1993, at the Copenhagen European Council, the EU defined the membership criteria, often referred to as the Copenhagen Criteria, which requires that every candidate country has to achieve:

- the stability of institutions guaranteeing democracy, the rule of law, human rights and respect for, and protection of, minorities (political criterion);
- the existence of a functioning market economy, as well as the capacity to cope with competitive pressure and market forces within the Union (economic criterion);
- the ability to take on the obligations of membership including adherence to the aims of political, economic and monetary union (acquis communautaire criterion).

Accession negotiations are under way with twelve countries, ten from Central and Eastern European Countries (Estonia, Latvia, Lithuania, Poland, the Czech Republic, Slovakia, Hungary, Slovenia, Romania, and Bulgaria). Negotiations started on March 31st 1998 with six applicant countries - Hungary, Poland, Estonia, the Czech Republic, Slovenia and Cyprus. On October 13th 1999, the European Commission recommended to open negotiations with Romania, the Slovak Republic, Latvia, Lithuania, Bulgaria, and Malta. This was endorsed by Member States at the Helsinki Summit on December 12th 1999, with negotiations starting in February 2000. The European Council in Gothenburg (June 15th and June 16th 2001) affirmed their objective to complete negotiations by the end of 2002. The countries should thus participate as full members in the European Parliament's elections of 2004. The European Council in its meeting in Laaken in December 2001 named ten candidate countries to become EU members in 2004. By the end of July 2002, eight of ten CEEC had at least 25 of the 31 chapters closed.[3]

The Single European Act of February 17th 1986 and the Treaty of Maastricht of February 7th 1992 are the legal basis of EMU. The Single European Act establishes the objectives of EMU and the Treaty of Maastricht lays down the criteria every country has to fulfill, if it wants to join EMU.

---

[3] See http://europa.eu.int/comm/enlargement/negotiations/pdf/stateofplay_july2002.pdf.

The four criteria are (TEC, Article 121):

- the achievement of a high degree of price stability; a member state has a price performance that is sustainable and an average rate of inflation, observed over a period of one year before the examination, that does not exceed by more than 1.5 percentage points that of, at most, the three best performing member states in terms of price stability;
- the sustainability of government finances; the planned or actual government deficit no higher than 3% of GDP at market prices and government debt around 60% of GDP at market prices;
- maintenance within the normal fluctuation margins of the exchange-rate mechanism of the European Monetary System (EMS), for at least two years, without devaluing against the currency of any other member state;
- the durability of convergence and of its participation in the exchange-rate mechanism is reflected in, for one year before entry, average nominal long-term interest rates that do not exceed by more than 2 percentage points that of, at most, the three best performing member states in terms of price stability.

According to the third criterion, new EU members can join EMU after at least two years of participation in the exchange-rate mechanism. Therefore, the CEEC may only join the EMU after the beginning of their third year of EU membership and not immediately after their accession to European Union.

Currently, none of the CEEC fulfill all the Maastricht criteria. Only Latvia and Lithuania fulfill the criterion of price stability. In all other CEEC inflation lies above the reference value. With respect to government finances the situation is better. Government deficit to GDP is below 3% in Bulgaria, Estonia, Latvia, Lithuania, and Slovenia. The criterion of government debt is fulfilled even better, in the year 2000/01 almost all CEEC had less than 60% of government debt to GDP ratios. Bulgaria being the only exception. As the CEEC can not be members of the European Monetary System, the third criterion is not applicable. However, in considering the exchange rate fluctuation of CEEC's currencies, vis-a-vis the Euro in the last two years, volatility is more than +/- 15 % for almost all CEEC. Only Estonia meets this exchange rate stability requirement. Finally, none of the CEEC have interest rates lower than the reference value. The Estonian interest rate comes closest to the EU standard (see Table 1).

Table 1: Maastricht-Convergence Criteria - CEEC, 2001

	price stability	government financial position		exchange-rate	long-term interest-rate levels
	consumer price index, percent change [1]	government budget deficit to gross domestic product (in percent of GDP)	government debt to gross domestic product [2] (in percent of GDP)	deviation against the Euro less than +/- 15%, 1999 - 2001 [3]	lending rate, in percent [4]
reference values	**3.3**	**3**	**60**	**yes**	**7.0**
Bulgaria	7.5	0.9	76.9	no	11.4
Czech Republic	4.6	7.1	17.3	no	7.6
Estonia	5.9	0.3	5.3	yes	7.3
Hungary	9.1	4.3	55.7	no	12.0
Latvia	2.5	1.8	14.1	no	8.5
Lithuania	1.4	1.7	23.7	no	8.9
Poland	5.6	4.3	40.9	no	17.9
Romania	34.1	3.5	22.9	no	51.3 [5]
Slovak Republic	7.4	4.5	32.4	no	11.4
Slovenia	8.5	1.2	25.8	no	14.0

[1] HCPI for EU-15. [2] Data of 2000. [3] instead of participation in the exchange-rate mechanism of the EMS, only EU member states can be member of the EMS. [4] long term interest rates for EU-15. [5] Treasury Bill Rate

Source: *European Commission* (2001a) for inflation and log term interest rates of EU-15, *European Commission* (2001b) for inflation and deficit of CEEC, *European Commission* (2001c) for government debt of CEEC, and *IMF* (2001) for exchange rates and lending rates of CEEC.

III. OCA Theory and EU Enlargement

A. Related OCA Research

The Optimal Currency Area (OCA) theory addresses the question whether a country benefits from joining a currency union. The establishment of a currency union has as a consequence the replacement of the national currency by a common currency. The exchange rate as an instrument to counteract asymmetric economic shocks is forgone. From this theory, criteria have been derived to help decide whether such a step is beneficial. The concept of the OCA goes back to *Mundell* (1961). Two countries, A and B, with a bilaterally fixed exchange rate are considered, where country B is hit by an asymmetrical negative demand shock. Prices and output in country B decrease, and unemployment results. According to Mundell, the adequate response for country B of monetary expansion would, under a fixed exchange rate regime, only be possible if country A would also adopt an expansive monetary policy. Absent the consensual monetary expansion labor mobility could also alleviate the problem. Workers moving from country B to A would reduce the excess supply of labor, reducing import demand in B and therefore reestablishing equilibrium in the current account.[4] Overall, fixed exchange rates or monetary union prove less advantageous, if countries face asymmetrical shocks and show little factor mobility. Since its introduction the OCA theory has been extended and several criteria added. Among others, *McKinnon* (1963) emphasized the meaning of the degree of openness for member countries and *Kenen* (1969) underlined the importance of product diversification.[5]

The main findings of the OCA theory show that when countries are different in economic structures, they are likely to face asymmetric shocks. In the absence of the exchange rate as an instrument, they need flexible labor markets (e.g. wage flexibility, labor mobility) so as to adjust for and prevent these shocks from leading to permanent unemployment. OCA theory also states that the cost of relinquishing the exchange rate instrument declines with the degree

---

4 For an illustrative and detailed presentation of the Mundell approach, see *De Grauwe* (2000) 6 ff. For a critique on the Mundell see *Maes* (1992).

5 For an overview of the theoretical and empirical OCA-literature see inter alia *Breuss* (1998) 183 ff; *Horvath* (2001b); and *Ishiyama* (1975).

of openness of the country. For very open countries the exchange rate instrument loses much of its effectiveness to influence output and employment, and therefore to correct for asymmetric shocks. Thus, very open (and typically small) countries bear lower costs joining a monetary union than large, very closed economies. Conversely, the benefits of a single currency increase with the degree of openness of a country, because a larger proportion of trade involves exchange rate transactions (see also *De Grauwe/Aksoy* (1999)).

The empirical application of OCA theory has been well covered in economic literature. The preparedness of member states for European Monetary Union has been tested several times. Among others, *Bayoumi/Eichengreen* (1993) carried out an analysis of supply and demand shocks in the member states of the European Union using a technique developed by *Blanchard/Quah* (1989). A detailed list of related empirical research can be found in surveys, e.g. *Breuss* (1998), pp. 184 - 185.

In the last few years, OCA theory has also been applied to the CEEC to discuss the question of joining EMU. The main issues in this literature are the timing of monetary union membership and the proper interim exchange rate regime. In this section, we provide an overview of the studies recently written on the former.

Breuss (1999) was one of the first to deal with the preparedness of the CEEC. Due to a lack of sufficiently long time series data, he concentrated on a survey of the theoretical and empirical OCA-literature and the analysis of how far the CEEC fulfill the Maastricht criteria.

De Grauwe/Aksoy (1999) investigated the nature of the asymmetric shocks in the countries Czech Republic, Slovak Republic, Slovenia, Hungary, and Poland over the period 1992 to 1995. They used a panel data model to determine the extent to which output growth (measured by GDP and IP) and employment in the CEEC have differed from the European Union. The goal was to separate the common (international) and the country specific (asymmetric) sources of shocks in output and employment, through the application of static and dynamic models. The static model showed that the contribution of common shocks to total variability was generally higher than country specific shocks, thus changes in output and employment tend to be dominated by common shocks. This was most pronounced for employment changes and much less so for industrial production, where common and country specific shocks were equally important. On average, changes in output and employment of the CEEC differ significantly from the EU. This difference lied in the time patterns of output and employment deviating substantially between the CEEC and EU countries. The dynamic model showed significantly different cycles for industrial production in all CEEC, except Slovenia. However, GDP and employment cycles had no significant time varying effects. They concluded that some Central and Eastern European countries were not part of an European OCA and that Slovenia represented the most ideal candidate for EMU.

Boone/Maurel (1999) analyzed the similarity of the CEEC business cycles to identify those countries that would not suffer from joining monetary union. The sample included five current EMU members, the EU as a whole, and the candidates of Czech Republic, Slovak Republic, Hungary, and Poland. Two criteria were used, the percentage of domestic business cycles explained by a common German or EU shock and the correlation of the domestic impulse responses. As a proxy for economic activity, time series data of monthly unemployment rates was used. The low quality of data was the weak point in this study. Labor market data from the CEEC is particularly unreliable.[6] To detrend the series, they applied the Hodrick Prescott filter. The analysis of the shocks was done in a two step process, first by identifying common shocks by computing ARMA regressions. The shock that affects Germany or the EU was the residual of the identified ARMA process. The second step was analyzing the extent to which the CEEC fluctuations were explained by the common shock by regressing the estimated unemployment series on the common shock. They found that the business cycles of the CEEC were similar enough to that of Germany and to a minor extent to that of the EU permitting an enlargement of the EMU. They showed that the percentage of CEEC business cycle fluctuations explained by a German shock was very high and the impulse responses were positively correlated. These findings suggest that the CEEC would not suffer from a common monetary policy.

Fidrmuc (2001) tested the endogeneity hypothesis of OCA criteria using the approach of *Frankel/Rose* (1998) in a cross-section of thirteen EU member states and five Central and Eastern candidate countries. According to the endogeneity hypothesis, business cycles are becoming increasingly similar across countries as a

---

6 See *UNECE* (2001b) p. 14.

consequence of close trade links, particularly high levels of intra-industry trade. Similar business cycles create good preconditions for policy integration and the creation of a currency area. These were evaluated using time series data from 1993 to 1999 for five central European countries Czech Republic, Hungary, Poland, Slovak Republic, and Slovenia, as well as of EU member states. Some caveats to this work are: First, the observation period was short relative to the length of the cycles. Second, the trade regime change has not taken place at one point in time but is continuous. The opening up of the markets in the CEEC vis-à-vis the EU took place sector per sector. Third, during the examination period different trade and exchange rate systems were in place which have influenced the data. This made it difficult to isolate the effects of individual regime shifts and draw accurate conclusions. Fidrmuc concluded that intra industry trade caused convergence of business cycles and an increase in bilateral trade intensity. Also, the OCA endogeneity hypothesis was supported, as intra industry trade is shown as positively correlated with total trade. The endogeneity of OCA criteria implied a comparable degree of business cycle harmonization of CEEC with EU countries as between current EU members over the medium term.

Horvath (2001a) developed the work of *Bayoumi/Eichengreen* (1983) and adopted the Blanchard Quah decomposition to identify supply and demand shocks to GDP for all the CEEC (with exception of Bulgaria and Romania) and the four largest EU members. He correlated the supply and demand shocks to analyze the extent of synchronization between the business cycles and used a uniform lag length of 2 and the first difference of the two variables (GDP and GDP deflator). These factors reduced the number of degree of freedom for tests of significance considerably. The applied method in this study does not seem to be ideal for the short time series available. He found that idiosyncratic shocks prevailed between the largest EU member states and the candidate countries, suggesting a potentially costly process of adjustment when these countries join the European Monetary Union.

Fidrmuc/Korhonen (2001) tested if the CEEC belong to an Optimal Currency Area with Europe using the same approach as *Horvath* (2001a). In contrast to *Horvath*, the sample was extended to the whole of the EU (except Luxembourg), three European non-EU member states, and selected non European countries. The sample included nine of the ten CEEC (one country more than Horvath).

They used quarterly data of GDP and GDP deflator, where available, or quarterly IP data. Some caveats to this study are: First, *Fidrmuc/Korhonen* mixed GDP and IP data so that they correlated the shocks found in GDP data with shocks found in IP data. Second, the data contained too few observations relative to the number of explaining variables. In addition to GDP or IP and inflation, they inserted three dummies for seasonal adjustment and chose four lags, leaving only a few degrees of freedom for tests of significance. Finally, *Fidrmuc/Korhonen* computed pairwise correlation coefficients for time series GDP and inflation for each CEEC with each of the EU countries, and compared correlation coefficients for time series with different lengths. Their main findings are that some accession countries showed a relatively high correlation of the underlying shocks with the Euro area. However, even for many advanced accession countries, the shocks remained significantly idiosyncratic.

Korhonen (2001) investigated the relationship between short-term business cycles in the CEEC and EU member states by applying vector autoregression models. His analysis was based on monthly time series data of industrial production and avoided having too few observations, relative to the number of explanatory variables. However, the data was less representative as industrial production accounts for less than half of production in the CEEC and the EU. A clear difference was found in the degree of correlation of candidate countries. For Hungary and Slovenia, Euro area shocks accounted for a large proportion of variations in industrial production, which indicates high integration. Also, the Czech Republic and Estonia were reasonable well integrated with the business cycle of the Euro area, while Lithuania and Romania appeared to have little integration. A lower level of integration implies that joining monetary union could result in larger costs, unless their business cycles converge closer with the Euro area.

Finally, *Boreiko* (2002) estimated the readiness of the ten CEEC for EMU or for unilateral Euro adoption using a fuzzy clustering algorithm based on variables suggested alternatively by the criteria of the Maastricht Treaty and OCA theory. The variables for the analysis on the basis of the OCA theory were the correlation in business cycles, the volatility of bilateral exchange rate of national currencies against the Deutsche Mark, the ratio of trade with the EU over trade with the world, and the differential of the CEEC's inflation to the EU-15. Business cycles are extracted from monthly

Industrial Production indices (except monthly unemployment for Bulgaria and quarterly GDP for Estonia) using the Hodrick-Prescott filter and, alternatively, the twelfth differences of the logs of the series. The correlation coefficients computed for the whole observation period of 1993 to 2001 were found to be low for the most of the CEEC. Hungarian and the Slovenian business cycles have the highest correlation with the German cycle to the extent of around 0.5. Correlations over subperiods of 1997 to 2001 and 1999 to 2001 identified substantial increases over time and this was interpreted as a tendency towards real convergence. However, these subperiods comprised, at most, of only one full business cycle and were consequently too short for sound conclusions concerning convergence to be drawn. The overall results of this analysis, according to OCA theory, showed the presence of three groups of accession countries. The highest converged group consisted of the Czech Republic, Hungary, Estonia, and Slovenia, followed by Latvia, Lithuania, and Romania and then Bulgaria and the Slovak Republic.

B. Measuring business cycles in the CEEC

1. Method

Several concepts and methods have been used to analyze business cycles. Four groups of methods can be distinguished: The direct measure of cycles from survey data, non-structural (or statistical) methods, structural (or theory based) methods, and multivariate methods. *Direct measurement* identifies business cycles by comparing the actual capacity utilization rate and the actual output with the degree of capital utilization and optimum output with the absence of tensions in the goods market. *Non-structural measures* include all methods that are based on statistical procedure rather than referring explicitly on an economic theory. The Hodrick-Prescott filter, as used in this paper, and the Beveridge Nelson decomposition are the most common examples of this type. In contrast the *structural methods* rely on specific economic theory and two broad groups can be distinguished within this category. First, multivariate structural methods combined with theoretical assumptions constitute the so-called Structural Vector Auto Regressions (SVAR), such as the approach developed by *Blanchard/Quah* (1989). Second, structural methods can be based on an aggregate production function. *Multivariate methods* of business cycle analysis consist of multivariate versions of non-structural or statistical approaches, such as multivariate Beveridge-Nelson decompositions and multivariate Hodrick Prescott filter.[7]

For this paper the use of the *Blanchard/Quah* decomposition was considered. This approach (a SVAR method) decomposes variations in price level and activity into supply and demand shocks. Supply shocks are assumed to have permanent effects on output, whereas demand shocks have only transitory effects. Both supply and demand shocks have only transitory effects on the price level. A supply shock depresses the price level, whereas a demand shock increases it.

The drawbacks of the *Blanchard/Quah* decomposition are that it is incapable of distinguishing between shocks to the goods and money market. No distinction is made between endogenous and exogenous shocks. A shock introduced through stabilization policies will appear in the same way as an external demand shock. The approach has often been challenged with respect to its identification restrictions. VAR methods require long time series data to overcome the detrimental small sample properties of this method (*Licandro*, 1998). Large continuous time series of data for emerging and transition economies, such as the CEEC, do not often exist and frequently exhibit structural breaks. Too short time series, structural breaks and different orders of time series integration rendered this method inappropriate.[8] Moreover the study would be subject to the same drawbacks as *Fidrmuc/Korhonen* (2001).

The *Blanchard/Quah* method as well as the *Beveridge/Nelson* (1981) decomposition were considered for the analysis of our data set. The former method could not be applied since the inflation rates of the CEECs were not of the same order. The *Beveridge/Nelson* decomposition – a less sophisticated univariate time series decomposition – proved to be inappropriate due to similar reasons.

Therefore, the widely applied Hodrick-Prescott filter was selected to decompose the time series into its trend and cyclical com-

---

7 See *Chagny/Döpke* (2001) for a comprehensive survey on methods to identify business cycles.

8 Real GDP must be integrated to the order of one (I(1)) and the GDP deflator integrated to the order of zero (I(0)) for applying the approach of *Bayoumi/Eichengreen*. A series is said to be integrated to the order of one, denoted I(1), if after taking the first difference a stationary process results.

ponents. The trend is identified by the following convex minimization.

$$\underset{\{\tau\}_t}{Min} = \sum_{t=1}^{N}(z_t - \tau_t)^2 + \mu\sum_{t=3}^{N}\left[(\tau_t - \tau_{t-1}) - (\tau_{t-1} - \tau_{t-2})\right]^2$$

The first term contains the difference between the original series z_t and the trend τ_t, which is interpreted as the degree of adjustment. The second term indicates the degree of variability by means of the second differences of the trend τ_t. The coefficient μ reduces the acceleration of the trend. If μ equals zero, the original series and the trend are equal. If μ tends toward infinity the trend will become linear. We have chosen μ to be equal to 1600, which is standard for quarterly data analyses.

In our analysis the cycle c_t is defined as the difference between the original time series, either GDP or IP, and its trend:

$$c_t = z_t - \tau_t$$

Cycles were identified by determining the turning points. The turning points have to be proceeded either by two subsequent negative or positive values of the level of growth.[9] Ideally, a whole set of variables, such as whole sale, investments, savings, etc. as suggested by *Moore* (1983)[10] would allow for a more sophisticated identification. However, due to a lack of data this was not possible.[11] Furthermore, business cycles of transition economies are harder to analyze as cycle length are often shorter and turning points are harder to identify due to phenomena such as two consecutive peaks. The *Sachs/Larrain* procedure was followed as closely as possible, so that an upturn was sustained as long as the next downturn could be separately identified by two consecutive negative values.

2. Data

This paper uses quarterly time series data of Gross Domestic Product (GDP) at constant 1995 prices and Industrial Production (IP) Indices of CEEC and EU member states. Data availability and quality is well known to be difficult, and as such time series of both

---

9 *Sachs/Larrain* (1995) 670 ff.

10 *Breuss* (1984) was one of the first to identify the Austrian business cycle by similar methods.

11 According to *Tichy* (1976) 45 ff. GDP is easily justifiable as a single business cycle indicator as changes in GDP reflect changes in many of the variables suggested by NBER.

indicators are used.[12] The results obtained from the two indicators are different due to factors like the sensitivity to external trade. Industrial sectors usually operate in more competitive markets, because their products are typically tradable. They are more strongly related to EU countries through trade and have to react more quickly to changes in the economies of the EU. Therefore, variations in the IP are expected to have higher correlation than GDP business cycles. The IP is less representative than GDP as it incorporates only 25 to 41 percent of the economic activities in the CEEC (1999 data, see *UNECE* (2001a), p. 106).

The main source of data for the Central and Eastern European candidate countries is the United Nations Economic Commission for Europe (UNECE), which has provided data of different lengths for different countries.[13] The IP data for the EU countries were obtained from the OECD (database "Main Economic Indicators"). IP data for Denmark and Luxembourg was obtained from Eurostat, as the OECD does not provide IP data for these countries. GDP data is also from Eurostat. GDP for the CEEC was measured in national currencies and for EU countries in million Euro. Other sources, such as the OECD, Eurostat and national statistical offices were considered as sources of data for the CEEC but the data was limited in its use. OECD data for the Czech Republic and Slovakia has substantial differences compared with data from other sources and Eurostat could only provide data for six of the ten CEEC. Availability and consistency were problems with data from national statistical offices.

Available quarterly GDP data for accession countries usually spans from 1994 or 1995 to the end of 2000 or 2001. Quarterly IP time series for the CEEC start uniformly at the beginning of 1993.[14] For most countries, the data therefore omits the period of recession related to transformation in the accession countries. We have used EU GDP data for the last ten years for consistency with the accession countries, even though for some EU countries longer time se-

[12] Cross correlations between GDP and IP are not applied. Correlations are only applied within the two subsets.

[13] This data set comprises not only GDP and IP time series but also data on the components of GDP at the spending side of national accounts (consumption, investment, ...) of all candidate countries except Slovenia.

[14] Quarterly IP data is used to facilitate the computation of correlations between the GDP and IP cycles.

ries data is available. For Germany, Ireland, Portugal and Sweden consistent quarterly GDP data is available from 1991, 1997, 1995, and 1993, respectively. Quarterly GDP data of Greece and Luxembourg was not available from Eurostat.

3. Empirical Results

In this paper we deconstruct quarterly GDP data of eight Central and Eastern European Candidates (CEEC) and twelve members of the European Union (EU) in their trend and cyclical components by applying the Hodrick-Prescott filter.[15]

The GDP data for Bulgaria could not be used because of a 29% decline in GDP between the end of 1995 and beginning of 1997 which was identified as structural break in the time series. Furthermore, in the years before and after this structural break, GDP alternated between short periods of increases and decreases, which could not be interpreted as the upswings and downswings of normal business cycles of a market economy. It has been concluded that the transformation process has not been completed in this country before the beginning of observation period but were still continuing and we have therefore decided to exclude Bulgaria from our analysis. For Romania, quarterly GDP data was only available from 1998:1 to 2000:3. This is clearly too short to enable business cycle analysis. Quarterly GDP time series of Luxembourg and Greece were not available and Irish GDP data was available from 1997. These three EU countries have also been excluded from our analysis.

The logarithm of GDP was used. A deconstruction of the main components of GDP has also been undertaken to explain the cycle of the GDP. All data was seasonal adjusted by using the Tramo Seats method.

Additionally, the paper deconstructs quarterly Industrial Production (IP) index data for all Central and Eastern European candidates, except Bulgaria, and fourteen EU members with the Hodrick-Prescott filter. Bulgarian IP data suffered from a similar problem as GDP data. The data showed a reduction of around 60 percent of industrial production in 1996, constituting a structural break. Before and after this break, as with the GDP data, very short periods of increases and declines were found, which did not reflect normal business cycles. Therefore this data was excluded from our analy-

[15] The computations were done using the computer software package E-Views 4.0.

sis. Luxembourg was also excluded because of the small size of its economy. In general, deconstructions were started at the beginning of the time series. The only exceptions to this were Latvia and Lithuania where a strong decline of the Industrial Production index was observed at the beginning of the observation period. This decline was interpreted as the residual part of recession as a result of economic transformation and not as a downswing of a business cycle. Therefore the deconstruction was started in 1994 and 1995 for Lithuania and Latvia respectively. All data was seasonally adjusted using the Tramo Seats method.

The results of the Hodrick Prescott decomposition are shown and will briefly be discussed country by country. The relationship between the cycles of the CEEC and EU countries will be discussed with reference to the OCA theory.

a.) Business Cycles in the CEEC Candidate Countries

Figure 1 and Figure 2 show the time of beginning and ending and the length of the business cycles derived from our analyses of GDP and IP in the CEEC. The length of GDP and IP cycles differ across countries, with peaks and troughs occurring at different times. As shown below, cycles in transition countries tend to be shorter than in fully developed market economies, possibly due to more frequent endogenous policy shocks caused by the stabilization of their economies. We can also observe that within individual countries GDP and IP cycles differ. The only common movement observed is the downswing in the second half of 1998 caused by a crisis in Russia influencing all cycles except Slovenian GDP. The Slovenian economy is relatively less intertwined with the Russian economy than many other eastern European economies. In Table 2, we show the correlation of the GDP and IP business cycles with each other and with cycles of the main components of GDP. The business cycles are analyzed on a country by country basis to explain the underlying relationships.

Figure 1: Lengths of GDP-cycles

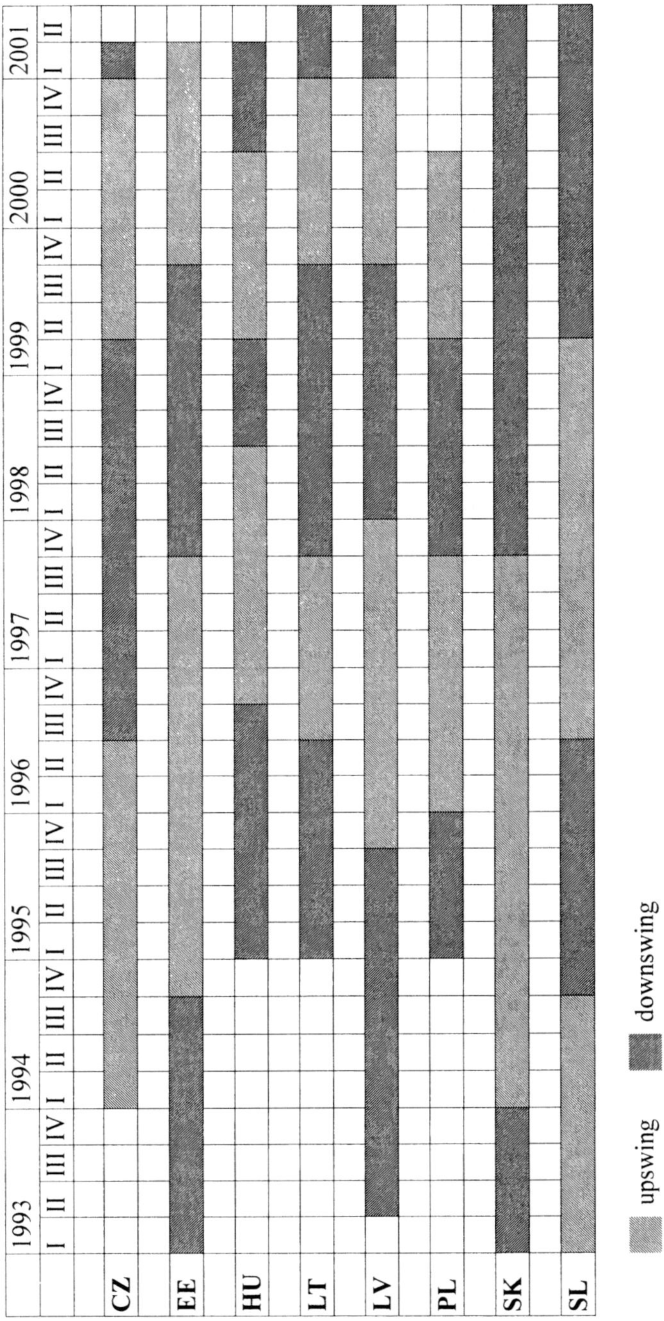

Figure 2: Lengths of IP-cycles

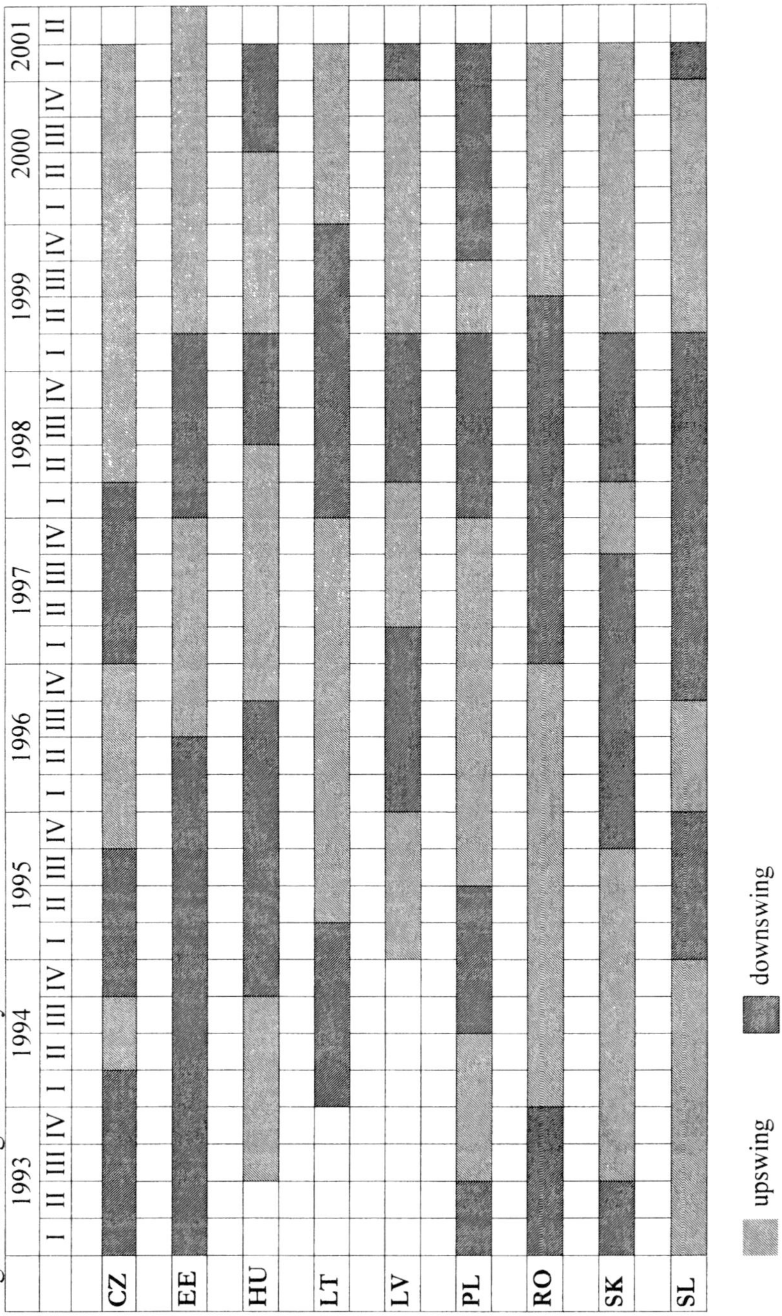

Table 2: Correlations of GDP cycle, IP cycle and GDP-component-cycles

	Czech Republic	Estonia	Hungary	Latvia	Lithuania	Poland	Slovak Republic	Slovenia
	correlation coefficients with GDP cycles							
private consumption	0.77	0.72	0.07	0.29	0.60	0.49	0.84	--
public consumption	0.24	-0.16	-0.24	-0.04	0.65	0.56	0.48	--
capital formation	0.93	0.84	0.19	0.29	0.74	0.56	0.61	--
Exports	0.51	0.63	0.15	0.69	0.79	0.31	-0.16	--
industry production	0.24	0.88	0.81	0.79	0.73	0.65	0.34	0.36

For the *Czech Republic,* one and a half GDP business cycles can be identified (two upswings from 1994:1 to 1996:2 and from 1999:2, one downswing from 1996:3 to 1999:1). The downswing took place during a currency and financial crisis in 1997 and the subsequent crisis in Russia in the second half of 1998. These cycles are strongly correlated with the cycles of investment and private consumption and, to a lesser extent, exports. The high correlation of investment was expected, as the investment to GDP ratio is the highest of all CEEC. The recession 1997 and 1998 was caused mainly by the reduction in investment caused by their sensitivity to financial crisis, the main reason for the downswing. The correlation with the consumption cycle is high because this is the largest GDP component. The business cycles derived from industrial production indices are different from GDP business cycles and their correlation is low because industrial production data does not contain investment and consumption activities as well as production activities of branches not included in the industrial sector. The industrial production business cycles are strongly correlated with the export cycle because industrial sectors are particularly exposed to external trade, as products are mainly tradable goods.

In *Estonia* we identified two complete business cycles (two upswings from 1994:4 to 1997:3 and from 1999:4, two downswings from 1993:1 to 1994:3 and 1997:4 to 1999:3). Further investigation shows strongly positive correlation with the cycles of the investment, private consumption, and export as well as mild negative correlation with government expenditure cycle. The correlation with exports is particularly meaningful, as Estonia is a small open economy. Russia used to be an important trade partner, until 1998, with over 10 percent of total exports. The cycle derived from industrial production is similar to the cycle derived from GDP and the two are highly correlated (around 0.88). The IP business cycles demonstrate similar correlations to GDP with the other variables examined.

Two and a half business cycles (two upswings from 1996:4 to 1998:2 and 1999:2 to 2000:2, three downswings from 1995:1 to 1996:3, from 1998:3 to 1999:1 and from 2000:3) were identified during the observation period in *Hungary*. The GDP business cycle is not correlated with any of its components.[16] A correlation of 0.8 indicates that the industrial production cycle is similar to the GDP cycle. The IP cycle is also relatively less correlated with the cycle of the components of GDP, in a similar way to in the Czech Republic.

The *Latvian* economy went through two complete cycles, with two upswings (from 1995:4 to 1997:4 and from 1999:4 to 2000:4) and two downswings (from 1993:2 to 1995:3 and from 1998:1 to 1999:3). The volatility of the business cycle is higher than in other countries and there is a high correlation with the export cycle. Similar to Estonia, exports play a major role in the Latvian economy and Russia used to be an important trade partner until 1998. Exports are highly dependent on the development of the Russian economy. Correlations with cycles of other GDP components are low or even slightly negative (e.g. government expenditure cycle). The IP cycle is highly related to the GDP cycle, with a correlation of 0.79.

For *Lithuania* we found also two complete cycles (two upswings from 1996:3 to 1997:3 and from 1999:4, two downswings from 1995:1 to 1996:2 and from 1997:4 to 1999:3). Exports have the highest relative correlation although government expenditures and investment are also highly correlated with the GDP cycle (above 60 percent). The IP cycle and the GDP cycles are correlated with 0.73. The IP cycle is quite strongly correlated with the export cycle. The influence of exports on the business cycle is high because Lithuania is a small open economy, with a high proportion of exports to GDP. Like for the economies of the other two Baltic states the exports to Russia used to be particularly important until 1998.

The analysis of *Polish* GDP revealed two complete business cycles (upswings from 1996:1 to 1997:3 and from 1999:2, downswings from 1995:1 to 1995:4 and from 1997:4 to 1999:1). We also found high correlation with the investment cycle, the government expenditure cycle and the private consumption cycle. The correlation with the export cycle is low, as Poland has the lowest of proportion of exports to GDP of all CEEC due to its large domestic market. The business cycles drawn from industrial production indi-

---

16 This is a relatively uncommon phenomenon for an industrialized economy and maybe be influenced by the transition to a market economy or statistical anomalies.

ces and from GDP have slightly lower correlation than in the Baltic states and Hungary.

As mentioned before, for *Romania,* a lack of quarterly GDP data meant that only industrial production business cycles could be derived. We have identified two business cycles from the available data, two upswings (from 1994:1 to 1996:4 and from 1999:3) and two downswings (from 1993:1 to 1993:4 and from 1997:1 to 1999:2). The recession in 1997 to 1998 can be explained by war in the former Yugoslavian countries and, to a lesser extent, the crisis in Russia.

In the *Slovak Republic,* we found a strong downswing after separation from the Czechoslovak Republic (1992), one upswing afterwards, and a second downswing from the end of 1997 to the end of the observation period. The GDP cycle is highly positively correlated with the investment and private consumption cycles and has slight negative correlation with export cycle. The Slovak industrial production business cycle is mildly correlated with the GDP cycle and the other variables for the same reasons as in the Czech Republic.

For *Slovenia,* a sharp decline was found in the GDP business cycle in 1992, at the beginning of the observation period, which is clearly a consequence of its separation from Yugoslavia and their short war. Following this downturn, a further one and a half cycles, with one upswings (from 1996:3 to 1999:1) and two downswings (from 1994:4 to 1996:2 and from 1999:2), were identified. Due to the lack of data, we can not analyze the various components of GDP for correlations. In Slovenia, the GDP business cycle was not influenced by the Russian crises, whereas the IP cycle was affected. The business cycles derived from industrial production and GDP are not highly correlated (36 percent) for similar reasons to the Czech Republic and Slovak Republic. The remarkably low relationship between the IP and GDP business cycles is interpreted as a sign of high state of development within the economies.

b.) Do the business cycles of the CEECs and the EMU members correlate?

In this section we investigate the relationship between the business cycles in the CEEC candidate countries and the EU member states to show the preparedness of the CEEC for joining EMU. According to Mundell OCA criteria, countries could benefit from joining a currency union if their business cycles are highly correlated. We have computed the correlation coefficients of both the GDP and IP business cycles between the CEEC and the EU countries. The boundary between relatively high and relatively low correlation lies at 0.5.

Table 3 shows the correlation of the GDP business cycles in the CEEC and the EU member states. According to the results of our analysis the business cycles in most of the CEEC are more or less strongly related to other CEEC, but only correlated to a minor extent with members of EMU. Only the cycles of the three Baltic states and Poland are strongly correlated with Finnish cycle. This is probably due to their short geographical distance and resulting significant levels of trade with Finland. Only the Hungarian business cycle is positively correlated with the cycles in the EMU countries Belgium, France, and Italy. The correlation with the German business cycle is also quite high but slightly lower than 0.5. On this basis, Hungary is the highest integrated candidate country. However, its integration can be judged as not strong enough to be a part of a European OCA. This result confirms the results of *Fidrmuc/Korhonen* (2001) which also identifies Hungary having the most synchronized business cycle. The Czech, Slovak and Slovenian business cycles are not positively correlated with cycles in any EMU member states. Negative correlations with a few EMU countries are displayed by the Czech and Slovak Republics. The Polish and Slovak business cycles, as well as the cycles of the three Baltic states, are related to the cycles of the EU member United Kingdom and negatively correlated with the one in Sweden, but these countries are not EMU members.

From these results, we conclude that none of the GDP business cycles of the CEEC are correlated enough to identify them as a part of a European OCA. Consequently, these countries would be unlikely to benefit from joining the European Monetary Union, as accession would cause high adjustment costs.

Table 3: Correlation matrix of GDP business cycles in the CEEC´s candidate countries and in the EU (to be continued)

	CZ	EE	HU	LV	LT	PL	SK	SL	AT	BE
Czech Republic (CZ)	1	-0.12	-0.38	-0.19	-0.06	0.08	0.50	-0.11	-0.10	-0.11
Estonia (EE)		1	-0.04	0.94	0.83	0.83	0.51	0.03	-0.12	0.41
Hungary (HU)			1	-0.07	-0.13	-0.18	-0.46	0.34	0.24	0.61
Latvia (LV)				1	0.85	0.90	0.49	0.01	-0.23	0.43
Lithuania (LT)					1	0.74	0.62	-0.08	-0.28	0.17
Poland (PL)						1	0.56	-0.02	-0.18	0.46
Slovak Republic (SK)							1	-0.29	-0.34	-0.15
Slovenia (SL)								1	0.01	0.40
Austria (AT)									1	0.21
Belgium (BE)										1
Denmark (DK)										
Finland (FI)										
France (FR)										
Germany (DE)										
Italy (IT)										
Netherlands (NL)										
Portugal (PT)										
Spain (ES)										
Sweden (SE)										
United Kingdom (UK)										

Table 3 (continued): Correlation matrix of GDP business cycles in the CEEC's candidate countries and in the EU

	DK	FI	FR	DE	IT	NL	PT	ES	SE	UK
Czech Republic (CZ)	0.28	-0.28	-0.57	0.23	0.24	-0.71	-0.30	-0.82	-0.15	0.31
Estonia (EE)	0.27	0.76	-0.09	0.18	0.29	0.37	0.15	0.34	-0.44	0.55
Hungary (HU)	0.23	0.13	0.75	0.46	0.57	0.18	-0.01	0.36	0.77	0.32
Latvia (LV)	0.27	0.84	-0.15	0.08	0.20	0.37	0.28	0.40	-0.52	0.57
Lithuania (LT)	0.16	0.79	-0.19	0.01	0.20	0.09	0.40	0.21	-0.45	0.44
Poland (PL)	0.36	0.68	-0.25	0.16	0.19	0.25	0.23	0.21	-0.60	0.61
Slovak Republic (SK)	0.26	0.25	-0.62	-0.01	0.16	-0.42	0.03	-0.39	-0.57	0.46
Slovenia (SL)	0.16	0.16	0.14	0.31	0.20	0.11	-0.15	0.16	0.18	-0.01
Austria (AT)	-0.11	-0.38	0.67	0.33	0.28	0.45	-0.38	0.39	0.43	-0.21
Belgium (BE)	0.38	0.43	0.39	0.59	0.59	0.35	-0.06	0.34	0.25	0.64
Denmark (DK)	1	0.25	-0.06	0.44	0.50	-0.07	0.25	0.02	-0.01	0.56
Finland (FI)		1	-0.04	0.04	0.24	0.27	0.52	0.36	-0.31	0.46
France (FR)			1	0.30	0.30	0.55	-0.08	0.61	0.66	-0.11
Germany (DE)				1	0.45	-0.02	-0.36	0.03	0.26	0.41
Italy (IT)					1	-0.03	-0.04	0.06	0.52	0.64
Netherlands (NL)						1	0.08	0.86	-0.02	-0.17
Portugal (PT)							1	0.34	-0.13	0.02
Spain (ES)								1	0.12	-0.12
Sweden (SE)									1	-0.03
United Kingdom (UK)										1

Furthermore, our results show the cycles of the *Czech Republic* and the *Slovak Republic* are positively correlated with each other. The reason for this is historical, as they were part of a common federal state until 1991. The Czech business cycle is not related to any other business cycle of CEEC. The Czech economy is a small open economy with external trade oriented towards the EU and with only a small proportion of exports to its former CMEA partners. The *Hungarian* cycle is slightly negatively correlated with the Slovakian cycle, with a coefficient of just below 0.5, and not correlated with cycles of any other CEEC. The *Slovenian* business cycles are not found to be correlated with any other candidate country, largely due to their distinctive economic policies during the transition period and in the last few years.[17] Their economic policy has been characterized by steady reform, thus avoiding shocks, combined with prudent exchange rate policy and balanced budgets. Moreover, the Slovenian economy is less connected to the Russian economy, being geographically further away and was therefore less influenced by Russian crises. Of the CEEC, the Czech, Hungarian and Slovenian economies are the most advanced and relatively more oriented towards the industrialized countries in the EMU. This is probably the reason for their low correlation with the business cycles of other CEEC. However, even these countries do not have sufficiently similar economic structures to EMU countries or synchronized GDP business cycles.

Our results also show another group of countries for which the cycles are more or less strongly correlated together. This group consists of the three Baltic states (Estonia, Latvia, and Lithuania), Poland and the Slovak Republic. All these countries also have positive correlation with the cycle of the EMU country Finland and the EU member United Kingdom, as well as negative correlation with the cycle of the non EMU country Sweden.[18] These countries are considered to be at a similar state of economic development, with similar structures, and consequently have synchronized GDP busi-

---

[17] If the correlation coefficients of Slovenian GDP cycle had been computed only with EU members for which GDP data is available for the same length as the Slovenian time series, these results would be different and the Slovenian cycle would have been related to Belgium, Germany, and Spain.

[18] The Slovak cycle is not directly related with the Finish cycle, but the Slovak Republic belongs to this group because of its strong synchronization of its cycle with that in the Baltic states.

ness cycles and equally high GDP per capita. This is a group of less advanced countries compared to the first group of the Czech Republic, Hungary and Slovenia with lower GDP per capita, different economic structures and cycles lesser synchronized with the cycles of EMU member states. As no statistical relationship with the larger EMU economies has been identified, it is unlikely these countries could benefit from joining EMU at the moment. However, the *Estonian*, the *Latvian* and the *Lithuanian* cycles are particularly strongly correlated with each other because these countries were previously part of a single country and this connection still influences their development. These three countries would benefit now from forming a currency union with each other.[19]

Table 4 displays the relationship of the IP business cycles in the CEEC's candidate countries with that in the EU member states. As expected, the correlation coefficients are higher on average than the correlations of the GDP business cycles, due to the higher level of international trade in industrial products. These results reveal that IP business cycles in most candidate countries are correlated with the industry cycle in Germany, the largest economy in European Monetary Union. In contrast to the GDP cycle, the IP cycle correlations indicate that these countries might benefit from forming a currency union with Germany. The only two exceptions are Romania and Lithuania, which is due to their relatively lower levels of trade integration with EMU member states. According to Mundell OCA theory, these countries are the only candidates, which should definitely remain outside of EMU. These results confirm the findings of *Korhonen* (2001).

[19] A third group of countries with similar business cycle consisting of Romania and Bulgaria may have been identified if sufficient data were available.

Table 4: Correlation matrix of IP business cycles in the CEEC's candidate countries and in the EU (to be continued)

	CZ	EE	HU	LV	LT	PL	RO	SK	SL	AT	BE
Czech Republic (CZ)	1	0.73	0.17	0.89	0.67	0.67	0.19	0.63	0.33	0.12	0.44
Estonia (EE)		1	0.25	0.73	0.43	0.77	-0.01	0.40	0.27	0.26	0.56
Hungary (HU)			1	0.03	-0.16	0.28	-0.09	0.28	0.53	0.86	0.39
Latvia (LV)				1	0.64	0.62	0.05	0.42	0.36	0.04	0.45
Lithuania (LT)					1	0.11	0.18	0.67	0.10	-0.20	0.16
Poland (PL)						1	0.11	0.36	0.38	0.35	0.65
Romania (RO)							1	0.51	0.13	-0.35	0.14
Slovak Republic (SK)								1	0.33	0.20	0.49
Slovenia (SL)									1	0.54	0.52
Austria (AT)										1	0.51
Belgium (BE)											1
Denmark (DK)											
Finland (FI)											
France (FR)											
Germany (DE)											
Greece (GR)											
Ireland (IE)											
Italy (IT)											
Netherlands (NL)											
Portugal (PT)											
Spain (ES)											
Sweden (SE)											
United Kingdom (UK)											

Table 4 (continued): Correlation matrix of IP business cycles in the CEEC's candidate countries and in the EU

	DK	FI	FR	DE	GR	IE	IT	NL	PT	ES	SE	UK
Czech Republic (CZ)	0.45	0.28	0.32	0.60	-0.37	0.25	0.53	0.13	0.01	0.08	0.42	0.12
Estonia (EE)	0.37	0.39	0.31	0.67	-0.41	0.05	0.35	-0.28	-0.23	0.28	0.29	-0.05
Hungary (HU)	0.38	0.63	0.34	0.76	-0.09	0.42	0.43	0.12	-0.60	0.34	0.39	0.17
Latvia (LV)	0.32	0.20	0.48	0.51	-0.21	0.06	0.41	-0.05	0.09	0.18	0.29	0.15
Lithuania (LT)	0.09	0.08	0.15	0.30	-0.24	0.11	0.30	0.07	0.28	-0.06	0.30	0.02
Poland (PL)	0.47	0.26	0.34	0.51	-0.37	-0.01	0.49	0.08	-0.11	0.28	0.29	0.29
Romania (RO)	0.27	0.00	-0.64	-0.06	-0.64	0.04	0.21	0.39	-0.01	-0.58	0.47	0.16
Slovak Republic (SK)	0.42	0.41	-0.02	0.54	-0.42	0.32	0.64	0.48	0.06	0.01	0.69	0.24
Slovenia (SL)	0.62	0.50	0.47	0.58	-0.16	0.12	0.32	0.07	-0.50	0.29	0.51	0.41
Austria (AT)	0.36	0.58	0.57	0.68	0.16	0.30	0.38	0.04	-0.51	0.64	0.35	0.23
Belgium (BE)	0.58	0.58	0.39	0.65	-0.35	0.27	0.58	0.12	-0.22	0.46	0.63	0.36
Denmark (DK)	1	0.58	0.21	0.56	-0.53	0.27	0.58	0.18	-0.27	0.29	0.70	0.15
Finland (FI)		1	0.36	0.77	-0.46	0.35	0.48	0.03	-0.38	0.40	0.65	0.01
France (FR)			1	0.47	0.28	-0.02	0.24	-0.18	-0.10	0.72	0.07	0.34
Germany (DE)				1	-0.30	0.47	0.51	-0.01	-0.41	0.35	0.49	0.03
Greece (GR)					1	-0.05	-0.37	-0.16	0.10	0.24	-0.53	0.01
Ireland (IE)						1	0.44	0.17	-0.09	-0.07	0.28	-0.28
Italy (IT)							1	0.54	0.05	0.39	0.70	0.35
Netherlands (NL)								1	0.32	-0.13	0.31	0.37
Portugal (PT)									1	-0.19	-0.27	-0.19
Spain (ES)										1	0.33	0.35
Sweden (SE)											1	0.34
United Kingdom (UK)												1

Again, the CEEC can be divided into three groups. The first consists of the two most advanced countries Slovenia and Hungary. Their IP business cycles are related together and to that of Austria, Finland and Germany. The Slovenian cycle is also positively correlated with Belgium and Denmark and, to a minor extent, France. This country seems to be the best prepared country, among the CEEC, for membership in the EMU. This result confirms the findings of *De Grauwe/Aksoy* (1999), who also identified Slovenia as the closest country to the EMU, with respect to the synchronization of shocks.

A second group consists of five countries whose business cycles are correlated with the Czech one. The three Baltic states, as well as Poland and the Slovak Republic belong to this group. Almost all of their IP business cycles are correlated to Germany and also, to a higher or lesser extent, to Belgium. Some of them are also positively correlated with Italy. This group can be described as medium advanced countries, with their IP cycles not so strongly correlated with each other as their GDP cycles.

The third group consists of Romania and Bulgaria. The Romanian business cycle correlates with different countries than the rest of the CEEC. It does not positively correlate with other candidate countries (except the Slovak Republic) or with EMU members, but has negative correlation with the French, Greek, and Spanish cycle. In this way, Romania can not be said to belong to a European Optimal Currency Area. Bulgaria also probably belongs to this group, but analysis of its business cycles is limited due to a lack of data. These countries could be described as the least developed countries, furthest away from being a part of a European OCA.

IV. Conclusions

In this paper we have discussed whether the CEEC could be part of a European Optimal Currency Area (OCA) with the current member states of the European Union (EU). This would mean increased economic benefits from joining the European Monetary Union (EMU). Criteria derived from OCA theory can be used to determine whether a group of countries may benefit from forming a monetary union. One of the OCA criteria is the similarity of business cycles among the participating countries. Therefore this paper extracted business cycles for the CEEC from Gross Domestic Product (GDP) and Industrial Production (IP) time series data and computed the respective cross correlation coefficients with that of the EU member states. The results have been interpreted in the light of the OCA-theory.

Our analysis did not result in clear-cut conclusions concerning membership of a European OCA. In analyzing GDP business cycles we found only some evidence that the three Baltic states (Estonia, Latvia, and Lithuania) could benefit from forming their own currency union. We found little evidence for the preparedness of the candidate countries to join EMU. The analysis of IP data revealed that all of the business cycles in the candidate countries (except in Romania and Lithuania) are related to the German cycle, with some correlation to other EMU members. Most EU member states industry cycles are also correlated with the German cycle. We conclude therefore that a large group of countries, with cycles correlating with Germany, might belong to a European OCA and could therefore benefit from joining EMU. However, Lithuania and Romania clearly do not belong to a European OCA.

It should be considered that the former communist countries of Central and Eastern Europe are still transition economies. Only Hungary, Poland, Slovenia, and the Slovak Republic have managed to re-achieve their 1989 levels of GDP after their transition related recessions. The change over to market economies is therefore not yet complete. Our investigations are based on data affected by far-reaching economic change and political reforms and it follows that interpretation of the results should be drawn with caution. It should also be noted that the economic importance of the CEEC in terms of the EU economy is quite small. The total GDP of the ten CEEC is 10.6 percent of GDP for the EU-15.[20] For the CEEC, it is more difficult and risky to join EMU than for the EU member states. According to the Maastricht Treaty, these countries have to become EMU members and each candidate country has to participate in the European Exchange Rate Mechanism II (ERM II) for at least two years. Moreover they have to fulfill all other Maastricht convergence criteria. None of the CEEC fulfill all of these at the moment. For the European Union to achieve its goal to admit the candidates in time for the next European Parliament elections (2004), the candidates would join EMU, at the earliest, in 2006. This raises the question of whether this change within a relatively short period will not be too costly for the CEEC, in terms of output.

---

[20] Cf. *EUROSTAT* (2001).

The Mundell OCA criteria are necessary, but should not be applied in isolation. A rather simplified method was used in our study, due to the limited availability and quality of data. This enables us only to analyze the current situation based on past experiences of the CEEC. The analysis itself does not allow for predictions on the future preparedness of the CEEC with respect to join the EMU.

References

Bayoumi T. / Eichengreen B. (1993), One Money or Many? Analyzing the Prospects for Monetary Unification in Various Parts of the World, in: CIDER Working Paper, No. C93-030, Berkley, 1993.

Beveridge S. / Nelson C. (1981), A New Approach to Decomposition of Economic Time Series into Permanent and Transitory Components with Particular Attention to Measurement of the 'Business Cycles' , in: Journal of Monetary Economics, 7, 1981, pp. 151 - 174.

Blanchard J. / Quah D. (1989), The Dynamic Effects of Aggregate Demand and Supply Disturbances, in: American Economic Review, Vol. 79, No. 4, 1989, pp. 655 - 673.

Boone L. / Maurel M. (1999), An Optimal Currency Area perspective of the EU enlargement to the CEEC, in: Discussion Paper No. 2119, Center of Economic Policy Research, 1999.

Boreiko D. (2002), EMU and Accession Countries: Fuzzy Cluster Analysis of Membership, paper presented at the conference Monetary Union: Theory, EMU Experience, and Prospects for Latin America, University of Vienna, April 14th - 16th, 2002.

Breuss F. (1984), Konjunkturindikatoren für die österreichische Wirtschaft, in: Monatsberichte des Österreichischen Instituts für Wirtschaftsforschung, issue 8/1994, Vienna, pp. 464 - 492.

Breuss F. (1998), Außenwirtschaft, Monetärer Teil, Schwerpunkt Wirtschafts- und Währungsunion, Verlag Springer, 1998, (SpringerNotes Wirtschaftswissenschaften).

Breuss F. (1999), Wann sind die MOEL reif für die Wirtschafts- und Währungsunion, in: *Breuss F.* (Coordination), Reifegrad der mittel- und osteuropäischen EU-Beitrittswerber, Austrian Institute of Economic Research, Vienna, 1999, p. 205.

Chagny O. / Döpke J. (2001), Measures of the Output Gap in the Euro-Zone: An Empirical Assessment of Selected Methods, in: Quarterly Journal of Economic Research, issue 3/2001, Business Cycle Research in the European Economic and Monetary Union, German Institute for Economic Research (DIW), Berlin, pp. 310-330.

De Grauwe P. (2000), Economics of Monetary Union, 4th Edition, Oxford University Press, New York, 2000.

De Grauwe P. / Aksoy Y. (1999), Are Central European Countries Part of the European Optimum Currency Area?, in: *De Grauwe P. / Lavroč V.* (eds.), Inclusion of Central European Countries in the European Monetary Union, Kluwer Academic Publishers, Boston/Dordrecht/London, 1999, pp. 13 - 36.

European Commission (2001a), Autumn 2001 Forecasts for 2001-2003, European Economy, Supplement A, No 10/11 - October/November 2001, Brussels, Belgium, 2001.

European Commission (2001b), "Economic Reform Monitor: Autumn 2001 Forecast", Issue 2001/4, November 2001, Brussels, Belgium.

European Commission (2001c), Regular Reports Progress towards accession, November 2001, Brussels, Belgium.

EUROSTAT (2001), The GDP of the Candidate Countries. Figures for the second quarter of 2001, Statistics in focus, economy and finance, Theme 2-42/2001, Luxembourg.

Frankel J. / Rose A. (1998), The Endogeneity of the Optimum Currency Area Criteria, in: Economic Journal 108, 1998, pp. 1009 - 1025.

Fidrmuc J. (2001), The Endogeneity of the Optimal Currency Area Criteria, Intraindustry Trade, and EMU Enlargement, in: LICOS Discussion Paper 105/2001, LICOS Center for Transition Economics, Katholieke Universiteit Leuven, 2001.

Fidrmuc J. / Korhonen I. (2001), Optimal Currency Area between the EU and Accession Countries: The Status Quo, paper presented at the East West Conference 2001 of Oesterreichische Nationalbank, November 4 to 6, 2001, Vienna.

Horvath J. (2001a), "Supply and Demand Shocks in Europe: Large-4 EU Members, Visegrad-5 and Baltic-3 Countries", Department of Economics, Central European University Budapest, Hungary, 2001, mimeo.

Horvath J. (2001b), The Optimum Currency Area Theory. A Review, Department of Economics, Central European University Budapest, Hungary, 2001, mimeo.

IMF (2001), International Financial Statistics, in: Wifo databank online (country"60P"M).

Ishiyama Y. (1975), The Theory of Optimum Currency Areas - A Survey, in: *IMF Staff Papers*, No. 22, 1975, pp. 344 - 383.

Kenen P. (1969), The Theory of Optimum Currency Areas: An Eclectic View, in: *Mundell R. / Swoboda A.* (eds.), Monetary Problems of the International Economy, University of Chicago Press, Chicago, 1969, pp. 41 - 60.

Korhonen I. (2001), Some empirical tests on the integration of economic activity between the Euro area and the accession countries, in: BOFIT Discussion Paper 2001/No. 9, Bank of Finland, Institute for Economies in Transition.

Licandro F. G. (1998), "Is MERCOSUR an Optimal Currency Area? A Shock Correlation Perspective", Paper presented at the ETC Congress, June 12, 1998, Preliminary Draft, *Mimeo*, Banco Central del Uruguay, Montevideo.

Maes I. (1992), Optimum Currency Area Theory and European Monetary Integration, Tijdschrift voor Economie en Management, 37(2), 1992, pp. 137-152.

McKinnon R. (1963), Optimum Currency Areas, in: American Economic Review, No. 53, 1963, pp. 717 - 725.

Moore G. (1983), Business Cycles, Inflation, and Forecasting, in: *Studies in Business Cycles*, No. 24, National Bureau of Economic Research, Cambridge 1983.

Mundell R. (1961), A Theory of Optimum Currency Areas, in: American Economic Review, Vol. 51, No. 4, 1961, pp. 657 - 665.

Sachs J. / Larrain F. (1995), Makroökonomie in globaler Sicht, Verlag Oldenburg, München, Wien, 1995.

Tichy G. (1976), "Konjunkturschwankungen. Theorie, Messung, Prognose", 1. Ausgabe, 1976, Verlag Springer, Berlin u.a.

UNECE (2001a), Economic Survey of Europe 2001 No. 1, prepared by the secretariat of the United Nations Economic Commission for Europe, Geneva 2001.

UNECE (2001b), Economic Survey of Europe 2001 No. 2, prepared by the secretariat of the United Nations Economic Commission for Europe, Geneva 2001.

Peter R. Haiss

Monetary Union and Enlargement – Constrained by the Financial Sector?

I. Introduction[1]

European Monetary Union (EMU) offers a variety of economic advantages to its members. The neighbouring countries have built close political, economic and financial bonds to the European Union (EU). The next wave of EU members, the so-called candidate countries, show a great interest into EMU with an eye on joining it. For both groups among the candidate countries, be it the Mediterranean group or the Central and Eastern European Accession Countries (CEECs), joining the euro zone is seen as an important way of gaining policy credibility. Lower risk premiums, lower interest rates, and lower transaction costs should be their benefit - at least in the long run.[2] Timing, conditions and prerequisites for that move, and short-term implications of the speculative kind, however, are still under debate.

Several factors have been heavily discussed with regard to the adoption of the euro by the accession countries in valuable contributions: trade integration, the optimal currency area theory (OCA), low levels of GDP, and the capacity to absorb financial transfers.

---

1 The opinions expressed are the authors' personal views and don't necessarily reflect those of the institutions he is affiliated with. Parts of the contribution are based on an earlier paper entitled "Major achievements and open issues in financial market transition of Eastern European Candidate countries, co-authored by *Gerhard Fink*, that was presented a the Fifth World Conference of the European Communities Studies Association (ECSA), Brussels, December 2000. The author would like to thank *Gerhard Fink* and *Markus Eller* of the Research Institute for European Affairs, Vienna University of Economics and Business Administration, and the participants at the ECSA Conference for valuable comments. Remaining errors are mine. The author would also like to thank *Günther Hochradl* of Bank Austria and *Roland Schwab* and *Alex Hooley* of Microsoft Austria who helped with the recovery after a computer breakdown. This article is devoted to my father *Alfred Haiss* whom I lost while writing this contribution and to my wife *Ulli Haiss-Berger* who gave me generous support during difficult times.

2 *Szapáry* (2001) 26; *Köhler/Wes* (1999) 3; *Frenkel et al* (1999) 4; while the focus here is on financial sector issues, it should be acknowledged that there are also positive implications through the transmission mechanism of international trade (higher growth, higher synchronization with economic cycles, higher use of the euro in trade invoicing); see *Bekx* (1998) for a discussion.

One of the major prerequisites to a functioning economy, i.e. a financial sector capable of intermediation, deserves renewed attention with regard to the interplay with EMU. This contribution tries to fill that gap.

The state of the banking industry is of major priority for the next wave of EU-members in their preparation for the following full participation in the eurosystem. A robust banking sector may ameliorate the impact of shocks. A weak banking system may generate or amplify liabilities elsewhere in the economy.[3] Most accession countries are well under way in adapting their monetary policy framework. Given that weak corporate governance capacities, low financial intermediation levels and inherently instable financial markets lead to asset bubbles and to a higher vulnerability to speculative attacks, these financial services sector issues need to be resolved before introduction of the Euro in the accession countries seems possible. It is therefore argued that EMU-enlargement should not be seen in unison, but rather as an integral part of financial sector integration.

This article progresses in the following way. In *section one*, the process and progress towards participation in E(M)U is reviewed with a special emphasis on the monetary and financial services context. The criteria and the chapters on free movement of services and capital as well as that on EMU of the ongoing membership negotiations are discussed. The current level of compliance with the acquis and remaining adjustment measures are depicted.

Section two highlights the link between EMU, types of capital flows and financial sector reform. Ongoing transformation of the financial services sector in its core (banks and capital markets) and prerequisite facets (i.e. regulatory and judiciary environment) are depicted with regard to repercussions to the accession countries forthcoming participation in EMU and later the eurozone. Size and governance issues are discussed. Special attention is devoted to the various types of capital inflows, likely change patterns with regard to type and tenure, typical reactions in financial services and resulting implications to systemic risk. The *Commission's* (2001b) evaluation of that reconstruction process is discussed in contrasting

---

[3] *Cunningham* (2001) 187.

its findings on the Copenhagen EU-entry criteria to the 2002-2003 Accession Partnership Priorities.

Section three deals with convergency as well as monetary and foreign exchange policies during the pre-accession phase (till EU-membership) and the accession phase (between EU-membership and the final introduction of the euro) in the accession countries. The current currency regimes are depicted, the future participation in the Exchange Rate Mechanism II (ERM II) and intermediate adjustment issues are discussed. It is argued that the advantages of flexible exchange rate strategies predominate in order to comply with real convergence. The reasoning is based on possible speculative attacks in case of narrow fluctuation bands combined with the lack of realignment options in ERM II. Issues of monetary size are discussed with regard to the susceptibility to volatile currency flows and the current match of the Maastricht convergency criteria. Institutional adjustment needs with regard to the later inclusion of the accession countries central banks in the organisational units of the European System of Central Banks (ESCB) are depicted. Finally, the last section contains a short conclusion .

II. Process and Progress in EMU Enlargement

The introduction of the euro and the conduct of the single monetary policy by the European Central Bank (ECB) have further *deepened* the integration within the European Community and its Member States. *Widening* the European Union by integrating new members adds another dimension to the overall economic policy framework.[4] Membership negotiations have already progressed considerably with two Mediterranean and ten Central and Eastern European (CEEC) candidate countries (further referred to as "accession countries").[5] That widening brings along the next step of deepening, as EU membership requires the adherence to the aims of EMU. Enlargement thus means commitment to finally adopting the

4 *ECB* (2001a) 51; *Padoa-Schippa* (2002) 1.

5 The CEECs comprise Bulgaria, The Czech Republic, Estonia, Hungary, Latvia, Lithuania, Poland, Romania, the Slovak Republic and Slovenia. The Mediterranean accession countries comprise Cyprus and Malta. Turkey is also officially recognised as candidate for accession, but conditions for the start of membership negotiations have not yet been met.

euro and has implications in the monetary field already at this stage.

A. The Accession Process

There is a clear distinction between participation in EMU, which is compulsory for all Member States, and full-fledged participation in the eurosystem within the euro zone.[6] The process of adopting the euro for accession countries is generally characterised by three successive stages as identified by the ECOFIN Council.[7] First the current *pre-accession phase* (till EU-membership becomes effective), then the *accession phase* (as an EU-member with EMU-derogation) and lastly the participation in the euro zone by *adoption of the euro*.

Box 1: Process Issues of Accession
Among the EU membership criteria are already several issues of direct relevance to the final adoption of the euro. Many EMU-requirements that must only be kept from the date of accession on have monetary implications already prior to accession. Before joining the eurosystem, new members have to spend about two years in the ERM-II convergence room and finally pass those criteria. Earlier euroisation has been ruled out by the Commission, the ECOFIN Council and the ECB.

Participation in EMU becomes binding for the accession countries with EU membership. EU-membership is based on other criteria (i.e. those set out by the Copenhagen European Council and further detailed by subsequent European Councils)[8] than the final adoption of the euro (i.e. convergency criteria prescribed by the Maastricht Treaty). The accession countries will enter the EU as EMU members with a derogation.[9] The acquis relevant for EU

---

6 *European Commission* (2000a) 27.

7 *ECOFIN* (2000) 1.

8 *European Commission* (2001b) 2; note the renewed focus on implementation and judicial capacity in the 2001 opinion.

9 A memberstate with a derogation is, according to article 122 of the Treaty, excluded from the rights and obligations within the European System of Central Banks (ESCB). This implies, amongst other things, that the member state in question will not participate in the eurosystem since the criteria for being able to do so have not yet been fulfilled.

accession already includes many aspects with direct relevance to the final adoption of the euro:[10]

- the *existence of a functioning market economy*, including that the financial sector is sufficiently developed to channel savings towards productive investment, free interplay and the absence of significant market entry and exit barriers within the financial industry and its clients;
- the *capacity to withstand competitive pressure and market forces in the medium term*, including the availability of a sufficient amount of capital at an appropriate cost for all types of economic agents, integration of the financial sector and the extent to which governments influence competitiveness through competition policy and state aids, among others; and
- the *capacity to take on the acquis and other obligations of membership in the medium term*, including the transposition and application of the acquis communautaire (internal market; free flow of capital, service etc.), judicial and administrative capacity, and adherence to the aims of economic and monetary union which candidate countries should implement by accession at the latest, in particular:
  - *completion of the orderly liberalisation of capital movements* and *achievement of macroeconomic stability;*
  - *prohibition of any direct public sector financing by the central bank*, including the prohibition of overdraft or any other type of credit facilities conceded to EC institutions, and of direct acquisition of public debt instruments by the ECB or the national central bank;
  - *the prohibition of privileged access of the public sector to financial institutions*, including the prohibition of any measure not based on prudential considerations establishing privileged access of EC bodies to financial institutions;
  - *central bank independence and goals set*, i.e. the national central banks must aim at price stability as their explicit objective, and there has to be absence of any external institution or body able to give instructions, approve, censor, be consulted or

---

[10] *ECB* (2000) 47; *ECOFIN* (2000); *European Commission* (1998) 2; *European Commission* (2002a); *Fink/Haiss* (2000b).

participate in central bank decisions (personal, institutional and financial independence of the respective national banks).

In addition to the above mentioned elements that must be adapted in the accession countries′ legislation *prior* to the date of accession, further elements *formally* only have to be complied *thereafter*, i.e. from the date of accession on, including:[11]

- *adherence to the aims of economic and monetary union;*
- commitment to *treat economic and exchange rate policy as* a matter of *common concern*;
- *co-ordination of economic policies* with member states through participation in Community procedures, including supervisory mechanisms;
- *avoidance of excessive government deficits* and *adherence to* the provisions of the *Stability and Growth Pact*;
- further adaptation of the national *central bank's statutes* with a view to integration in the European System of Central Banks (ESCB);
- *progress towards* the fulfilment of the *Maastricht convergence criteria* (on public finances, inflation, exchange rates and long term interest rates).

After accession, New Member States will also be expected to join the ERM II for at least two years, subject to a common accord on the central parity and fluctuation band.[12]

While formally not applicable, the latter set of criteria will already have an impact prior to accession due to the following reasons: time lags between policy setting and market acceptance; the renewed focus of the Commission on implementation rather than on just formal law adjustment; the already high level of economic and political integration and the already de-facto unilateral linking of the accession countries′ currencies to the euro (see below).

Both the Commission and the ECB have drawn clear distinctions between participation in EMU and adoption of the euro as a single currency.[13] New Member States are not expected to adopt the single currency upon accession, even though they will be taking

---

[11] *European Commission* (1998); *European Commission* (2002a).

[12] *ECOFIN* (2001); for a discussion, see III.B.

[13] *European Commission* (1998); *ECB* (2000).

part in the 2nd stage of EMU with a derogation.[14] According to article 122 of the Treaty, Member States with a derogation are excluded from the rights and obligations within the European System of Central Banks (ESCB). Such new Member States will not transfer their monetary sovereignty upon accession to the EU.[15]

The candidate countries cannot adopt the euro upon accession,[16] because the Maastricht Treaty requires an assessment of the sustainability of the government's financial position to be performed before accession.[17] The other reason is that the candidate countries will not have participated in the Exchange Rate Mechanism (ERM) for two years, which is not open to the candidate countries prior to accession to the EU.[18] The shortest possible time span between EU-membership and the EU Council decision on adoption of the euro by the respective accession group thus is about two years. It is difficult to assess how long technical preparations for the adoption of the euro might take. Greece needed roughly nine months to prepare. Should the first round of accession take place in 2004/2005,[19] this would imply that the euro could be adopted by these countries at about 2007 at the earliest.[20]

The accession countries will adapt their currency regimes to be compatible to ERM II, or they could be induced to go for a fixed

---

14 *ECB* (2000) 46.

15 *European Commission* (2002a).

16 As was initially thought by Estonia and Slovenia; see *Köhler/Wes* (1999) 11.

17 *European Commission* (1998).

18 Some countries considered applying prior to EU-accession; *European Commission* (2000b) 40.

19 The Göteborg Summit in June 2001 confirmed that the EU regards 2004 as the target date for the first round of accession. According to the Laeken Summit in December 2001, this first round might encompass all the candidate countries except Bulgaria and Romania. In order to participate in the elaboration of the EU's financial framework for the period 2007-2013, accession by 2005 at the latest is a precondition; see *Richter* (2002) for a review.

20 *Hochreiter/Wagner* (2001); *Eikenberg/Zukowska – Gagelmann* (2001). Previous interpretations of this two year schedule also accepted shorter time spans. For a discussion see *section III. B.* on criteria and options in the accession phase or *Task Force `Enlargement` of the European Parliament* (1999) 10.

link to the euro. The latter would pretty much resemble unilateral euroisation. Imported stability, resulting in attracting foreign direct investment (FDI) and reduced interest rate levels are typically quoted as rationale for euroisation.[21] A fixed exchange rate for a country in structural transition, with a business cycle not yet fully aligned with that of the euro zone, would deprive that country of its independent monetary policy and unduly constrain fiscal policies during the catch-up phase.[22] There are significant dangers in narrowly pegging the exchange rate while liberalizing the financial sector.[23] According to the Commission, this way is not foreseen in the resolution to the ERM II (97/C 236/03). Equally ECOFIN and ECB made it clear that any unilateral adoption of the single currency would run counter to the underlying economic reasoning of EMU in the Treaty, which foresees the eventual adoption of the euro as the final step of a structured convergence process within a given multilateral framework.[24] The stages foreseen by the Treaty for the adoption of the euro as discussed in the following.

B. Relevant Chapters in Negotiation

Many of the regulatory elements depicted as crucial to the later introduction of the euro are covered in the ongoing EU-membership negotiation process. The relevant regulatory approximation is mainly covered in the chapters on free movement of services, on free movement of capital and on EMU, although there are various spill over effects from other chapters, for example competition.[25] The current status as of March 2002, according to *Commission*

---

21 *Schrader* (1999) 12; *Wyplsosz* (2002) 1; *Mundell* (2000) 160f argues that the EU should accept (only) countries to fix their currency versus the euro once they achieved convergence on inflation targets and have been inside the ERM. For a discussion of euroisation, see for example *Nuti* (2000) or *Wójcik* (2002).

22 *FBE* (2002) 9; *Hochreiter/Wagner* (2001); based on 1992-1998 data, *Frenkel et al.* (1999) 18, finds that even symmetric shocks might cause major adjustment problems for CEECs without refuge to the exchange rate mechanism.

23 *Dickson/Mullineux* (2001) 221.

24 *ECOFIN* (2000); *ECB* (2001b) 115.

25 For a review of the regulatory approximation process of financial services issues in general, see *Lannoo/Salem* (2001) 95f.

(2002a) communication,[26] is reviewed in the following. Pre-accession economic programmes have been designed bearing in mind the requirements for economic and monetary union.[27]

Box 2: Euro-Issues in EU Enlargement Negotiations
The chapters on free movement of services and capital have been provisionally closed with all candidate countries but Romania by March 2002; the EMU chapter with all but Bulgaria and Romania. The candidate countries will have to enter the EU with fully liberalized capital movements. In previous enlargement rounds, New Members entered with the possibility of retaining restrictions on capital flows for about ten years. Transitional periods on certain financial services issues were granted. Most candidate countries' national banks are not yet fully independent. According to the Stability and Growth Pact, candidate countries have to avoid excessive budget deficits already in the pre-accession phase.

1. Free Movement of Services

The chapter on free movement of services refers to several fields of relevance to EMU, including banking, insurance, investment services and securities markets. It has not been opened for negotiation with Romania by April 2002. With the other 11 candidates, the chapter has been provisionally closed. For several of these, transitional periods of up to five years have been agreed, e.g., for reaching minimum levels of guarantees for banking deposits or investor protection. A number of candidates have been accorded exemption from the banking acquis for very small institutions. A significant amount of work remains to be done in the complex area of financial services. Derogation's on capital movement could have a direct impact on the Treaty-based right of establishment and freedom to provide services.

With regard to the administrative capacity and monitoring, the establishment of an effective regulatory infrastructure is particularly important in order to implement the acquis and ensure an efficient and well-supervised financial sector. The Commission is monitoring very closely the supervisory arrangements for financial services in the candidate countries.

---

26 *European Commission* (2002a).

27 *European Commission* (2001b) 2.

Table 1: Free Movement of Services: Transitional Arrangements in Financial Services Issues

BG	exclusion of co-operative credit and savings societies until end 2007
CY	exclusion of co-operative credit and savings societies until end 2007
CZ	none
EE	lower levels of bank deposit guarantee and investor compensation until end-2007
HU	exclusion of two specialised banks, lower level of investor compensation until end 2007
LV	exclusion of credit unions, lower levels of bank deposit guarantee and investor compensation until end 2007
LT	exclusion of credit unions, lower levels of bank deposit guarantee and investor compensation until end 2007
MT	none
PL	exclusion of credit unions and a specialised bank; lower level of investor compensation until end- 2007
RO	not yet opened
SK	lower level of investor compensation until end 2006
SL	lower level of capital require-ments for savings and loan under-takings until end 2004

Source: *European Commission* (2002a).

2. Free Movement of Capital

The chapter on free movement of capital includes several fields of direct relevance to the functioning of EMU: payments and transfers of money over the borders, transactions allowing transfer of ownership of assets and liabilities, investments in companies and real estate or portfolio investments, cross-border credit transfers and prevention of money laundering. It has been opened for Romania and is now provisionally closed with the other eleven countries. Transitional arrangements concern mainly the access of non-residents of various kinds to land or farmland, which does have some bearing with regard to the availability of real estate as lien in granting credits by foreign banks. The capital liberalisation process will be completed upon accession to the EU, given that no other transition periods have been requested.

Several accession countries still uphold restrictions to short-term capital flows (see the Accession Partnership Priorities discussed below). Capital flows have to be completely liberalised prior to EU accession because this move is thought to reflect their ability to cope with competitive pressure and market forces within the EU.[28] Some of the accession countries are already OECD members. That membership requires almost completely free capital movements.[29] A comparison with previous enlargement rounds is quite revealing. Spain and Portugal entered the EU with the possibility of retaining restrictions on capital flows over more than ten years. In this respect the current enlargement round is different.[30] When Portugal and Spain joined, the liberalisation of short-term capital flows led to strong inflows of short-term capital. Once the remaining restrictions to short-term capital flows are abandoned, the financial sectors′ intermediative capacity is crucial.

3. EMU

The negotiation chapter on EMU deals with issues pertaining to the prohibition of direct public sector financing by the central bank and of privileged access of the public sector to financial institutions, with the alignment of national bank status, the administrative capacity of the national bank and finance ministry and with macroeconomic stability. Participation in EMU presupposes the adoption of the Single Market acquis by the candidate countries, in particular of the acquis on free movement of capital as was the case for present member states. With regard to legislation on central banks, all features of central banks′ independence (institutional, personal, functional and financial) should be effective at the time of accession to the EU.[31]

Negotiations on this chapter have been concluded with ten countries (all except Romania and Bulgaria) by April 2002. The EMU-chapter was opened with Bulgaria in March 2002. It has not been decided by April 2002 to open negotiations with Romania. Independence of the national banks (for all but Hungary and Slovenia) and corporate governance issues resulting from direct public sector financing and/or privileged public access to financial institutions and weak administrative capacities remained major

---

[28] *ECB* (2000) 48.

[29] *FBE* (2002) 3.

[30] *Halpern/Wyplosz* (2001) 6.

[31] Article 109 (ex Article 108 of the Treaty); *ECB* (2000) 47.

concerns.[32] The variety of independence issues range from causes of dismissal for members of the national bank board (Latvia), its composition (Bulgaria; Poland has to ban participation of government representatives in the Monetary Policy Council and overcome mounting internal political opposition), to personal, financial and institutional independence (Czech Republic). An opt-out status of the kind granted to the United Kingdom and Denmark being disregarded for the candidate countries, no transitional periods or special arrangements are therefore permitted, nor have they been requested by any of the countries with which negotiations have been carried out until April 2002.[33]

According to the *Commission* (2002b), independence of the central banks in the accession countries should be supplemented by co-ordination between the respective monetary and fiscal authorities, i.e. between the national banks and the finance ministries, in order to reduce possible vulnerabilities in the financial sector and on the macroeconomic side.[34] Due to political pressure in the Czech Republic and Poland, the ECB seems to be concerned that some accession countries make steps back on progress already achieved in central bank independence and price stability statutes.[35]

---

32 *European Commission* (2001a); *Dvorsky* (2002) 83, 92. For a review of earlier evaluations, see *Lannoo / Salem* (2001).

33 *European Commission* (2002a).

34 *European Commission* (2002b) 7.

35 *Padoa-Schioppa* (2002) 5, referring to a resolution by the Sejm (Polish Parliament) that puts the blame for unemployment and low growth on the national bank and aims at refocusing monetary policy towards growth and employment creation.

Table 2: Compliance with the Acquis on the EMU-Chapter According to the Commission (2001) Progress Report

	BG	CY	CZ	EE	HU	LV	LT	MT	PL	RO	SK	SL
prohibition of direct public sector financing by central bank					X			X		X	X	X
prohibition of privileged access of the public sector to financial institutions										X	X	
alignment of national central bank status (goal & independence)	X	X	X	X		X	X	X	X	X	X	
administrative capacity of national bank, ministry of finance etc.	X						X	X				
macroeconomic stability								X		X		

Source: *European Commission* (2001a). X= problem area, blank = o.k.

With regard to the adoption of the acquis in the areas of macroeconomic stability, a further requirement has to be taken into consideration. Membership negotiations have to be based on the current acquis at the time, which is a kind of „moving target approach." Therefore, the Stability and Growth Pact (SGP), which became part of the acquis in 1997, also has to be considered relevant. The SGP[36] aims towards balanced national budgets and fixes the upper limit of the acceptable annual budget deficit under normal circumstances at three percent of gross domestic product (GDP) at market prices. This is only to be surpassed in case of extraordinary economic shocks and for finite tenure. Accession countries have to endeavour to avoid excessive government deficits already in the pre-accession phase.[37] These disciplining effects of the SGP confront the accession countries with considerable restrictions in their fiscal autonomy.[38] Accession countries have to adjust their macro-policies according to those of EU members (price stability, transparent pricing mechanisms, long term interest rates) and should have macroeconomic programmes consistent with those prevailing in the euro area in their medium-term policy agenda.[39] The Commission refers to the level of annual budget deficits in the annual evaluations. It applies this measure similar to the original Copenhagen criteria. It is up to the Council to decide about the appropriateness of the budget deficit and to implement sanctions.[40]

III. Financial Sector Issues

The smooth functioning of banking and financial markets is of utmost importance for successful integration of the accession countries, first into the EU and at a later stage into the eurosystem. In order to create conditions for financial stability and sound banking systems, accession countries will have to implement the EU directives in the banking and financial area before accession.[41] These include the rules on capital adequacy, insolvency, the adoption of accounting standards, effective prudential supervision, set-

---

[36] *Breuss* (1998, 2000).

[37] *Task Force 'Enlargement' of the European Parliament* (1999) 8.

[38] *Welfens* (1999); *Cooper/Kempf* (2000); *Pelkmans/Gros/Ferrer* (2000) 111.

[39] *ECB* (2000).

[40] *Breuss* (1998, 2000).

[41] *ECB* (2000) 48.

tlement finality and the avoidance of moral hazard problems. A variety of other issues are also necessary for the smooth functioning of financial markets, for example a functioning judiciary system, an established land and mortgage market, reasonable bankruptcy procedures and a market-oriented corporate governance system. Only countries in which the financial sector can bear the intense competition of the common market and in which the banking sector is capable of acting as a counterpart of the eurosystem can enter EMU.[42] There is an interesting disparity on the actual evaluation of the maturity of the accession countries financial sector. The factual evaluation of the susceptibility to speculative attacks due to weaknesses in the financial sector seems to depend on the data and measure applied.[43] In the following, relevant financial services issues and evaluations are discussed.

Box 3: Financial Sector Issues in EMU-Enlargement
The generally favourable official evaluation for most candidate countries contrasts considerably with the remaining adjustment measures prioritized in the 2002-2003 Accession Partnerships. Most CEECs financial markets are small, the level of financial intemediation is low, bank asset quality is poor, supervision and governance is insufficient and judiciary problems prevail. In case these issues are not fully resolved prior to EU membership, their resolution is postponed into the following accession phase to the eurosystem. In the short run banks will only have a minor impact on economic growth. Financial intermediation will grow fast, abundant liquidity may lead banks to increase credit. If these markets are opened and fully liberalised, they are prone to speculative bubbles. Foreign dominance may considerably improve that situation till the time of formal evaluation.

42 *FBE* (2002) 8.

43 Two oppositive views are for example represented by *Reininger/Schardax/Summer* (2002) and the *European Commission* (2002b); this may be based on data limitations for the CEEC, different data applied or different interpretation. *Darvas/Szapáry* (2000) 34, for example, discuss channels of capital flows, but the data set does not include private sector borrowing.

A. Financial Sector Transformation

Financial sector transition has emerged as a very dramatic process characterized by some highly applauded success stories. But even more often "unexpected" collapses of seemingly decent institutions happened, at times accompanied by systemic breakdown. Compared with achievements in macroeconomic stabilization, economic liberalization and privatisation of state owned enterprises (SOE), the overall track record of transition in the financial services sector is much less impressive. Some banking systems have achieved miracles thanks to a handful of farsighted technocrats and entrepreneurs. The absence of strong external and internal governance structures also provided a fertile ground for abuse of depositors' and shareholders' rights, hijacking of management control, transfer of state assets into dubious hands and other imprudent behaviour of various stakeholders.

It has to be acknowledged that the organizational setting and the capacity of financial institutions in the CEECs before the collapse of communism was quite different from those in market economies,[44] and also varied from country to country. Hungary, Poland and former Yugoslavia started to reform the banking system in the second half of the 1980s; Bulgaria, Czechoslovakia and the Baltic states had rather sterile economic structures with a central bank engaged also in financial transfers among firms, a foreign trade bank, savings institutions and a few other specialised banks.

After 1990, the new state owned commercial banks were created by transferring existing loans from the portfolio of the central bank. These banks started life with an inherited overhang of troubled assets (also referred to as the "stock problem"), which in most cases were highly concentrated on a few large enterprises in a single or a few industries.

A wave of new bad debt had to be swallowed by the banks, and later on by the respective taxpayers via repeated recapitalisations. The reasons for this "flow problem" were delayed company restructuring, hesitant implementation of bankruptcy procedures, misguided voucher privatisation and continued interference of "vested interests" of powerful stakeholders (including governments) during the transition process. In the absence of prudential

---

[44] *Zwass* (1979).

regulation the number and size of greenfield financial institutions grew rapidly. Many of those lacked capital, knowledge, prudence or a combination thereof. Due to stakeholders' vested interests and apparent power structures, bank managers were inclined to under-report non-performing loans until a program of rehabilitation was announced. Several governments were falling into the trap of repeated recapitalisations. Hungary and the Czech Republic spent more of 10% of its GDP in several rounds of banking sector rehabilitation; Bancorex, the flagship bank in Romania, was recapitalised five times before final liquidation.[45]

The CEECs also had to re-establish capital markets and respective institutions (stock exchanges, investment houses, supervisory agencies etc.). Formal privatisation under mass-voucher schemes led to initial grossly inflated equity markets in some countries, most notably the Czech Republic, with major corrections following suit and a market capitalization relative to GDP of only 22% in 1999. A combination of gradual liberalization of foreign portfolio investment and parallel enforcement of stringent listing requirements and information dissemination rules proved more successful in the case of Hungary and Poland. Equity market capitalisation also remains low with 19% of GDP (PL) and 33% (H) compared to EU-countries at the lower end of the scale like Portugal or Ireland with 60-70%.[46]

---

[45] *Bokros* (2000) 4.
[46] *Cohrs/Nick* (2000) 3.

Table 3: Foreign Banks in Selected CE- countries

Foreign participation in percent of total bank assets			Foreign Controll	Return on Equity		Problem Loans/Total Loans		Cost-to-income Ratio	
	12/1994	12/1999	12/1999	Foreign banks 1996-98	Domestic banks 1996-98	Foreign banks 1996-98	Domestic banks 1996-98	Foreign banks 1996-98	Domestic banks 1996-98
Czech Republic	5,8	47,3	50,7	14,4	- 1,6	18,8	28,5	70,9	40,5
Hungary	19,8	59,5	80,4	16,1	-26,0	10,6	15,1	62,4	113,0
Poland	2,1	36,4	52,8	24,1	- 0,1	11,1	9,2	50,9	59,9
Total	7,8	44,0	59,9	19,3	-5,0	13,7	17,1	59,9	62,1

Source: *Fink/Haiss* (2000b); Data: *Mathieson/Schinasi* (2000), p. 153, p. 166.

During the last years mostly significant progress in implementation of the EU *acquis* could be observed, while the first eight years of reform were characterised by slow and hesitant action. *Foreign banks* were finally allowed to take over troubled CEEC banks as majority owners. As a result, the financial sector seems to be more advanced in countries like Hungary and Estonia (to a lesser extent Poland) that allowed strong foreign equity involvement in the banking sector. More than half of the banking market in the CEECs is in the hands of foreign-owned banks. In Hungary, Poland, the Czech Republic, Estonia and Latvia, more than 70% of the local banking market is served by foreign-owned banks, with the level on the rise.[47] Although control by a reputable foreign strategic partner seems to be by far the most successful way of stabilising and modernizing the economy it is often impeded by many economic and political sensitivities.[48]

The *critical element* is not to sell majority stakes to a foreign bank. What matters is *the transfer of real management control and responsibility to prudent strategic partners that intend to run the bank as financial intermediary and not as portfolio manager.* That happened in case of the Czech Investicni a Postovni Banka (IPB). A foreign buyer (Nomura) was able to privatise gains, whereas the losses were finally socialized.[49] Banking systems in the CEECs now rely on strategic shareholdings by better-regulated banks, most of which are from the EU.

B. Reconstruction of the Financial Sector Still in Progress

Banking reform had its ups and downs and is still an ongoing issue in all CEECs. Most accession countries have established all the *institutions* needed to perform the financial market *functions. An increasingly sophisticated legal and regulatory framework was established.* There remains a lot to be done in *implementation* and *enforcement capacity* to make the financial system tick in a way that it contributes to economic growth, which so far is generated by factors outside the banking system, and to create an effective and

---

[47] *Jones* (2001) 50.

[48] With OTP in Hungary and BKO BP in Poland, even the largest (retail) banks of advanced financial services sector reformers remained in state hands for an extended period.

[49] *Bokros* (2000) 11; the case is still pending in the courts.

stable framework for monetary policy. Frequently, asset stripping of faltering banks could not be avoided. Initial recapitalisations could not prevent moral hazard. It is not easy to see how banks which have difficulties to manage themselves can exert a positive influence on the management of corporations and increase the efficiency of firms.[50]

Besides relatively *immature governance structures*, the financial sector in the CEECs is also plagued by other weaknesses. *Financial markets in most of the CEECs are small* in relative and absolute terms (and in some countries still declining) due to several reasons: The neglect of financial intermediation under communism and also during the first years of transition, low level of GDP per capita, mostly a small number of population of the country concerned, and successive waves of excessive lending followed by a credit crunch and finally high risk aversion after bank failures.

---

50 *Vincentz* (2002) 27.

Table 4: Banking Intermediation in the Candidate Countries

Year	BG	CY	CZ	EE	HU	LV	LT	MT	PL	RO	SK	SL	TR
	Bank Assets in Percent of GDP												
1998	35%		120%	56%	69%	47%	28%	194%	58%	36%	85%	74%	79%
1999	36%		123%	62%	69%	50%	30%	206%	59%	31%	92%	76%	103%
2000	38%	264%	128%	68%	70%	62%	31%	208%	63%	29%	96%	81%	94%
	Domestic Credit to Private Sector in Percent of GDP												
1998	9%	106%	58%	23%	23%	16%	13%	89%	25%	16%	67%	34%	21%
1999	11%	113%	53%	24%	25%	17%	15%	94%	29%	11%	50%	37%	20%
2000	12%	119%	49%	24%	29%	21%	13%	98%	30%	9%	46%	39%	21%
	Non-Performing Loans in Percent of Total Loans												
1998	12%		20%	1%	6%	5%	13%	9%	11%	72%	44%	5%	7%
1999	18%	8%	22%	2%	3%	6%	13%	14%	14%	53%	41%	5%	10%
2000	11%	8%	25%	1%	2%	5%	11%	14%	15%	5%	15%	5%	9%

Data: *European Commission* (2002b) supplemented by *EBRD* (2001).

Note: year-end (stock) data on bank assets, domestic credit and sour credits mixed with annual (flow) data on GDP.

The initial expansion was clearly assisted by imprudent behaviour of well-connected "invisible hands". Many banks in the CEECs now rather act like fee-earning brokers by trying to link their business partners directly rather than taking risk.[51] Compared with established market economies, a low level of reported financial intermediation through banks can be observed in most candidate countries. While the average stock market capitalisation of the euro area is about 84% of GDP, the CEECs on average roughly reach one fifth. Bank assets relative to GDP ranged from 31% in Lithuania to 128% in the Czech Republic in 2000. In most CEECs the ratio is only about one fourth of the euro-area level of 240% of GDP.[52] Moreover, the majority of credits granted are rather short-term as evidenced by banks′ assets structure.[53] Domestic credit relative to GDP ranges from 9% in Romania to 48.2% in Slovakia, while it is about 100% in Portugal and Spain. The Slovak Republic had to move bad bank debt amounting to another 14% of GDP into the public sphere in 2000.[54] The presumably high bank asset ratios for the Czech and Slovak Republics are inflated by a considerable load of sour credits (ranging from 1% in Estonia to 25% in the Czech Republic) still inherent in the financial sector and/or now resting on public books as contingent liabilities .

From the relatively small degree of financial intermediation, several conclusions can be drawn. For one, *in the short run domestic banks cannot have a strong impact on economic efficiency* of the CEEC economies. Interest rate and credit channels are not well developed yet.[55] For two, *abundant liquidities may lead banks to increase credit, causing a mismatch* if capital flows were to reverse themselves and foreign currency liabilities were matched by domestic currency assets and/or short-term inflows were turned into longer-term credit.[56] For three, from the current low level, *financial intermediation might grow considerably*. New customer and product groups will be targeted, especially retail banking (i.e. servicing households and SMEs, where asymmetric information and inexpe-

---

51 *Fink/Haiss* (2000b).

52 *European Commission* (2002b) 8.

53 *European Commission* (2002b) 8.

54 *Backé/Barisits/Fidrmuc/Reininger/Schardax/Wojcik* (2001) 81.

55 *Backe/Fidrmuc/Reininger/Schardax* (2002) 35.

56 *Wyplosz* (1999) 241.

rience are common) receives a lot of renewed attention. Given the prevailing lack of adequate financial sector supervision as indicated by the *Commission* (2001b) for many accession countries,[57] rising banking intermediation may carry potentially higher systemic risk.[58]

C. The Official Evaluation of the Reconstruction Process

In spite of the remaining problems, progress in the transition of the financial services sector shows that reforms pay off. The credit for this success belongs mainly to the people of those countries themselves. Undoubtedly the process was significantly promoted by the prospect of EU membership. In combination with the IMF/World Bank Financial Sector Assessment Programme (FSAP) the EU accession criteria and the EBRD transition indicator scores[59] provided the benchmarks. EU support with information and finance provided incentives. Without the Agenda 2000 and the consequent acquis screening financial sector reform possibly would have collapsed.

From the Commissions' annual progress reports and from joint Commission/Member Candidate assessments of economic policy priorities, short-term and medium-term accession priorities are derived in the form of Accession Partnership Agreements (APA). These allow for a stepwise solution of the remaining problems, provided that the respective candidate countries governments have the ability and will to implement them.[60]

There are interesting *differences between the Commissions´* views expressed in the *general conclusions of the Regular Reports´ Strategy Paper*[61] (whereas only Bulgaria and Romania are regarded as not having a functioning market economy; Romania also is seen as not having the capacity to withstand competitive pressure and market forces within the Union in the medium term) *and the more detailed analysis therein and* especially with regard to the Com-

---

[57] *European Commission* (2001b, 2001c).

[58] *Thießen* (2000) 14.

[59] *Stern et al* (1999) e.g. 24, 40 and 202ff; *Adams et al* (1999) 155ff.

[60] For reviews of previous progress reports, see *Fink/Haiss* (2000a, 2000b).

[61] *European Commission* (2001b).

missions′ *2002-2003 Accession Partnership Priorities.*[63] In that Regular Report, the *Commission* (2001b) finds that for all candidate countries, according to the "economic" and "other obligations of membership" criteria, "Financial intermediation is still overall at a low level in the CEEC-10 economies. The sector contributes little to the financing of investment in what should be a growing private sector. Intermediation is particularly low and inefficient in Bulgaria, Romania and Lithuania. In general, further progress is needed before accession, as a proper working of the transmission mechanism for monetary policy would require higher levels of more efficient intermediation. The expansion of the financial sector has been accompanied by improved supervision in the banking sector, but supervision of the other parts needs to improve, not only on regulations but also on the administrative capacity and independence of supervisors.

In the financial sector, the bank privatisation agenda is completed in a number of candidates such as Estonia, Hungary, Latvia and the Czech Republic. It has advanced in Lithuania, Romania, Poland and Slovakia and is lagging considerably behind in Slovenia. Concerning the state-owned banks not intended for privatisation, it is important that governments do not interfere with their operating practices and credit policies. For other parts of the financial sector, progress in privatisation is hesitant and uneven across candidates. The completion of land reform with the creation of a functioning land market lingers in many CEEC-10. This is hindering the development of land and housing markets and of construction, with unfavourable implications for the labour markets and financial intermediation." Moreover, there is a need to improve administrative capacity in economic and monetary union.[64] By grouping the financial services sector issues among the 2002-203 *Accession Partnership Priorities*[65] by frequency of item and country, a ranking emerges that is quite different from the country grouping as reported in the Strategy Paper of the *Commissions′* (2001b) Regular Report. That difference *highlights the quality of many central issues still pending in the financial sector*.

---

62 *European Commission* (2001c).

63 *European Commission* (2001c).

64 *European Commission* (2001b) 14f.

65 *European Commission* (2001c).

Reinforcement of supervision and the development of monitoring and regulatory bodies in financial services are among the pending priorities for 11 of the 12 candidate countries (all but Hungary; see table 5). According to the experience from the Asian (1997) crisis, such institutional features are very important determinants of economic performance. Failure to impose proper regulatory and legal control over the operation of the financial sector will have real consequences.[66] All CEEC accession countries are still facing difficulties in setting-up crucial elements of the legal and institutional framework needed for the functioning of a market economy. While the degree of legal certainty is considered high for Estonia and Hungary in the 2001 Regular Report,[67] this is not yet the case for the other countries. Without a functioning land market, implemented bankruptcy laws and a functioning judiciary, financial institutions functioning has to remain shallow.[68] Progress in these areas is crucial before accession, the reform agenda is not yet complete as confirmed by the ECB.[69] Given the relative progress made in Slovakia recently, the provision of official credits which are conditional upon financial sector reform seems to provide positive triggers in that matter.[70]

One interpretation of the soft stance on the mostly premature financial sector could be that derogations or other transition arrangements for financial services sector issues are likely to come up for several countries. That would not match the current status of negotiations as discussed above. Along this line, there have been calls for either far-reaching exceptions to the acquis or for long transition periods for the CEECs to improve "creative" development of the respective capital markets.[71] The other interpretation could be that the accession phase to the eurosystem will be used to overcome financial services sector problems that might still be pending for the New Members *after* accession to the EU due to a

---

66 *Dickson/Mullineux* (2001) 220.

67 *European Commission* (2001b) 11.

68 *The European Commission* (2002b) 11, quotes in more detail: contract enforcement and loan recovery, collateral availability and seizure, corporate financial disclosure, corporate accounting and auditing rules.

69 *Padoa-Schioppa* (2002) 4.

70 *Katzman/Mullen* (2001) 21.

71 *Lannoo/Salem* (2001) 120.

soft evaluation of the Copenhagen criteria. In that case the financial sector might be regarded as a matter not to be resolved completely *before* membership in the EU, as this possibly could delay accession. With full membership and informal derogation in financial sector adjustment, it remains questionable *whether restricted competition will be effective enough to guarantee accelerated moves towards efficiency and good governance*. The risk is that *financial sector reform* might informally be *derogated* but *free movement of capital* already *implemented* upon accession to the EU by the New Members. *It is therefore suggested to let the market take the whole at accession, to have free capital movement established together with unrestricted foreign strategic investment in the financial services sector.*[72] Another issue to be resolved is the appropriation of currency regimes as discussed in the following.

---

72 *Fink/Haiss* (2000b).

Table 5: Financial Sector Issues in the Accession Partnership Priorities 2002-2003 (to be continued)

	Economic Criteria – To Dos	**Ability to Assume the Obligations of Membership –To Dos**
BG	- maintain macro-economic stability and continue to promote economic growth and competitiveness - improve the functioning of the financial sector and in particular strengthen the banking sector - improve and accelerate bankruptcy and liquidation procedures - establish a functioning land market - develop SME´s access to finance on appropriate terms	- services: reinforce supervision of financial services - capital: prevent the use of the financial system for money laundering. - company law: upgrade accounting and auditing standards & practices and urgently enhance enforcement of industrial property rights - competition: enforce state aid and anti-trust rules - agriculture: put in place necessary conditions for capital markets in the rural and agricultural sectors
CZ	- improve the operation of the commercial register - improve bankruptcy legislation and its implementation - resolve bad loan problem in a transparent and efficient way - continue fiscal reforms, incl. pension system financing reforms	- services: complete alignment in insurance, reinforce supervision of financial services - capital: abolish existing anonymous accounts - company law: enforce industrial property rights - competition: ensure enforcement of state aid and anti-trust rules - EMU: urgently align national bank independence - justice and home affairs: establish cooperation in fight against financial crime and corruption, in particular money-laundering
EE	- complete land reform and land registration	- services: align financial services legislation and reinforce supervision of financial services, esp. securities markets - capital: urgently align legislation on payment systems and ensure implementation; align legislation in direct investment - competition: enforce state aid and anti-trust rules - justice and home affairs: continue fight against organised crime and strengthen capacities to deal with money laundering

Table 5 (continued): Financial Sector Issues in the Accession Partnership Priorities 2002-2003 (to be continued)

	Economic Criteria – To Dos	**Ability to Assume the Obligations of Membership –To Dos**
HU	- health care reform and railway restructuring to reduce budget impact - create conditions for efficient agricultural land market - improve SMEs access to credit	- capital: urgently implement FATF recommendations on money laundering; phase out anonymous savings books - competition: ensure enforcement of state aid and anti-trust rules, including incompatible aid schemes, esp. fiscal aids - justice and home affairs: strengthen fight against organised crime and money laundering
LV	- strengthen land market and finalise land and property register - stimulate domestic and inward investment	- services: reinforce supervision of financial services and ensure independence of supervisory body - capital: comply with recommendations of FATF (money laundering) - company law: urgently strengthen enforcement of industrial property rights - competition: ensure enforcement of state aid rules - justice and home affairs: strengthen law enforcement in fight against organised crime, esp. money laundering
LT	- reduce unemployment - social security reform in a sustainable way for public finances - privatise remaining state owned banks - ensure implementation and enforcement of legislation on enterprise restructuring and bankruptcy, esp. by training in enterprise risk assessment and evalu-ation of company restructuring - complete land titling, registration and land market development	- services: develop monitoring and regulatory bodies for financial services - capital: urgently amend restrictive legislation on FDI; strengthen surveillance and regulatory bodies; liberalise progressively short-term capital movements; ensure implementation of recommendations of FATF - company law: establish central register of legal entities and strengthen enforcement capacities of industrial property rights - competition: ensure enforcement of state aid and anti-trust rules - justice and home affairs: ensure effective implementation of anti-money laundering measures

Table 5 (continued): Financial Sector Issues in the Accession Partnership Priorities 2002-2003 (to be continued)

	Economic Criteria – To Dos	**Ability to Assume the Obligations of Membership – To Dos**
PL	- maintain macroeconomic and budgetary stability - progress in structural reforms, including privatisation of remaining state-owned financial institutions - restructure railway aiming at budgetary sustainability - improve functioning of the land market and complete development of property register	- services: develop monitoring and regulatory bodies in financial services - capital: urgently amend sectoral legislation restricting FDI, liberalise short-term capital movements, ensure implementation of FATF recommendations (money laundering) - company law: urgently upgrade industrial property enforcement - competition: ensure enforcement of state aid and anti-trust rules - taxation: urgently develop IT systems for exchange of e-data with EMU; consolidate the independence of the National Bank - justice and home affairs: address money laundering and economic crime
RO	- establish macroeconomic stability - continue privatisation, stimulate investment, implement bankruptcy procedures - speed up creation of a functioning land market by completing the issuance of land titles and strengthen property rights - develop a policy framework for rural credit and financial infrastructure	- services: align legislation of securities markets and reinforce supervision of financial services - capital: implement recommendations of FATF - company law: enforce industrial property rights - competition: ensure enforcement of state aid and anti-trust rules - industrial policy: improve the access of enterprises (esp. SMEs) to investment finance - justice and home affairs: align acquis in money laundering, fight corruption and organised crime

Table 5 (continued): Financial Sector Issues in the Accession Partnership Priorities 2002-2003

	Economic Criteria – To Dos	**Ability to Assume the Obligations of Membership –To Dos**
SK	- ensure sustainability of public finances by tackling expenditure reform, esp. of health and pension systems - complete financial sector restructuring, privatise banks & insurance companies - implement bad-debt recovery mechanisms and implement bankruptcy and investment promotion legislation - complete establishment of efficient land and capital markets	- services: align and implement directives on financial services legislation and reinforce supervision of financial services - capital: relax restrictions on institutional investors, strengthen and co-ordinate the supervisory institutions and procedures, comply with the recommendations of the FATF - company law: train judiciary and prosecuters - competition: ensure enforcement of state aid and anti-trust rules - justice and home affairs: fight against organised crime and fraud and strengthen the capacity to deal with money laundering
SL	- restructure the financial sector by completing the privatisation process of state-owned banks and by privatising the insurance company - improve the efficiency of the land registration system	- services: reinforce the supervision of financial services, complete alignment of legislation on investment services - capital: abolish remaining restrictions on short-term transactions in order to complete liberalisation of capital flows and ensure compliance to recommendations of FATF - company law: enforce industrial property rights - competition: implement state aid control
	Note: FDI = foreign direct investment;	FATF = Financial Action Task Force, esp. on money laundering

Source: compiled by the author from: *European Commission* (2001c).

IV. Nominal and Real Convergence

Box 4: EMU Convergence and Speculative Bubbles
So far current account deficits were covered by privatisation-related FDI. The final solution to the worrying "twin deficits" of the current account and budgetary is growth, not FDI. Future current account deficits will be financed by portfolio investment and short term credit. These inflows can easily be reversed and will be intermediated by a weak financial system. Volatile flows of speculative funds might lead to sharp fluctuations in the exchange rate, create asset bubbles and exercise a disturbing influence. With the CEECs monetary volume only 3% of the eurozone, even minor capital flows may be problematic. Most accession countries already have currency regimes in line with the ERM-II requirements and can be regarded as extended eurozone. For those candidate countries that are in a fixed currencyboard relation to the euro and/or are very small, the step back towards a free float only to fix again after about two years upon entry into the eurosystem sounds a complicated matter of principle.A tight fix to the euro during the ERM-II period may avoid speculative attacks for them. The group of candidate countries with flexible currency regimes should stick to the full +/- 15% ERM-II band to avoid speculative attacks. On the convergency criteria, problems are most obvious with regard to inflation and interest rates. On the debt criteria, contingent liabilities and measurement uncertainties blur the picture for now.

A. Monetary and Foreign Exchange Policy Issues

The ECB stresses that candidate countries should have macroeconomic programmes consistent with those prevailing in the euro area in their medium-term policy agenda, although price stability, the sustainability of public finance, exchange rate stability in the framework of participation in the ERM and the convergence of interest rates are not mandatory for EU accession.[73] The ECB is not recommending a particular monetary policy strategy, but only recommends that the aim to maintain price stability should be the ultimate compass.[74] As can be referred from the table, the accession countries share a close proximity in currency regimes. Over time, a

[73] *ECB* (2000) 44.

[74] *Padoa-Schioppa* (2002) 3.

two-corner solution developed with exchange rate regimes either relatively flexible or very rigid.[75] Many accession countries have been moving towards more flexible exchange rate regimes in order to better accommodate capital inflows.[76] On the other hand, some of the smaller CEECs have a fixed peg or a currency board, partly attributed to the "fear of floating".[77] A growing number of accession countries already follow exchange rate strategies that are in line with the ERM II requirements and only a few (e.g. LAT, MAL, TKY) will have to modify their policies to make them compatible with ERM II membership.[78] Fully floating exchange rates, crawling pegs and pegs against anchors other than the euro are rendered incompatible versus the ERM II by the ECOFIN and the ECB.[79] Given that most of their currencies are already linked in one way or another to the euro, the candidate countries can already be regarded as an „extended eurozone" (which also includes several countries in the Balcans).[80] With joining EU and progressively liberalising capital flows, accession countries will become less and less able to target their exchange rate without ‚importing' their monetary policy from the euro area.[81] New Members will have to treat their economic and currency policy as a matter of common concern.

---

75 *Halpern/Wyplosz* (2001) 5.

76 *European Commission* (2002b) 6; *Wyplosz* (1999) 243.

77 *Hochreiter/Wagner* (2001).

78 *Padoa-Schioppa* (2002) 4.

79 *ECOFIN* (2000).

80 *Köhler/Wes* (1999) 2 already argued that euro soon would become an attractive vehicle currency and reserve asset for the candidate countries.

81 *Duisenberg* (1999) 6.

Table 6: Currency Regimes

Candidate	Monetary Policy Goal and Currency Regime
BG	exchange rate stability; currency board (EUR/ DM) with Lev 1.95583 per euro since July 1997
CY	monetary stability, pegged to the euro with a band of +/- 2.25% since 1992
CZ	foreign exchange stability (headline inflation targeting); managed floating, net of administered prices: euro as reference currency since Mai 1997
EE	exchange rate stability; currency board (EUR/ DM) with EEK 15.699664 per euro since June 1992
HU	foreign exchange stability, +/- 15% band vs. Euro widend from +/-2.25% in May 2001
LV	price stability; fixed peg to SDR[82] since Feb.1994 (0.8 Lats per SDR)
LT	exchange rate stability; currency board; in Feb. 2002, the euro replaced the US-$ as anchor
MT	foreign exchange stability; peg to currency basked since 1971 (EUR 56.8 %, US-$: 21.6 %, GBP: 21.6 %); +/- 0.25% band
PL	price stability; managed floating, headline inflation target with euro as reference since April 2000
RO	foreign exchange stability; managed floating with euro as reference currency since August 1992
SK	foreign exchange stability; managed floating, core inflation target with euro as reference currency since October 1998
SL	foreign exchange stability; managed floating with annual M3 growth target; euro as reference currency since 1992
TR	inflation target, free float with peg to currency basket ($ 1 + EUR 0,77)

Source: *Eller/Haiss* (2002a).

1. The ERM II and Implications

The ERM could accommodate the main features of a number of exchange rate regimes, provided their commitments and objectives are credible and in line with those of the ERM II.[83] As the ERM II only allows for a defined deviation of the participating currencies from a certain parity to the euro, systems which are flexibly managed, crawling pegs or pegs to other currencies than the euro would have to be abandoned and follow the euro with normal fluctuation margins of up to +/-15%. Currency regimes that are a fixed peg or a managed float with the euro as reference anchor can be integrated into the ERM II. Crawling pegs in their current format imply a me-

[82] Special Drawing Right (G7-weighted reference value).

[83] *ECOFIN* (2000).

chanic or automatic adjustment of the parity in periodic intervals and thus are not compatible to the criteria for ERM II, according to which the parity has to be fixed in principle and can only be adjusted with the involvement of all members, including the ECB.[84] New Member States will be expected to participate in this mechanism for at least two years without exceeding the agreed upon band versus the euro.[85] Narrower bands can be formally agreed at the request of the non-euro member state or declared as a unilateral commitment of the respective non-euro area central bank.[86] After widening the margins in the ERM-I to +/- 15% in 1993, the DKR held a +/-2.5% band and most other ERM-I-currencies stayed within fluctuation margins of +/-4.5%.

In the accession countries, monetary and exchange rate polices have also to cope with issues related to the catching-up process. Large foreign direct investment (FDI) inflows and goal conflicts between price stability and foreign exchange rate stability in the case of high productivity gains in tradeable goods can press a currency towards revaluation.[87] For a detailed discussion of the so-called Balassa-Samuelson-Effect, see the chapters by *Fritz Breuss* and *Kronberger/Mahlberg* in this volume. Avoiding real exchange rate misalignments and excessive nominal exchange rate fluctuations may pose a systemic challenge for those accession countries' national banks which operate a flexible exchange regime.[88] A real revaluation might worsen the trade balance and slow down GDP-growth, restructuring and convergence. During the 1997 currency crises, the Czech Republic had to abandon the peg to the DM/US-$-basket following speculative attacks due to weak fundamentals, financial sector problems and insufficient restructuring.[89] Therefore, more flexible systems seem appropriate. In June 2001, Hun-

---

84 *Eurpoean Commission* (2000b) 38f.

85 *FBE* (2002) 8. The Treaty speaks of "the observance of the normal fluctuation margins provided for by the exchange rate mechanism of the European Monetary System, for at least two years, without devaluing against the currency of any other member state." *Pelkmans/Gros/Ferrer* (2000) 118.

86 *Wyplosz* (2002) 4; *Breuss* (2000) 38.

87 *Buiter/Grafe* (2001) 7; *Köhler/Wes* (1999) 14.

88 *ECB* (2000) 44; *Halpern/Wyplosz* (2001) 2.

89 *Kopits* (1999) 9.

gary widened the Forint-band to +/-15% based, arguing, that the wider exchange rate band will significantly reduce the dangers and speculative attacks the previous rigid narrow-band exchange rate system was exposed to.[90]

2. Current Account Financing

For the accession countries, current account deficit improved from 5.6% of GDP (1999) to 5.2% (2000) and further to 4.3% (2001, 2002e) in spite of a deterioration in the terms of trade.[91] A major macroeconomic policy challenge remains in keeping prospectively high and growing current account deficits (2003e: growing to 4.7% again)[92] within the range where sound external financing can be secured.[93] The "twin deficit" of external accounts and of the budget raises worries about the sustainability of the real appreciation of the CEECs currencies.[94] The solution to deficits is not necessarily fiscal policy but mainly growth. According to the *Fink* (1993) debt model, the government debt quota (general government debt relative to GDP) depends on two factors: on the deficit quota (current account relative to GDP or budget deficit to GDP) and on GDP growth.[95] With a nominal GDP growth of slightly above 5% a country can afford a 3% deficit quota without infringing the 60% government debt benchmark. If GDP growth slows down below 5%, the deficit quota also has to be reduced. In case the economy grows faster, the country can afford a higher deficit. With a constant deficit quota and constant GDP growth, public debt converges to its threshold value. The issue to be dealt with is the GDP growth rate necessary to cover the current account deficit at a certain interest rate.

In almost all cases, the current account imbalance was covered significantly by foreign direct investment (FDI). Average annual

---

90 *Magyar Nemzeti Bank* (2001), 2. In the meantime, the crawling peg was replaced by a band vs. the euro.

91 *European Commission* (2001b); *European Commission* (2002c) 51. To a considerable extent, this improvement is explained by a decline in Poland as a consequence of ist domestic demand concentration. See *European Commission* (2002c) 6, for details.

92 *European Commission* (2002c) 51.

93 *European Commission* (2002b) 5.

94 *Wyplosz* (2002) 1.

95 *Fink* (1993) 261.

FDI inflows in the accession countries range from 1.2% of GDP in Slovenia to 7.4% of GDP in Lithuania in 1996 to 2000.[96] Because of privatisation, nearly half of the FDI flows have been directed to non-tradable sectors such as financial institutions (banks) and public utilities (e.g. telecommunications). Greenfield investments are increasing in some countries and represent over half of FDI in Bulgaria and dominate in Hungary. The privatisation component of FDI dominated total aggregate inflows during the last years. Now the accession countries are facing increasing capital inflow of three types: foreign direct investment, investment financed by foreign credits and foreign portfolio investment. Especially short-term foreign credit and portfolio investment have to be considered, given that they provide a potential basis for speculative attacks.[97] This is discussed in the following.

3. Speculative Bubbles

In evaluating current account deficits, besides the structure and mix of foreign direct investment (FDI) it is necessary to compare their development relative to portfolio investment and to the stability and maturity of the financial sector. Growing current account deficits are a latent concern as possible triggers for capital flight.[98] In the short term, many accession countries will still be able to rely on privatisation-based FDI inflows in order to cover their current account deficits to a considerable degree.[99] High levels of FDI substituted for domestic financial intermediation and domestic savings so far.[100] This may increase the foreign debt burden of companies and in turn raise the credit risk of their domestic banks in case these companies are not adequately hedged.[101] The considerable in-

---

96 *European Commission* (2002b) 5.

97 *Buiter/Grafe* (2001).

98 See *Wirtschaftsblatt* 19.04.2001: A6 and *Wirtschaftsblatt* 20.04.2001: A6.

99 *European Commission* (2002b) 5.

100 *Vincentz* (2002) 11.

101 *European Commission* (2002b) 9. According to *Reininger/Schardax/Summer* (2002) 22, the corporate sector's net foreign exchange position in percent of total credit received from the domestic banking system and foreign creditors reached about 49% in Poland, 43% in Hungary and 29% in the Czech Republic in 2000.

volvement of foreign banks may provide a certain protection in that respect.[102]

Foreign capital inflows will remain high in the medium term, but the mix will change and that has important implications. Future foreign capital inflows into the accession countries are estimated at about 4% of the annual GDP (before EU subsidies).[103] *With FDI-attracting privatisation coming to an end, foreign capital inflows rather will show up in the format of* short-term *credits and portfolio investment of the non-strategic, trading-oriented kind.* Around the time when a formal judgement on the convergency criteria needs to be established, current account deficit financing may have to increasingly rely on these debt-creating, more short-term, and easier to reverse capital inflows.[104] These types of capital flows lead to a higher fluidity and inherent danger of destabilisation from the creation of asset bubbles and the reinforcement of procyclical behavior.[105] In Poland, Hungary and the Czech Republic, the actual shares of foreign portfolio investors are estimated to amount to about 60% to 75% in 2000 already.[106] The corporate sectors′ net foreign exchange lending ranges between 29% to 49% for these countries.[107] The relationship between the total level of private

---

[102] Empirical evidence on these issues is inconclusive. *Beck* (2000) for example found that foreign bank penetration may also tend to rather increase the volatility of capital flows.

[103] *Vincentz* (2002) 13. Note that according to *Richter* (2002), the accession countries will most likely resume a net contributor position to the EU budget at least during their first year of membership. Even thereafter, the net financial transfers from the EU budget as measured as a percentage of the accession countries GDP is estimated at just about 1% annually.

[104] *European Commission* (2002b) 5.

[105] For herding behaviour, see *Fink/Haiss* (2001). For the causal link between excessive short-term indebtedness and financial crises in emerging markets see *Lamfalussy* (2000) 172. For the interplay between macroeconomic policy and capital flows and the prospect of a future "bumpy ride" see *Dickson/Mullineux* (1999).

[106] *Reininger/Schardax/Summer* (2002) 40.

[107] *Reininger/Schardax/Summer* (2002) 22; *Vincentz* (2002). According to *Darvas/Szapáry* (2000) 36, in the case of Hungary, the steady growth of the share of foreign exchange credits in the total borrowing of enterprises may reflect the growing importance of multinational companies.

sector's foreign assets and the size of net capital flows in and out of these countries therefore deserves special attention.[108] The upshot could be short-term inflows and outflows of speculative funds, leading to sharp fluctuations in the exchange rate and resulting problems in the domestic financial sector and the real economy.[109]

Additional risk potentials may result from domestic banks intermediating these increasing amounts of foreign capital inflows.[110] Such capital inflows typically lead to a lending boom and a financial or real estate bubble.[111] As long as the financial sector is strong and viable, this extra stress can be born. An *efficient and competitive financial sector* is not only the basis of effective monetary policy, but also a guarantee for low risk of capital transactions. Due to the prevailing low level of financial intermediation in the accession countries, small absolute and relative size of financial markets, poor bank asset quality with high fractions of non-performing and/or short-term loans, immature supervisory and governance structures, and crucial elements missing in the proper legal environment (functioning judiciary, land markets and bankruptcy procedures), this is not the case yet in most of the accession countries.[112] Monetary policy making in the accession countries is quite challenging due to the uneven functioning of monetary transmission channels, as the interest rate and credit channels are not well developed yet.[113] It is difficult to judge what the financial sectors' intermediatory capacity will be in 2007. At this time entry into the eurosystem may be at stake and the financial sector capabilities will be judged. According to the recent past, it seems that the domestic banking system at least in several CEECs does not successfully intermediate foreign short-term funds to productive investments in

---

[108] *Motamen-Samadian/Croft* (2000) 153.

[109] *Schularick* (2002) 3.

[110] *European Commission* (2002b) 10.

[111] *Fink/Haiss* (2001); *Hochreiter/Wagner* (2001). *Dickson/Mullineux* (2000) 236, argue that once speculators get to work the crisis will feed on a lack of confidence in domestic financial institutions, exacerbated by increases in the domestic rate of interest in an attempt to protect the currency.

[112] See *Eller/Haiss* (2002a).

[113] *Backé/Fidrmuc/Reininger/Schardax* (2002) 35.

the privat sector for now.[114] Should the accession countries join the EU with this *premature financial sector*, it might be *easy for speculative foreign portfolio investors to influence asset prices, create asset bubbles and exercise a disturbing influence on the real economy.*[115]

Phasing out of remaining controls on the movement of capital also has to be considered in this respect, although it remains a controversial issue.[116] The Commission warns that the complete liberalisation of capital markets could raise potential vulnerabilities if capital inflows should be poorly intermediated by the domestic financial sector or if they should exceed the absorptive capacity of the respective economies.[117] Capital inflows that are not channelled into productive investments might lead to speculative bubbles under these circumstances.[118] Experience has shown that the most serious difficulties arise during the final phases of inflation convergence if capital controls have already been lifted[119] and that emerging economies remain exposed to volatile capital flows.[120]

Following an initial contagion effect, markets tend to become more sensitive to the underlying fundamentals of the economy.[121] Already the investment (inflow) and divestment (outflow) of – in international terms comparatively small, in CEEC-terms quite large - amounts could induce economic shocks.[122] In this case the small and underdeveloped financial markets of the member candidate countries could be taken hostage by large foreign portfolio investors which easily can influence asset prices and trigger stock exchange crashes by investing and withdrawing relatively small

[114] *Reininger/Schardax/Summer* (2002) 44.

[115] *Hochreiter/Wagner* (2001) 15; *Szapáry* (2001) 28; *Wyplosz* (1999) 241.

[116] *Halpern/Wyplosz* (2001) 6.

[117] *European Commission* (2002b) 5; for a general discussion, see *Wyplosz* (1999) 243, arguing that capital controls can play a crucial role, provided their role is neither inflated nor minimized.

[118] *European Commission* (2002b) 5; *Dickson/Mullineux* (1999) 225.

[119] *Pelkmans/Gros/Ferrer* (2000) 118.

[120] *Szapáry* (2001) 27.

[121] *Darvas/Szapáry* (2000) 40.

[122] *Fink/Haiss* (2000b) 6; for a review of types of contagion, see *Darvas/ Szapáry* (2000) 29.

amounts of capital. That impression also is supported in comparing broad money in the CEECs and the current eurosystem.

Portfolio investments or company acquisitions that are midsize in European terms may already have an impact on the respective CEECs exchange rate, given their small monetary volume. Aggregate M1[123] of all ten CEE accession countries is about equal to the Austrian level (or twice the level of Greece) and amounts to about 2.7% of the eurozone M1. An approximation of aggregate M3 of the ten CEE accession countries is slightly above the Austrian equivalent and amounts to about 3.1% of the current eurozone. Poland alone accounts for about half of the monetary volume. Even considering the volume of euros held in the CEECs of about EUR 7.5 bn to EUR 15 bn only marginally changes that picture.[124] In the CEECs, broad money also is smaller relative to GDP than in the current eurozone.

Table 7: Broad Money

Country / Zone	M1 (1999) in bn Eur	M3* (1999) in bn Eur	M3* (1999) in % GDP
Poland	23,52	62,37	43,1%
Czech Republic	13,03	37,59	75,4%
Hungary	8,41	21,21	46,2%
Slovenia	1,73	9,13	52,6%
Romania	1,82	8,21	25,7%
Bulgaria	1,53	3,76	32,3%
Slovak Republic	0,80	2,72	64,6%
Lithuania	1,24	2,11	21,1%
Estonia	1,16	2,06	42,7%
Latvia	0,98	1,60	27,2%
CEEC-10	54,22	150,75	46,2%
Euro-11-zone without Greece	1.964,00	4.791,50	78,2%
Euro-12-zone with Greece	1.988,50	4.909,50	78,6%
Greece	24,50	118,00	
Austria	55,82	139,48	
Austria in % of Euro-12-Zone	2,8%	2,8%	
CEEC-10 in % Euro-12-Zone	2,7%	3,1%	
PL in% Euro-12-Zone	1,2%	1,3%	

Source: *Eller/Haiss* (2002b).* for EST, LAT, LIT, SK: M2 as proxy for M3

[123] M1 = currency in circulation – cash + sight deposits

[124] Deutschmark-holdings in the CEECs and Turkey were estimated at DM 50-100, with 30-40% resting in Turkey alone. *Sinn/Westermann* (2001) 30, argue that deutschmarks returning from the candidate countries might partly have led to a fall in the euro exchange rate vis-a-vis the US-dollar. See also *Stix* (2001) and *Judson/Porter* (2001) for issues of foreign currency holdings.

A negative example is the development of the financial sector in Turkey in spring 2001. That incident postponed Turkeys possible accession considerably and thereby depicts the necessity of a mature banking sector and of appropriate corporate governance.[125] These are matters of concern for the accession countries because the complete fulfilment of the Copenhagen criteria regarding the financial sector is an essential step towards creating a solid basis for future non-inflationary economic growth.[126] The inherent instability of the accession countries financial markets is a determining challenge of monetary policy.[127] In the presence of potentially strong and reversible capital inflows, monetary policy cannot foster the required real exchange rate stability.[128] As the CEECs approach EU accession, they will need to avoid the perils of too much or too little exchange rate variability when capital flows are likely to be large and volatile.

For candidate countries with a euro-based currency board (Bulgaria, Estonia, Lithuania), adoption of a *very tight version of ERM during the accession phase may prevent currency related speculative pressure.*[129] Otherwise they would have to move from fixed to a transitory flexible currency regime for about two years of ERM-II membership, just to fulfil the requirements for the final fix. Slovenia could be included in this group due to its negligible economic size and the fact that in practice Slovenia limits exchange rate movements severely.[130] No one ever cared whether San Marino, the Vatican State or Monte Carlo have met the convergency criteria – so why bother with the smaller of the candidate countries? For larger accession countries that operate under a flexible currency regime, the situation looks different.

In ERM II, there is no realignment mechanism serving as a "safety valve" to adjust bilateral parities as there was in ERM I. Adjusting the central parities was used on and off in ERM I. This exemplified the lack of convergence, but also provided the flexibil-

[125] *Cunningham* (2001) 190.
[126] *Duisenberg* (1999) 4.
[127] *Mooslechner* (2000) 565.
[128] *Feldman/Watson* (2000) 25.
[129] *Wyplosz* (2002) 8.
[130] *Wyplosz* (2002) 5.

ity necessary to smooth the common process of convergency.[131] The Delors-plan effectively dropped the realignment mechanism in ERM-I by announcing the "irrevocable freezing." By removing that safety valve, a flexible barrier became a fixed one, inviting speculative attacks. *For candidate countries which operate a flexible exchange regime, narrower bands might cause similar speculative pressure and could prove problematic.*[132] The +/- 15% ERM-II-band should not be tightened for them. "In the run up to accession and entry into ERM II, a country may also experience an increase in temporary capital flows as interest rates are bid down toward levels prevailing in the euro zone and markets speculate about entry central parities. These so-called convergence plays can induce surges in inflows that are quickly reversed once arbitrage opportunities disappear or a credible exchange rate is announced."[133] Even otherwise sufficient currency reserves might not provide an adequate cushion against a fundamental and, in view of the market, „correct" speculation. During the Russian crisis, Poland discovered that even rather wide bands did not provide a shield from speculative attacks in the face of a sudden shift in market sentiment.[134] Providing a realignment mechanism (be it by pre-announcing "likely conversion rates") might be a solution. It remains to be seen whether such issues will be reflected in the interpretation of the nominal convergency criteria.

---

131 *Gensberg* (1991) 744.

132 *Corker/Beaumont/van Elkan/Iakova* (2000) 1.

133 *Corker/Beaumont/van Elkan/Iakova* (2000) 14; *Köhler/Wes* (1999) 15.

134 *Szapáry* (2001) 27.

Table 8: Convergency Criteria

	Price stability avg. of period, % yoy			**Interest rates 10Y bonds 1)**	**Exchange rate stability deviation from parity 2)**		**Fiscal balance, 3) % of GDP**			**General govt debt, 3) % of GDP**		
	2000	2001e	2002f	Last	Last	Max (2Y)	2000	2001e	2002f	2000	2001e	2002f
Reference value	**2.8**	**3.3**	**2.8**	**7.3**		**+/-15%**	**-3.0**	**-3.0**	**-3.0**	**60.0**	**60.0**	**60.0**
Bulgaria	10.1	7.9	7.0	5.2	0	-1.3	-1.1	-1.0	-0.8	83.8	72.5	68.3
Czech Republic	3.9	4.7	3.8	5.5	14.0	-6.0	-4.0	-3.2	-3.0	29.2	29.0	30.5
Estonia	4.0	5.8	4.5	4.7	0.0	0.0	-0.7	1.1	-1.2	6.6	6.2	5.8
Hungary	9.8	9.2	5.2	6.7	5.4	-4.5	-3.5	-5.0	-5.2	56.1	51.5	49.1
Latvia	2.7	2.5	3.2	10.7	2.6	2.6	-2.8	-1.9	-2.8	10.0	12.2	11.4
Lithuania	1.0	1.3	3.3	7.9	8.1	8.1	-2.8	-1.4	-1.6	28.3	29.0	28.4
Poland	10.1	5.5	3.8	8.3	8.4	-8.7	-2.7	-6.3	-4.2	43.8	38.0	37.5
Romania	45.7	34.5	27.4	34.9	-31.4	-31.5	-4.1	-3.7	-3.3	29.2	31.2	32.2
Slovakia	12.0	7.3	4.3	7.8	4.0	-2.0	-6.8	-7.2	-6.7	32.9	42.7	42.0
Slovenia	8.9	8.5	6.6	11.1	-7.1	-7.1	-1.4	-1.3	-2.5	25.1	25.4	26.0

1) If available, shorter maturities taken for: Bulgaria, Estonia, Latvia, Lithuania, Romania, Slovakia; Reference: Bunds+15 bp.

2) Parity here: last 3-year average exchange rate against EUR.

3) Definitions may differ from the ESA 95 rules applied by the EU. One-off increases from financial sector cleansing may not be included.

Source: *Böttcher Deutsche Bank Research* (2002).

B. Criteria and Options in the Accession Phase

Candidate countries will have to conform to the convergence criteria for participation in the eurosystem. This will be decided after accession to the EU. The degree of sustainable convergence will be assessed every two years according to a standing set of criteria laid down in Art. 121 of the Treaty of the European Union and the Protocol on the Convergence Criteria.[135] The ECB made it clear that real convergence (structural adjustment) and nominal convergence (fulfilment of the Maastricht convergency criteria) should be pursued in parallel.[136] In its opinion, no extra criteria are required from accession countries compared to those that were applied to all countries that adopted the euro so far.[137] The criteria will not be applied in a simplistic or mechanistic fashion, as ultimately a judgement will have to be passed.

The great strides that the accession countries' peoples made should be acknowledged in that respect. Since 1992, the accession countries' dynamic GDP growth exceeds that of the EU. High gains in productivity accelerate the catching-up process. Strong trade links with the EU have been established and business cycles show signs of convergence.[138] Average GDP per capita on purchasing power standards (PPS) basically remained at the 1996 level of 35% for all 13 candidate countries.[139] Large within-country regional disparities still exist. Unemployment and ongoing restructuring remains a major issue for the accession countries. Future growth depends on continued high investment-to-GDP ratios, continued foreign capital inflows, rising domestic private sector savings and a further increase in productivity. The catching-up process will be paralleled by sectoral shifts and economic fluctuations. Economic policy needs to be especially attentive to financial sector consequences of growth variations in order to avoid overheating and

---

135 *Halpern/Wyplosz* (2001) 4; The evaluation of the institutional criteria (e.g. central bank independence, prohibition of direct public sector financing by the central bank etc.) were dealt with in section one (entitled relevant chapters in negotiation) of this contribution.

136 *ECB* (2000) 41.

137 *Padoa-Schioppa* (2002) 6.

138 *Kager* (2002) 7; *Fidrmuc/Schardax* (2002) 33f.

139 *European Commssion* (2002b) 3.

boom-bust cycles which frequently are a prelude to current account and financial sector mismatches.[140] Once these macroeconomic stability issues have been overcome according to the EU-entry Copenhagen criteria, the Maastricht convergency criteria become formally relevant for further integratory steps within EMU.

Sustainable convergence with regard to the *exchange rate criterion* is judged by reference to the observance of the normal fluctuation margins provided for by the ERM of the European Monetary System. Candidate countries currencies′ must have remained within ERM-II for at least two years prior to the assessment within the fluctuation band. No significant exchange market tensions and no change in the central parity against the euro on the initiative of the candidate country must have happened within that time span.[141] Both the margin and the time horizon provide room for interpretation. It is generally accepted that a +/- 15% margin applies, although this widened band was not considered a satisfactory test of currency stability in previous assessments.[142] In the judgement on the initial eurosystem members in 1998, the two year period was defined as running from March 1996 to February 1998, which is 23 months. The Finnish Markka and the Italian Lira joined the ERM in autumn 1996, that is about 17 months prior to the cut-off point. Both were assessed as if their currencies had taken part in the ERM for the full two years.[143] It remains to be seen how "biting" this criteria is really applied or if it is just taken as a means of political interpretation and leeway as in the case of Sweden.[144]

---

140 *European Commission* (2002b) 4.

141 *Halpern/Wyplosz* (2001) 4.

142 *Task Force ′Enlargement′ of the European Parliament* (1999) 9, "Instead, the Commission applied the criterion of +/- 2.25% around the *median* currency, which *′allows for deviations greater than 2.25% against the exchange rates of the remaining ERM currencies′ and ′appears most consistent with the actual working of the ERM after the introduction of the +/- 15% fluctuation bands…*".

143 *Task Force ′Enlargement` of the European Parliament* (1999) 10.

144 Not having been within the ERM for two years while meeting the other Maastricht criteria so far gave Sweden a face-saving way of staying outside the eurosystem without the formal option of „opting out". Once public opinion in Sweden turns in favour of the euro, the length of the actual ERM-test period applied might be worthwhile watching with re-

None of the accession countries currencies could formally join the *ERM II mechanism* yet, so this criteria cannot be met. While the accession countries' currencies strongly devalued against the euro up to 1994, since 1999 they show a moderate nominal appreciation.[145] Besides the Romanian Lei, all CEE accession countries' currencies stayed within a +/- 15% fluctuation band around the euro during the last two years. Estimates of average annual real appreciation for the years to come amount to about 3.5%.[146] Within two years, this is equivalent to about half of the ERM-II bandwidth. With continuing high growth prospects and reinforced capital inflows, further upward pressure on the CEECs exchange rates can be expected.[147] That could absorb the remaining half of the ERM II bandwidth.[148] Alternatively, inflation will rise above the EMU average. A trade-off between exchange rate stability and the inflation target will characterise the ERM-II membership period for the candidate countries.

On the *inflation* side, only Latvia and Lithuania meet the average of the lowest three EU plus 1,5%-measure in 2000 and 2001. In a long-term-view, aggregate inflation rates for the CEECs have been falling with the exception of regional crises triggers (the Baltics and Romania in the early nineties, Bulgaria and Romania in 1997).[149] Trend core inflation continues to be higher and dominated by increases in indirect taxes and administered prices in many accession countries.[150] In 2000 and the first half of 2001, a main immediate cause of returning inflation was the high increase in oil prices. The subsequent easing of oil prices brought inflation down in most accession countries. Particularly worrying are cases where the monetary policy framework and the pass-through structural features are largely contributing to inflation inertia. There are positive developments in Hungary , with the new exchange rate and monetary framework, while Slovenia is lagging behind according to

---

gard to implications towards the accession countries' aspirations of joining the eurozone.

145 *Kager* (2002) 4.

146 *Halpern/Wyplosz* (2001) 19.

147 *European Commission* (2002b) 6.

148 *Halpern/Wyplosz* (2001) 19.

149 *Kager* (2002) 3.

150 *European Commission* (2002c) 5.

the 2001 Regular Report.[151] The Balassa-Samuelson effect (real convergence price pressures) as well as the remaining adjustments of administered prices might be taken into consideration in evaluating the accession countries' inflation rates. The reason is that the Maastricht inflation criteria seems to be harsher for the accession countries than it was for the initial members.[152] The fast growing accession countries could have a considerably higher inflation rate than the euro zone even while pegging tightly to the euro and without running up external balances.[153] Besides paying attention to the catching-up needs in evaluating inflation, suggestions were also made to define the permissible inflation deviation with reference to the average inflation rate of the euro zone instead of to the three EU members with the lowest inflation.[154] It remains to be seen whether such suggestions will be included in the measurement of inflation by the Council judgement.[155] Differentiated treatment compared to the original members might violate the principle of equal treatment. Fears were also raised with regard to more restrictive effects of monetary policy in the core EMU countries compared to the accession countries, with the cost of reduced GDP growth for the core. Price and wage flexibility seems to be higher in the accession countries than in some current members. Due to the small economic size of the accession countries, the effect on the EU inflation rate is rather negligible.[156]

With regard to *long-term interest rates*, only for four countries (Czech Republic, Hungary, Poland, Slovenia) the official yardstick of 10-year governmental bond rates are available. For the remaining CEECs, shorter maturities have to be applied as proxies. Besides Romania, many accession countries meet the proxy benchmark (German Bunds plus 15 basis points) or are not too far. Interest rate differentials have been narrowing. The Commission seems to be concerned with continuing upward pressure on accession countries' interest rates, as it advocates fiscal restraint to keep in-

---

[151] *European Commission* (2001b) 11.
[152] *FBE* (2002) 11.
[153] *Pelkmans/Gros/Ferrer* (2000) 119; *Fidrmuc/Schardax* (2002) 45.
[154] *Szapáry* (2001) 29.
[155] *Padoa-Schioppa* (2002) 6.
[156] *Hochreiter/Wagner* (2001).

terest rates low and to limit potentially destabilising capital inflows.[157]

In aggregate accumulated *public debt* relative to GDP, only Bulgaria exceeds the 60% benchmark. On the *annual budget deficit* criteria, results are mixed and levels remain relatively high. The *Commission* (2001b, 2002b)[158] expressed concern that the general government deficit, measured in terms of the European System of Accounts (ESA 95), has deteriorated somewhat from about 3% of GDP to 3.5% for the candidate countries. Large one-off increases were recorded in the latecomers to financial sector reform. Under ESA 95 rules, these costs have to be taken into account in the general government net balance the year it is incurred.[159] The process of cleansing the accounts of the politically sensitive state-owned enterprises and of the banking system brings hidden liabilities of the public sector to the surface.[160] In the Czech Republic, non-performing loans worth an estimated Kc 228 bn have been transferred to the Konsolidacni Agentura, the successor to Konsolidacna Banka, in connection with the privatisation of state-owned banks.[161] In 2001, a monthly outlay of roughly Kc 25 bn to clean up bad financial sector debt led to a significant deterioration of the Czech central government budget. The fiscal cost of cleaning up banks caused a readjusted 2001 budget deficit of about 7% in the Czech Republic and of 6.4% in Slovakia. Besides these repeated one-off costs, there also is a rapid build-up of a large volume of contingent liabilities in the form of government loan guarantees amounting to Kc 104 bn in 1996 to 2000, with 75% of the total carrying a 90% or greater default risk.[162] For some accession countries the scope for fiscal expansion is limited by conditions for IMF/World Bank loans. In case of Slovakia, payment release on such a loan is condi-

---

[157] *European Commission* (2002b) 6.

[158] *European Commission* (2001b) 11; *European Commission* (2002b) 7.

[159] *European Commission* (2001b) 11; despite increasing transparency in accession countries ′ public finances, their deficits are neither fully comparable across countries, nor yet fully in line with EU definitions, according to *European Commission* (2002c) 7.

[160] *Pelkmans/Gros/Ferrer* (2000) 112.

[161] *Katzman/Hoey* (2002) 20.

[162] *Katzman/Hoey* (2002) 21.

tional of defined measures of financial sector restructuring.[163] In the long run the fiscal balance is imperative, as countries with big deficits most likely run into speculative difficulties and their currencies will be in trouble.[164]

A number of countries are experiencing difficulties implementing reforms which are key to medium-term sustainability of public finances that could indicate a future worsening of their fiscal position.[165] Hungary and Slovakia have healthcare sector reform among their 2002 Accession Partnership Priorities in order to support meeting the Copenhagen economic criteria for EU-accession. The same applies to railway restructuring in Poland and Hungary. Some non-transparent fiscal practices are returning in Hungary. Poland's municipal reform has not been accompanied by a realistic plan to pay for the costs of municipal services, and overly lax government fiscal policy has been accompanied by a very restrictive central bank policy.[166] In some countries the reform of social security is too timid or still at an early stage, such as in the Czech Republic, Slovakia and Slovenia. However, the experience of Portugal, Spain and Italy provides a good example that once the political will to achieve fiscal convergence is proven by strong initial implementary steps, financial markets start to anticipate a probability that the countries in question will succeed.[167]

Evaluating the current score of the accession countries, it becomes clear that problems are most obvious with regard to inflation and interest rates. While aggregate public debt on average is lower than in the eurozone, annual budget deficits provide mixed results and measurement uncertainties remain.[168] There seems to be room for improvement on the budget deficit criteria till the time is ripe for a formal evaluation. Two approaches could be applied in course of the formal evaluation: either taking account of the special circumstances as was the case in evaluating Italy and Belgium, or fundamentalistic-strict. The decision will be an expression of the difficult balance between the different positions of the current

---

[163] *Katzman/Mullen* (2001) 9, 21.
[164] *Mundel* (2000) 158.
[165] *European Commission* (2002b) 6; *Hölscher* (2000) 195.
[166] *Böttcher* (2002) 14.
[167] *Pelkmans/Gros/Ferrer* (2000) 111.
[168] *European Commission* (2002c) 7.

members. The impact on EU members that remained outside the eurosystem for the time being (Sweden, Denmark and the United Kingdom) also has to be considered.[169]

C. Institutional Issues

Given the comparatively small size of the accession countries′ economies (M3 at about 3.1% of the EU-12 eurozone), the contribution of these countries to the enlargement of the euro′s economic and financial base and the eurozones′ global economic impact with regard to size is quite limited.[170] Even the impact of enlargement by countries that have not achieved sufficient economic and institutional stability might be mitigated economically by that small size factor. The political or journalistic interpretation could be quite different and could weaken the international role of the euro. Large transfers from the core E(M)U to the accession countries could lead to higher eurosystem government debt levels.[171] In case of economic turbulence in the accession countries, it might be difficult for the ECB and the EU to detach itself from economic support for a variety of reasons: Short-term intervention cost might be lower than long-term recovery cost; large-scale investment of EU-firms might turn into sunk costs; industry peer group pressure within EU; enlargement might come to a political halt, if other accession countries′ voters don't feel accepted any more, etc. In addition, the links between the euroized accession country and the EU/ECB are quite advanced, any break could also challenge the high level of mutual EU-accession countries′ intertwinedness. This remaining bailout risk may have been among the reasons why the Commission and the ECB both turned down early euroization.[172]

As EMU-members with a derogation, New Members to the EU will be autonomous in their monetary, economic and fiscal policy in principle. All EU members have to treat their economic policies as a matter of common concern, which requires a high degree of coordination.[173] Along with EU-accession goes the institutional

---

169 *Haiss* (1995) 66.

170 *van Eden et al* (1999) 70.

171 *van Eden et al* (1999) 70.

172 *Pelkmans/Gros/Ferrer* (2000) 129f advocate early euroization for small CEECs with weak monetary institutions.

173 *Breuss* (1998) 202.

integration of the respective central banks into the European System of Central Banks (ESCB). Their governors will join the *General Council* of the ECB during the accession phase.[174] Among the tasks of the General Council are the strengthening of cooperation, the monitoring of the functioning of the exchange rate mechanism and providing advice in the fixing of bilateral parities within the ERM. The General Council comprises of all EU states national central banks as well as the President and the Vice-President of the ECB. The other four members of the ECBs′ executive council have no voting on the General Council. Currently there are seventeen, with twelve new members that would be 29. This does not yet include Croatia, Turkey and the four non-voting members. This size calls for requests about operational efficiency.[175] *Upon introducing the euro, the New Members national banks′ governors also get a vote on the ECBs key decision making body, the Governing Council, which will expand from its current 18 members (6 executive board,12 eurozone national bank governors) to 28 or more.*

It is not just sheer size or the concern for operational efficiency of the respective boards, it is also their makeup that is at stake. For one, the relative size and voting power of the Executive Board would be weakened.[176] For two, the economies of the accession countries will still more resemble that of Ireland than that of Germany or other core euroland countries. They are small, high-growth and high-structural-inflation countries. Especially the Governing Council might become split up between half a dozen of "core" countries and about a dozen of post-emerging (high on structural fund receipts, growth and inflation, but small) nations.[177] Under the current rule set, that post-emerging group would have enough votes to set interest rates while accounting for roughly one fifth of eurolands′ GDP. With each member having one vote, several power plays among the participating countries may be a cause

---

[174] *ECB* (2000) 50.

[175] *FBE* (2002) 12.

[176] *Baldwin/Berglöf/Giavazzi/Widgrén* (2001) 35.

[177] *Baldwin/Berglöf/Giavazzi/Widgrén* (2001) 32.

of concern for the current EU members.[178] Examples are: many small against a few large, or CEECs versus current benefactors from structural funds. Several solutions have been proposed. *Rotation* would be an imitation of the U.S. Federal Reserve System, where there is a split between permanent and non-permanent members and rotation among the non-permanent ones.[179] *Representation* along International Monetary fund lines and *delegation* to an independent committee are further alternatives. In the case of delegation, the Governing Council would be turned into a mere consultative body.[180] Considering political implications, it seems likely that the provision made in Article 5 of the Nice Treaty that allows the voting structure of the ECB to be changed without the need for a new treaty will be evoked.

IV. Review and Conclusion

This contribution discusses the inclusion of the accession countries into EMU and later the eurosystem with an emphasis on repercussions to financial sector capabilities and potential volatilites of capital flows. European Monetary Union (EMU) offers a variety of economic advantages to its members. Joining the euro zone is seen as an important way of gaining policy credibility for the candidate countries. Participation in the eurosystem should in principle offer various economic advantages, at least in the long run. Timing, conditions and prerequisites for that move, and short-term implications of the speculative kind are still under debate. In any market economy, the financial sector is one of the key elements, acting as a vehicle for mobilizing private savings and allocating them to investments.[181] A financial sector capable of intermediation, one of the major prerequisites to a functioning economy, deserves renewed attention. This contribution tries to fill that gap.

In *section one*, the process and progress towards participation in E(M)U is reviewed with a special emphasis on the monetary and financial services context. The criteria and the chapters of the ongoing membership negotiations with direct relevance to the later introduction

---

178 *FBE* (2002) 12. The European Banking Federation even refers to this issue as causing resistance from current members to expand EMU membership under the current rule set.

179 *Pelkmans/Gros/Ferrer* (2000) 131; *Kern* (2000) 9.

180 *Baldwin/Berglöf/Giavazzi/Widgrén* (2001) 33.

181 *Corbett* (1990); *Levine* (1997); *Porter* (1992).

of the euro are discussed. The current level of compliance with the acquis and remaining adjustment measures are depicted. It is argued that, although certain elements of the relevant acquis *formally* only have to be complied after the date of accession to the EU, some of them will have an impact already prior to accession. It is concluded that if capital inflows should be poorly intermediated by the domestic financial sector, liberalisation of capital movements could raise potential vulnerabilities. With regard to the EMU-acquis, independence of the respective national banks and corporate governance issues resulting from direct public sector financing remain major concerns to be adapted prior to EU-accession.

Section two highlights the interlink between EMU, types of capital flows and financial sector reform. Ongoing transformation efforts of the financial services sector in its core (banks and capital markets) and prerequisite facets (i.e. regulatory and judiciary environment) are depicted. Emphasis is put on repercussions to the accession countries forthcoming participation in EMU and later the eurozone. Size and governance issues are discussed. Special attention is devoted to the various types of capital inflows, likely change patterns with regard to type and tenure, typical reactions in financial services and resulting implications to systemic risk. The *Commission*'s (2001b) evaluation of that reconstruction process is discussed in contrasting its findings to the 2002-2003 Accession Partnership Priorities. Several conclusions are drawn. Firstly, in the short run domestic banks cannot have a strong impact on economic efficiency of the accession countries. The low level of development of the credit channel poses a challenge for monetary policy making.[182] Secondly, abundant liquidities may lead to a mismatch in banking sectors' asset allocation under certain conditions. Thirdly, financial intermediation growth might turn into a lending bubble with capital flows that are insignificant for the size of the euro zone but large in local levels possibly disrupting the catch-up process. With regard to the *Commissions'* (2001b) Regular Report,[183] it seems that the generally favourable official evaluation for most accession countries contrasts considerably with the remaining adjustment measures in the financial services sector prioritised in the

---

[182] *Backé/Fidrmuc/Reininger/Schardax* (2002) 35.

[183] *European Commission* (2001b).

2002-2003 Accession Partnerships.[184] If there are no formal derogations to EU-membership negotiated, the accession phase to the eurosystem thereafter might be used to overcome remaining financial services sector problems. In that case, financial sector reform might informally be derogated but free movement of capital might already implemented upon accession.

Section three deals with convergence issues as well as with monetary and foreign exchange policies during the pre-accession phase (till EU-membership) and the accession phase (between EU-membership and the final introduction of the euro) in the accession countries. The current currency regimes are depicted. Future participation in the Exchange Rate Mechanism II and intermediate adjustment issues are discussed. With regard to the compatibility of monetary policy strategies during ERM II a distinction is drawn between currencies that are already in a close fix to the euro, and currencies that are in a flexible relationship to the euro. For the currency-board group it is argued that a fixed relationship should be continued in order to avoid speculative inflows. For the "flexible" group it is argued that they should not narrow the +/- 15% ERM-II band without being able to take shelter via a realignment mechanism. Otherwise there is a danger that speculators are going to play convergency games.

Further in section three, issues of monetary size are discussed with regard to the susceptibility to volatile currency flows and the current match of the Maastricht convergency criteria. Institutional adjustment needs with regard to the later inclusion of the accession countries central banks in the organisational units of the European System of Central Banks (ESCB) are depicted. With the privatisation process nearing completion, it is argued that current account deficit financing may have to increasingly rely on more short-term, debt creating, and easier to reverse capital inflows. The susceptibility for speculative attacks is intensified by the premature financial sector in most accession countries. Continued financial sector reforms are central to ensure that these issues do not lead to speculative bubbles and boom-bust cycles. Similar conclusions are drawn from the current match of the nominal convergency criteria. While the aggregate government debt level is below EU averages,

---

184 *European Commission* (2001c).

the criteria on inflation, interest rates and annual budget deficit look less favourable. Besides repeated costs of cleaning up the banks bad debts, there also is a rapid build-up of large volumes of contingent liabilities from government loan guarantees and pending reforms in the healthcare, pension, railway and other sectors which are key to medium-term sustainability of public finances. Given the small economic size of the accession countries relative to the eurozone, any economic effect of enlargement on the eurozone itself is considered rather small. This even applies if the accession - countries have not achieved sufficient economic and institutional stability at the time of accession.

It is argued in the contribution, that the state of the banking industry is of major priority in the preparation for EU and later eurosystem integration of the next wave of EU-members. A robust banking sector may ameliorate the impact of shocks, but a weak banking system may generate or amplify liabilities elsewhere in the economy.[185] Most accession countries are well under way in adapting their monetary policy framework. Given that weak corporate governance capacities, low financial intermediation levels and inherently instable financial markets lead to asset bubbles and to a higher vulnerability to speculative attacks, the conclusion is drawn that these financial services sector issues need to be resolved before introduction of the Euro in the accession countries. Strengthening the interest rate and credit channels via structural reforms within the financial sector remain important tasks for monetary policy.[186] EMU-enlargement should not be seen in unison, but rather as an integral part of financial sector integration.

After ten years of transformation it is getting more and more difficult to blame the communist heritage for the state of the financial markets in the CEEC accession countries. The banking sector in several of the candidate countries still can be considered as a sector where capital disappears. A financial system capable of intermediation is key for two reasons. It is crucial for meeting the nominal Maastricht convergency criteria because it fortifies an interest-rate based monetary policy transmission and aids in stabilizing the macroeconomic environment. It is also crucial for real convergence by promoting investment and saving possibilities.

---

[185] *Cunningham* (2001) 187.

[186] *Backé/Fidrmuc/Reininger/Schardax* (2002) 35.

Given the recurring financial sector problems, there seems to be an argument for rather flexible exchange rate regimes to accommodate for potential economic shocks and speculative tensions in the run up to EMU. However, there is no "one-size-fits-all" exchange rate regime. What can be generalised is that the strength of the political commitment to pursue sound fiscal, monetary and income policies will be crucial.[187] In the case of Greece, the commitment to achieving the Maastricht criteria and the consequent visible improvement of internal and external balances reduced the perceived risk attached to this country quite considerably.[188]

Although the heavy adaptation of the real sector and of foreign trade structures are well under way, there remains a crisis scenario for a *fast* integration of the accession countries into the eurozone due to financial sector and monetary volume considerations. The precarious combination of large current account deficits, high weight of portfolio investments and low money supply relative to the Eurozone could induce a capital flight and speculative attacks on narrow fluctuation bands. Therefore a quick participation of the CEECs in EMU does not seem very reasonable without the preceding sustained consolidation of the financial sector. While the process of strengthening the banking system and developing domestic financial markets is likely to take some time, it will be accelerated by progress in integration with the EU.[189] Setting a timeframe to the fulfilment of the Maastricht convergence criteria might provide an anchor during a potentially turbulent phase in financial markets, avoiding adverse shocks in an environment of free capital movement. But such a step should be accompanied by adequate structural measures in order not to trigger volatility rather than calm it. The development of proven early-warning crisis indicators for growth fluctuations, for the quality of banks' loan portfolios and for foreign financing may prove useful.[190] Including such issues in the screening process should uncover any remaining deficiencies. This will guarantee that at the time of accession, the New Members should possess a framework that is compatible with a smooth functioning of the EMU. By 2007/2008, most of the present accession countries may already have had a number of years to adjust and con-

---

[187] *Szapáry* (2000) 29.

[188] *Darvas/Szapáry* (2000) 48.

[189] *ECB* (2000) 41.

[190] *European Commission* (2002b) 4, 9.

verge with the EU. Their experience will have to be taken into consideration in the decision about full-fledged entry to the eurosystem. Enlargement is a major step in peaceful political integration in Europe. For the EU, in economic terms it is a rather small step. For the accession countries, it will be a big step both in economic and political terms.

References

Adams Ch. / Mathieson D. / Schinasi G. (1999), International Capital Markets, International Monetary Fund, Washington, DC, Sept. 1999.

Backé P. / Barisitz S. / Fidrmuc J. / Reiniger T. / Schardax F. / Wojcik C. (2001), Entwicklungen in ausgewählten Reformländern, in: OeNB Berichte und Studien 1/2001, pp. 74-92.

Backé P. / Fidrmuc J. / Reininger T. / Schardax F. (2002), Price Dynamics in Central and Eastern European EU Accession Countries, in: OeNB Working Paper 61/2002.

Baldwin R. / Berglöf E. / Giavazzi F. /Wildgrén M. (2001), Preparing the ECB for Enlargement, in: Policy Paper No. 6, Centre for Economic Policy Research, 2001, http://www.cepr.org .

Beck R. (2000), The Volatility of Capital Flows to Emerging Markets and Financial Services Trade, in: CFS Working Paper no. 2000/11, Center for Financial Studies, http://www.ifk-cfs.de/pages/veroef/cfswor/abstr/00_11/conten_d.htm .

Bekx P. (1998), The Implications of the Introduction of the euro for non-EU countries, in: Euro Papers No. 26, July 1998, http://europa.eu.int/comm/dgII .

Bokros L. (2000), Experience and Perspectives of Financial Sector Development in Central and Eastern Europe, Paper, presented at the Austrian National Bank and the Joint Vienna Institute Conference on Completing Transition: The Main Challenges, Vienna, Nov. 2000.

Böttcher B. (2002), Financing issues dominate negotiations calendar, in: EU Enlargement Monitor No. 7, April 17, 2002, Deutsche Bank Research, http://www.dbresearch.com .

Breuss F. (1998), Außenwirtschaft Band II, Monetärer Teil, Schwerpunkt Wirtschafts- und Währungsunion, Springer, Vienna 1998.

Breuss F. (2000), Wann sind die MOEL reif für die Wirtschafts- und Währungsunion?, in: *Breuss F. / Fink G. / Griller St.* (eds.), Vom Schuman-Plan zum Vertrag von Amsterdam, Springer, New York 2000, pp. 205-235.

Buiter W. / Grafe C. (2001), Central Banking and the Choice of Currency Regime in Accession Countries, in: SUERF Studies 11, 2001.

Cohrs Th. / Nick F. (2000), The Visegrad Countries, in: The 2000 Guide to Visegrad Countries, HypoVereinsbank / Euromoney, London, Sept. 2000.

Cooper R. / Kempf H. (2000), Commitment and Stabilization Policy in a Monetary Union, Wirtschaftspolitische Blätter 5-6(47), 2000, pp. 598-606.

Corbett J. (1990), Policy Issues in the designing of banking and financial systems for industrial finance, in: European Economy 43, 1990, pp. 225-237.

Corker R. / Beaumont C. / van Elkan R. / Iakova D. (2000), Exchange Rate Regimes in Selected Advanced Transition Economies – Coping with Transition, Capital Inflows, and EU Accession, in: IMF Policy Discussion Paper DP/00/3-EA, International Monetary Fund, April 2000, http://www.imf.org/external/pubs/cat/longres.cfm?sk=3569.0 .

Cunningham A. (2001), Assessing the stability of emerging markets economies' banking systems, Financial Stability Review, Bank of England, Dec. 2001, pp. 187-191.

Darvas S. / Szapáry G. (2000), Financial Contagion in Five Small Open Economies: Does the Exchange Rate Regime Really Matter?, in: International Finance 3:1, 2000, pp. 25-51.

Dickson D. / Mullineux A. (1999), Macroeconomic policy and capital flows: evidence from transforming economies of Central and Eastern Europe, in: *Mullineux A. / Green Ch.* (eds.), Economic Performance and Financial Sector Reform in Central and Eastern Europe, Edward Elgar Publ., Cheltenham 1999, pp. 221-242.

Dickson D. / Mullineux A. (2001), The Asian financial crisis and lessons for CEE economies, in: *Dickson D. / Mullineux A.* (eds.), Financial and Monetary Integration in the New Europe, Edward Elgar Publ., Cheltenham 2001, pp. 202-223.

Duisenberg W. (1999), EU enlargement, some views from the ECB, 2001, http://www.ecb.int./key/sp991015.htm.

Dvorsky S. (2002), Measuring Central Bank Independence in Selected Transition Countries, in: OeNB Focus on Transition 2, 2002, pp. 77-95.

EBRD (2001), Transition Report, European Bank for Reconstruction and Development, London 2001.

ECB (2000), The Eurosystem and the EU enlargement process, in: Monthly Bulletin 2, European Central Bank, 2000, pp. 39-51.

ECB (2001a), The economic policy framework in EMU, in: Monthly Bulletin 11, European Central Bank, 2001, pp. 51-62.

ECB (2001b), Annual Report 2000, Frankfort 2001.

ECOFIN (2000), Exchange-Rate Strategies for Accession Countries, Council Conclusions following the 2310st Council meeting, Brussels, 7 November 2000, in: Press Release 12925/00.

van Eden H. / de Groot A. / Ledrut E. / Romijn G. / de Souza L. V. (authors) / *Patterson B.* (editor) (1999), EMU and Enlargement: a review of policy issues, in: Economic Affairs Series Working Paper ECON 117 EN, European Parliament, Directorate-General for Research, December 1999, http://www.europarl.eu.int/workingpapers .

Eikenberg K. / Zukowska-Gagelmann K. (2001), Euro for the East – nicht ohne reale Konvergenz, Europa-Volkswirtschaft, Hypovereinsbank, March 2001, http://www.hypovereinsbank.de/Category=/Research/Themen/Trends .

Eller M. / Haiss P. (2002a), Anpassungsmaßnahmen am Weg der EU-Beitrittskandidaten in die Wirtschafts- und Währungsunion, in: Wirtschaftspolitische Blätter 2, 2002, pp. 181-193.

Eller M. / Haiss P. (2002b), Integrationstheoretische, aussenhandelsseitige und finanzsektorspezifische Analyse der Teilnahme der Mittel- und Osteuropäischen Länder am Euro-Währungsraum, in: Osteuropa Wirtschaft 2, forthcoming June 2002.

European Commission (1998), Enlarging the European Union, Reports on progress towards accession by each of the candidate countries, Composite Paper, Nov 4, 1998, http://europa.EU.int/comm/dg1a/ enlarge/index.htm .

European Commission (2000a), Strategy Paper-Regular Report from the Commission on Progress towards Accession by each of the Candidate Countries, Nov. 8, 2000, http://europa.eu.int/comm/enlargement/report_11_00/index.htm .

European Commission (2000b), Enlargement Papers No. 1, Seminar on Currency Boards in the context of EU accession, May 2000, http://europa.eu.int/comm/economy_finance/document/enlargement/elpidxen.htm.

European Commission (2001a), Regular Report from the Commission on Progress towards Accession by each of the candidate countries / Chapter 11 – Economic and Monetary Union, Nov. 2001, http://europa.eu.int/comm/enlargement/malta/chap11/index.htm .

European Commission (2001b), Strategy Paper/Regular Report from the Commission on Progress towards Accession, Nov. 2001, http://europa.eu.int/comm/enlargement/report2001/index.htm .

European Commission (2001c), Accession Partnerships 2002 – Proposal for a Council Decision on the principles, priorities, intermediate objectives and conditions contained in the Accession Partnership with the Accession Countries, 13 November 2001, http://europa.eu.int/comm/enlargement/report2001/acc_partn.htm .

European Commission (2002a), Enlargement of the European Union – Guide to the Negotiations Chapter by Chapter http://europa.eu.int/comm/enlargement/negotiations/chapters/negotiationsguide.pdf.

European Commission (2002b), Report on macroeconomic and financial sector stability developments in candidate countries, European Economy – Enlargement Papers No. 8, April 2002, http://europa.eu.int/comm/economy_finance .

European Commission (2002c), Economic Forecasts for the Candidate Countries Spring 2002 by Directorate General for Economic and Financial Affairs, in: European Economy – Enlargement Papers No. 9, April 2002, http://europa.eu.int/comm/economy_finance .

FBE (2002), EU and EMU Enlargement, in: FBE Letter 8, Feb. 2002, European Banking Federation, Bruxelles, http://www.fbe.be .

Feldman R. / Watson M. (2000), Central Europe From Transition to EU Membership, in: Finance & Development, Sept. 2000, p. 25.

Fidrmuc J. / Schardax F. (2002), More "Pre-Ins" ante Portas? Euro Are Enlargement, Optimum Currency Area, and Nominal Convergence, in: OeNB Focus on Transition 2, 2002, pp. 28-47.

Fink G. (1993), Über die Mechanik des Schuldenmachens, Bankarchiv 4, 1993, pp. 261-269.

Fink G. / Haiss P. (1998), Seven Years of Financial Market Reform in Central Europe, in: *Balling M.* (ed.), Corporate Governance in Central and Eastern Europe, SUERF Studies 3, Société Universitaire de Recherches Financières, Amsterdam 1998, pp. 53-95.

Fink G. / Haiss P. (2000a), Accession Countries Banking Markets from an EU Perspective, Part 1 in: Bankarchiv 1, 2000, pp. 29-38; Part 2 in: Bankarchiv 2, 2000, pp. 122-128.

Fink G. / Haiss P. (2000b), Major Achievements and Open Issues in Financial Market Transition of Eastern European Candidate Countries, Paper presented at the Fifth European Commission / European Community Studies Association (ECSA) World Conference, Brussels, Dec. 2000.

Fink G. / Haiss P. (2001), Lemming Banking: Conflict Avoidance to eliminate Excess Capacity by Herd Instinct?, in: Bankarchiv 1, 2001, pp. 9-20.

Frenkel M. / Nickel Ch. / Schmidt G. (1999), Some Shocking Aspects of EMU Enlargement, in: Deutsche Bank Research Note RN-99-4, http://www.debresearch.com .

Haiss P. (1995), Die EU braucht eine rasche Ostvertiefung, in: Wirtschaftspolitische Blätter 1, 1995, pp. 65-71.

Halpern L. / Wyplos Ch. (2001), Economic Transformation and Real Exchange Rates in the 2000s: The Balassa-Samuelson Connection, in: Economic Survey of Europe 1, 2001, pp. 227-239, http://heiwww.unige.ch/~wyplosz .

Hölscher J. (2000), Central banking and financial stability in transition countries, in: *Karmann A.* (ed.), Financial Structure and Stability, Physica, Heidelberg 2000, pp. 186-200.

Hochreiter E. / Wagner H. (2001), The Road to the Euro – Exchange Rate Arrangements in European Transition Economies, Paper presented at the Europäisches Forum Alpbach 2001, Aug. 2001, forthcoming in: Annuals of the American Academy of Political and Social Science, 2002.

Jones C. (2001), Top 100 CEE Banks – region loses core banks to outsiders, in: The Banker 11, 2001, pp. 50-55.

Judson R. / Porter R. (2001), Overseas Dollar Holdings: What Do We Know?, in: Wirtschaftspolitische Blätter 4, 2001, pp. 431-440.

Kager M. (2002), EU enlargement at the point of no return, Paper presented in Brussels, 25 April 2002, http://www.bankaustria.com .

Katzman M. / Mullen F. (2001), Country Report Slovakia, The Economist Intelligence Unit, London, November 2001.

Katzman M. / Hoey J. (2002), Country Report Czech Republic, The Economist Intelligence Unit, London, January 2002.

Kern St. (2000), Eastward enlargement of the EU and EMU – implications for the Euro?, in: EMU Watch No. 88, 2000, http://www.dbresearch.com .

Kopits G. (1999), Implications of EMU for Exchange Rate Policy in Central and Eastern Europe, in: Working Paper WP/99/9, International Monetary Fund, January 1999, Washington, D.C.

Köhler H. / Wes M. (1999), Implications of the euro for the integration process of the transition economies in central and eastern Europe, in: EBRD Working Paper No. 38, March 1999, http://www.ebrd.com.

Lamfalussy A. (2000), Financial Crises in Emerging Markets, Yale University Press, New Haven 2000.

Lannoo K. / Salem T. (2001), The Emerging Regulatory Framework for Banking and Securities Markets in the CEECs, in: *Schröder M.* (ed.), The New Capital Markets in Central and Eastern Europe, Springer, New York 2001, pp. 85-124.

Levine R. (1997), Financial Development and Economic Growth: Views and Agenda, in: Journal of Economic Literature 35, 1997, pp. 688-726.

Mathieson D. / Schinasi G. et al (2000), International Capital Markets, in: IMF World Economic and Financial Surveys, 2000.

Mundell R. (2000), Exchange Rate Arrangements in Central and Eastern Europe, in: *Arndt S. / Handler H. / Salvatore D.* (eds.), Eastern Enlargement: the Sooner, the Better?, Austrian Ministry for Economic Affairs and Labour, Vienna 2000, pp. 158-165.

Mooslechner P. (2000), Die schwierige Interaktion von Geldtheorie und Geldpolitik, in: Wirtschaftspolitische Blätter 5-6(47), 2000, pp. 563-572.

Motamen-Samadian S. / Croft G. (2000), Capital flows and their impact on stability of emerging markets, in: *Motamen-Samadian S./ Garrico C.* (eds.), Emerging Markets, Macmillan Press, London 2000, pp. 136-153.

Nuti M. (2000), The Costs and Benefits of Euro-Isolation in Central-Eastern Europe before or instead of EMU Membership, in: *Arndt S. / Handler H. / Salvatore D.* (eds.), Eastern Enlargement: the Sooner, the Better? Austrian Ministry for Economic Affairs and Labour, Vienna 2000, pp. 171-194.

Padoa-Schioppa T. (2002), Accession Countries on the Way to the euro: A Central Banker's View, Speech at the Conference on Economic Policy Directions in the OECD Countries and Emerging Markets: Analysing the Experiences, Warsaw, 21 March 2002, http://www.ecb.de/key/02/sp020322.htm .

Pelkmans J. / Gros D. / Ferrer J. (2000), Long-Run Economic Aspects of the European Union's Eastern Enlargement, in: WRR Scientific Council for Government Policy Working Document W 109, The Hague, September 2000.

Porter M. (1992), Capital Disadvantage: America's Failing Capital Investment System, in: Harvard Business Review, Sept-Oct. 1992, pp. 65-82.

Reininger T. / Schardax F. / Summer M. (2002), Financial System Transition in Central Europe: The First Decade, in: SUERF Studies No. 16, Société Universitaire Européenne de Recherches Financières, Vienna 2002.

Richter S. (2002), The EU Enlargement Process: Current State of Play and Stumbling Blocks, in: WIIW Current Analysis and Country Profiles No. 17, April 2002.

Schrader A. (1999), From dollarization to euroization? The euros´ potential outside EMU, HypoVereinsbank Volkswirtschaft/ Strategy & Trend Research, 1999, http://www.hypovereinsbank.de.

Schularick M. (2002), Poland, Monetary Convergence / Poland, 08/30/2001, Deutsche Bank Research, http://www.dbresearch.com .

Shirreff D. / D'Amato E. / Lyons R. / White Ch. (2000), Central Europe: Beware – bad banks in operation, in: Euromoney 9, 2000, pp. 68-103.

Sinn H.-W. / Westermann F. (2001), Why has the euro been falling?, in: CESifo Working Papers No. 493, May 2001, http://www.CESifo.de .

Stern N. / Lago R. / Fries St. / Commander S. / Hellman J. / Raiser M. (1999), Transition Report, European Bank for Reconstruction and Development, London, Nov. 1999.

Stix H. (2001), Fremdwährungsbesitz in Zentral und Osteuropa: Umfrageergebnisse, in: Bankarchiv 11, 2001, pp. 899-905.

Szapáry G. (2001), Transition Countries Choice of Exchange Rate Regime in the Run-Up to EMU Membership, in: Finance & Development 6, June 2001, pp. 26-29.

Task Force 'Enlargement' of the European Parliament (1999), Economic and Monetary Union (EMU) and enlargement. Briefing

No. 34, 1999, http://www.europarl.eu.int/enlargement/briefings/34a2_en.htm .

Thießen U. (2000), Banking Crises in Transition Countries – Theory and Empirical Evidence: The Case of Russia, in: DIW Discussion Paper No. 193, Berlin, January 2000, Deutsches Institut für Wirtschaftsforschung, http://www.diw.de .

Vincentz V. (2002), Entwicklung und Tendenzen der Finanzsysteme in Osteuropa, Osteuropa Institut München, in: Working Paper No. 237, 2002, http://www.lrz-muenchen.de/~oeim.

Welfens P. (1999), EU-Osterweiterungen: Vorteile, Konflikte, Strategieprobleme, in: Wirtschaftspolitische Blätter 1-2/1999, pp. 123-129.

Wójcik C. (2002), A Critical Review of Unilateral Euroization Proposals: The Case of Poland, in: OeNB Focus on Transition 2, 2002, pp. 48-76.

Wyplosz Ch. (1999), Summary on Financial Flows, in: *Gács J. / Holzmann R. / Wyzan M.* (eds.), The Mixed Blessings of Financial Inflows, Edward Elgar Publ., Cheltenham 1999, pp. 239-245.

Wyplosz Ch. (2002), Euroisation. Revue Elargissement 26, April 29, 2002, http://www.dree.org/elargissement .

Zwass A. (1979), Money, Banking & Credit in the Soviet Union & Eastern Europe, London 1979, Macmillan.

List of Authors

Prof. *Michael J. Artis*, Department of Economics, European University Institute, Italy.

Mag. Dr. *Harald Badinger*, Research Institute for European Affairs, Vienna University of Economics and Business Administration (Forschungsinstitut für Europafragen der Wirtschaftsuniversität Wien).

Univ.-Prof. Dr. *Fritz Breuss*, Research Institute for European Affairs, Vienna University of Economics and Business Administration (Forschungsinstitut für Europafragen der Wirtschaftsuniversität Wien).

Mag. Dr. *Barbara Dutzler*, Research Institute for European Affairs, Vienna University of Economics and Business Administration, *since September 2002:* Federal Ministry of Finance, III/14, Vienna (Forschungsinstitut für Europafragen der Wirtschaftsuniversität Wien, *seit September 2002:* Bundesministerium für Finanzen, III/14, Wien).

Mag. *Gerhard Fenz*, Lecturer at the Research Institute for European Affairs, Vienna University of Economics and Business Administration (Forschungsinstitut für Europafragen der Wirtschaftsuniversität Wien).

Univ.-Prof. Dr. *Stefan Griller*, Research Institute for European Affairs, Vienna University of Economics and Business Administration (Forschungsinstitut für Europafragen der Wirtschaftsuniversität Wien).

Dr. *Rudolf Habacht*, Oesterreichische Nationalbank, Financial Markets Analysis and Surveillance Division, Vienna (OeNB, Abteilung Finanzmarktanalyse, Wien).

Dr. *Peter R. Haiss*, Lecturer at the Institute of European Studies and at the Vienna University of Economics and Business Administration.

Prof. *Andrew Hughes Hallett*, Department of Economics, Vanderbilt University, Nashville.

Dr. *Walter Hoffenberg*, Oesterreichische Nationalbank, Payments Systems Division, Vienna (OeNB, Zahlungsverkehrsabteilung, Wien).

Dr. *Ralf Kronberger*, The Austrian Federal Economic Chamber, Department for financial fiscal and trade policy, Vienna (Wirtschaftskammer Wien, Abteilung für Finanz- und Handelspolitik).

Mag. Dr. *Bernhard Mahlberg*, Research Institute for European Affairs, Vienna University of Economics and Business Administration, *since September 2002:* Institute for Industrial Research, Vienna (Forschungsinstitut für Europafragen der Wirtschaftsuniversität Wien, *seit September 2002:* Industriewissenschaftliches Institut, Wien).

Dr. *Aurel Schubert*, Oesterreichische Nationalbank, Statistics Section, Vienna (OeNB, Hauptabteilung Statistik, Wien).

Dr. *Nicola Viegi*, Lecturer at the Department of Economics, University of Strathclyde, Glasgow.

SpringerRecht

Birgit Schoißwohl

Staatshaftung wegen Gemeinschaftsrechtsverletzung: Anspruchsgrundlage und materielle Voraussetzungen

Zugleich ein Beitrag zur Gemeinschaftshaftung

2002. XIX, 512 Seiten.
Broschiert **EUR 74,90,** sFr 116,50
ISBN 3-211-83775-2
Schriftenreihe des Forschungsinstituts für Europafragen der Wirtschaftsuniversität Wien / Research Institute for European Affairs Publication Series, Band 18

Die Europäische Staatshaftungsjudikatur zählt zu den meistdiskutierten europarechtlichen Themen. Dieses Buch legt eine extensive rechtsvergleichende Analyse der Staatshaftungssysteme Österreichs, Deutschlands, Frankreichs und Englands vor. Es vermittelt durch die Darstellung der in diesen Rechtsordnungen bei Umsetzung der Staatshaftungsjudikatur diskutierten Lösungen praxisorientiertes Wissen. Weiters bietet die Autorin durch eine tiefgreifende Diskussion der haftungsrechtlichen Grundlagen der gemeinschaftsrechtlichen Staatshaftung eine umfassende Ergänzung. Die auf einzelne Rechtsfragen und Sachverhaltskonstellationen konzentrierte Darstellung der Rechtsprechung Europäischer Gerichte zur Gemeinschaftshaftung vermag überdies Hilfe für die Rechtspraxis im Verfahren der Haftungsfeststellung zu leisten.

Stefan Griller, Fritz Breuss, Erich Vranes

The Banana Dispute

An Economic and Legal Analysis

2003. Approx. 300 pages.
Softcover **approx. EUR 64,09,** sFr 99,50
(Recommended retail price)
This Euro-price is recommended for Germany and includes 7 % VAT.
ISBN 3-211-83727-2
Schriftenreihe des Forschungsinstituts für Europafragen
der Wirtschaftsuniversität Wien / Research Institute
for European Affairs Publication Series, Volume 19
Due January 2003

The "Banana dispute" represents one of the central cases in international trade. It has led to several precedents on the international (WTO), EC and national level. It thus constitutes the mandatory starting point for any in-depth study of the WTO system and transatlantic trade relations. Moreover, this dispute casts new light on classic issues of European law, especially the relationship of EC, national law and state liability.
This treatise is the most comprehensive published to date, and also an easily accessible one. The study is supplemented by an economic analysis of the welfare effects of the EC banana import regime for the EC domestic market, and interdisciplinary conclusions for future amendments of the WTO enforcement system.
This book will be of equal interest to practitioners, academics and students of international economic relations.

SpringerWienNewYork

A-1201 Wien, Sachsenplatz 4–6, P.O. Box 89, Fax +43.1.330 24 26, e-mail: books@springer.at, www.springer.at
D-69126 Heidelberg, Haberstraße 7, Fax +49.6221.345-229, e-mail: orders@springer.de
USA, Secaucus, NJ 07096-2485, P.O. Box 2485, Fax +1.201.348-4505, e-mail: orders@springer-ny.com
EBS, Japan, Tokyo 113, 3–13, Hongo 3-chome, Bunkyo-ku, Fax +81.3.38 18 08 64, e-mail: orders@svt-ebs.co.jp

SpringerLaw

Stefan Griller, Birgit Weidel (eds.)

External Economic Relations and Foreign Policy in the European Union

2002. IV, 500 pages.
Softcover **EUR 84,53,** sFr 131,50
(Recommended retail price)
This Euro-price is recommended for Germany and includes 7 % VAT.
ISBN 3-211-83726-4
Schriftenreihe des Forschungsinstituts für Europafragen der Wirtschaftsuniversität Wien / Research Institute for European Affairs Publication Series, Volume 20

The challenges of globalisation call for a strong role of the European Union as an international actor. Despite its economic importance, the EU has not been able to assert a corresponding influence on the course of international politics. The artificial distinction between external economic relations, as a subject of the supranational first pillar, and foreign policy, as a subject of the intergovernmental second pillar undermines consistent policy-making and significantly weakens the EU's performance on the international scene.
This book illustrates the inextricable link between political and economic aspects of external relations and the constitutional dimension of this area. Provided with a thorough analysis of competence and representation issues the reader will gain a more profound understanding of the complex area of EU external relations.

SpringerWienNewYork

A-1201 Wien, Sachsenplatz 4–6, P.O. Box 89, Fax +43.1.330 24 26, e-mail: books@springer.at, www.springer.at
D-69126 Heidelberg, Haberstraße 7, Fax +49.6221.345-229, e-mail: orders@springer.de
USA, Secaucus, NJ 07096-2485, P.O. Box 2485, Fax +1.201.348-4505, e-mail: orders@springer-ny.com
EBS, Japan, Tokyo 113, 3–13, Hongo 3-chome, Bunkyo-ku, Fax +81.3.38 18 08 64, e-mail: orders@svt-ebs.co.jp

Springer-Verlag and the Environment

WE AT SPRINGER-VERLAG FIRMLY BELIEVE THAT AN international science publisher has a special obligation to the environment, and our corporate policies consistently reflect this conviction.

WE ALSO EXPECT OUR BUSINESS PARTNERS – PRINTERS, paper mills, packaging manufacturers, etc. – to commit themselves to using environmentally friendly materials and production processes.

THE PAPER IN THIS BOOK IS MADE FROM NO-CHLORINE pulp and is acid free, in conformance with international standards for paper permanency.